TEACHING TODAY

AN INTRODUCTION TO EDUCATION

Eighth Edition

David G. Armstrong
Late of the University of North Carolina at Greensboro

Kenneth T. Henson
The Citadel

Tom V. Savage
Santa Clara University

Merrill
is an imprint of

Upper Saddle River, New Jersey
Columbus, Ohio

Library of Congress Cataloging-in-Publication Data

Armstrong, David G.
    Teaching today : an introduction to education / David G. Armstrong, Kenneth T. Henson, Tom V. Savage.—8th ed.
        p. cm.
    Includes bibliographical references and index.
    ISBN 978-0-13-159552-1
    1.   Teaching—United States. 2.   Education—Study and teaching—United States. 3.   Teaching--Vocational guidance—
United States.   I. Henson, Kenneth T.   II. Savage, Tom V.   III. Title.
    LB1775.2.A75 2009
    370.010973—dc22

                                                                                                    2007042685

Vice President and Executive Publisher: Jeffery W. Johnston
Executive Editor: Darcy Betts Prybella
Development Editor: Amy J. Nelson
Editorial Assistant: Nancy J. Holstein
Project Manager: Sarah N. Kenoyer
Production Coordinator: Mary Tindle, S4Carlisle Publishing Services
Design Coordinator: Diane C. Lorenzo
Cover Design: Bryan Huber
Cover Image: Jupiter Images
Operations Specialist: Susan W. Hannahs
Director of Marketing: Quinn Perkson
Marketing Coordinator: Brian Mounts

This book was set in Goudy by S4Carlisle Publishing Services. It was printed and bound by Edwards Brothers.
The cover was printed by Phoenix Color Corp.

Photo Credits: Anthony Magnacca/Merrill, pp. 1, 2, 30, 258; John Neubauer/PhotoEdit Inc., p. 56; Scott
Cunningham/Merrill, pp. 83, 84, 108, 202; Anne Vega/Merrill p. 138; Patrick White/Merrill p. 170, 284; Liz Moore/Merrill,
p. 201; Laima Druskis/PH College, p. 232; Bob Daemmrich/The Image Works, p. 312; SyracuseNewspapers/Frank
Ordoñez/The Image Works, p. 340

Pearson Education Ltd.
Pearson Education Singapore Pte. Ltd.
Pearson Education Canada, Ltd.
Pearson Education–Japan

Pearson Education Australia Pty. Limited
Pearson Education North Asia Ltd.
Pearson Educación de Mexico, S.A. de C.V.
Pearson Education Malaysia Pte. Ltd.

Merrill
is an imprint of

10 9 8 7 6 5 4 3 2 1
ISBN-13: 978-0-13-159552-1
ISBN-10:   0-13-159552-0

DEDICATION

The quality of any journey is enhanced by your companions. Throughout our careers we have been fortunate to have companions who have helped us celebrate the successes and cope with the detours. We dedicate this edition to our spouses. Thank you Sharon and Marsha for being there and for your constant encouragement.

TVS

KTH

PREFACE

Welcome to the Eighth Edition!

Because education is one of the critical components in society, the quality of education is the subject of much debate. This debate is often passionate and complex. Therefore, as we enter the 21st century, education is in an age of reform. Every aspect of education from the preparation of teachers to the quality of preschool is the focus of reform. These reform proposals have the potential to dramatically change education as we know it. However, change can be positive or it can be negative. Therefore, education today poses many challenges and opportunities. One thing is certain—the status quo is not acceptable.

The responsibilities of those involved in education include evaluating proposals for change and making sure that the interests of students are upheld. The nation needs quality teachers who have a clear grasp of basic issues—motivating us to write the eighth edition of *Teaching Today*.

We have had exciting and productive careers in education and we have found teaching to be an exciting and rewarding profession. We hope to encourage the best and the brightest of our nation to accept the challenge to be teachers. However, to enter the teaching field as a challenging responsible individual, pre-service teachers must understand that there are thorns that go with the roses. There are challenges to being a teacher. Perhaps that is what makes the successes so sweet. Therefore, in *Teaching Today* we have tried to provide a strong dose of reality. We want individuals to realize that there are many conflicting points of view. There is not a national consensus about the goals of education or how they should be accomplished. Although we recognize that there might be some who find this conflict and the prospect of profound change disconcerting, we believe that many are invigorated by this prospect, and realize that they can play an important role in shaping the lives of students and the future of society.

In preparing the eighth edition, we have emphasized topics that are relevant to the world you will enter as an educator. In addition to basic information about these topics, we have attempted to give alternative perspectives on these issues so that you can better analyze, reflect, and decide. You can go beyond the text to pursue these topics on the MyEducationLab site (www.myeducationlab.com) and at other locations on the World Wide Web.

This text provides opportunities for you to reflect on issues and develop your personal perspectives. We have also included opportunities for you to develop an Initial Development Portfolio that will help you record your growth toward becoming a professional educator.

Organization of This Text

Both undergraduate and graduate students have used earlier editions of *Teaching Today* as they seek to develop a broad understanding of the complex world of education. This edition organizes content under three major headings, as listed and described below.

Part 1 *The Changing Profession.* If there is one constant in contemporary education, it is change. There are many proposals for change from various different sectors. Chapter 1 focuses on the changing nature of education and those forces that influence the change. Chapter 2 emphasizes the process of becoming a professional educator and the possible roles that educators play. Chapter 3 discusses specific proposals for reforming schools.

Part 2 *Working with Students.* Chapter 4 presents information on selected characteristics of students and patterns of development that influence student learning. Chapter 5 focuses on the great diversity of students found in contemporary classrooms. This diversity includes cultural diversity, students with exceptionalities, and students who are gifted and talented. Chapter 6 discusses what is taught and how it is taught. The basic topics are curriculum and instruction. Chapter 7 emphasizes assessment. In an age of accountability, it is important for teachers to know how data is gathered and whether students have learned.

Part 3 *Forces Shaping Educational Policies and Practices.* This is the most extensive section. It discusses a number of forces. Chapter 8 focuses on the history of education so that teachers can understand how educational practices and policies were developed. It is important to note that we define history as not just one story, but as a number of stories. Specifically, we present a story of Native American education and a story of African American education. Chapter 9 discusses the role of school in society and different perspectives through which education can be viewed. Chapter 10 focuses on specific educational philosophies and how they influence educational policy and practice. Chapter 11 emphasizes how the role of technology is changing education. Chapter 12 presents legal issues relating to the rights and responsibilities of teachers and students. Finally, Chapter 13 discusses the critical dimension of who governs education and how education is financed.

New to This Edition

New, Revised, and Reorganized Chapters.

- New Chapter 13 *Who Controls and Finances Education?* focuses on two critical components of education: governance and finance.

- The previous chapter on Social and Philosophical Perspectives has been divided into two chapters for a more comprehensive resource:

  - New Chapter 9 *What Is the Role of School in Society?* and

  - New Chapter 10 *How Do Philosophical Perspectives Influence Education?*. The previous chapters on diversity and exceptional learners has been revised and combined into

- Chapter 5 *How Has Diversity Changed?*, to offer students one strong, streamlined and updated chapter.

- Chapter 6 *What is Taught and How Is It Taught?* has been revised, updated, and combined with the previous chapters on curriculum and the instruction, to offer a concise resource for today's learners.

"A Day in the Life . . ." attempts to capture some of the rewards and challenges that teachers face. This feature asks the reader to consider the values of successful teachers. Readers then examine a "Disposition Check" section that provides an understanding of the teacher's disposition and offers questions for the reader to reflect on. The scenarios are based on the stories of real teachers.

A DAY IN THE LIFE . . . Looking Beyond Test Scores

In many classes there are students who surprise you. Such was the case of Juana. Juana was a Hispanic girl whose parents did not speak English. At the beginning of the year, Pat Taylor noticed on Juana's cumulative records that her IQ score was listed as in the mid 80s. Pat had expected her to be one of those students who needed extra help and struggled with school work.

Such was not the case! Juana turned out to be an enthusiastic student who did everything well. On all of her assignments and tests she was near the top of the class. She was one of the classroom leaders who was quick to help other students who needed help. She was especially helpful in translating material for the two limited English-speaking students in the classroom. In short, she became one of Pat's favorite students.

As the year progressed, Pat wanted to make sure Juana's abilities were recognized and that she was encouraged to pursue education beyond high school. There was a special academic enrichment program in the school that was supposed to take the most talented students and provide them with some challenging and academically enriching experiences. Pat decided that Juana was a perfect candidate for the program and that it would provide her with experiences that would help her obtain a scholarship for college. Pat wrote the school counselor a glowing letter of recommendation for Juana.

Today the school counselor met with Pat. The counselor started by telling Pat how impressed she was with Pat's recommendation and the samples of Juana's work that had been submitted. "However," the counselor continued, "I don't think she is a good candidate for the enrichment program. I wouldn't want her to be placed in a program where she might have trouble keeping up with the other students." "Wait a minute," responded Pat, "She is motivated, enthusiastic and demonstrates good task persistence. She is doing just fine competing with the other students in my class." "Well, yes," said the counselor, "However, one of the criteria for admission is an above average IQ and her score is just in the 80s."

Pat was absolutely livid. Wasn't the real test of ability how a person performed rather than a score on a test given several years ago? What was education all about if it wasn't finding talent in students and encouraging them to excel?

However, the counselor was not moved. Rules were rules and Juana simply did not qualify.

 Disposition Check

Sometimes students are labeled and misjudged by criteria of questionable validity. Teachers have a responsibility to look beyond first impressions or isolated bits of data. Teachers who are committed to students and who do develop attachments to students are often frustrated by the inability of others to get beyond labels and strict rules.

1. As you review this situation consider what dispositions were being demonstrated by Pat?
2. What dispositions were being demonstrated by the school counselor?
3. How might your dispositions lead to conflict with others in the school?

Part I   The Changing Profession

will be observed and interpreted and have consequences beyond the immediate situation. For example, if you display great anger when a learner makes a mistake in class, you may find class members increasingly fearful of volunteering responses to your questions. On the other hand, if you are willing to experiment and share your errors, your classroom will become a safe place where your students will become scientific risk-takers (Phelps, 2006). If you teach in a middle school or high school, behaviors you have displayed in one class quickly become known and affect your relationships with other classes you teach.

History

The interaction you have with class members over a term or an entire year develops a class history. A class history is a kind of culture that is unique to each class of students and results from an ongoing record of interaction between the teacher and students. The manner in which you relate to learners, plan instruction, and react to unpredictable events creates this history.

Differences in particular class histories explain why apparently similar behaviors by different teachers do not always produce similar results. For example, you might find that a quiet word may stop inappropriate behavior, but another teacher using this approach can find that it fails to correct the situation. As you think about developing your own teaching style, you will not find it productive to simply mimic another teacher's behavior. Your class members will have a history that may vary considerably from the history of learners of the teacher you are trying to emulate. As a result, your learners will have a different interpretation of your actions.

What Do You Think?

As you review the complexities of the teaching situation, reflect on the following:
* How do you cope with unpredictable events?
* Which of the dimensions of the classroom worry you most?
* Can you think of an example when the history established by the teacher with a group of students has impacted teaching and learning?

COPING WITH SELECTED CHANGES

Education is a part of society, not separate from society. As society changes, education must also change. Just a few years ago personal computers, the World Wide Web, cell phones, and satellite television did not exist. Now, we find it hard to imagine life without them. These technological innovations have an impact on educational practices. There have been changes in the composition of the student population. Increased mobility means that schools in every part of the nation are likely to have a diverse student population. The underlying values and beliefs of students are likely to be quite different than those of students just a few decades ago. Unfortunately, education is often slow to change and adapt to new realities. As a future teacher, you need to realize that education must change to accommodate new realities. Over time, the role of the teacher may significantly change. You need to be aware of some of the changes that are taking place in education and consider how they may impact teaching and learning. For instance, see this chapter's *Video Viewpoint* feature to see how cell phones impact teaching and learning today.

"What Do You Think?" key questions in each chapter provide reflection opportunities that prompt readers to consider their viewpoint based on their chapter reading.

Focus Features

Video Viewpoints 2–1

Charles Best

WATCH: In this *Nightline: Up Close* video segment, Michel Martin interviews a teacher, Charles Best, who came from a privileged background, attended prestigious schools, and chose to become a teacher in the New York public schools. Charles Best then had an idea about finding funding for teacher ideas and created a Web site: www.donorschoose.org. This segment includes a discussion of the motivation of a person to choose teaching, as well as an innovative way to provide resources for teachers who most need them.

THINK: Discuss with your classmates or write in your teaching journal your responses to the following questions:

1. What do the interviewer's questions infer about the status of teaching in the United States?
2. What does this segment indicate regarding equal educational opportunities for all students?
3. What does this segment indicate about the rewards of teaching?

LINK: Can you think of other creative ideas to address educational issues?

To view this video, go to the Video Viewpoints DVD and click on this chapter's video: "Charles Best."

ABC News and *Video Viewpoints*. *Videos* bring to life current and controversial education issues discussed throughout the text. Here you can answer questions, apply your responses to your professional philosophy, or engage in group discussion.

Critical Incidents. Located in several chapters, this issues-oriented feature presents readers with opportunities to engage in higher-level thinking as they reflect on situations faced by today's teachers.

Critical Incident

Teaching to the Test

Maria is a first-year teacher. She wants to develop lessons that interest and motivate her students. Recently, her principal visited her classroom for an observation. Following the lesson, the principal said, "You had an interesting lesson and everybody in your class was engaged. However, you need to remember that test scores are very important here. Our parents expect us to post high test scores and we cannot afford to let them slip. We expect that all of the students in your classroom will do well on the test. If I were a parent and asked you how today's lesson ties to the testing program, what would you say?"

1. *What are your reactions to the principal's comments?*
2. *Should teachers be teaching to the test?*
3. *Is there an inconsistency between having interesting lessons and meeting standards?*
4. *How would you respond?*

Web Extension 3–1

Consortium for Policy Research in Education (CPRE)

The Consortium for Policy Research in Education (CPRE) is a group that links policy researchers from the University of Pennsylvania, Harvard University, Stanford University, the University of Michigan, and the University of Wisconsin–Madison. At this site, you will find a link labeled "publications." If you click on this link, you will be taken to an extensive list of reports and articles, many of which deal with issues related to systemic reform. Systemic reform requires the efforts of all school members (Moss & Faison, 2006).

http://www.cpre.org/

Web Extensions. To deepen their understanding of chapter content, these features include useful, quality Websites and their description that prompt readers to learn more about topics by visiting the sites, searching the content, and finding supplementary information on chapter content.

MyEducationLab

Your Class. Your Career. Everyone's Future.

"Teacher educators who are developing pedagogies for the analysis of teaching and learning contend that analyzing teaching artifacts has three advantages: it enables new teachers time for reflection while still using the real materials of practice; it provides new teachers with experience thinking about and approaching the complexity of the classroom; and in some cases, it can help new teachers and teacher educators develop a shared understanding and common language about teaching. . . ."[1]

As Linda Darling-Hammond and her colleagues point out, grounding teacher education in real classrooms—among real teachers and students and among actual examples of students' and teachers' work—is an important, and perhaps even an essential, part of training teachers for the complexities of teaching today's students in today's classrooms. For a number of years, we have heard the same message from many of you as we sat in your offices learning about the goals of your courses and the challenges you face in teaching the next generation of educators. Working with a number of our authors and with many of you, we have created a website that provides you and your students with the context of real classrooms and artifacts that research on teacher education tells us is so important. Through authentic in-class video footage, interactive simulations, rich case studies, examples of authentic teacher and student work, and more, **MyEducationLab** offers you and your students a uniquely valuable teacher education tool.

> Chapter 9   What Is the Role of School in Society?   237
>
> provided by families related to educational readiness tend to vary by social class and family background. One study found that a substantial number of 3-year-olds from poor families were 9 months or more behind in language and intellectual development (Ballantine, 2001).
>
> Several research studies support the value of early childhood education. Among the benefits found for preschool are that those who have preschool experience are less likely to later need special or remedial classes, they have a lower school dropout rate and a lower incident of retention in grade, and they make significant academic gains in such subjects as mathematics and reading. One early childhood education study discovered that the greatest return on investment is providing preschool for 3- and 4-year-old children of low-income families (Ballantine, 2001).
>
> More than half of the nations of the world fund early childhood education for 3- through 5-year-olds. Some nations, such as Israel and China, begin early childhood education earlier and have made it mandatory (Ballantine, 2001). Many attempts have been made to extend mandatory education to the preschool years. For example, the Goals 2000 Project, supported by the Bush and Clinton administrations during the 1990s, emphasized the importance of preschool and contained a "ready to learn" initiative directed at preschoolers.
>
> However, proposals for increased or mandatory preschool in the United States have been met with considerable opposition. Much of the opposition comes from those who see this as an infringement by the schools on the roles and responsibilities of the family (Bracey, 2003).
>
> **Working with Parents**
> Go to MyEducationLab and select the topic "Family and Community." Read the article "Beyond Instruction." Respond to the questions that are included in the module. Some of the questions are designed to prepare you for your licensure examination.
>
> **Conflict Between Education and Religion**
> Because both education and religion have a deep interest in the development of youth, conflicts are inevitable. Historically, the conflict between education and religion led to the rise of the private schools, especially Catholic schools. Early on, it was perceived that the public schools were furthering Protestant beliefs so that Catholic leaders felt they had no choice but to create their own school systems.
>
> Over time, legal decisions clarified the separation between church and state. However, this did not eliminate the conflict between church and state. In fact, in some places public schools were viewed as antireligious.
>
> A conflict involving education and religion is the current controversy relating to the science curriculum and the teaching of evolution versus intelligent design. Many religious leaders have long viewed the teaching of evolution as contrary to their religious beliefs. In 1919, the World's Christian Fundamentals Association was formed to oppose the teaching of evolution. Since that time, many efforts have been made to restrict the teaching of evolution; the most famous was the Scopes trial in the 1920s (Altenbaugh, 2002). The basic argument has centered on the idea that "creationism" is a religious theory, not a scientific one. Therefore, teaching creationism amounts to teaching a religious doctrine.
>
> In 1999, the Kansas state school board adopted a science curriculum that essentially replaced evolutionary theory with "intelligent design." Many scientists see intelligent design as just another name for creationism. Proponents claim that intelligent design is not creationism but an alternative theory for explaining the origins of life that should be taught

MyEducationLab is easy to use! Wherever the MyEducationLab logo appears in the margins or elsewhere in the text, you and your students can follow the simple link instructions to access the MyEducationLab resource that corresponds with the chapter content. These include:

Video: Authentic classroom videos show how real teachers handle actual classroom situations.

Homework & Exercises: These assignable activities give students opportunities to understand content more deeply and to practice applying content.

Case Studies: A diverse set of robust cases drawn from some of our best-selling books further expose students to the realities of teaching and offer valuable perspectives on common issues and challenges in education.

---

1. Darling-Hammond, l., & Bransford, J., Eds. (2005). Preparing Teachers for a Changing World. San Francisco: John Wiley & Sons.

Simulations: Created by the IRIS Center at Vanderbilt University, these interactive simulations give hands-on practice at adapting instruction for a full spectrum of learners.

Student & Teacher Artifacts: Authentic student and teacher classroom artifacts are tied to course topics and offer practice in working with the actual types of materials encountered every day by teachers.

Readings: Specially selected, topically relevant articles from ASCD's renowned *Educational Leadership* journal expand and enrich students' perspectives on key issues and topics.

Other Resources:

Lesson & Portfolio Builders: With this effective and easy-to-use tool, you can create, update, and share standards-based lesson plans and portfolios.

News Articles: Looking for current issues in education? Our collection offers quick access to hundreds of relevant articles from the New York Times Educational News Feed.

MyEducationLab is easy to assign, which is essential to providing the greatest benefit to your student. Visit *www.myeducationlab.com* for a demonstration of this exciting new online teaching resource.

Instructor Support

Supplements to the text are available to the instructors who adopt this text. Those supplements include:

- **Instructor's Manual/Media Guide and Test Bank** provides chapter-by-chapter instructional and media resources, available on the Instructor Resource Center.
- **PowerPoint slides** are available on the Instructor Resource Center.
- **Computerized Test Bank** questions give instructors access to multiple choice, short answer, and essay questions for each chapter. These questions are available on the Instructor Resource Center.
- **Instructor Resource Center**
  Instructor supplements can be accessed at our Instructor Resource Center located at *http://www.pearsonhighered.com*. The Instructor Resource Center opens the door to a variety of print and media resources in downloadable, digital format. Resources available for instructors include:
  - Instructor Manual/Media Guide and Test Bank,
  - Computerized Test Bank, and
  - PowerPoint slides.
  Your one-time registration, available under the Instructor Support tab opens the door to Pearson's premium digital resources. You will not have additional forms to fill out or multiple usernames and passwords to remember to access new titles and/or editions. Register today and maximize your time at every stage of course preparation.

For instructors who have adopted this text and need additional registration help, please contact your sales representative or call Faculty Services at 1-800-526-0485. We look forward to hearing from you.

Acknowledgements

Several individuals have helped shaped the eighth edition of *Teaching Today*. We are grateful for the helpful comments of several professionals who reviewed the seventh edition and preliminary versions of new and revised chapters. Those include Dwight Allen, Old Dominion University; Donna Adair Breault, Illinois State University; Jean Camp, University of North Carolina at Greensboro; Debra J. Chandler, University of South Florida; Leigh Chiarelott, Bowling Green State University; Lydia Carol Gabbard, Eastern Kentucky University; Alan Garrett, Eastern New Mexico University; Fred H. Groves, University of Louisiana at Monore; Melissa Marks, University of Pittsburgh at Greensburg; and Angelia J. Ridgway, University of Indianapolis.

In addition, we are especially grateful for the help of professionals at Merrill. Those include Debbie Stollenwerk, Christina Robb, and Amy Nelson. They always provide valuable insight that helps make the text much better. Finally, we want to recognize our spouses who tolerate our long hours at the computer and those occasional outbursts when things do not go as expected. Thank you for your patience.

TVS
KTH

BRIEF CONTENTS

CONTENTS

SPECIAL FEATURES

A Day in the Life. . .

Video Viewpoints

Web Extension

Critical Incident

MyEducationLab

ABC NEWS AND VIDEO VIEWPOINTS

Now available on the DVD included with every copy of *Teaching Today: An Introduction to Education*, Eighth Edition!

Engage your readers through ABC news video segments, available on the *Video Viewpoints: ABC News DVD*, focusing on controversial educational issues that illustrate chapter content relevancy and bring chapter content to life. ABC News *Video Viewpoints* features within the text indicate when a video is available and offer a short summary of each episode with discussion questions.

Chapter 1

Pushing Your Buttons: No Cell Phones Allowed

Advances in technology create new issues that educators must confront. This video segment discusses the problems created by the widespread use of cell phones. Some schools have banned cell phones and confiscate them when they are brought to school. However, parents believe that safety issues require that they be in contact with their children.
Running Time: 6:08
Page 13

Chapter 2

Charles Best

This video profiles the work of Charles Best. Best is a New York City teacher who saw the need to do more for public school students. He created a website to help link teachers with needs to potential donors.
Running Time: 19:47
Page 46

Teacher Shortage

This video segment explores the problem of the teacher shortage. It makes the point that raising standards in an attempt to improve education will not accomplish much if classrooms are taught by unqualified teachers.
Running Time: 2:12
Page 50

Chapter 3

Controversial School Voucher Program

In this video, John Stossel of *20/20* makes the argument for school vouchers. He is critical of the current educational system and teacher associations.
Running Time: 9:40
Page 67

No Child Left Behind

This video discusses some of the problems with No Child Left Behind. It focuses on a high-performing model school in Utah that was labeled as in "need of improvement."
Running Time: 2:54
Page 73

Chapter 4

Home Room: One Last Chance

This video discusses the Seed Charter School in Washington, D.C. The founders of the school believed that major changes not normally addressed in charter schools were needed. They took the bold step of creating a boarding school so that they could take the students out of the environment. This video raises questions about what is really needed to improve achievement.
Running Time: 20:04
Page 92

"Stinky": Robotics and Immigration

This video presents a fascinating case of students from a Phoenix, Arizona, high school. This high school is 92% Hispanic and 87% of the students qualify for the free-lunch program. The school entered an underwater robotics competition against such prestigious universities as MIT. It was discovered that all of the students on the robotics team were undocumented immigrants.
Running Time: 19:45
Page 103

Chapter 5

When Students Are Hungry: A Teacher's Mission

Sometimes teachers are unaware of the needs that students bring to school. This video presents the case of a teacher who did not realize that she had students in her class who were hungry. She learned that a prerequisite to success is sufficient nutrition.
Running Time: 5:49
Page 111

Chapter 6

The Test

The drive for accountability has led to an emphasis on high-stakes tests. The video focuses on the Florida Comprehensive Assessment test. A passing grade on this test is required for high school graduation. Arguments pro and con are discussed.
Running Time: 19:38
Page 151

Homework

The reform movement in education has highlighted homework as an important component of school improvement. However, this video makes the point that homework might not be as important as some think. Some parents are beginning to complain that excessive homework is interfering with other activities that are important for development.
Running Time: 6:19
Page 160

Chapter 7

Uses and Misuses of Standardized Tests

The use of standardized tests is a key element of the accountability movement. This video discusses the SAT as a tool for college admission. The validity of the test is questioned and the uses and misuses of standardized tests are discussed.
Running Time: 19:58
Page 175

Chapter 8

The Reunion

The impact of major changes in education is often overlooked. This video segment interviews students from a kindergarten class in 1960. This was the first group to experience school integration. This interesting video provides a perspective on how this social experiment impacted their lives.
Running Time: 39:35
Page 217

Chapter 9

Science vs. Religion

Tensions between basic institutions in society are bound to arise. This video discusses the tension between religion and education over the debate about teaching evolution. This video segment covers the debate in Kansas regarding the science standards and the inclusion of "Intelligent Design" in the science curriculum.
Running Time: 19:47
Page 238

Chapter 11

Caught Cheating Using Cell Phones

This video discusses how increased pressure on students has led to increased cheating. This video is a summary of an investigation of several high schools and colleges across the nation. It raises disturbing questions about societal practices that contribute to the perspective that cheating is acceptable.
Running Time: 13:12
Page 301

Chapter 12

Action, Reaction, and Zero Tolerance

Making decisions as an educator on legal issues is not always simple and clear cut. The zero tolerance policy has been instituted in many schools as an effort to curb violence. This video illustrates that implementing this principle might not be as clear as many assume. It begins with the case of two 8-year-old students who were criminally charged for terrorist threats for playing "Cowboys and Indians" with paper guns.
Running Time: 19:11
Page 319

Chapter 13

Failing Grade

The story of why some schools fail can be complex. This video investigates the case of a failing school district. Some of the blame can be placed on poor management. In an attempt to address the problems, a number of measures were taken including the state taking over the operation of the school district and turning over the high school to Edison Schools. The video illustrates the difficulty in trying to apply simplistic solutions to complex problems.

Running Time: 20:45
Page 348

THE CHANGING PROFESSION

CHAPTER 1

HOW IS EDUCATION CHANGING?

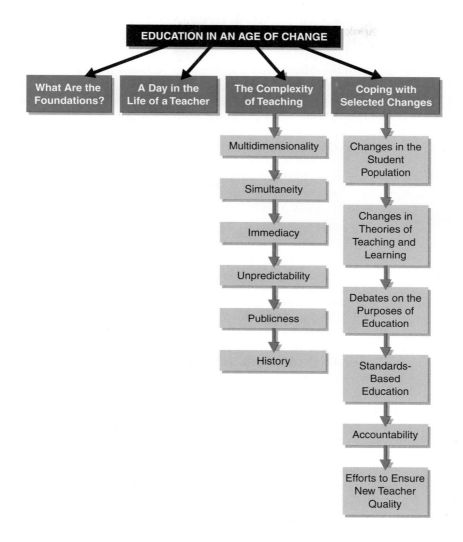

EDUCATION IN AN AGE OF CHANGE

- What Are the Foundations?
- A Day in the Life of a Teacher
- The Complexity of Teaching
  - Multidimensionality
  - Simultaneity
  - Immediacy
  - Unpredictability
  - Publicness
  - History
- Coping with Selected Changes
  - Changes in the Student Population
  - Changes in Theories of Teaching and Learning
  - Debates on the Purposes of Education
  - Standards-Based Education
  - Accountability
  - Efforts to Ensure New Teacher Quality

OBJECTIVES

This chapter will help you to

- identify basic foundational questions related to education.
- describe many of the realities teachers face each day.
- point out characteristics that add to the complexity of teachers' responsibilities.

- explain how changes related to characteristics of learners, knowledge about teaching and learning, views of education's purposes, curriculum standards, and demands for learner and teacher accountability affect teachers' work today.
- describe advantages of developing a professional-development portfolio.

INTRODUCTION

Welcome to the interesting world of education. Education is one of the basic institutions of society. The quality of education in a given society has a direct link to that nation's social, economic, and political health. As a result, it is a subject of intense interest by a variety of individuals ranging from the parents and guardians of young children to business and political leaders on the national stage.

Those considering teaching will find teaching a demanding, exciting, rewarding, and frustrating profession. And that is just in one day! There is nothing more rewarding than to see students' eyes suddenly widen as they get it and to see the excitement that is generated when students succeed, knowing you have played an important role in their lives. However, it is equally frustrating to see students with potential waste that potential and remain unmotivated or even hostile to learning and intellectual growth.

Teaching is often labeled society's "essential" profession. As a teacher, you have an impact on the most valuable resource in society, the youth of the nation. It is not unusual for individuals who are honored for their contributions to society to single out a teacher who had an impact on their lives. Without good teachers there would not be good engineers, physicians, attorneys, scientists, musicians, politicians, and others who contribute to the overall health of a society.

There is certainly no shortage of ideas about what education should be and what teachers should do. Because all citizens have had some personal experience with education, they tend to view themselves as "experts." For example, one of the authors has found that the reactions of individuals vary according to how he introduces himself. If he introduces himself as a "researcher" or a "writer," there is usually a relatively low-key response. However, if he introduces himself as a "teacher," people often launch into a discussion about what needs to be done to improve education! You will find that these ideas about education vary tremendously. As you analyze individual proposals, you will encounter many suggestions that are supported by compelling evidence and have great potential for enhancing the quality of learners' experiences in school. On the other hand, you are certain to encounter other prescriptions for improvement that, if implemented, might actually diminish the quality of school programs. One of your challenges as an educator will be to distinguish between school-improvement proposals with legitimate prospects to make schools better and more dubious propositions with little potential to make positive changes.

The Satisfactions of Teaching

To get a perspective on the satisfactions of teaching go to MyEducationLab and select the topic "Teaching Profession" and read the article "The Satisfactions of Teaching." In this brief article, Elliot Eisner, a professor at Stanford University, highlights six aspects of teaching that lead to satisfaction. Answer the questions that accompany the article. Some of the questions are written specifically to prepare you for your licensure examination.

WHAT ARE THE FOUNDATIONS?

Understanding the current status of education and evaluating proposals for improvement require an understanding of the foundations of education. The foundations comprise the set of historical, philosophical, social, legal, and cultural assumptions that form a logical base for decisions about schools and schooling. As a preparation for making informed decisions about competing school-improvement ideas, you will find it useful to know something about questions associated with the foundations of education. Some examples associated with selected foundation categories follow:

- *Social and philosophical foundations. What is the good society, and how should education contribute to that society?* (Many debates about changes in education are really debates among people who have different views of what constitutes the good society. Debates about what should be taught and who should be taught are two areas of conflict in the social and philosophical foundations.)
- *Historical foundations. Where did current school practices and traditions originate, and are they still important?* (Current school practices did not come about because a group of experts sat down and worked from a blank slate. Historical developments have greatly influenced our educational system. Your task is to determine the extent to which these historical influences still have merit.)
- *Political foundations. Who has the power to decide priorities and to influence how schools operate?* (You will find that some proposals for changes in the ways schools conduct their business are directed at the wrong audience. For example, "Letters to the Editor" on topics related to education are often directed to "teachers" when they should be directed at the school board or state legislators who are making the rules. You and others interested in school reform need to know who has the power to make decisions that will result in desired modifications.)
- *Curriculum foundations. What is taught, and why is it taught?* The term *curriculum* is used to describe the overall framework for an instructional program. (You will find that much debate about the quality of education centers on what is taught in the schools. There is much consensus around the idea that the curriculum must keep up-to-date with technological changes. However, much more contention rages around other issues. Should more be required of learners at earlier ages? How much content about different cultures should be included? Should young people be allowed to learn in their primary language? Are some subjects "frills" that can be eliminated?)
- *Instructional foundations. What is good teaching?* The term *instruction* refers to teaching approaches that are used to help learners achieve the overall purposes that are outlined in the curriculum. (The issue of good teaching is central to any debate about education. You will find that not everybody defines "good teaching" in the same way. For example, some people want teachers to embrace findings of recent research into how the brain operates and processes information. Others favor approaches based on other research or theoretical perspectives. One issue you will need to confront concerns striking a balance between (a) requiring teachers to follow certain common instructional patterns and (b) allowing teachers flexibility to implement instructional approaches of their own choosing.)
- *Legal foundations. What are the legal and ethical rights and responsibilities of teachers and learners?* (In recent decades there has been much litigation relating to education. Proposals for change have to take into account legal principles that influence the actions of teachers and school administrators.)

What Do You Think?

Take a couple of minutes to respond to the following questions.
- How are the foundations interrelated?
- How might an understanding of the foundations help you make an informed decision about becoming a teacher?

(continued)

Throughout this text we will address these basic foundations of education. They are central to discussions about educational change. Understandings you develop related to these questions will help you better evaluate specific educational change proposals.

There are numerous misconceptions about the life of the teacher. Some see it as a relatively easy job with few intellectual demands. For example, a friend of one young woman preparing to be an elementary teacher asked, "What's difficult about teaching someone that $2 + 2 = 4$?" One individual challenging the need to complete courses in order to obtain a teaching credential remarked, "All you need to know to be a teacher is how to read the teacher's guide." It is relatively common for individuals in interviews for admission to teacher-preparation programs to state, "Oh, I know I'll be a good teacher because I've done lots of babysitting and teaching in church school." In fact, some recent proposals for reforming education seem to presume that, other than subject matter, there is little a teacher needs to know.

What is teaching really like? You have spent thousands of hours as a learner in classrooms and you may have spent time observing teachers. You may have spent considerable time working with youngsters in a variety of other settings. As a result, you may think you have a clear grasp of the role of the teacher. However, it is probable that at this point in your professional development you still have a somewhat restricted view of what teachers do.

As a recipient of instructional services and as an observer, you have experienced only the visible actions of teachers as they communicated with their learners. The reality is that many excellent teachers are so good at what they do that they make teaching look easy to observers. They move smoothly through the curriculum, their learners are engaged in lessons, and few disruptions interfere with the instructional process. What you probably were not able to discern during your observations were (1) the thinking and the decision making involved in lesson preparation and (2) the teachers' prior efforts to understand the interests and motivations of individuals resulting in lesson strategies that learners found meaningful. Often, too, good teachers make small, important, and sometimes invisible-to-observers adjustments to changing classroom situations that keep learning on track. As a result, what you may have seen as a seamless, almost effortless activity actually involved a complex interplay of actions requiring application of sophisticated learner-understanding and interpersonal-communication skills.

The unobserved aspects of the public performance of good teachers may be only one of the surprises you will encounter as you start work in the profession. We have often heard former students comment, "There is so much I don't know." Many people are surprised at how much time is taken up by activities that don't involve direct work with learners. Among them are responsibilities associated with

- planning lessons,
- record keeping and other administrative duties,
- participating in special school events (back-to-school nights, parent-teacher meetings, athletic contests, school dances, graduation exercises, and so forth),
- serving on various committees,
- participating in professional group activities, and
- communicating with parents or guardians.

The types of activities you will be involved with will vary according to the age level of your learners and the nature of your school and school district. What might be an issue in one place may not be an issue in another. For example, the special characteristics of your school may make it essential that you quickly come to an understanding of the political climate. This understanding might be less critical in another setting. If you teach at the secondary level, you may be expected to serve as an adviser or a sponsor for a school organization or to assist at athletic events. If you teach in an elementary school, you may spend time monitoring learners on the playground or in the lunchroom.

There are no ordinary days in teaching, and there are no typical schools. As a result, place-to-place and day-to-day differences make it difficult to describe the reality of a day in the life of a teacher. However, we thought it worthwhile to make the attempt. We observed a randomly chosen elementary teacher for a single day we make no claim that this scenario generalizes to this teacher's other days or to other teachers in other settings. Our purpose is not to suggest that this day is typical. Rather, our intent is to prompt you to reflect on some aspects of teaching that you may not have considered.

> **Web Extension 1–1**
>
> ## New Teacher Web Page
>
> The Web offers an excellent opportunity for you to extend your understanding and to find resources that can assist you in accomplishing your professional goals. A good place to start is the New Teacher Web page. This site provides specific information about a variety of topics such as finding a job, substitute teaching, and becoming a professional in the classroom.
>
> http://www.new-teacher.com/

Throughout the text we have placed "A Day in the Life . . ." features. These features are based on actual experiences of teachers. Our intent is to give you a glimpse into the rewards and frustrations that accompany being a teacher. In all of these instances we have identified the teacher as "Pat Taylor." See this chapter's "A Day in the Life: A Typical Day."

THE COMPLEXITY OF TEACHING

As you review the day described, consider the variety of things to which Pat Taylor had to attend. When you begin your career in the classroom, your duties will embrace much more than simply teaching lessons. You may find yourself emotionally stretched as you

Sybil Shelton/PH College

Classrooms are very public, multidimensional environments that require alert and active teachers.

A DAY IN THE LIFE . . . A Typical Day

Students in Pat Taylor's elementary school are expected to arrive by 8:30 a.m. However, the day for Pat and the rest of the teachers begins much earlier because school regulations require teachers to be present no later than 8:00 a.m. Many teachers are in the building by 7:30 a.m. or earlier, working on room decorations, preparing lessons, making copies, taking care of administrative work, and preparing for the instructional day. On this morning Pat spends time completing paperwork from the district personnel department relating to validation of summer-term courses taken at a local university.

Pat learns that a parent has called the school. Her child is ill and will miss several days of school. Pat has been asked to prepare assignments that the parent can pick up and use with the child at home. The parent does not want her son to fall behind. Another surprise event this morning is the unexpected arrival of another parent. This parent is concerned about her child's progress, and Pat and the parent spend some time discussing the situation. Phone calls from parents, unexpected arrivals, and other early-morning events are typical of what is encountered most mornings. On some days, there are scheduled early-morning meetings of the entire faculty. What all this means is that there are few days when Pat has uninterrupted time in the morning to work in the classroom.

We are visiting Pat early in the fall when the district regularly holds its annual "Back-to-School Night." During this event, each teacher gives parents an overview of the curriculum and teacher expectations. Pat knows that the explanation will need to be repeated at least twice so that parents with more than one child can visit at least two classrooms. Even though the event does place an additional burden on the teachers, Pat welcomes the opportunity to make contact with parents. Establishing positive rapport now can pay off later in the year.

Pat is expected to pay close attention to the public relations' importance of the back-to-school event, and extra time will have to be spent making the room attractive and stimulating. This morning, with the time that is left, samples of student work are put on the bulletin boards.

The children arrive, and things begin to move quickly. During the first part of the morning, Pat moves the class smoothly through the curriculum. Class members are generally on task, and things go well. Recess time arrives, and students quickly exit the classroom. Pat gathers material and books that have been used and puts them away. Then, after a quick check to make sure all material is ready for the rest of the morning, it is time for a quick trip to the lounge for a cup of coffee and conversation with other teachers.

Recess time passes quickly. Pat and the other teachers position themselves outside their doors to monitor students as they return to the classrooms. A couple of problems have occurred during recess. One of the girls has a skinned elbow that needs attention, so Pat sends the youngster to the office. In time past, the school nurse would have handled this situation, but because of budget cuts, a nurse is available only one day a week. As a result, the school secretary calls the parents and gets permission to bandage the elbow.

Pat also has to deal with a complaint brought by several children who claim that some students were not behaving properly on the playground during recess. Pat informs them that the matter will be addressed. These assurances seem to satisfy them, and the class is soon back to work. As learners work independently, Pat holds a brief conference with those involved in the recess incident. A warning with a firm tone of voice seems to achieve the desired outcome.

As the morning passes, some class members experience difficulty staying on task because their attention spans shorten. In response to this situation, Pat moves around the classroom working with different groups and refocusing learners' attention on what they are supposed to be doing. Lunch come as a welcome break.

The lunch period begins with a trip to the cafeteria. Joking and light conversation with other teachers make the time go swiftly. A quick trip to the mailbox reveals some messages and an announcement about Back-to-School Night that needs to be sent home with the students that afternoon. The lunch break is

. . . continued

concluded with a hurried gathering of equipment needed for the afternoon science lesson. As usual, several items are missing. This discovery prompts a quick search and some adjustments to the original lesson plan.

After arriving back in the classroom before it is time for the class members to return, Pat quickly cleans up things left out from the morning. A few notes are added to the plan book as reminders of things that must be done tomorrow.

Pat is still making preparations for the afternoon when the bell rings and students line up outside the classroom. They are still excited from lunch and the few minutes they have spent on the playground. They are talking loudly. To calm them, Pat instructs them to go quickly to their seats and sit quietly. Then, Pat takes a favorite children's book from the desk and begins to read aloud. There are a few groans when the reading stops.

It is time for the next lesson. This lesson and those that follow go well, but the rest of the school day seems to pass slowly. The class is restless and less attentive. Pat knows this is a typical pattern, and many afternoon activities feature active learner participation in the hope that this will keep class members focused and involved. A few minutes before the dismissal bell, Pat stops all instructional activities. He asks members of the class who have been assigned as workers to perform their duties. Books are placed in the bookshelves, paper are collected, and he takes time to make last-minute announcements and to give reminders about homework. Pat distributes the papers that need to be sent home and dismisses the class.

Today Pat has bus duty. After a hurried walk to the bus loading zone, the behavior of students who ride buses is monitored. Once all the buses have left, Pat heads back to the classroom.

The first order of business is to gather the papers that need to be taken home and corrected. Next, lessons for the next day are reviewed, and reminders about what needs to be done are jotted in the margins of the daily plan book. Then it is time to create, gather, and organize supplementary material that will be used. Some materials for tomorrow need work, and these are placed in the "take-home" bag. Over an hour has passed since the last child boarded the bus. Finally, Pat locks the door and heads home, carrying papers to be graded and lessons to be planned.

 ## Disposition Check

In recent years, studies about teachers have extended beyond just skill acquisition to the area of teacher dispositions. Teacher dispositions are defined as those attitudes, values, and perceptions that influence teacher behavior and decision making. In the "Day in the Life . . ." feature we will ask you to consider teacher dispositions.

This scenario indicates that the day in the life of a teacher is a very busy one. Teaching is a profession where the attitudes and dispositions of the teacher have a powerful influence on the lives of students. Teachers soon learn that they are the most important variable in the classroom. Their moods create the daily "weather." Teachers have tremendous power to make a student's life exciting or unpleasant. In the face of pressure, teachers must remain calm and professional as they face unexpected events and unplanned interruptions. As professionals, teachers cannot afford to "lose it."

Reflect on Pat's day.
1. What attitudes and dispositions were present?
2. What disposition do you think are important for success in teaching?
3. Which of these dispositions do you possess?

learn to cope with these many responsibilities. Walter Doyle (1986) suggests that the following features combine to make the role you will play as a teacher particularly complex:

- Multidimensionality
- Simultaneity

- Immediacy
- Unpredictability
- Publicness
- History

Multidimensionality

Multidimensionality refers to the idea that teachers' responsibilities range across a broad array of duties. When you teach, you have to know how to multitask. In addition to planning and delivering instruction, you have to diagnose learning difficulties, spot misconceptions, monitor learner progress, make on-the-spot adjustments, respond to unanticipated events, administer standardized tests, attend meetings, keep accurate records, relate to parents, work productively with colleagues, and create materials. You may wonder, "How am I supposed to do all of these things and still teach?"

Perhaps the biggest challenge you will face as a teacher is responding adequately to young people in your classes who come to you with different backgrounds, motivations, aspirations, needs, abilities, and learning styles. Some of them will have the prerequisite skills and abilities to achieve success; some will not. Some learners will come from backgrounds that differ from your own. Some will come to school as cheerful, well-rested individuals, but others may be tired and angry. Although many young people you teach are likely to see you as a caring and supportive mentor, a few may see you as a threatening adult who cares little for the things they deem important.

Simultaneity

Simultaneity refers to the idea that many things happen at once in the classroom. When you stand before students, you need to watch for indications of comprehension, interest, and attention. You should listen carefully to answers to determine their relevance and to spot misconceptions and signs of confusion. While providing assistance to one learner, you must, at the same time, monitor the behavior of the rest of the class. You also need to devise ways to keep members of your class focused on your lesson when you must deal with an unexpected interruption such as a message from the office requiring you to provide an immediate written response. Over time, you will grow in your ability to prioritize and respond immediately to multiple stimuli.

Immediacy

Immediacy refers to a classroom reality that features situations that require you as a teacher to respond at once. Often you will not have the luxury of placing things on hold until you have the time and energy to deal with them. The need to act quickly in complex situations places great stress on teachers. This kind of stress is likely to be particularly acute when you are new to the profession and inclined to worry about whether you have made appropriate decisions.

The immediacy character of the classroom requires you to develop good judgment. You cannot learn these kinds of decision-making skills from reading a book. However, you can prepare yourself by thinking about kinds of situations that might develop in the classroom and by considering possible responses you might make. Henson (2004) labels this practice proactive teaching and provides activities to develop proactive skills. In essence, teachers must be problem solvers (Martinez, 2006). The process of simulating responses will help you develop higher levels of comfort when confronted with making real decisions in your own classroom.

Unpredictability

Unpredictability refers to teachers' challenges in working with learners whose reactions do not always follow consistent patterns and with situations that may unexpectedly interfere with established routines. Neither you nor your learners are programmable computers who respond in consistent ways to similar situations. This reality contributes to making teaching both interesting and challenging. Individual learners and classes respond to the same stimuli in different ways. You will soon learn that a lesson that works well with one class may not be effective with learners in another.

Risk taking is an important indicator of professionalism (Phelps, 2006). Unpredictability results not just from differences among individual learners but from unexpected distractions and interruptions that occur when you are teaching. Unexpected visitors, a call over the intercom, a fire drill, a suddenly ill member of your class, or an unusual change in the daily schedule are events that often intrude just as you are trying to make an important point in your lesson.

How should you respond to unpredictable events? The answer will vary depending on your personality, philosophical views, and general orientation to teaching. In other words, different teachers respond to similar situations in various ways. For example, one of your colleagues might interpret an unexpected learner response as an act of defiance, whereas you might see it as a manifestation of nothing more than a lack of understanding. There probably will be occasions when you will view unanticipated occurrences as frustrating disruptions and other occasions when you may see them as providing interesting, though unexpected, learning opportunities.

How should you respond to unpredictability? Do you need to have things follow a predictable pattern? Do you get upset if things do not always go as planned? You need to think about your answers to these questions. Although you need to work to ensure that your classroom runs smoothly, unpredictable events will happen and will upset the best of plans. You need to be ready for this reality. If you are uncomfortable in situations that feature unpredictability, you might want to consider a career other than teaching.

Publicness

Publicness refers to the idea that teaching is a profession that occurs in an arena that allows recipients of the instructional process to monitor every classroom action their instructor takes. When you teach, you are operating in an environment where your learners can observe your every move. Young people are keen observers, and they will soon make personal decisions about what you are "really like." Your mannerisms, enthusiasms, biases, and values will become public knowledge in no time. Some members of your class will quickly learn what pleases you and what upsets you.

The particular character of your interaction with learners is strongly influenced by the interplay between your actions and your learners' interpretations of those actions. A ripple effect often follows your actions in the classroom. In other words, your actions will be observed and interpreted and have consequences beyond the immediate situation. For example, if you display great anger when a learner makes a mistake in class, you may find class members increasingly fearful of volunteering responses to your questions. On the other hand, if you are willing to experiment and share your errors, your classroom will become a safe place where your students will become scientific risk-takers (Phelps, 2006). If you teach in a middle school or high school, behaviors you have displayed in one class quickly become known and affect your relationships with other classes you teach.

History

The interaction you have with class members over a term or an entire year develops a class history. A class history is a kind of culture that is unique to each class of students and results from an ongoing record of interaction between the teacher and students. The manner in which you relate to learners, plan instruction, and react to unpredictable events creates this history.

Differences in particular class histories explain why apparently similar behaviors by different teachers do not always produce similar results. For example, you might find that a quiet word may stop inappropriate behavior, but another teacher using this approach can find that it fails to correct the situation. As you think about developing your own teaching style, you will not find it productive to simply mimic another teacher's behavior. Your class members will have a history that may vary considerably from the history of learners of the teacher you are trying to emulate. As a result, your learners will have a different interpretation of your actions.

What Do You Think?

As you review the complexities of the teaching situation, reflect on the following:
* How do you cope with unpredictable events?
* Which of the dimensions of the classroom worry you most?
* Can you think of an example when the history established by the teacher with a group of students has impacted teaching and learning?

COPING WITH SELECTED CHANGES

Education is a part of society, not separate from society. As society changes, education must also change. Just a few years ago personal computers, the World Wide Web, cell phones, and satellite television did not exist. Now, we find it hard to imagine life without them. These technological innovations have an impact on educational practices. There have been changes in the composition of the student population. Increased mobility means that schools in every part of the nation are likely to have a diverse student population. The underlying values and beliefs of students are likely to be quite different than those of students just a few decades ago. Unfortunately, education is often slow to change and adapt to new realities. As a future teacher, you need to realize that education must change to accommodate new realities. Over time, the role of the teacher may significantly change. You need to be aware of some of the changes that are taking place in education and consider how they may impact teaching and learning. For instance, see this chapter's *Video Viewpoint* feature to see how cell phones impact teaching and learning today.

**Video Viewpoints
1–1**

Pushing Your Buttons: No Cell Phones Allowed

WATCH: This *20/20* video segment on the controversy regarding the presence of cell phones in school illustrates how changes in society and technology have impacted the classroom in ways that were not anticipated. In this instance, the debate concerns even allowing students to bring cell phones to school. This video illustrates the difficulty that many schools have in coping with new technology.

THINK: Discuss with your classmates or write in your reflective journal your responses to the following questions:

1. Which is your response to the attempt to ban cell phones from schools?
2. How do you respond to the arguments against cell phones?
3. How do you respond to the concerns of the parents?
4. What do you think would be a reasonable solution?

LINK: What are some other innovations that have the potential to impact the classroom?

 To view this video, go to the Video Viewpoints DVD and click on this chapter's video: "Pushing Your Buttons: No Cell Phones Allowed."

Changes in the Student Population

One of the most significant changes in society has been an increase in diversity. Because of population mobility and international interdependence, you are almost certain to be teaching in communities in which schools enroll young people from varied cultural and language backgrounds. Many adults and policymakers have not grasped the significance of this change. By the year 2020, half of the nation's public school students will be minorities but only about 5% of the teachers will be minorities (Meyer & Rhodes, 2006). School leaders today struggle as they attempt to help the general public understand that the characteristics of learners in today's schools differ markedly from those enrolled just a decade or two ago.

Today's schools enroll many young people from homes in which the primary language spoken is not English. Nearly 50 million children in the schools are nonnative speakers of English and are still working toward complete fluency in the language. This figure represents more than a 95% increase in such learners from those enrolled in academic year 1991–1992 (Padolsky, 2002). In some states, these young people comprise high percentages of the total school population. In California, for example, fully one-fourth of the young people in grades K–12 are nonnative speakers of English. Other states with schools that enroll extremely high percentages of these learners are Texas, Florida, New York, Illinois, and Arizona (Kindler, 2002). As a teacher you will face tremendous challenges in creating an environment in which all learners can succeed and in which there is open communication between the school and parents or guardians of these young people.

Attempts to respond to this diversity in the classroom have led to several important changes. Many schools have bilingual education programs, where learners are taught in their native language for at least a part of the day until they become proficient in English. There has been a major emphasis on multicultural education, a perspective that holds that school programs should present learners with instruction that honors and respects the contributions of many individual cultures to our nation and world.

James Banks (2001), a leading expert on multicultural education, points out that growing ethnic and cultural diversity requires rethinking school curricula. He believes that all learners should develop multicultural perspectives. Banks wants school curricula to accurately describe how different cultural groups have interacted with and influenced Western civilization.

Supporters of multicultural education have begun to exert a serious influence on educational practices. For example, many school textbooks now include multicultural content, and many states mandate the inclusion of multicultural content in the curriculum. Not everyone supports the idea that more multicultural perspectives should be included.

Critics of multicultural education worry that, at best, multicultural content replaces important substantive content in the curriculum or, at worst, it tears down the basic values of our national heritage and leads to national disunity (Schlesinger, 1995). They fear that traditional Western writers such as Shakespeare will be eliminated from the curriculum and the teaching of history will be distorted.

Bilingual education also has both supporters and critics. Advocates contend that learners' education should not be delayed until they acquire English proficiency. The Bilingual Education Act of 1968 was developed as a program to help nonnative speakers of English study school subjects in their home languages until they develop adequate proficiency in English. This arrangement allows young people to continue to master school subjects at the same time as their facility with English develops. Research on the bilingual arrangement supports the view that learning in one's primary language improves feelings of self-worth and helps develop an understanding of one's own culture (Macedo, 1995).

Critics contend that the effectiveness of bilingual education has not been validated (Ravitch, 1995). They believe that a common language promotes national unity. Some opponents of bilingual education also object to its high cost. Still other critics contend that allowing young people to learn in their home language delays their acquisition of English.

Some critics of bilingual education suggest that learners who come to school speaking home languages other than English should be enrolled in total immersion programs (Ravitch, 1995). Total immersion programs attempt to speed nonnative speakers' acquisition of English by involving them in instructional programs that surround them with English-language instructional programs. The controversy over bilingual education has sparked an effort to have English declared as the official language of the United States. Some supporters of this idea would like to take money currently spent on bilingual education and reallocate it to pay for total immersion programs for learners.

What Do You Think?

- What is your response to the arguments regarding multicultural content in the curriculum? What evidence can you cite to support your view?
- How do you think the schools should accommodate students who speak a language other than English? Do you think bilingual education or immersion is the best approach? Why?

Another type of diversity that has had an impact on the classroom is the increasing presence of learners with a range of mental and physical challenges in the classroom. Inclusion refers to a commitment to the view that learners, regardless of unique personal characteristics (disabilities, for example), not only have a legal right to services in the regular classroom but they are welcomed and wanted as members of these classes. For many years, the traditional practice was to separate these learners in special education classrooms. Today special education teachers, who have received special academic preparation related to teaching learners with varying disabilities, increasingly work with regular classroom teachers in designing and delivering instruction to these learners.

Changes in Theories of Teaching and Learning

How individuals learn has been the subject of debate for centuries. There is still much that we do not know about the human brain and what causes learning to occur. We do know that the brain is incredibly complex. In recent years new insights into the brain and into the nature of what is termed "intelligence" have influenced educational practice. Today many teachers are implementing instructional programs that are strongly influenced by research related to (1) constructivism and (2) multiple intelligences.

Web Extension 1–2

Education Week on the Web

• ◆

This is the home page for a Web version of a publication that provides weekly information about a variety of educational issues. It is a good way to keep current on contemporary issues and emerging trends.

http://www.edweek.org

Constructivism

Constructivism is based on the principle that individuals cannot simply be given knowledge. Rather, individuals must create knowledge as they interact with the world around them. Their constructions of knowledge are rooted in their prior knowledge. Your learners' knowledge will grow as they compare new information with what they already know. The theory holds that the mind is constantly searching for patterns and attempting to resolve discrepancies. The social and cultural contexts within which learning takes place also heavily influence what is constructed or learned.

Constructivism has several important implications. One is that the conditions that best facilitate learning are what might be described as learner-centered and problem-centered. This means that as a teacher you need to provide learners with complex, complete, "authentic" problems. Once this is done, guidance is provided to class members to help them gain the knowledge needed to solve the problems. This contrasts with more traditional approaches that introduce learners to small pieces of information that, in time, are put together into a whole.

For example, a traditional approach to teaching elementary children arithmetic emphasizes lessons requiring them to memorize multiplication tables. The expectation is that the information will prove useful at some future date when they need to apply these skills to solve problems that are important to them. By way of contrast, a constructivist approach to teaching multiplication tables might begin by presenting learners with a problem that requires multiplication skills in order to find a solution. The students work together to consider what they need to know to solve the problem. If you are using a constructivist approach, you help class members note patterns and develop a generalization on how multiplication processes work. The idea is to teach multiplication in the context of "real" problems when your learners need this skill.

In the same vein, constructivist approaches to teaching topics such as punctuation and spelling are embedded with larger story-writing activities that provide learners with a real need to know this kind of content. The general approach has led to a reading philosophy commonly referred to as whole language instruction, which features lessons in which reading, writing, speaking, and listening are taught as a single, integrated process. Youngsters in the earliest grades are urged to write stories and then read them to others. The focus is on encouraging them to use language, to look for patterns, and to learn writing and spelling conventions as they are needed.

Storytelling is another activity that constructivist teachers use, and it works well with students of all ages and abilities. Former Virginia Teacher of the Year,

Scott Cunningham/Merrill

An increased emphasis on accountability has led to increased testing of students.

Mary Bicouvaris (see Henson, 2004, p. 250) explains, "The smartest students love storytelling; the weakest ones worship it."

Another assumption of constructivism is that members of your class need to be actively engaged in the learning process. They must actively seek solutions to problems and share ideas. Because the social and cultural context is important, and because it is not likely that any one individual can find the solution working alone, often your learners will work in pairs or in teams. As a result, lessons built around constructivism principles may involve members of your class in considerable talking and movement.

Constructivism also has changed conceptions of assessment, the process of ascertaining what members of your class have learned. If you are teaching according to this perspective, you will be interested in assessment procedures that focus on how well class members can solve problems and in their ability to explain what they have discovered and learned. You will be less interested in traditional tests that often measure largely what learners remember about what they have been told.

As you may have already noted, these approaches differ from certain popular present-day assessment practices. The current emphasis on accountability, the idea that teachers and schools should be held directly responsible for teaching specific information to specific learners, has relied heavily on the use of standardized tests. Standardized tests are tests developed by testing experts to test a large population of students. They specify conditions under which they are to be used. The items included in the standardized tests have been tested on a reference group and often have a set of "norms" that allow comparison of a single student to a larger population of students. The emphasis on standardized testing has caused many teachers to focus on the information that might be tested and to use practices that run counter to constructivist learning.

Accountability concerns also have led to the creation of highly controlled instructional approaches. In these approaches, the role of the teacher is to follow a provided script. Constructivists argue that this type of instruction does not take into account prior knowledge of learner differences and is based on the old idea that learning has to proceed in small, predictable steps.

Multiple Intelligences

Another important change that has influenced education relates to conceptions of intelligence. Throughout history, debates have focused on the nature of intelligence (Woolfolk, 2001). Traditionally, intelligence has been viewed as a single trait that can be measured by an Intelligence Quotient or IQ test. The IQ test assumes that if a person is smart in one area, he or she will be smart in other areas as well. People with higher IQ scores are assumed to have more of the "intelligence trait" and hence to be able to achieve more success in challenging academic endeavors.

In recent years, there has been growing support for the idea that intelligence has many facets or that there are multiple intelligences. According to this view, intelligence is not a unitary trait but rather consists of a number of separate categories. A person may have different levels of ability in individual categories. That is, a person may be smart in certain categories of intelligence and not so smart in terms of certain other categories. Most people are thought to have combinations of strengths rather than just a strength in one area and weakness in all others. Howard Gardner (1999), a leading authority in multiple intelligences, has identified at least nine distinct kinds of intelligence:

- **Logical-mathematical intelligence.** People with strengths in this area are good at seeking meaning through analytical processes that involve the use of abstract symbols.
- **Linguistic intelligence.** People with strengths in this area are especially adept at making sense of the world through language.
- **Musical intelligence.** People with strengths in this area have the capacity to communicate and create meaning that involves consideration of sound.
- **Spatial intelligence.** People with strengths in this area have facility in perceiving, transforming, and re-creating visual images that contribute to their understanding of their world.
- **Bodily-kinesthetic intelligence.** People with strengths in this area are good at using muscular and other body systems to respond to situations and to solve problems.
- **Interpersonal intelligence.** People with strengths in this area are particularly good at recognizing and responding to feelings and motivations of others.
- **Intrapersonal intelligence.** People with strengths in this area heavily weigh their own personal capacities and attitudes when determining which course of action to follow in a given situation.
- **Naturalist intelligence.** People with strengths in this area are especially good at making inferences based on classifications and analyses of features of the physical world.
- **Existential intelligence.** People with strengths in this area seek insights regarding ultimate issues such as the meaning of life and how their own existence does or should fit into this scheme.

Yet another dimension to the conception of multiple intelligence has been added by Daniel Goleman (1995). Goleman defined what he calls emotional intelligence as the ability to exercise self-control, remain persistent, and be self-motivating. Individuals with high levels of emotional intelligence have developed expertise in five key areas:

- **Mood management.** A person's ability to handle feelings in ways that are appropriate to and relevant for a situation.
- **Self-awareness.** A person's ability to know feelings he or she is sensing and to discriminate among them in meaningful ways.
- **Self-motivation.** A person's ability to organize feelings in ways that allow self-directed activity in behalf of a goal to go forward, even in the face of self-doubts and distracting temptations.
- **Empathy.** A person's ability to recognize verbal and nonverbal cues of others and to be sensitive to their feelings.
- **Managing relationships.** A person's ability to work productively with others to resolve conflicts, to maintain open lines of communication, and to negotiate compromises.

Multiple-intelligence theories have implications for you as a teacher. Perhaps the most important is the need to avoid labeling learners according to their IQ scores. Scholars who have studied multiple intelligences point out that there are many ways an individual can be gifted. Another implication is that you need to vary your instructional program in ways that excite and challenge learners with strengths in varying kinds of intelligences. This reality means that you need to vary your modes of presentation. A lesson that is perfectly appropriate for a learner with great strength in the area of linguistic intelligence may not well serve the needs of another learner who is weak in this area but strong in spatial intelligence.

Debates on the Purposes of Education

As you strive for excellence in education and seek to defend your instructional decisions, one of the realities you will face is that people hold wildly different views regarding what schools and educators should be doing (Clincy, 1998). You will find that different individuals often give quite varied answers to questions such as:

- What subjects should our schools emphasize?
- Should we be primarily concerned about preparing academically proficient individuals for higher education?
- Should we be producing individuals with marketable vocational skills?
- Should schools be addressing social justice issues?
- To what extent should schools address persistent social problems such as substance abuse and healthy living?
- To what extent should schools be developing moral and ethical character?
- Should there be standardized expectations for all learners, or should there be a focus on the development of the unique potential of individuals?
- What should the schools do to prepare individuals for their citizenship responsibilities?

The normal perspective in response to these issues has been that it is a part of the responsibility of the schools to address important societal concerns. When there is a prominent health concern, such as AIDS, new programs are added to schools. When there is an increase in crime, there is a call for schools to spend more time on morality and character education. In times of national crisis, more emphasis on citizenship is promoted. When the economy dips, schools are expected to produce skilled workers who can immediately enter the workplace as productive employees. Almost always, parents are worried about whether their children are being prepared to gain admission to higher education.

Because individuals have varying priorities, proposals to improve or reform education reflect a tremendous diversity. Throughout the history of American education there have always been voices criticizing the schools and calling for reform. For example, in the 1940s and 1950s, books such as *Crisis in Education: A Challenge to American Complacency* (Bell, 1949), *Educational Wastelands: The Retreat from Learning in Our Public Schools* (Bestor, 1953), *The Diminished Mind: A Study of Planned Mediocrity in Our Public Schools* (Smith, 1954), and *Quackery in the Public School* (Lynd, 1953) leveled criticisms against the schools that in some ways are similar to those we continue to hear today. During the late 1950s and 1960s, American space failures following the 1957 appearance of *Sputnik*, a satellite launched by the former Soviet Union, were blamed on poor education, and a decade of pressure for school reform followed. In the 1970s the focus changed to a concern about potential damage that highly structured school programs might be doing to children. The view of schools as repressive, unimaginative places was reflected in widely read books, including *How Children Fail* (Holt, 1964), *Death at an Early Age* (Kozol, 1967), *Teaching as a Subversive Activity* (Postman & Weingartner, 1969), and *Crisis in the Classroom* (Silberman, 1970).

One thing you will discover is that many critics of the schools have little knowledge of the history of educational reform efforts. It is interesting to hear contemporary critics call for a return to the schools of the past, a suggestion that implies that nobody complained about the quality of the schools we had 10, 20, 30, or more years ago. As the list of titles introduced in the previous paragraph attests, the idea that there was a "golden age" just a few years ago when everybody agreed the schools were excellent simply is nonsense. There has never been a time in our educational history when everybody believed our schools were performing appropriately.

Because people have varied views about which aspects of schooling are important, the evidence used to measure the success of schools varies according to purposes that are given priority. For example, in recent decades some groups have measured the success or failure of schools by using the scores of students taking college entrance exams such as the Scholastic Achievement Test (SAT), international tests of learner achievement, and most recently, standardized achievement tests. Obviously, these indicators of school success focus on just a few of the purposes of education. Some critics contend that these indicators are poor measures of many important educational goals.

Standards-Based Education

As policymakers have attempted to respond to a call for school improvement and reform, they have been frustrated by the lack of valid and reliable data upon which to judge the success of schools. These frustrations have led to support for standards-based education. Standards-based education is an attempt to develop clear, measurable descriptions of what learners should know and be able to do as a result of their education. These descriptions typically take the form of goals to reach or levels of proficiency to be attained (Noddings, 1997). Educational specialist Elliot Eisner (1999) notes that one basic motivation behind the standards-based movement is to hold schools accountable. Accountability is facilitated when there are common standards that allow schools, classrooms, teachers, and learners to be compared. Most states and many professional associations have spent considerable time and effort defining standards.

There are several different types of standards. Performance standards relate to the identification of levels of proficiency that given groups of learners are expected to attain. For example, a performance standard in reading might state that all learners will attain a certain level of reading proficiency. Content standards describe what teachers are supposed to teach and what young people in their classrooms are expected to learn (Noddings, 1997).

Many national subject-matter groups have developed content standards for what they believe to be essential learning in their subjects. Many states also have developed academic content standards for most of the subjects commonly taught in their schools.

Proponents of clearly defined content standards believe that once standards are specified, measurements can be developed that will provide data that can be used to evaluate school performance and to guide the allocation of scarce resources. They argue that this information is important to provide the public with information relative to the excellence of their schools and teachers. It is assumed that this will prompt teachers to higher levels of performance and provide parents with more information that they can use in selecting schools for their children.

Not everyone agrees that standards-based education is a good idea. Elliot Eisner (1999), for example, suggests that this approach is based on a faulty understanding of the educational process. He argues that proponents of standards-based education inappropriately view schooling as something like a horse race or an educational Olympics that emphasizes competition among individuals rather than as an enterprise designed to develop the distinctive talents and abilities of individuals. C. Thomas Holmes (2006, p. 58) says that "Standardized test results should be used for identifying areas in curriculum that need improvement, not for holding students accountable."

The focus on standards represents a fundamental shift in the traditional ways educational decisions have been made. It is a particular challenge to the tradition of local control. Local control has meant that curriculum decisions and school improvement efforts (1) have been made at the local community level and (2) attempts have been made to match improvement efforts with local priorities and interests (Stake, 1999). Standards applied across the entire nation or across an entire state effectively remove control from local school authorities. Robert Stake acknowledges that whole states and the entire nation do have a legitimate interest in what every child is learning. However, he argues that this does not mean that every child should learn exactly the same content.

Stake's concern raises this critical question: Who should determine the content standards for the schools? Should a group appointed by politicians such as the president, members of Congress, or governors determine them? Should the standards be decided by a group of business leaders or academic professors in higher education? Is the role of education to supply a trained workforce for industry, or should programs be designed with the expectation that all learners will qualify for admission to a college or university? At times in recent years, members of all of these groups have been involved in efforts to define educational content standards.

Efforts to establish standards have often led to divisive debates. For example, when national standards for history were proposed, there was widespread support for the project. However, once the original standards were published, many people, even those who had originally supported the project, quickly rejected them as too multicultural and unpatriotic. Hence, the seemingly logical and innocent idea of clearly defining expectations for learners quickly assumed political overtones.

In another instance, when science standards were proposed in California, a group of Nobel Prize winners in science criticized them and proposed their own set of standards. Because of their high profile, the media disseminated their views widely, and a debate was under way. Critics pointed out that a Nobel Prize does not necessarily confer on the winner a store of validated knowledge about what is appropriate for young people to learn at different grade levels. Others attacked the Nobel Prize winners' assumption that every public school learner should master science content at a sophistication level necessary to qualify for admission to the most selective universities.

One of the most significant changes brought about by standards-based education has been a tremendous increase in the emphasis on testing in every subject and at every grade

Critical Incident

Teaching to the Test

Maria is a first-year teacher. She wants to develop lessons that interest and motivate her students. Recently, her principal visited her classroom for an observation. Following the lesson, the principal said, "You had an interesting lesson and everybody in your class was engaged. However, you need to remember that test scores are very important here. Our parents expect us to post high test scores and we cannot afford to let them slip. We expect that all of the students in your classroom will do well on the test. If I were a parent and asked you how today's lesson ties to the testing program, what would you say?"

1. *What are your reactions to the principal's comments?*

2. *Should teachers be teaching to the test?*

3. *Is there an inconsistency between having interesting lessons and meeting standards?*

4. *How would you respond?*

level (Stake, 1999). Much of this assessment consists of high-stakes testing. This means that the results of assessments have important consequences. Scores may strongly influence the promotion or retention of learners, and retention adversely affects minority youths more than mainstream students (Holmes, 2006). Scores also influence the graduation of high school students, the evaluation and the salaries of teachers, and the levels of funding individual schools receive. Because low learner scores can have extremely negative effects, today teachers spend considerable time helping students master content that will be assessed on high-stakes tests. Today, high-stakes testing is prevalent throughout the world (Cancoy & Tut, 2005). In some schools where you might accept employment, you and your colleagues may sense pressure to "get test scores up." For an example, see the *Critical Incident: Teaching to the Test* feature. Such pressures have the potential to narrow the extent of the taught curriculum. In effect, the curriculum becomes that content most likely to be emphasized by standardized-test makers. Some critics of standardized testing assert that this tendency has given anonymous test-makers more power over the content of the curriculum than they legitimately should have.

Accountability

The concept of accountability relates closely to standards-based education. Standards are developed to indicate what schools should be teaching and the level of performance that learners should be attaining. Accountability frequently is related to issues such as the financing and control of the schools. In many places, schools that do not demonstrate attainment of certain learner performance levels, usually measured by standardized tests, face certain consequences. For example, they may lose a portion of their funding, the principals may be replaced, learners may be allowed to transfer to other schools, and the schools or districts may even be placed under state control. In some places, a tendency has developed for teacher evaluations to be based not on general observations of their classroom performance, but rather on their learners' test scores.

Accountability has developed in response to several concerns. One relates to education costs. Educational expenditures are a significant portion of any state budget. As education costs have increased, policymakers have demanded that schools be held responsible for spending the money in ways that result in improved learning. However, the accountability emphasis might end up costing the state more money for education. Some states have ruled that if the state establishes standards for student graduation, it is then responsible for providing an appropriate education for all students. This has been called "adequacy funding" and estimates are that this method of funding is more costly than current methods.

When considering debates regarding accountability, you need to separate the general concept of accountability from the issue of measurements that are used to make judgments about teachers and school programs. For example, few educators oppose the general idea of accountability. When you begin teaching, you will find that the majority of your colleagues are sincerely interested in using resources carefully and in working to ensure that students get the best education possible. Issues teachers have with accountability center not on the idea itself, but rather on what is used to determine whether educational services are as good as they should be. In particular, teachers argue against using standardized-test scores as the only accountability measure.

One problem with using standardized-test scores is that a judgment about a teacher's instructional effectiveness is based on what a learner does on a single day of standardized testing. Critics claim that this is too limited a sample of the learner's levels of understanding to be taken as overall evidence of what he or she has learned. In addition, critics point out that test scores depend on several variables other than the quality of instruction they receive. Further, many variables are beyond an individual teacher's control. Some variables that may affect learners' test scores and that are not subject to teacher influence include the following:

- The home language of individual learners (Learners who speak a language at home other than English sometimes have difficulty scoring well on standardized tests.)
- The income and educational levels of learners' families (Learners' home situations affect their school learning. There are huge differences in reading material found in individual learners' homes, levels of parental education and, hence, parental capacities to help with homework, noise levels in the home, and so forth. Scores on standardized tests are highly correlated with the socioeconomic status of parents. Therefore, they are probably a better indicator of parental status than teacher performance.)
- The quality of learning materials provided to supplement instruction (Are books available that are appropriate for the grade level? Is content of the adopted books consistent with content assessed on standardized tests?)
- The nature of the school's facilities (Is classroom lighting adequate? Are classrooms well insulated from outside noise? And so forth.)

Even assuming none of the above differences existed, problems are still associated with using learners' scores on tests as accountability measures. Critics point out that these tests are poorly suited to stand as academic-success indicators. Because so many learners take standardized tests, individual items must be presented in a form that allows for quick, mechanical scoring. This tends to limit test content to fairly unsophisticated information that can be assessed using item formats that require learners to use less complex thinking levels. They fail to challenge learners to use the sophisticated thinking processes they need to engage more difficult content. Another problem is that to avoid penalties for their teachers and schools, some administrators require students to spend so much time preparing for these tests that they do not have time to integrate what they are learning or apply their new knowledge (Cankoy & Tut, 2005).

How might accountability data be gathered in ways that more appropriately respond to some difficulties associated with overuse of standardized-test results? Some critics of present practices propose that data on such topics as school dropout and graduation rates, college acceptance rates, follow-up studies of graduates, teacher-turnover rates, school safety issues (such as the number of suspensions and discipline incidents), and other variables need to be considered in addition to test scores. The problem is that gathering this information can be time-consuming, difficult, and expensive.

In summary, you are certain to encounter continued discussions of concerns related to standards and accountability when you enter the profession. You and other professionals will face challenges as you seek to ensure that adopted standards are consistent with the purposes of education and that the measurements used for accountability purposes are valid and fair.

Efforts to Ensure New Teacher Quality

The focus on standards has not been confined to the K–12 schools. In recent years, a broadened accountability interest has embraced development of standards for beginning teachers. Accompanying assessments seek to evaluate higher education programs based on how well their graduates meet those standards. In previous years, state authorities issued teaching certificates to newcomers based only on their completion of a prescribed sequence of college courses. Today, many states are moving to performance-based systems that judge candidates' readiness in terms of their ability to perform in the classroom in ways consistent with adopted professional standards.

Interstate New Teacher Assessment and Support Consortium

More than 30 states participate in a consortium called the Interstate New Teacher Assessment and Support Consortium (INTASC). INTASC has identified 10 principles that beginning teachers should know and be able to do. Yours may be one of the many states that now use these principles as a basis for organizing teacher-preparation programs and for issuing teaching licenses. These principles, referred to as the INTASC Model Core Standards, follow (Interstate New Teacher Assessment and Support Consortium [INTASC], 1992):

Standard 1 (S1). The teacher understands the central concepts, tools of inquiry, and structures of the discipline(s) he or she teaches and can create learning experiences that make these aspects of subject matter meaningful for students.

Standard 2 (S2). The teacher understands how children learn and develop, and can provide learning opportunities that support their intellectual, social, and personal development.

Standard 3 (S3). The teacher understands how students differ in their approaches to learning and creates instructional opportunities that are adapted to diverse learners.

Standard 4 (S4). The teacher understands and uses a variety of instructional strategies to encourage students' development of critical thinking, problem solving, and performance skills.

Standard 5 (S5). The teacher uses an understanding of individual and group motivation and behavior to create a learning environment that encourages positive social interaction, active engagement in learning, and self-motivation.

Standard 6 (S6). The teacher uses knowledge of effective verbal, nonverbal, and media communication techniques to foster active inquiry, collaboration, and supportive interaction in the classroom.

Standard 7 (S7). The teacher plans instruction based upon knowledge of subject matter, students, the community, and curriculum goals.

Standard 8 (S8). The teacher understands and uses formal and informal assessment strategies to evaluate and ensure the continuous intellectual, social, and physical development of the learner.

Standard 9 (S9). The teacher is a reflective practitioner who continually evaluates the effects of his/her choices and actions on others (students, parents, and other professionals in the learning community) and who actively seeks out opportunities to grow professionally.

Standard 10 (S10). The teacher fosters relationships with school colleagues, parents, and agencies in the larger community to support students' learning and well-being.

Web Extension 1–3

INTASC Standards

More information about the INTASC standards and about content standards that have been developed for particular subjects can be accessed at the INTASC Web site.

http://www.ccsso.org/Projects/Interstate_New_Teacher_
Assessment_and_Support_Consortium

As you continue through your teacher-preparation sequence, you will gain the knowledge and skills you need to meet these standards. From time to time, you may wish to review your own professional development in terms of your growing ability to understand and perform in ways consistent with the INTASC Model Core Standards.

Praxis Assessments for Beginning Teachers

Educational Testing Service (ETS) developed the Praxis series of assessments to evaluate individuals preparing for careers in teaching at various points in their professional development. Many states and universities use results of these tests as a basis for making program-entry decisions; awarding teaching certificates, licenses, or credentials (documents making it legally possible for a person to teach in a state's schools); and determining whether beginners' levels of teaching performance are acceptable. Currently, 35 states use some or all of the assessments as a credential requirement.

Praxis has three different assessment categories. Praxis I consists of academic skills assessments. These tests are used early in the academic careers of students who wish to pursue education careers. They seek to determine whether prospective teacher candidates have adequate reading, writing, and mathematics skills.

Praxis II assessments provide information about teacher candidates' knowledge of the subject(s), important pedagogical knowledge, and knowledge of important learning and teaching principles. In many places, teacher candidates must receive certain minimum scores before they will be issued teaching licenses, certificates, or credentials.

Praxis III is a classroom-performance assessment that usually takes place during the first year of teaching. Local assessors use nationally validated criteria to observe and make judgments about a teacher's performance. Results often are used to help newcomers to the profession prepare professional improvement plans.

As you go through your professional development program, you may find it particularly useful to keep in mind some categories assessed by the Praxis II assessments. Because Praxis II assessments are used in a large majority of the states, at some point in your program you may be required to take these tests. Even if you are not required to do so, the Praxis II categories describe aspects of practice that are important for you to master as you work to become a professional educator.

Some of the topics covered in the Principles of Learning and Teaching Test include how learning occurs, learner motivation, learner diversity, different instructional approaches, planning instruction, effective communication, the role of the school in the community, debates on best teaching practices, major laws relating to learner and teacher rights, and personal reflection on teaching practices.

Web Extension 1–4

Investigating Praxis

More detailed information on the Praxis series of assessments and even sample questions can be found on their Web site.

http://www.ets.org/praxis

Key Ideas in Summary

- Because education is viewed as such an important societal institution, it is the subject of much debate and numerous proposals for change. Because there is no national consensus regarding the purposes of education, you are likely to find disagreements and inconsistency among proposals to improve the schools.

- School policies and practices are influenced by answers to important questions associated with the foundations of the education profession. These questions include those associated with (1) social and philosophical foundations, (2) historical foundations, (3) political foundations, (4) curriculum foundations, (5) instructional foundations, and (6) legal foundations.

- Teachers' roles require them to discharge diverse responsibilities. These include (1) planning lessons, (2) maintaining records, (3) attending special school events, (4) working on committees, (5) participating in professional groups' activities, and (6) communicating with parents and guardians.

- The complexity of teaching relates to its *multidimensionality* (the idea that responsibilities range across a broad variety of duties), *simultaneity* (the need for teachers to work in an environment in which many things occur at the same time), *immediacy* (the necessity to respond at the same time to multiple events), *unpredictability* (the need to work in an environment in which learners' behaviors do not always follow consistent patterns), *publicness* (the need to work in an arena that is subject to constant monitoring by others), and *history* (the need to cope with classroom patterns or culture that have resulted from previous teacher-learner interactions).

- As a teacher today, you will confront challenges that change over time in important ways. These challenges require you to be flexible and to be willing to modify your teaching approaches in light of new conditions and situations.

- Instructional approaches tied to *constructivism* and *multiple intelligences* are examples of those you may encounter early in your career. Constructivism refers to the idea that people cannot simply be given new knowledge. For knowledge to become meaningful, learners must create understanding through interactions that involve prior knowledge and knowledge that is presented to them for the first time. Multiple-intelligence theory holds that intelligence is not a unitary trait. Rather, there are various kinds of intelligences, and individuals are likely to be "smarter" in terms of some intelligence types than others.

- Over time, there have been numerous debates about the appropriate purposes of schooling. There has never been a time in our educational history when everyone agreed on what constitutes a good education. You may expect to encounter debates about what we need to do to "make schools better" throughout your career in the profession.

- Today, there is great interest in establishing public standards against which to measure learners' academic progress. These standards often are accompanied by testing programs that seek to assess how well young people are mastering the prescribed content. Increasingly, school leaders and teachers are being held accountable for learner performance on these tests. Some people argue that this trend irresponsibly forces teachers to "teach to the test."

- In recent years, legislators and others responsible for overseeing the schools have become greatly interested in the issue of teacher quality. The Interstate New Teacher Assessment and Support Consortium (INTASC) is an example of an entity created as a result of this interest. INTASC has developed a set of expectations for new teachers known as the *INTASC Model Core Standards*. These standards lay out knowledge and behavioral expectations for beginning teachers. Many colleges and universities use these standards as a framework for constructing their teacher-preparation programs.

- The *Praxis* series of assessments represents another response to the desire to ensure that new teachers meet acceptable minimum standards of quality. Many states require all prospective teachers to take these tests. Individual Praxis tests are given at three points during a teacher's professional development sequence: (1) a basic understanding and skills test is given as a precondition to formal entry into the professional component of a teacher education program; (2) a test over subject matter and pedagogical knowledge is given as a prerequisite to awarding teacher certificates, licenses, or credentials; and (3) a classroom-performance assessment is given during a new teacher's first year in the classroom.

- You may wish to keep an *initial-development portfolio* as you go through your teacher-preparation program. The portfolio allows you to organize information, reflect on it, and make decisions about what important information you already know and what important information you need to obtain to adequately prepare yourself for the classroom.

Reflections

1. In this chapter, you learned that many debates about education are rooted in different perceptions about what is a good society and how education should contribute to that society. What are your views of the good society? How does your view of the good society influence your views of what education should be?

2. Schools reflect society, and changes in society influence education. What do you see as two or three changes that are occurring in society that will have an important impact on schools and education? What impact do you think they will have? How do you propose to react to these changes?

3. Review material in the chapter dealing with *constructivism*. If you decided to embrace this approach, what would your lessons be like? What is your response to constructivism, and why do you feel this way? Do you recall any of your own teachers operating in ways that are consistent with this approach? What did they do that you liked or disliked?

4. Sometimes today's critics paint pictures of so-called "golden ages" when the schools were excellent and everybody was happy with our educational system. In this chapter you learned that, contrary to the pronouncements of these critics, there has never been a time when there has been an absence of debate about the quality of our educational system. During your career, you are virtually certain to encounter some people who will tell you, "Our schools are much worse than they used to be." How will you respond to people who share this view?

5. The INTASC standards and Praxis examinations have become important components guiding the preparation and licensure of teachers. What is your reaction to them? How will you use information you now have about the INTASC standards and the Praxis examinations as you continue your preparation for classroom teaching?

Field Experiences, Projects, and Enrichment

1. Interview a teacher who has taught for at least 10 years. Select someone who teaches at a grade level and in a subject area you would like to teach. Ask this person to reflect on the kinds of criticisms of teachers and schools he or she has

heard over the years. What has been the general nature of this criticism? Have all critics complained about the same things? What remedies have been proposed? How have this teacher and his or her teaching colleagues dealt with these criticisms? Share responses with others in your class.

2. Observe a teacher and look for instances of *multidimensionality, unpredictability, simultaneity, immediacy,* and *history.* After your observation, ask the teacher what impact these have on planning and instructing. Which of these variables does the teacher think provided the most challenges during his or her first year of teaching? What advice does the teacher have for a newcomer to the profession who will be dealing with these challenges for the first time? Share your findings with others in your class.

3. In this chapter you read a brief explanation of *emotional intelligence.* Educators are becoming increasingly interested in this topic. To enrich your own understanding, use a good search engine such as Google at http://www.google.com, enter the search terms *emotional intelligence,* and conduct an Internet search. You will find dozens of sites with good information. One you may particularly wish to visit is the EQ International Site on Emotions, Emotional Needs, and Emotional Intelligence at http://www.eqi.org. At this site, you can follow a link to a massive table of contents including topics such as conflict resolution, emotional awareness, emotional literacy, emotional intelligence, and emotional needs. Review information at one or more Internet sites. Then, prepare a short report for others in your class that will expand their understanding of emotional intelligence.

4. Research the state standards and state assessment programs for the grade level(s) and subject(s) you plan to teach. Your instructor will be able to help you locate this information. Many state departments of education put this information on their Web sites. Then, think about these questions: Did you find any surprises? Do you agree with them? Why or why not? To conclude the exercise, prepare a personal plan of action in which you outline some specific things you intend to do to gain the knowledge and expertise you will need to deal with any standards (and related tests) for which you do not feel your present preparation is adequate.

5. Take the 10 principles outlined by the INTASC standards and create an *Already Know/Want to Learn/Learned* chart. For each standard make three columns. At the top of the first, write "Know." At the top of the second column, write "Want to Learn." At the top of the third column, write "Learned." Begin by entering what you think you already know about the principle in the first column and what you want or need to learn about it in the second column. As you progress in your development, write what you learn about each principle in the third column. You may wish to keep this in a professional-development portfolio as documentation of what you have learned.

◆ ──

References

Banks, J. (2001). *An introduction to multicultural education* (3rd ed.). Boston: Allyn & Bacon.

Bell, B. I. (1949). *Crisis in education: A challenge to American complacency.* New York: Whittlesey House.

Bestor, A. (1953). *Educational wastelands: The retreat from learning in our public schools.* Urbana, IL: University of Illinois Press.

Bicouvaris, M. (2004). In K. T. Henson, *Constructivist teaching strategies for diverse middle-level classrooms.* Boston: Allyn & Bacon.

Cankoy, O., & Tut, M. A. (2005). High-stakes testing and mathematics performance of fourth graders in North Cyprus. *The Journal of Educational Research, 98*(4), 234–244.

Clincy, E. (1998). The educationally challenged American school district. *Phi Delta Kappan, 80*(40), 272–277.

Doyle, W. (1986). Classroom organization and management. In M. Wittrock (Ed.), *Handbook of research on teaching* (3rd ed., pp. 392–431). New York: Macmillan.

Eisner, E. (1999). The uses and limits of performance assessment. *Phi Delta Kappan*, 80(9), 658–660.

Gardner, H. (1999). *Intelligence reframed: Multiple intelligences for the 21st century*. New York: Basic Books.

Goleman, D. (1995). *Emotional intelligence*. New York: Bantam Books.

Henson, K. T. (2004). *Constructivist teaching strategies for middle-level classrooms*. Boston: Allyn & Bacon.

Holmes, C. T. (2006). Low test score plus high retention rates equal more dropouts. *Kappa Delta Pi Record*, 42(2), 56–58.

Holt, J. (1964). *How children fail*. New York: Dell.

Interstate New Teacher Assessment and Support Consortium. (1992). *Model standard for beginning teacher licensing, assessment and development*. Washington, DC: Council of Chief State School Officers.

Kindler, A. L. (2002). *Survey of the states' limited English proficient students and available educational programs and services: 2000–2001 summary report*. Washington, DC: National Clearinghouse for English Language Acquisition & Language Instruction Educational Programs.

Kozol, J. (1967). *Death at an early age*. Boston: Houghton Mifflin.

Lynd, A. (1953). *Quackery in the public school*. Boston: Little, Brown.

Macedo, D. (1995). English only: The tongue tying of America. In J. Noll (Ed.), *Taking sides: Clashing views on controversial educational issues* (8th ed., pp. 249–258). Guilford, CT: Dushkin.

Martinez, M. E. (2006). What is metacognition? *Phi Delta Kappan*, 87(9), 696–699.

Meyer, C. F., & Rhodes, E. K. (2006). Multiculturalism: Beyond food, festival, folklore, & fashion. *Kappa Delta Pi Record*, 42(2), 82–87.

Noddings, N. (1997). Thinking about standards. *Phi Delta Kappan*, 79(3), 184–189.

Padolsky, D. (2002). *Ask NCELA no. 8: How has the English language learner (ELL) population changed in recent years?* http://www.ncela.gwu.edu/askncela/08leps.htm.

Phelps, P. (2006). The 3 Rs of professionalism. *Kappa Delta Pi Record*, 42(2), 67–71.

Postman, N., & Weingartner, C. (1969). *Teaching as a subversive activity*. New York: Delacourte.

Ravitch, D. (1995). Politicization and the schools: The case against bilingual education. In J. Noll (Ed.), *Taking sides: Clashing views on controversial educational issues* (8th ed., pp. 240–248). Guilford, CT: Dushkin.

Schlesinger, A. (1995). The disuniting of America. In J. Noll (Ed.), *Taking sides: Clashing views on controversial educational issues* (8th ed., pp. 227–236). Guilford, CT: Dushkin.

Silberman, C. E. (1970). *Crisis in the classroom*. New York: Random House.

Smith, M. (1954). *The diminished mind: A study of planned mediocrity in our public schools*. Chicago: Greenwood Press.

Stake, R. (1999). The goods on American education. *Phi Delta Kappan*, 80(9), 668–672.

Woolfolk, A. (2001). *Educational psychology* (8th ed.). Boston: Allyn & Bacon.

Chapter 2

What Does It Take to Become a Professional Educator?

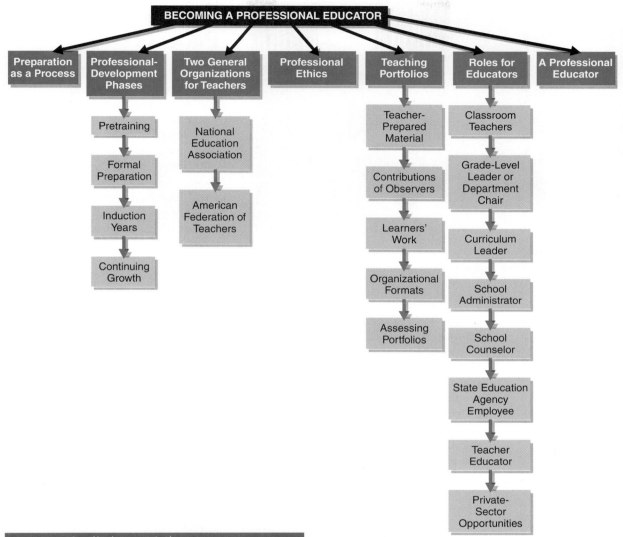

BECOMING A PROFESSIONAL EDUCATOR

- Preparation as a Process
- Professional-Development Phases
  - Pretraining
  - Formal Preparation
  - Induction Years
  - Continuing Growth
- Two General Organizations for Teachers
  - National Education Association
  - American Federation of Teachers
- Professional Ethics
- Teaching Portfolios
  - Teacher-Prepared Material
  - Contributions of Observers
  - Learners' Work
  - Organizational Formats
  - Assessing Portfolios
- Roles for Educators
  - Classroom Teachers
  - Grade-Level Leader or Department Chair
  - Curriculum Leader
  - School Administrator
  - School Counselor
  - State Education Agency Employee
  - Teacher Educator
  - Private-Sector Opportunities
- A Professional Educator

OBJECTIVES

This chapter will help you to

- explain why teacher preparation is better thought of as a career-long process rather than as a series of steps having a definite end.

- describe important phases in a typical teacher-development process.

- suggest ways that information from such national teacher organizations as the National Education Association and the American Federation of Teachers can help beginning teachers adjust to their new profession.

- define dimensions of ethical behavior in the education profession.

- explain benefits associated with the development of teaching portfolios, and describe components in these documents.

- point out examples of the variety of roles that are found within the education profession.

- state the challenges and rewards of teaching.

Scott Cunningham Merrill

Preparation programs are designed to prepare teachers for success in complex, multicultural environments.

PREPARATION AS A PROCESS

Think about what the word *preparing* means in the phrase "preparing for teaching." When you learned to ride a bicycle, you reached a point when someone let you go and you could confidently ride. A profession does not work this way. You do not wake up one day shouting, "Eureka! I know all I need to know about this business." Professionalism is a deliberative, developmental experience. Veteran teacher educator Patricia Phelps (2006, p. 69) says that helping students develop professionalism is "the most challenging aspect of preparing new teachers." When you prepare for teaching, you develop a commitment to career-long growth (Steffy, Wolfe, Pasch, & Enz, 2000). Your initial preparation program helps you to start learning the kinds of things necessary to continue learning.

Members of individual professions share common values and perspectives. For example, there are ethical standards to which members of the teaching profession subscribe. A shared commitment to certain ethical practices, a concern for the development of the capacities of all learners who come to school, and a sense that education should be a high-priority concern for the entire society have led educators to band together in large and powerful organizations. These include the **National Education Association (NEA)** and the **American Federation of Teachers (AFT).** These groups help set national and state education agendas.

In recent years, public discussion of education has focused increasingly on performance of both learners and teachers. As a new teacher, you will be entering a profession that attracts much public scrutiny, and it is likely that you will be asked to provide evidence that documents your performance. In many places, teachers are being asked to prepare teaching portfolios for this purpose.

As you begin work as an educator, you probably will be surprised by the diversity of the field. People who begin as classroom teachers have knowledge and skills that equip them to pursue many interesting career paths. Some of these options exist within formal education systems and related governmental agencies; some are in the private sector. These options provide you with a wonderful opportunity to find a role in education that fits you well.

PROFESSIONAL-DEVELOPMENT PHASES

Your professional development as a teacher did not begin when you entered your teacher-preparation program. The roots of your decision go all the way back to your personal set of prior experiences, your thoughts about them, and the decisions you made that ultimately resulted in your taking steps to pursue a program leading to a teaching certificate, license, or credential.

Though your teacher-preparation program will contribute to making you a professional, the preparatory process will continue throughout your career. As you think about entering the profession, you may find it helpful to know something about four important phases that characterize teachers' professional lives. They are

- the **pretraining phase,**
- the **formal-preparation phase,**
- the **induction-years phase,** and
- the **continuing-growth phase.**

Pretraining

Your personal experiences and the attitudes you developed before enrolling in any teacher-preparation courses reflect an influence of the pretraining phase of your professional development. Your attitudes probably derive in part to views that your family members hold. In addition, your feelings about teaching may have been affected by your teachers, your classmates, and experiences you had when you were in elementary, middle, and high school. Influences of your own schooling experiences are to be expected, given that the typical high school graduate has spent more than 10,000 hours in K–12 classrooms.

Memories of your own school days may not be as helpful as you think. Schools and learners today vary tremendously. You may find that the schools you see during your preparation program are quite different from those you attended. The young people, too, may differ from those with whom you went to school, and you may find that some instructional techniques that your favorite teachers used (and that you liked) do not work well with other learners in other settings. You need to keep an open mind about what constitutes "good teaching" and recognize that practices that are enthusiastically received by learners in some places may not be appropriate for learners in others.

Formal Preparation

You are using this text, so you are probably in the formal-preparation phase of your professional development. Though there are some differences from institution to institution, there are common features in most teacher-preparation programs. In part, these common features have been developed in response to guidelines of state and national accrediting bodies such as the **National Council for Accreditation of Teacher Education (NCATE).** Preparation programs often have these three basic parts:

- core studies,
- teaching specialization(s)/academic major(s), and
- professional education.

Core Studies

In addition to the specific content areas you will be expected to teach, you are expected to be familiar with information that educated adults know. The **core-studies component** of teacher-preparation programs is designed to accommodate this need. Typically, core-studies requirements ask students to take a specified number of content courses from mathematics, the sciences, the liberal arts, and the fine arts. These courses constitute about 30% to 40% of a typical bachelor's degree program.

Teaching Specializations/Academic Majors

If you are preparing for a career in elementary schools, you will be expected to teach information from a variety of content areas. You may also have a particular **teaching specialization** such as reading or mathematics that you have studied in some depth as part of your preparation program.

Prospective middle school teachers may have teaching specializations or a formal **academic major,** and future high school teachers almost always have an academic major. If you are preparing to teach in high school, you probably intend to teach courses in your academic major. You may also be assigned to teach at least a few courses in other subject areas. (Requirements related to teaching outside of the academic major vary greatly; however, a certain minimum number of college or university courses are often required.)

Professional Education

The **professional-education component** of your preparation program seeks to give you the expertise needed to deliver instruction and manage learners. In recent years, there has been a trend toward having more of this component of the preparation program offered in K–12 schools. Prospective teachers today spend much more time in the schools than was the case 10 or 20 years ago. The goal is to smooth the transition from the world of the college or university to the world of the K–12 school. Many programs today provide opportunities for prospective teachers to engage in some supervised instruction of learners in the schools at various stages throughout their preparation program. Historically, preparation programs provided prospective teachers with virtually no direct contact with K–12 schools until student-teaching experience, a capstone experience that often did not occur until the term just before graduation.

You may have already had some experience teaching K–12 students as part of your own preparation program. If not, you probably will soon have an opportunity to do so. Successes you experience will be confidence builders. They can also broaden your appreciation of the many kinds of learners in the schools, and they can challenge your capacity for honoring and responding professionally to the diversity you probably will encounter. Work in the schools, particularly when it is approached seriously, can be a wonderful beginning to a successful teaching career.

• •

State Licensing Standards
Go to MyEducationLab to learn about getting your license, beginning your career, and understanding your state license standards. This site also addresses passing the licensure exam and portfolios.

- What are the specific standards for obtaining a credential in the state of interest to you?
- What is the balance of content courses, teacher education courses, and field work?

• •

Induction Years

The first years in teaching are sometimes called the **induction-years phase.** This term implies that no one assumes you will arrive on the job fully formed as a professional educator. It is another recognition that professionals are involved in a process of career-long development and that the early years are times of particularly intense learning. Much learning during the first few years of teaching centers on adapting to the special characteristics of the school, the learners, the surrounding community, the prescribed curriculum, the available resources, and the interpersonal relationships among the teachers.

Even new teachers from the finest preparation programs experience stress during the initial years of teaching. Beginners sometimes miss the support university supervisors and supervising teachers provided them during student teaching. Many school systems recognize this problem, and some respond by assigning experienced mentor teachers to work with newcomers. Some states now have laws requiring school districts to provide this kind of support to new teachers.

Much discussion about challenges facing newcomers to the profession used to focus on the first year of teaching. Today, educators recognize that beginners take several years to settle comfortably into their new roles. Increasingly, school leaders are thinking about ways to provide special assistance during the first 2 to 4 years of teachers' professional service. Some states permit teacher-education students to graduate, but they withhold teacher certification until the new teachers have experienced a successful year of supervised internship. Other states are planning to adopt this practice.

What Do You Think?

- What is your response to the idea of extending the teacher-preparation process?
- What do you think would be helpful to teachers during their first years of teaching?

Continuing Growth

Professional development does not end with your induction into the profession (Shechtman, Levy, & Leichtentritt, 2005). It is a career-long, self-improvement process (Flowers, Mertens, & Mulhall, 2002). You will have a number of alternative professional-development approaches to pursue when you are in your continuing-growth phase. These include

- staff-development opportunities,
- college and university courses, and
- work associated with professional organizations.

Staff Development

You may find yourself employed in one of the many school districts that organize extensive **staff-development** activities for teachers. Districts commit funds to these activities as part of their efforts to enhance the overall quality of instruction. The term **in-service education** often is applied to these efforts. These programs often feature special sessions to introduce new teaching techniques, introduce well-known educational speakers, give workshops to prepare materials or modify curricula, or "share" sessions in which participants exchange materials and ideas.

It is likely that you will be required to attend some staff-development sessions; others may be optional. In some districts, teachers receive staff-development credits, and when they have accumulated enough credits, they qualify for higher salaries. Some schools provide workshops during the school day that enable teachers to work with parents. These workshops tend to have positive academic impact. For example, using a survey of 18 elementary and secondary schools in seven states, Sheldon and Epstein (2005) reported that dramatic achievement gains occurred when schools offered such workshops and assigned homework that required students to show and discuss their skills with their parents.

College and University Courses

You may elect to take college and university courses to build your professional knowledge base. Many institutions offer night courses so teachers may take them during the school year. It is common for colleges and universities to have extensive summer-session offerings for teachers. You can often use college and university courses to fulfill requirements for an advanced degree. Frequently, school districts award increases in salaries to teachers who complete specified courses or fulfill advanced-degree requirements.

As you consider possible courses you might take during your early years in the classroom, think first about taking those that will help you meet specific challenges you might be facing in the classroom. You should focus on selecting courses that will directly help you with your work rather than those designed to meet advanced-degree requirements. You may be in the profession for a long time. There will be plenty of time to complete an advanced-degree program after you have addressed some more pressing gaps in the knowledge you need to succeed in the classroom.

Involvement with Professional Groups

You will find that many professional organizations sponsor meetings that include sessions designed to improve teachers' expertise. These groups often offer professional-development opportunities of various kinds, including workshops or more formal sessions in which individual presenters share ideas. Some professional organizations focus on specific subject areas and specific categories of learners. Some sources you may wish to contact for further information include:

- American Alliance for Health, Physical Education, Recreation, and Dance (AAHPERD)—http://www.aahperd.org/
- Council on Exceptional Children (CEC)—http://www.cec.sped.org

The National Education Association is the largest of the general organizations for teachers.

The U.S. National Education Association of the United States

- International Reading Association (IRA)—http://www.reading.org
- International Society for Technology in Education (ISTE)—http://www.iste.org
- Music Teachers National Association (MTNA)—http://www.mtna.org
- National Art Education Association (NAEA)—http://www.naea-reston.org/
- National Association for Gifted Children—http://www.nagc.org/
- National Business Education Association (NBEA)—http://www.nbea.org/
- National Council for the Social Studies (NCSS)—http://www.ncss.org/
- National Council of Teachers of English (NCTE)—http://www.ncte.org/
- National Council of Teachers of Mathematics (NCTM)—http://www.nctm.org/
- National Middle School Association (NMSA)—http://www.nmsa.org/
- National Science Teachers Association (NSTA)—http://www.nsta.org/

Joining a professional group gives you an opportunity to meet people with shared interests. Members often get productive new ideas from even casual conversations with others in the group. Many professional organizations sponsor the publication of journals that feature excellent, practical how-to-do-it articles.

TWO GENERAL ORGANIZATIONS FOR TEACHERS

In addition to the many specialty organizations that serve teachers with particular grade-level or subject-area interests, two national organizations represent the more general interests of the teaching profession. These organizations are

- the National Education Association (NEA) and
- the American Federation of Teachers (AFT).

These organizations perform many services for their members. They help explain teachers' work to the public at large. They engage in lobbying activities seeking legislation thought to advance the interest of their members and opposing legislation thought to have negative implications for teachers. They provide opportunities for classroom practitioners to keep abreast of new knowledge as it relates to their professional development and practice. They also often specify standards of appropriate or ethical practice.

National Education Association (NEA)

The NEA is the larger of the two major teachers' organizations. Though today the NEA does recognize the strike as one legitimate weapon that teachers can use as they seek improved conditions of practice and better salaries, in general the organization conceives of teachers as members of a learned profession such as law and medicine. Because these professionals have a long tradition of

Philip James Corwin/CORBIS-NY

Teachers in many parts of the nation have been involved in political action demonstrations as a means of communicating their needs and wants to those in power.

Web Extension 2–1

The National Education Association

You will find much information about the National Education Association (NEA) at the organization's Web site. Click on a link titled "For and About Members." This link will take you to a page that includes additional links to information of interest to future teachers, beginning teachers, support staff in the schools, retired teachers, and other groups. You will find information of potential interest to you as a prospective educator by following links titled "Beginning Teachers" and "Future Teachers." At this site, you can also find a listing of the NEA's mailing address should you wish to initiate correspondence with the group about a topic that interests you.

http://www.nea.org/

Web Extension 2–2

The American Federation of Teachers

This site is the home page of the American Federation of Teachers (AFT). You will find information about a wide range of activities the group undertakes in support of its members. Click on the link titled "PreK–12 Teachers." This link will take you to a page that includes a link titled "Teachers." Click on this link to go to a page with information about becoming a teacher, staff-development opportunities for teachers, and ideas for working with learners in the classroom.

http://www.aft.org/

self-governance, the NEA has had a tradition of supporting policies that give teachers more control over their professional lives. This implies a role for teachers in such areas as preparation of new teachers, qualifications for hiring teachers, appropriate content of courses, selection of learning materials, and identification of instructional methods.

American Federation of Teachers (AFT)

The American Federation of Teachers (AFT), a union affiliated with the AFL-CIO, views teachers as occupying positions similar to those of employees of large corporations. The AFT points out that teachers, unlike professionals such as lawyers, rarely are self-employed. Nearly all of them work for institutions (school districts). This employment reality creates a situation in which many teachers work at sites distant from the lead administrators in their districts. In the view of the AFT, this creates a need for teachers to have a strong organization to counter the possibility that distant administrators may make decisions that disadvantage teachers and learners.

The AFT has long embraced the strike as a legitimate bargaining tool. It seeks negotiated decisions that maximize teachers' benefits and restrict arbitrary exercise of administrative power. Negotiated agreements tend to specify in considerable detail the responsibilities and rights of both teachers and administrators. When there are differences of interpretation related to these agreements, an arbitration system is followed that is similar to those used in traditional labor-management disputes (see Essex, 2002).

The issue of teacher strikes is one that elicits heated exchanges between supporters and opponents. People opposed to strikes often argue that they undermine teachers' images. They fear that strikes will alienate middle- and upper-class citizens who traditionally have been among public education's strongest supporters. Disgust with strikes could lead these citizens to oppose needed funding for the schools.

Supporters of strikes often observe that people in general are simply unaware of the pressures teachers face. For example, they point to obligations many state legislatures have placed on teachers to raise learners' achievement levels in the absence of new commitments of state revenues to help them get the job done. Proponents of strikes contend that people may "talk a good line" about the need to improve schools, but little real action is likely without pressure such as can be exerted by a strike.

What Do You Think?

- Do strike actions threaten teachers' credibility with parents and other influential members of the community? Why or why not?
- Should the question of whether or not teachers should strike be answered "yes" in some instances and "no" in others? If so, under what circumstances might strikes be appropriate? Under what conditions might they be inappropriate?
- Have you or any of your family members been involved in a strike, particularly one involving schools? If so, what were the reactions of various groups of people who had a stake in the outcome?
- How do you personally feel about strikes by teachers? Have you had personal experiences that have led you to your position on this issue?

PROFESSIONAL ETHICS

One of the marks of a profession is that the practitioners of that profession follow a code of ethics. Ethics refers to a moral code or standard embraced by individuals or groups. In the "helping" professions, such as teaching, an underlying principle of that moral code is that those in the profession act in accordance with the well-being of the client in mind rather than personal concerns or satisfactions. In law, an attorney should act in a manner that is best for the client regardless of how the attorney feels about the guilt or innocence of the person. In medicine, a physician should act in the best interest of the patient and not those of the physician, the hospital, or pharmaceutical companies. In teaching, it requires considering what is best for a student. For example, it might be personally satisfying to seek revenge on a student who has interrupted your lesson by misbehaving. However, as a teacher, you must consider your response in terms of what would be best for the education of the student.

The National Education Association Code of Ethics identifies two major areas of ethical responsibility, those related to the students and those related to the profession (see Figure 2–1). We have divided the area into three areas of ethical concerns for educators. The first are the interactions and relationship with the students, the second is fulfilling professional responsibilities, and the third is in relationships with others such as teachers and parents.

Figure 2–1   **Code of ethics of the education profession.**

PREAMBLE

The educator, believing in the worth and dignity of each human being, recognizes the supreme importance of the pursuit of truth, devotion to excellence, and the nurture of democratic principles. Essential to these goals are the protections of freedom to learn and to teach and the guarantee of equal education opportunity for all. The educator accepts the responsibility to adhere to the highest ethical standards.

The educator recognizes the magnitude of the responsibility inherent in the teaching process. The desire for the respect and the confidence of one's colleagues, of students, of parents, and of the members of the community provide the incentive to attain and maintain the highest possible degree of ethical conduct. *The Code of Ethics of the Education Profession* indicates the aspirations of all educators and provides standards by which to judge conduct.

The remedies specified by the NEA and/or its affiliates for the violation of any provision of the Code shall be exclusive and no such provisions shall be enforceable in any form other than one specifically designated by the NEA or its affiliates.

(continued)

Figure 2–1 Code of ethics of the education profession. (*continued*)

Principle I

Commitment to the Student

The educator strives to help each student realize his or her potential as a worthy and effective member of society. The educator therefore works to stimulate the spirit of inquiry, the acquisition of knowledge and understanding, and the thoughtful formulation of worthy goals.

In fulfillment of the obligations to the student, the educator—

1. Shall not unreasonably restrain the student from independent action in the pursuit of learning.
2. Shall not unreasonably deny the student access to varying points of view.
3. Shall not deliberately supress or distort subject matter relevant to the student's progress.
4. Shall make reasonable effort to protect the student from conduct harmful to learning or to health and safety.
5. Shall not intentionally expose the student to embarrassment or disparagement.
6. Shall not on the basis of race, color, creed, sex, national origin, marital status, political or religious beliefs, family, social or cultural background, or sexual orientation unfairly:
   a. Exclude any student from participation in any programs.
   b. Deny benefits to any student.
   c. Grant any advantage to any student.
7. Shall not use professional relationships with students for private advantage.
8. Shall not disclose information about students obtained in the course of professional service, unless disclosure serves a compelling professional purpose or is required by law.

Principle II

Commitment to the Profession

The education profession is vested by the public with a trust and responsibility requiring the highest ideals of professional service.

In the belief that the quality of the services of the education profession directly influences the nation and its citizens, the educator shall exert every effort to raise professional standards, to promote a climate that encourages the exercise of professional judgment, to achieve conditions which attract persons worthy of trust to careers in education, and to assist in preventing the practice of the profession by unqualified persons.

In fulfillment of the obligation to the profession, the educator—

1. Shall not in an application for a professional position deliberately make a false statement or fail to disclose a material fact related to competency and qualifications.
2. Shall not misrepresent his/her professional qualifications.
3. Shall not assist entry into the profession of persons known to be unqualified in respect to character, education, or other relevant attribute.
4. Shall not knowingly make a false statement concerning the qualifications of a candidte for a professional position.
5. Shall not assist a noneducator in the unauthorized practice of teaching.
6. Shall not disclose information about colleagues obtained in the course of professional service unless disclosure serves a compelling professional purpose or is required by law.
7. Shall not knowingly make false or malicious statements about a colleague.
8. Shall not accept any gratuity, gift, or favor that might impair, or appear to influence professional decisions or actions.

Source: Adopted by the NEA 1975 Representative Assembly. Reprinted with the permission of the National Education Association.

The first area is especially important in education because we are dealing with impressionable students, acknowledged to be among the most vulnerable "clients." As a teacher, you are in a position to have a profound influence on their future well-being. You are also in a position of considerable power. That power needs to be exercised in an ethical and responsible manner.

You influence the lives of students not only through academic learning, you influence their moral and ethical development through your actions. Students are keen observers of teacher behavior. Everyday events have a great impact on them. For many students, teachers are significant adults in their life. What teachers do and say has a profound influence on them. This is an awesome responsibility that should not be taken lightly. As a teacher, you need to think beyond the bounds of your own self-interests.

One of the elements of a profession is that the practitioners of that profession have acquired a unique set of skills through their professional preparation. These are skills that would generally not be found in the general population. Therefore, ethical concerns in the realm of professional responsibilities include such things as being prepared for class, making sure that all students have an opportunity to learn, presenting content that is accurate, and making sure that student assessments are valid and free of bias and distortion.

Relationships with others in fulfilling the role of teacher can lead to some of the most difficult ethical dilemmas. For example, what do you do if you perceive that another teacher is not following professional standards of teaching? What should you do if a school administrator asks you to do something that you do not think is in the best interests of the students or violates an ethical principle? For example, one of the authors was called in to mediate a situation where a school principal was observed drinking and even becoming inebriated during the school day. A couple of teachers had exhibited courage in acting on their ethical principles by bringing this potentially dangerous situation to the attention of others in spite of incurring the displeasure of other teachers and the school district administration.

Ethical issues usually do not have easy right or wrong answers. They often involve a conflict of two or more values or moral principles. Behaving ethically means that you do the "right" thing, not just the expedient or the easy thing.

You will not get very far into your career of teaching without facing ethical dilemmas. In teaching, ethical considerations seem to be around each corner. For example, what should be given priority in responding to discipline problems, the needs of the individual or the needs of the group? How should you handle the dilemma of being required to teach to the test because the school is being judged by test scores yet it is apparent that the students need something different? It is normal that you will have some favorite students. When does that favoritism cross the line and become unethical? What should you do when you believe that another teacher is acting in ways that are harmful to students? What should you do if students share that they are contemplating doing something that will be harmful to them. Read this chapter's *A Day in the Life* as our focus teacher, Pat, faces these types of ethical questions.

TEACHING PORTFOLIOS: DOCUMENTING PERFORMANCE

In Chapter 1, "How is Education Changing?" you learned about features of an *initial-development portfolio*. An increasing number of teachers regularly keep **teaching portfolios** to document their performance and as aids to professional development. Portfolios of this type seek to document accomplishments and to record reflections gathered over a period of time and in a variety of situations (Hom, 1977). A teaching portfolio can give you a means of

A DAY IN THE LIFE . . . The Human Side of Teaching

It is a beautiful, crisp day late in the fall. The leaves are falling from the tress and everyone is looking forward to the coming holidays. However, Pat Taylor is preoccupied in the drive to school. One of Pat's students has been withdrawn lately and has stopped participating in class. Yesterday, on a writing assignment, the student hinted that it would be appropriate for children who were neglected at home to run away.

Pat is unsure about what to do. Was this just a piece of fiction created for this assignment? Was it just a typical adolescent feeling of loneliness? Was the student really experiencing neglect at home? Should a conference be held with the student or would the student see this as a violation of trust between the student and teacher? Should the administration or the school counselor be brought into the situation? Would it be appropriate to contact the parents and have a conference?

Pat began to reflect on the hidden dimensions of teaching. Because teachers are involved in the lives of impressionable youth, they cannot ignore the human side of teaching. This often creates ethical and moral dilemmas that do not have easy answers. Pat wondered if people really knew how many nights teachers spent worrying about students in their classroom.

Some of the older teachers seemed to have developed an immunity or even a callousness that seemed to allow them to shed these concerns and just focus on teaching as another job. However, Pat wasn't sure that was the right approach.

Disposition Check

The human side of teaching has a powerful influence on both students and teachers. When teachers face moral and ethical choices, skills are not relevant. Ultimately, it is their attitudes and values that are most influencial. The personal involvement and the concern of teachers about their students create ethical and moral dilemmas that may not be present for those who do not care. Surveys of students indicate, however, that students identify their favorite teachers more on their personal, caring qualities than on their teaching skills.

Reflect on this ethical dilemma.

1. *What attitudes and values seem to be influencing Pat?*
2. *What do you see as the most important values to consider in this situation?*
3. *How do you feel about the power teachers have over the lives of students?*
4. *Are your dispositions up to the challenge?*

There is some assistance that you can use in identifying the ethical principles that guide the professional practice. Perhaps the most familiar is a **Code of Ethics of the Education Profession** adopted by Representatives Assembly of the National Education Association in 1975 (see Figure 2-1). You should look through this code and identify the key principles.

Additional guidelines can be found in court decisions that relate to the actions of educators. For example, court decisions have addressed the rights of teachers when ordered by the administration to stop teaching content they considered inflammatory, the rights of teachers to write a letters to editors criticizing the local school district, the responsibilities of teachers when they suspect child abuse, and what teachers should do when they obtain information that a student might be contemplating suicide. Chapter 12 covers these and other important legal decisions that impact teacher behavior.

playing an active role in your own assessment (Tillman, Hart, & Ferguson, 2002). Hence, they act to increase your awareness of your cumulative growth needs as well as of the successes you have enjoyed when working with learners in the classroom.

If you decide to maintain a teaching portfolio, some key components you need to include are examples of instructional units you have developed, tests you have prepared, assignments you have made, and other materials you have devised. You probably will also wish to include samples of papers, projects, and other work prepared by members of your class. You will also add information and comments made by people who have observed your work and have prepared formal assessments of your teaching. Typically, your portfolio will also include some of your own written reflections. Material in this section of the portfolio gives you an opportunity to think about what went well (and why) and to consider possible modifications to what you might do if you find yourself not satisfied with certain aspects of the instructional actions you are reviewing.

Not all teaching portfolios organize information into the same set of categories, but most include examples of

- teacher-prepared material,
- contributions of observers, and
- learners' work.

Teacher-Prepared Material

If you are putting together a teaching portfolio, you will use the "teacher-prepared" section to state your own views about characteristics of good teaching. You will probably describe the learners with whom you work and some contextual constraints that affect your performance (e.g., local and state regulations, kinds of materials available, and problems associated with facilities). You may also wish to refer to specific learning objectives you are using to guide your instruction.

You may also choose to mention your preferred instructional and evaluation methodologies. This part of the portfolio is an appropriate place to display examples of instructional units, tests, and lesson plans. You may want to include examples of below-average, average, and above-average work that has been graded. These materials showcase your ability to differentiate among learners whose performances reflect varying achievement levels. You can also include information related to specific actions you have taken to deal with exceptional students and with others with special learning characteristics and needs. Finally, you will want to include reflections about the adequacy of your instructional performance.

Contributions of Observers

You may teach in a school where principals or other administrators regularly evaluate you. It is possible, too, that your school may use a **peer-evaluation system,** in which teachers observe and evaluate lessons taught by other teachers. You will want to include in your portfolio all information you receive that relates to formal evaluations of your classroom performance. Opinions and other reactions from learners and comments from parents, if available, represent other desirable categories of information.

Learners' Work

You also will want to include some evidence related to how well young people you teach have performed on learning assessments, such as class records of learners' scores on quizzes and examinations. In addition, depending on the age level of your learners and the subject(s) you teach, you may find it useful to add learner essays, models, term papers, and completed projects.

Organizational Formats

Several schemes for organizing portfolios have been adopted. An approach developed by James Green and Sheryl Smyser (1996) features five basic categories:

- *Personal background.* In this section, you provide details about your educational and professional experiences, with special reference to your current teaching responsibilities.
- *Context information.* In this section, you discuss the physical characteristics of the classroom, the specific nature of your learners, the adequacy of instructional materials, and other environmental factors that may affect how you teach and how members of your class learn.
- *Instruction-related information.* In this section, you include information about your lesson plans and unit plans and provide examples of materials and instructional aids you have developed. This part of the portfolio gives you an opportunity to include comments and reflections about the adequacy of your instructional approaches, especially about how those approaches have influenced what your students have learned.
- *Responses to special needs of individuals.* This section gives you an opportunity to describe actions taken to individualize instruction to meet specific student needs. Here you will include examples of differentiated assignments, varied learning materials, and alternative assessment procedures.
- *Contributions to the overall mission of the school.* This section allows you to display evidence that demonstrates how your actions have contributed to improving the teaching and learning environment of the entire school. You might include information such as professional-development objectives and plans for meeting them and committee work focusing on schoolwide and communitywide educational-reform issues.

Assessing Portfolios

Similar kinds of information do not appear in every portfolio. Hence, to some degree, assessment procedures need to be tailored to the specific portfolio that is being evaluated. One of the challenges in assessing portfolios concerns the issue of consistency or reliability. Guidelines should allow different reviewers to apply a similar standard in assessing a given portfolio. For example, if reviewers are expected to assign portfolios a rating of "unsatisfactory," "satisfactory," or "outstanding," these terms need to be clearly defined so that different raters will apply them in the same way. This need is often accomplished through the development of a **scoring rubric.** The scoring rubric specifies in considerable detail how a portfolio would look when assigned one of the available rating points. See Figure 2-2 for an example.

Using an appropriate scoring rubric, the portfolio reviewer looks for behaviors that reflect the teacher's expectations, noting any behaviors that are at odds with them. For example, a reviewer might look at what the teacher has described as key features of "good teaching" as a backdrop for considering evidence in the portfolio. Are materials presented in the portfolio consistent with the stated vision of good teaching? Does the provided information support the view that practices were consistent with stated priorities?

You will find that teacher evaluation based on portfolios has important advantages over traditional schemes that depend on data gathered from one or two classroom observations. By gathering information from multiple sources over a considerable period, you can build a portfolio that has the potential to provide a much more comprehensive picture of your classroom performance than could be attained through only one or two classroom visits by an outside observer.

Figure 2–2   **Example of a scoring rubric for portfolio assessment.**

The developer of this scoring rubric prepared it for use with teaching portfolios focusing on teachers' use of a specified set of one state's mandated "advanced technology competency." Note how the scoring rubric helps define the three rating points: "Needs Work," "Satisfactory," and "Exemplary."

Needs Work	The portfolio fails to include data in support of each identified competency. Examples that are provided fail to make a compelling case that the associated competency has been mastered. Teacher reflections, where present, are written in vague, general terms that fail to address specific issues and problems associated with mastering required competencies. The organizational scheme is not clear or, alternatively, it has not been consistently implemented throughout the portfolio.
Satisfactory	The portfolio exhibits examples that address all advanced technology competencies. These examples display evidence sufficient to support that mastery of essential features/components or each competency has occurred. A clear organizational scheme is evident, and it is executed consistently throughout the portfolio. Reflections focus clearly on complexities associated with mastering competencies, though some reflect deeper, more-reasoned consideration than others.
Exemplary	The portfolio exhibits strong and overwhelming evidence that each advanced competency has been mastered. A rich array of pertinent evidence is presented to support the mastery claim for each competency. Examples provided are multiple, varied, and appropriate. A clear organization scheme is evident, and it is executed carefully throughout with no "thin" sections. Reflections respecting all competencies evidence a solid grasp of issues and careful, rational analyses of problems and, perhaps, unexpected "easy stretches" associated with the mastery of each.

ROLES FOR EDUCATORS

Approximately one of every six Americans is a student in a public school. School systems employ millions of people to serve the needs of these young people. People employed in the schools work in diverse environments, and they perform varied functions. When you think about the education profession today, you refer not just to teachers but to people playing all of the roles that must be discharged as part of our society's effort to help young people grow toward productive and personally satisfying patterns of adult living.

Classroom Teachers

Teachers are by far the largest single category of employees in the schools. In the United States today, slightly more than 3 million people are employed as teachers in the public schools. By 2011, this number is expected to grow to approximately 3.6 million (Hussar, 2002).

Because initial-preparation programs for educators focus primarily on helping prospective newcomers get ready for roles in the classroom, you probably already know that teachers are the key players in schools. Their professional expertise unites important subject-area knowledge, planning and organizational skills, and abilities to motivate learners. They develop their capacity to respond to individual learner needs. Over time, they become skilled in articulating and defending their teaching practices to parents, interested community members, political leaders, and others. Learn about one person who chose teaching as a career, motivates others, and helps provide resources to other teachers in this chapter's *Video Viewpoints* feature.

Video Viewpoints 2–1

Charles Best

WATCH: In this *Nightline: Up Close* video segment, Michel Martin interviews a teacher, Charles Best, who came from a privileged background, attended prestigious schools, and chose to become a teacher in the New York public schools. Charles Best then had an idea about finding funding for teacher ideas and created a Web site: www.donorschoose.org. This segment includes a discussion of the motivation of a person to choose teaching, as well as an innovative way to provide resources for teachers who most need them.

THINK: Discuss with your classmates or write in your teaching journal your responses to the following questions:

1. What do the interviewer's questions infer about the status of teaching in the United States?
2. What does this segment indicate regarding equal educational opportunities for all students?
3. What does this segment indicate about the rewards of teaching?

LINK: Can you think of other creative ideas to address educational issues?

 To view this video, go to the Video Viewpoints DVD and click on this chapter's video: "Charles Best."

Soon you may belong to a **teaching team.** A teaching team consists of a group of teachers who draw on one another's strengths and insights to prepare programs and to deliver instruction that is responsive to learners' needs. Teaming requires teachers to have good collaboration skills as well as sound backgrounds in their subject fields and in various teaching methodologies (Lapan & Hays, 2006). Different schools use teams in different ways including (a) faculty groups as a whole, (b) grade-level teams, (c) vertical teams, (d) school-leadership teams, and (e) site-based management teams (Wheelan & Kesselring, 2006).

Teachers also function as leaders who are charged with making changes and adjustments to improve the quality of the learning environment (Lambert, 2002). To maintain a sharp professional edge, you will want to keep up with new knowledge related to effective teaching techniques and developmental aspects of learners, and new knowledge related to your subject(s). Developing a pattern of regular reading of professional journals can help you keep up-to-date. As noted previously, you will find that active participation in professional groups can be a useful part of your continuing-education agenda.

Web Extension 2–3

Phi Delta Kappa and Kappa Delta Pi

Phi Delta Kappa and Kappa Delta Pi are international honorary societies in education. Each organization publishes materials designed to help new teachers make a smooth entry into their new profession. Information related to Phi Delta Kappa is available at:

http://www.pdkintl.org

Go to this Web address and click first on "Professional Development." This will take you to a page with other links. Click on the one titled "New Teacher Connection." At the New Teacher Connection page you will be able to access an advice column for new teachers, ideas new teachers have found useful in their classrooms, and information about working with challenging learners.

Information related to Kappa Delta Pi is available at:

http://www.kdp.org

Go to this Web address. Click on "KDP Store." This will take you to a page with other links. Click on "subscriptions." At the subscriptions page, you will find ordering information for a number of Kappa Delta Pi publications. You might be especially interested in subscribing to *New Teacher Advocate*. This inexpensive newsletter features helpful tips and inspirational reflections for new teachers.

Grade-Level Leader or Department Chair

Many elementary schools have **grade-level chairs** with responsibilities for leading all teachers in the building who teach the same grade. In many middle schools and high schools, a person serving as the **department chair** plays a similar role. In high schools, this individual exercises leadership in a specific subject area (e.g., English, social studies, mathematics, or science). In middle schools, most teaching teams are interdisciplinary. Duties vary, but grade-level leaders often engage in such activities as ordering supplies, evaluating new teachers, coordinating staff-development opportunities, and disseminating information about school policies. In general, grade-level leaders and department chairs act as liaisons between school administrators and other teachers.

Typically, grade-level leaders and department chairs are selected from among the most experienced teachers. They have credibility both with their teaching colleagues and with school administrators. In some schools, grade-level leaders and department chairs teach a reduced load to allow them time to perform other assigned duties. They may receive extra salary, and they often work more days each year than regular classroom teachers.

Curriculum Leader

The position of **curriculum leader** may also be titled curriculum director, curriculum supervisor, or curriculum coordinator. By whatever title it is known, this position features leadership in such areas as curriculum planning, in-service planning, and instructional-support planning. If you work in small school districts, you may find that a single curriculum leader has responsibilities for several subject areas and grade levels and may even continue to teach part-time. If you are a member of the teaching staff in a larger district, individual curriculum leaders may be responsible for only a few grade levels or a single secondary-level subject area. In larger school districts, curriculum leaders often do not teach. In many districts, curriculum leaders have offices in the central administrative headquarters of the school district where they work.

Curriculum leaders are professionals who are familiar with up-to-date trends in the grade-level areas and/or subject areas for which they are responsible. They are in a position to influence the nature of the instructional program throughout the district in their areas of responsibility. Many curriculum leaders hold advanced degrees, work a longer school year than teachers, and receive higher salaries.

School Administrator

Traditionally, school administrators have started their careers as classroom teachers. A few school districts around the country have begun to appoint school administrators who have had prior leadership experience in business or the military services. Administrative positions often require holders to have completed a master's degree and to have met other specified administrative certification, licensure, or credentialing requirements.

Administrative positions exist both at the school level and at the central district administrative level. Typical administrative positions at the school level are assistant principal and principal. Examples of positions often found at the central administrative headquarters of a school district include director of personnel, assistant superintendent, and superintendent.

Over the past two decades, administrators' roles have increasingly involved providing instructional leadership. Pressures on administrators to increase learner achievement have made instruction-related concerns high on administrators' lists of professional priorities. To accomplish this purpose, successful administrators work hard to create a culture in their schools that makes it easy for teachers to enjoy working together and to engage in teaching practices that foster improved learner performance (Fullan, 2002).

More traditional duties of administrators include preparing budgets, developing schedules, preparing paperwork for state and federal authorities, and evaluating teachers and other staff members. They also function as official representatives of the schools to the community. Consequently, they must have good public relations skills. School administrators usually work a longer school year than teachers and are also paid higher salaries.

School Counselor

Some school counselors begin their careers as classroom teachers. There is debate within the professional community of counselors about whether school counselors should have had classroom teaching experience before becoming counselors. Those who support the idea argue that such experience gives the counselor a better understanding of what learners have experienced in their classrooms. Others argue that teaching is basically a controlling function and that counselors who have been teachers may not be able to change their roles from that of a controller to that of a listener and a facilitator.

Most states require counselors to complete academic course work beyond the bachelor's degree. Many prospective counselors enroll in master's degree programs with a school-counseling emphasis. In addition to personal and academic counseling, school counselors also are expected to perform a number of administrative tasks. Sometimes counselors are responsible for establishing the master teaching schedule for a school, and they are often in charge of all standardized testing. They must spend considerable time attending special meetings.

Counselors usually work a longer school year than teachers, and they are paid more. Time available for working with individual students often is surprisingly limited.

State Education Agency Employee

All states have education departments or agencies largely staffed by professionals with backgrounds in education. State education agencies hire people with a variety of backgrounds for diverse purposes. For example, subject-area specialists coordinate curriculum guidelines and in-service training throughout the state for teachers in specific subjects (e.g., English, social studies, music, science, mathematics, vocational education, or physical education). Typically, state education agencies also have assessment specialists who coordinate statewide testing programs. In addition, they usually staff teacher-certification or licensure specialists who work with colleges and universities to ensure that teacher-preparation programs are consistent with state regulations.

Many state education agency employees have had considerable prior experience working in the schools. Large numbers have at least a master's degree, and many have doctoral degrees. Often state agency employees have to travel to meetings at various locations throughout the state they serve. Usually, these employees are on the job 12 months of the year and are paid salaries that are higher than those of classroom teachers.

Teacher Educator

Successful teachers sometimes seek opportunities to share their expertise with future teachers. One way for them to do this is to become a teacher educator. Teacher educators are former teachers. They have assumed new responsibilities as instructors of and academic mentors for people preparing for careers as classroom teachers. Most teacher educators are faculty members of colleges and universities, though a few are employed by large school districts. Almost always, teacher educators hold doctoral degrees.

The role of the teacher educator is varied and complex. Although exemplary teaching contributes to success as a faculty member in teacher education, still more is necessary. As university faculty members, teacher educators must demonstrate initiative in improving preparation programs, stay current on findings of researchers, conduct research, and write for publication. In addition, they must seek opportunities to make presentations at regional and national meetings, maintain good working relations with other departments and with the schools, serve on many committees, maintain good links with state education agencies, and counsel students. All of these obligations require processing of massive quantities of paperwork.

Teacher educators typically are employed for 9 months a year. Many of them have opportunities to also work during the summer months. Salaries are not particularly high; in fact, some beginning teacher educators are paid less than some experienced public school classroom teachers. Although beginning salaries of teacher educators tend to be modest, top salaries for experienced teacher educators are higher than those paid to classroom teachers.

Private-Sector Opportunities

For a variety of reasons, some teachers decide to leave the classroom after just a few years. If you decide to leave teaching, will your teacher-preparation be of any value? Yes it will. There are employment options outside of the public schools for individuals with backgrounds in teaching.

Publishers of textbooks and other instructional materials hire people with backgrounds in education to work both as editors and salespeople. The expertise they bring from their background in the classroom helps firms ensure that materials they develop and market are appropriately designed. In addition, an important element of credibility is added when the salesperson says that he or she has been a classroom teacher.

Large firms, some of which have large training divisions, also hire people with backgrounds in education to work in their employee training programs. The term **human resource development,** often abbreviated **HRD,** frequently is used to describe the corporate training function. If you are interested in education and training in the private sector, go to your library and find a publication called *Training and Development*. It is the official journal of the **American Society for Training and Development (ASTD),** a professional organization for educators in private industries.

A PROFESSIONAL EDUCATOR

As we reach the conclusion of this chapter on becoming a professional educator, it is useful to reflect on what is required of a teacher in contemporary society. Individuals are finding that because you enjoy working with young people or because you enjoy the subject matter you teach are not sufficient conditions for choosing this profession. Becoming a professional educator requires you to be a lifelong learner. You need to realize that no one knows all there is to know about teaching and we are learning more every year. Becoming a professional educator can be a difficult journey as you proceed through all of the requirements to obtain a credential and continue to grow through in-service workshops and additional course work. Then you hear critics claim that teaching is a "soft job" with lots of time off and that schools are filled with intellectually inferior individuals.

Becoming a professional educator requires that you understand something of the complexities of interpersonal relationships you develop with students, parents, and other professionals. At times these relationships are highly satisfying and at other times they are very frustrating. Few things in life are more rewarding than to see the light go on when a student finally understands. Then you realize that the rewards of teaching are found in the impact you have on the lives of individual students. It is very satisfying to be a part of a committed faculty that develops innovative programs and influences the lives of students on a daily basis. However, it is equally frustrating when you have students who seem to have given up and it is distressing to observe other educators who just seem to be going through the motions.

The fact of the matter is that every year, many individuals decide that teaching is not for them. Although there is always some turnover expected in any profession, some teachers leave because they have discovered that teaching did not live up to their erroneous preconceptions of what is required of a professional educator. To a degree, at least, some of these erroneous impressions result from the mistaken notion that they "know all about teaching" because, after all, they had extensive experience as students. Another part of this turnover results from individuals who believe that anybody can teach and that there is nothing they need to learn. When they encounter the frustrations of unmotivated students who do not share their enthusiasm for their subject, they become disenchanted. This chapter's *Video Viewpoints* feature highlights the reasons for frequent teacher turnover.

The authors want you to know that their experience as public school teachers and their opportunities to work with students in a variety of settings have been personally rewarding. We believe that teaching is one of the most important professions and we are excited when we see bright and dedicated individuals move into the teaching profession and find satisfaction and success.

As you proceed through this text, we challenge you to continually reflect on the knowledge base of the profession and evaluate how this knowledge contributes to your development as a competent and compassionate professional.

Video Viewpoints 2–2

Teacher Shortage

WATCH: This ABC News segment discusses the shortage of teachers. Michele Norris highlights the reasons for the turnover of teachers in the public schools and the efforts to address this shortage.

THINK: Discuss with your classmates or write in your teaching journal your responses to the following questions.

1. What do you think the impact will be on the profession of teaching if individuals with inadequate preparation are hired as teachers?
2. Do you agree that standards are meaningless if teachers are not qualified?
3. What is the teacher supply in the region where you would like to teach?

To view this video, go to the Video Viewpoints DVD and click on this chapter's video: "Teacher Shortage."

Key Ideas in Summary

- The phrase "preparing for teaching" does not suggest that the process of preparation has a definite ending point. Rather, it implies that preparation is a career-long process of professional growth and adaptation.

- Teachers' professional development has four important phases. These include (1) the *pretraining phase*, (2) the *formal-preparation phase*, (3) the *induction-years phase*, and (4) the *continuing-growth phase*.

- The pretraining phase of teachers' professional development essentially represents a time when their attitudes and predispositions toward teaching are shaped by family influences and other life experiences. These experiences often give prospective teachers a set of expectations about teachers and their work and a limited view of what teachers do.

- The formal-preparation phase of teachers' professional development divides into three parts. *Core studies* include academic content that educated adults are expected to know, regardless of their college or university major. The *teaching specialization(s)/academic major(s)* component embraces content of the academic major (in the case of prospective secondary teachers) or academic content of the several school subjects they will teach (in the case of prospective elementary teachers). The *professional-education* component consists of preparation experiences related to instruction, evaluation, and management of school learners.

- The *induction years*, the first years of fully licensed classroom teaching, present important challenges to many teachers. During this period, teachers learn to adapt to the particular characteristics of their learners and to the special characteristics of their schools and communities.

- The *continuing-growth phase* of a teacher's career provides many opportunities for continued professional development. Among them are (1) staff-development opportunities sponsored by local school districts and local, state, and national professional associations; (2) college and university courses; and (3) possibilities for involvement with local, state, and national units of major professional groups.

- Two large national organizations represent the general interests of the teaching profession. The largest of these is the *National Education Association (NEA)*. Another important general organization for teachers is the *American Federation of Teachers (AFT)*, a group that is affiliated with organized labor.

- Because teachers are dealing with some of the most vulnerable in society, impressionable youth, high ethical standards are required of teachers. Those standards mean that professional teachers must be more than just knowledgeable adults. They must understand that being a part of a profession requires that they follow the ethical standards of the profession. The National Education Association has developed a *Code of Ethics of the Education Profession*. It obligates teachers to certain patterns of behavior with respect to their learners and with respect to the teaching profession.

- In recent years, there has been growing interest in the use of *teaching portfolios* to document teachers' accomplishments. Teaching portfolios attempt to gather evidence that attests to teachers' effectiveness and performance over time and in a variety of situations. Teaching portfolios often include examples of teacher-prepared materials, comments of people who have observed the teacher's work, and samples of their students' work.

- The profession of education has many roles. People with initial preparation for classroom teaching may find themselves employed at some point in their careers in roles such as: (1) classroom teachers, (2) grade-level or department chairs,

(3) curriculum leaders, (4) school administrators, (5) school counselors, (6) state education agency employees, (7) teacher educators, (8) textbook editors or salespersons, or (9) trainers in business or industry.

- Becoming a professional educator is a process that never ends. There is always more to learn about students and teaching. Individuals need to understand that a professional educator must be a lifelong learner. The profession of teaching includes both deep satisfactions and frustrations. A knowledge base is required of individuals who enter a profession, and those who do not understand this knowledge base are likely to encounter difficulty in their quest to become competent professionals.

For Your Initial-Development Portfolio

At the end of each of the remaining chapters we have provided prompts to help you think about artifacts that you might include in your portfolio related to the chapter. You may choose to identify your responses to items in the chapter such as the Margin Notes or your responses to some of the reflection questions at the end of the chapter. You may also consider observations you make in classrooms or materials you prepare for teaching. We suggest that you select a couple of items that you think best represents your thinking and development and include those in your portfolio.

As you develop a portfolio, one choice you need to make is to identify an organizational framework. We suggest using the INTASC standards discussed in Chapter 1. These are standards for beginning teachers that have been used by numerous states, so identifying material related to your development on these standards can be very useful.

1. What materials and ideas that you learned in this chapter will you include as "evidence" in your portfolio? Select up to three separate items of information. Number them 1, 2, and 3.
2. Think about why you selected these materials. As you do so, consider these issues:
   - specific uses you might make of this information as you plan, deliver, and assess the impact of your teaching;
   - the compatibility of the information with your own priorities and values;
   - any contributions this information can make to your development as a teacher; and
   - factors that led you to include this information as opposed to some alternatives you considered, but rejected.
3. Place a check in this chart to indicate the INTASC standard(s) to which each of your items of information relates.

ITEM OF EVIDENCE NUMBER	S1	S2	S3	S4	S5	S6	S7	S8	S9	S10
1										
2										
3										

4. Prepare a written reflection in which you analyze the decision-making process you followed. In your comments, mention the INTASC standard(s) to which your selected material relates.

Reflections

1. In this chapter, you learned that pretraining influences of families and prior experiences of prospective teachers often give them certain attitudes and perspectives on the education profession. Such influences may have influenced your own views. For example, think about how you would answer these questions:
   * What do good teachers do?
   * What is the ideal school like?
   * What kind of behaviors do you expect to characterize learners you will teach?
   Now, take time to think about where you acquired these perspectives. How sure are you that your present ideas represent an accurate picture of the teaching profession? How might you test the adequacy and accuracy of some of your present impressions?

2. Are there general concerns that teachers share regardless of (a) where they teach in the country, (b) the nature of their learners, or (c) the subjects they teach? Or, are situation-to-situation differences so profound that it makes little sense to talk about national patterns? Given your responses to these questions, what value do you attach to membership in national organizations for teachers such as the National Education Association and the American Federation of Teachers?

3. Review the *Code of Ethics of the Education Profession*. (See Figure 2–1.) Look carefully at Principle I, "Commitment to the Student." Which three of these commitments do you think will present you with the greatest challenges? What actions can you begin taking now to help you to meet these obligations?

4. Suppose you were asked to prepare a *teaching portfolio* that, among other things, had to include information related to how well people in your class were mastering content associated with your state's required curriculum. What kind of information might you include? What would you like to see in a *scoring rubric* designed to assess the quality of your portfolio?

5. Review information presented in the chapter about roles other than classroom teaching that are potentially open to individuals who have completed teacher-preparation programs. (Some of these roles require additional academic preparation.) Which of these roles interest you? What do you find appealing about them? Are your views based on extensive knowledge about the real day-to-day work of people in these roles, or are your opinions based only on general impressions about what they do? How might you go about learning more about these roles and about specific steps you might need to take to qualify for them?

Field Experiences, Projects, and Enrichment

1. Interview a teacher who has been in the profession for at least 15 years. Ask this person to describe his or her preparation for teaching and any in-service or other developmental activities he or she has experienced over the years. Make a report to your class on this topic: "The Professional Life Space of a Teacher: One Person's Experience."

2. Contact an administrator in the central office of a local school district who has responsibilities for staff development. (Your course instructor may be able to suggest the name of an appropriate person.) Try to obtain information about (1) the kind of in-service development the school district expects of its teachers and (2) the kind of in-service opportunities the school district provides to its teachers. Report your findings to others in your class.

3. Some people argue that teachers should have higher ethical standards than the population as a whole. Others suggest that this kind of a standard ensures that only atypical people will serve in the classrooms and that such individuals will be unrealistic models for young people. Organize a class debate on the issue, "Resolved That Teachers Must Be More Ethical Than Typical Citizens."

4. Many teachers today keep teaching portfolios. In this chapter, you learned about some design features that characterize many teaching portfolios. To broaden your understanding of teaching portfolios, enter the term "teaching portfolios" into a good Web search engine such as Google (http://www.google.com). Follow several of the links, and use the information you find as the basis for a report that features these basic categories:
   * design formats,
   * kinds of evidence included,
   * the nature of teachers' reflective commentary, and
   * your own reactions to the information. (Include specific references to ideas you have learned that you will use in your own teaching portfolios.)

5. Many large corporations have large employee-education staffs. The American Society for Training and Development is a professional organization to which many educators belong. Look at several issues of this group's journal, *Training and Development*. How would you compare and contrast articles from *Training and Development* with those appearing in journals that are directed at audiences of school teachers? (Your instructor may be able to suggest some journals you should review.) Present your findings in the form of a short paper.

References

Essex, N. L. (2002). *School law, 2nd ed.* Boston: Allyn & Bacon.

Flowers, N., Mertens, S. B., & Mulhall, P. F. (2002). Four important lessons about teacher professional development. *Middle School Journal, 33*(5), 57–61.

Fullan, M. (2002). The change leader. *Phi Delta Kappan, 59*(8), 12–20.

Green, J. E., & Smyser, S. O. (1996). *The teaching portfolio.* Lancaster, PA: Technomic.

Hom, A. (1977). *The power of teacher portfolios for professional development.* New York: National Teacher Policy Institute. www.teachnet.org/TNPI/research/growth/hom.htm

Hussar, W. J. (2002). *Projections of education statistics to 2011.* Washington, DC: National Center for Education Statistics.

Lambert, L. (2002). A framework for shared leadership. *Educational Leadership, 59*(8), 37–40.

Lapan, S., & Hays, P. A. (2006). Collaborating for change. In K. T. Henson, *Curriculum planning: Integrating multiculturalism, constructivism, and education reform* (3rd ed.). Long Grove, IL: Waveland Press.

Phelps, P. (2006). The 3 Rs of professionalism. *Kappa Delta Pi Record, 42*(2), 67–71.

Shechtman, Z., Levy, M., & Leichtentritt, J. (2005). Impact of life skills training on teachers' perceived environment and self-efficacy. *The Journal of Educational Research, 98*(3), 144–152.

Sheldon, S. B., & Epstein, J. L. (2005). Involvement counts: Family and community partnerships and mathematics achievement. *The Journal of Educational Research, 98*(4), 196–206.

Steffy, B. E., Wolfe, M. P., Pasch, S. H., & Enz, B. J. (2000). *Life cycle of the career teacher.* Thousand Oaks, CA: Corwin Press.

Tillman, B. A., Hart, P. M., & Ferguson, S. M. (2002). Using student portfolios with the NMSA/NCATE Guidelines and Praxis III Framework. *Middle School Journal, 33*(5), 14–19.

Wheelan, S. A., & Kesselring, J. (2006). Link between faculty group development and elementary, student performance of standardized tests. *The Journal of Educational Research, 98*(6), 323–330.

CHAPTER 3

WHAT ARE THE PROPOSALS FOR SCHOOL REFORM?

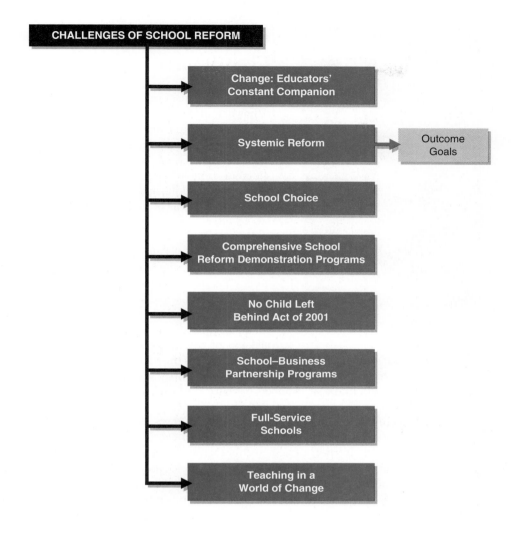

CHALLENGES OF SCHOOL REFORM

- Change: Educators' Constant Companion
- Systemic Reform → Outcome Goals
- School Choice
- Comprehensive School Reform Demonstration Programs
- No Child Left Behind Act of 2001
- School–Business Partnership Programs
- Full-Service Schools
- Teaching in a World of Change

OBJECTIVES

This chapter will help you to

- recognize that change will be a constant feature of your professional life as a teacher.
- describe characteristics of *systemic reform*.
- cite examples and describe features of selected approaches to providing parents, guardians, and learners with *school choice*.

- explain how the *No Child Left Behind Act of 2001* influences schools and school practices.
- describe examples of approaches to change teacher-compensation plans.
- explain purposes of *school–business partnerships*.
- describe characteristics of *full-service schools*.

Teaching in a world of change requires the use of
new skills such as teaching using technology.

Anthony Magnacca/Merrill

CHANGE: EDUCATORS' CONSTANT COMPANION

How do you react to change? Do you desire stability?
What is it about the role of teacher that you find attractive? You need to think about these questions as you consider a career in education. As you seek answers, you may
discover that schools are evolving in some ways that are
different from what you experienced during your own
elementary, middle, and high school years. You need to be
comfortable with a professional environment that continues to alter in response to changing social and political
environments.

At least in the near future, the rate of change is not
likely to slow. Modifications in schools and school practices
are a reflection of larger societal changes. Schools do not
stand apart from society but are influenced by the ebb and
flow of events and changes in the larger community. For
example, the increasingly diverse cultural and ethnic
makeup of our nation's population of young people has
tremendous implications for education. Across the nation, more and more schools include
learners from a variety of cultures, ethnicities, and languages. When you enter the profession, you will find that members of your class bring with them a wide spectrum of backgrounds and abilities.

Technology is another factor that fuels changes in schools. New digital wonders present new opportunities and provide tools you can use to organize your instruction and
interact with learners. These technological marvels also bring you face-to-face with
important moral and ethical issues. For example, young people from more affluent families are much more likely to have computers in their homes than learners from less affluent families. If school-based instruction depends more and more on access to computer
technology, does this situation give an unfair advantage to youths from more economically
advantaged families? If so, should public money be spent to purchase additional computers so learners from impoverished families can check them out and take them home?
These questions continue to be debated.

The accelerating rate of social change and a growing public awareness of the need for
our schools to prepare young people to accommodate new conditions have attracted the attention of political leaders. During the past several decades, more and more elected officials
have discovered that education is a political issue that resonates with the public. As a result,
they have been quick to enter into debates centered on education and to propose legislation
that purports to improve the schools.

The increasing politicization of educational issues raises important value-
laden questions that you and other citizens must answer in the years ahead. They
include:

- What should be the purposes of education in a democratic society?
- Who should control education?
- What should young people learn at school?
- What characteristics should "good" teachers have?
- Should teachers be held accountable for student learning?

What Do You Think?

- What is your view of the purposes of education?
- Where did you get your views of the purposes of education?

You may find that specific agendas drive answers to central questions. As a professional, you need to be a "player" in discussions related to changes in school policies and practices. To prepare yourself for this kind of proactive involvement, you need to develop (1) a sound understanding of issues that have prompted suggestions for change, (2) an appreciation of the particular interests that will be served when a change is implemented, and (3) a commitment to proposals that are consistent with your own professional values.

As you learned in Chapter 1, suggestions that schools need to be changed or reformed have been with us for many years. The most recent wave of change and reform proposals began with the publication of *A Nation at Risk: The Imperative for Educational Reform* (National Commission on Excellence in Education, 1983). This document detailed potential threats to the nation that might follow declines in test scores and increases in dropout rates. The report concluded:

> We report to the American people that while we can take justifiable pride in what our schools and colleges have historically accomplished and contributed to the United States and the well-being of its people, the educational foundations of our society are presently being eroded by a rising tide of mediocrity that threatens our very future as a Nation and a people. (p. 10)

The report perpetuated the myth that the schools of the past were excellent but now were failing. Looking back over two decades, it is quite clear that the report's alarmist rhetoric was at odds with reality. The threats that were cited in the report have not materialized, and, the United States currently stands as the world's dominant economic and political power. Educational programs that our schools provide have contributed to our country's continued development.

Although data have failed to confirm many of the conclusions of *A Nation at Risk*, the report's recommendations continue to influence public perceptions and debates about education policy. Many people, including policymakers, persist in seeing American public schools as failures. Although large numbers of individuals hold this attitude about schools in the nation as a whole, they often have higher opinions of their local schools. For example, polls of public attitudes toward schools report that most parents rate their local school quite high, but schools in general much lower.

If history is a guide, you will find debates about improving education to be a feature of your professional world throughout your career. You will find that many discussions focus on arguments between people who hold competing ideas regarding school practices and educational purposes. See Figure 3-1 for two very different sets of ideas. As you look at these lists, you might think about differences in proposals for school improvement that people committed to list "A" and list "B" would recommend. Also see this chapter's *Critical Incident* to read about one music teacher's experience at a school board meeting.

What Do You Think?

- Which list seems closest to your values and beliefs?
- What would be the implications for teaching that follow from your preferences?
- How does education currently measure up against your list?

Critical Incident

Is My Subject Now a Frill?

My name is Sook-ja Kim. I'm about eight months through my second year of teaching at Centennial Middle School. I direct the school orchestra and teach orchestra classes. For the most part, I've had a great experience.

Last month, I took my students on a two-day trip to the state orchestra competition. We went to the state capital, about 100 miles away. The students raised money for the trip, and we had plenty of parents along to help. These kids had really worked hard for this contest experience, and I was absolutely thrilled when we received a "1" rating, the highest awarded.

As soon as the award ceremony was over, I hurried back to the hotel and called my principal. She was delighted at the good news. Centennial's orchestra had never before received such a high rating. In fact, the principal was so excited that she immediately called the superintendent, who has been concerned for some time that our district's music program has not been as strong as it should be. The news about our 1 rating was very welcome.

A few days after I returned to school, I got a nice letter of congratulation from the superintendent. The letter included an invitation for me to attend a school board meeting, where I was to receive public thanks for the honor brought to the district by our orchestra's high rating.

On the evening of the school board meeting, it was fairly late when the board president asked me to stand. He and other board members said some very nice words about what had been accomplished by the Centennial orchestra. I appreciated hearing nice comments about how much the district approved of what I had accomplished in just two years. At the conclusion of these remarks, each member of the school board came over to shake my hand. I felt I had arrived at some kind of professional pinnacle.

The next item on the agenda was an open forum for citizens' comments. The first speaker deflated my fine feelings in a hurry. He said that the school district was spending too much money on frivolous, nonacademic subjects such as music. He indicated that the two days my orchestra kids had spent participating in the state contest had robbed them of two days of serious instruction in English and mathematics. He said this kind of thing provided just one more reason to support an effort he and a group of citizens were mounting to replace the present school board with people who would emphasize what he called *serious* academics.

I left the meeting feeling depressed. I've worked so hard this year, but now I know that there are people in town who think my entire function is unnecessary. I have a really bad taste in my mouth about this. I just don't know what I'm going to do.

1. *Are some subjects in the curriculum more important than others?*

2. *Do you think that schools spend too much time and effort on activities outside the core academic subjects?*

3. *What do you think are the essential subjects that should be included in the school curriculum?*

4. *How would you defend the importance of the subject you plan to teach?*

Figure 3–1 **Competing ideas about school practices.**

List A	List B
• Achievement is promoted by high standards, competition, and comparative assessments of students, teachers, and schools.	• Achievement is facilitated through cooperation, trust, confidence, and support between teachers and students
• Competition stimulates individuals to higher levels of performance.	• Cooperation provides the stimulus for developing higher levels of achievement for all students.
• Performance standards and frequent assessments ensure better outcomes.	• Assessment needs to be a collaborative effort between students and learning in order for it to be a learning experience that enhances academic growth.
• The curriculum should be structured around a common core of knowledge that reflects our cultural heritage.	• Curriculum should be organized around diverse knowledge that reflects the pluralistic nature of society and the world.
• A major purpose of education is to maintain the stability of the social, economic, and political order.	• Education should be evaluated on the basis of how it helps individuals improve and transform the social order.
• Education should be evaluated on the basis of preparing individuals for their role in society.	• The purpose of an educational system is the extent to which it helps all students achieve their potential.
• Merit should be rewarded and individuals should proceed through education solely on the basis of their ability and talent.	• By themselves, additional monetary resources are not sufficient to improve achievement, but they are necessary in order to bring about significant change.
• Additional investments in education will not increase student learning and are not necessary in order to bring about educational reform.	

As you may recall from Chapter 1, reform efforts calling for accountability and standardized testing have been among those having the most widespread influence on school practices. Over the past 20 years, school authorities have faced increasing pressure to raise public learners' scores on required tests. Supporters of this kind of disclosure take the position that wide dissemination of scores introduces an element of competition into the educational enterprise that acts to improve teachers' and schools' levels of performance.

This argument presumes that low test scores are reliable indicators of "problem schools." Critics challenge this assumption. Scores, they argue, tell the public nothing about the conditions that led to them (Popham, 2003). The reality is that poor levels of learner performance on tests may have multiple causes. A comprehensive attempt to understand why learners may not have done well requires answers to questions such as these:

- Is there evidence that teaching was appropriate?
- Were learners exposed to a curriculum that varied markedly from what was tested?
- Were the teachers qualified to teach the tested material?
- Does the school have a safe environment?
- Did learners have access to high-quality instructional materials?
- Did learners have opportunities to do schoolwork in supportive home and family environments?
- Were families or support agencies adequately meeting learners' nutritional needs?
- Were learners healthy, particularly on the day they took the test?
- Were the tests given to excited youngsters on the last school day before a holiday?

Reform of education requires teacher collaboration to plan for systemic change.

When you have answers to these questions, you are in a position to work with others to take needed remedial action. When all you have to work with are numbers representing learners' scores, you lack information you need to change conditions that will improve achievement levels (Popham, 2003). If you do not reflect on critical variables that may have influenced the test scores of your students, there is a danger that any changes you make will be narrowly focused and will not be responsive to all difficulties learners face. You may make changes that waste valuable resources and that fail to address the multiple causes of problems.

SYSTEMIC REFORM

Real improvement of instruction and of school programs results from responses that attack a number of clearly identified problem areas at the same time. These comprehensive solutions may include changes related to (1) administrative arrangements, (2) the nature of instructional materials, (3) the degree of support provided by learners' families, (4) the degree to which teachers are free to select instructional approaches that are well-suited to their learners' needs, and (5) the general nature of the classroom and school environment. The term that is applied to efforts to respond proactively to multiple

---

Web Extension 3–1

Consortium for Policy Research in Education (CPRE)

The Consortium for Policy Research in Education (CPRE) is a group that links policy researchers from the University of Pennsylvania, Harvard University, Stanford University, the University of Michigan, and the University of Wisconsin–Madison. At this site, you will find a link labeled "publications." If you click on this link, you will be taken to an extensive list of reports and articles, many of which deal with issues related to systemic reform. Systemic reform requires the efforts of all school members (Moss & Faison, 2006).

http://www.cpre.org/

problems is **systemic reform.** Some responses associated with systemic reform have generated support for efforts to:

- promote greater use of outcome goals,
- support the idea of school choice,
- redesign teacher responsibility and compensation schemes, and
- implement federal Comprehensive School Reform Demonstration programs.

Outcome Goals

Today, many education reformers support establishing **outcome goals.** Goals of this type emphasize the results or effects of instruction. For example, one outcome goal for primary-grades arithmetic might reference the learners' need to master basic operations and number facts.

The trend in support of outcome goals represents a shift away from a focus on **input goals.** Input goals relate to individual components of the school program that, collectively, are thought to produce desirable outcomes. For example, an input goal related to primary-grades mathematics might refer to the need to have an up-to-date arithmetic text available for each child to use.

In the past, comparisons among schools focused heavily on input goals. Sometimes school-to-school comparisons were made on the basis of evidence such as the number of computers in the classrooms, the percentage of teachers with advanced degrees, and the availability of recently published texts and other instructional materials. Input information says little about what learners are gaining from their experiences in school programs. For example, if a school had a large up-to-date library, an observer using input goals might conclude this was a "good" school. An observer who was committed to looking at outcome measures might say, "Wait a minute. What evidence is there that learners are profiting from the library and everything else going on in this building?"

You may be tempted to conclude that inputs are unimportant. This is not so. Adequate resources, such as qualified teachers and up-to-date texts, are important if learning is to occur. However, your focus should be on the impact these collective resources have on learners. In brief, high-quality inputs are a necessary but not a sufficient condition for educational excellence.

In recent years, many efforts have been made to identify high-quality learning outcomes for all subject areas. For example, excellent work of this kind has been done by national subject-area specialty organizations such as the National Council of Teachers of English (NCTE), the National Council of Teachers of Mathematics (NCTM), the National Council for the Social Studies (NCSS), and the National Science Teachers Association (NSTA). Increasingly, commercial publishers are incorporating outcome standards developed by these groups in texts, software, and other learning materials. These standards also are influencing content of teacher-preparation programs.

Another trend in efforts to reform schools is the new importance attached to **rigorous assessment** procedures. Rigorous assessments require learners to demonstrate sophisticated thinking skills. They stand in contrast to forced-choice techniques such as true–false and matching tests that often do not assess higher-order learning. One approach to evaluating learners' performances that is now attracting much interest is **authentic assessment** (Spady, 1994; Wiggins, 1989).

About half of today's high school students surveyed say that their school does not challenge them to do their best work (McCarthy & Kuh, 2006). Authentic assessment requires learners to demonstrate what they have learned in a way that has much in common with how a proficient adult might deal with this content. In a traditional class, you might ask learners to write an essay about possible consequences of locating a new factory close to a residential neighborhood. In authentic assessment, you might ask members of your class to provide documentation and testimony to a committee playing the role of a zoning board (and you might actually invite a zoning board member or two to participate in the exercise).

Advocates view authentic assessment as a more valid approach for holding teachers and schools accountable for the attainment of worthwhile educational standards than standardized tests. Detractors contend that authentic assessments rely too much on teacher judgments and are therefore too subjective. In addition, they do not provide data that can be used to compare students; therefore, they do not facilitate accountability. (For more information about authentic assessment, see Chapter 7, "How Do We Know Students Have Learned?")

In recent years, there has been broad public support for the idea of using results of standardized tests as a measure of educational quality (Cancoy & Tut, 2005). Although the public does not support the use of a single test to evaluate a school's performance, outcome measures of this type are part of a category you will often see referred to as *high-stakes tests*. This description refers to the significant consequences of scores on these tests for learners, teachers, and schools. For example, scores can (1) influence learners' chances to be admitted to certain colleges and universities, (2) affect a teacher's employment status or salary, and (3) reflect either positively or negatively on a school's overall reputation.

The bottom line for you as you think about outcome assessment is that you and your colleagues will be expected to present evidence that your students are learning. Your school is unlikely to be labeled "good" or "successful" based only on your claim that you have exemplary resources, bright and cheery classrooms, and teachers who have advanced degrees. In essence, the public demands answers to two key questions: (1) What have the young people learned? and (2) What evidence have you to support this claim?

SCHOOL CHOICE

Historically, most children have attended schools located within a particular **attendance zone.** Such a zone, prescribed by local school districts, typically requires learners to attend schools within certain areas of their community. In the case of elementary schools, the authorized buildings often are located in neighborhoods close to learners' homes. Learners must meet very special sets of conditions to get permission to attend a school outside of their normal attendance zone.

School choice supporters challenge the traditional attendance-zone arrangement. They see school choice as a key ingredient in improving educational quality. Proponents of school choice view schooling as a product. The product will be made better when the "producers" (i.e., individual schools) compete for "clients" (i.e., learners) in a competitive marketplace. These proponents claim that when such a scheme is in place, parents and guardians will choose to send their children to "good" schools, and "poor" schools will lose students and the state funds that accompany them. As a result, poor schools will have to improve or they will cease to exist. Therefore, competition and choice will bring school improvement with little or no extra cost.

Proponents of school choice also argue that this approach has excellent potential to respond well to diverse student needs. It is difficult for a single school to develop programs that are responsive to the special characteristics of all students. School choice allows parents and students to consider many different schools and to select one that they believe represents a best fit with the priorities of each family. These factors have the potential to increase both student and parent satisfaction with schools. In addition, teachers and administrators might find that they have a better environment for teaching because they do not need to try to accommodate every diverse point of view.

In summary, among advantages claimed for school choice are the following:

- School-choice policies have the potential to allow learners from low-income families to avoid mediocre, overcrowded inner-city schools.
- Families' interest in education may increase because they play an active role in selecting the schools their children attend.
- Competition among schools for students will improve the quality of all schools.
- Children attending schools that have been selected from among several alternatives potentially will find themselves in learning environments better matched to their needs than schools within their traditional mandatory-attendance areas. (Wells, 1990)

Not everyone agrees that school choice is a good idea. Critics challenge the idea that schools that lose enrollment will improve. Schools that lose students also lose the state support money that is associated with enrollment. Hence, the "poor" schools will be expected to make themselves more effective, but they will have even less money to do so than they had at the time they were perceived to not be doing a good job. Critics of school-choice plans argue that setting a higher standard at the same time as support money decreases makes little sense.

Others point out that choosing a school is not like choosing a car. Many variables must be considered in deciding if a school is "good." Because there are no valid rankings of school quality, those choosing a school often do so because of variables such as convenience, advertising, or religious preference. Therefore, it does not follow that competition will stimulate educational improvement.

Opponents also argue that school choice is not truly an option for all parents and guardians. Only affluent parents and guardians find it possible to transport their children to distant schools lying far outside normal attendance-zone areas. Parents and guardians with fewer resources depend on having schools that are either fairly close to their homes or accessible by their children as a result of well-established school bus routes. The difficulty of getting children to out-of-area schools does not make school choice a real option for many families.

Critics of school choice also wonder about the impact of such an approach on teachers' decisions about where to accept employment. Many conditions affect learners' academic performance (condition of the building, availability of up-to-date instructional resources, parental support at home, noise levels in and around the school, etc.). When a school-choice program is in place and individual schools face the threat of losing learners and state financial support, teachers may avoid accepting employment in schools where, for various reasons, learners' performance levels on standardized tests have not been as high as those of learners in other schools. The possibility is very real that school-choice programs may establish a system of teacher incentives that causes them to not serve those students who are most in need of the best teachers.

There are several approaches to school choice. Those approaches include vouchers, charter schools, open enrollment, and magnet schools. These approaches differ in some signficant ways.

Voucher Plans

Vouchers represent one approach to implementing school choice. In a voucher plan, parents and guardians receive tax money that they can use to pay for the education of their children at a school of their choice. Suppose a state pays individual schools $7,500 per year for each child. In a voucher system, a parent or guardian would receive a voucher in this amount for each school-aged child in the household. Once the parent or guardian decides which school the child will attend, this voucher is turned over to officials at that school. The officials deposit the money in the school's account and use it as part of the school's instructional and operational budget. This arrangement forces schools to compete for students and, in theory, would reward those schools doing well by attracting more students.

The voucher idea has been the focus of intense debate for several years. Much of the debate centers on different assumptions about the role of schools in a highly diverse democratic society. Educational-policy researcher Henry Levin (2002) points out that schools have a dual role of providing both private and public benefits.

The private benefits are related to the rights of parents to rear their children in a manner that they see fit. Therefore, those who give private benefit priority contend that because schools play an important role in child rearing, parents should be able to choose schools that best meet their philosophical, religious, and political lifestyles.

One important public benefit concerns schooling as a promoter of social cohesion. Society needs to reproduce the institutions of a free society. An effort must be made to provide students the experiences to assist them in developing knowledge, behavior, and values so they can participate in the social and political institutions that provide the foundation for a pluralistic democratic society. Hence, the state has an interest in reducing social and ethnic stratification and in making sure that all students have a common set of educational experiences.

Supporters of vouchers counter that parents are in the best position to seek an appropriate balance between education's private and public benefits. They argue that decisions individuals make when confronted with competing alternatives are superior and more satisfying than decisions made by employees of bureaucracies.

Another argument advanced by supporters is that vouchers will prompt the development of alternative educational opportunities for learners from less-affluent families who currently are trapped in low-performing schools. Vouchers, they argue, will accord less-affluent parents the same privileges of choice that have long been available to more-affluent families.

Critics argue that there are important negatives associated with vouchers. Voucher plans have the potential to lead parents and guardians to focus on issues other than the quality of a school's academic programs. Some choices they make may lead to an increased stratification of society along social class, political, and religious lines. For example, some parents or guardians may decide to send their sons and daughters to a particular school because of the makeup of the learner population or the availability of religious instruction. Such decisions represent choices based on criteria other than instructional-program quality.

In order to make good choices, parents and guardians need good information. Because variables other than qualities of school programs can affect learners' standardized-test scores, it is questionable that such scores represent high-quality indicators of school quality. Yet, when parents and guardians inquire about the relative quality of programs at individual schools, supporters of vouchers often respond, "look at test scores."

Opponents of vouchers question the assumption that a voucher system will result in alternative schools springing up to serve the needs of learners from low-income families. As evidence, they point to a voucher system in Milwaukee. The dollar value of vouchers offered to parents and guardians for each learner was higher than the amount the Milwaukee Public Schools received to support the instruction of each enrolled student. In spite of the dollars for which new, alternative schools could compete, few new schools appeared to take advantage of this opportunity to serve students from less-affluent families (Carnoy, 2000).

Voucher opponents point out that, in places where vouchers have been tried, religious schools, usually Catholic, are the dominant choices. This raises constitutional issues relating to subsidization of religious training. In an important 2002 U.S. Supreme Court decision, the Court upheld the constitutionality of vouchers given by the Cleveland Scholarship and Tutoring Program. The Court said that program was neutral with respect to religion because it simply provided a wider range of options to the existing choice options in a failing school district (Levin, 2002).

Critics of vouchers raise concerns related to fairness, particularly in situations in which vouchers can be used to pay for educational services provided by private schools. Private schools can select the learners they admit. If they choose to do so, they can admit only the most able learners and turn away youngsters who need special kinds of educational services. Opponents argue that if use of vouchers to pay for private-school educational services becomes widespread, over time public schools will be left with disproportionately high enrollments of learners with disabilities.

In summary, numerous attempts have been made to promote vouchers. The jury is still out on their effectiveness and impact on society. Supporters argue that vouchers have the potential to put in place a much-needed system of competition among schools that, over time, will improve the quality of programming throughout our educational system. Opponents argue that, instead of improving the schools, widespread use of vouchers may undermine social cohesion, interfere with issues related to church–state separation, and divert resources in ways that would make less-advantaged learners worse off than they are today. Learn more about both sides of this issue in this chapter's *Video Viewpoints* feature.

> ### Web Extension 3–2
>
> #### *Education Week* on the Web
>
> *Education Week*, a leading publisher of articles related to education, maintains this site. You will find a link labeled "archives." If you click on this link, you will be taken to a search engine. Enter the term "vouchers" in the search engine. You will be presented with an extensive list of articles from recent issues of *Education Week* that relate to vouchers. You can read them online.
>
> http://www.edweek.org/

Video Viewpoints 3–1

Controversial School Voucher Program

WATCH: This *20/20* episode focuses on the issue of vouchers. John Stossel, the host, clearly favors a voucher system and believes vouchers to be a key ingredient in school reform. He emphasizes the need for choice and the power of competition in bringing about change. Included, however, are some comments from those opposed to voucher systems. They contend that competition does not necessarily work in education and that voucher systems take needed money for change away from the schools that need it most.

THINK: Discuss with your classmates or write in your reflective journal your responses to the following questions:

1. Do you think that competition is a key element in bringing about change in schools? Why or why not?
2. Do you think vouchers are the best way of bringing about choice? Why or why not?
3. In addition to the points made in the video segment, what are some other issues surrounding vouchers that should be discussed?

LINK: What is the current status of vouchers and other choice programs?

 To view this video, go to the Video Viewpoints DVD and click on this chapter's video: "Controversial School Voucher Program."

Charter Schools

Another approach to providing school choice is reflected in the movement to establish **charter schools.** Charter schools are nonsectarian public schools of choice that are allowed to operate with freedom from many of the regulations that apply to traditional public schools. Groups such as parents, teachers, businesses, and community leaders can submit a proposal or a charter to the authorizing agency for permission to start a charter school. The agencies that approve charter schools vary from state to state and might include local school boards, intermediate school district boards, and state boards of education. If approved, the group submitting the charter usually is authorized to operate for some periods of time, usually from 3 to 5 years. At the conclusion of that period of time, the charter can be removed if the approving agency determines that the provisions of the charter are not being met. Charter schools have been supported by the Bush administration as an acceptable alternative to low-performing schools.

Local school boards are often viewed as poor authorizers of charter schools because they are often hampered by charter-adverse individuals and interest groups (Palmer & Gau, 2005). Arizona has a state board for charter schools that approves applications and in Indianapolis, the mayor approves charters. In some instances, institutions of higher education have been given the authority to approve them.

Charter schools have proven to be a more acceptable method of school choice than vouchers. Currently, 40 states have legislation authorizing the establishment of charter schools. As of fall 2006, the states with the most charter schools were Califronia (625), Arizona (466), Florida (391), Ohio (293), Texas (269), and Michigan (241). Across the nation an estimated 3,977 charter schools were serving about 1,149,000 students. However, this still represents only about 2% of the total public school population (Education Commission of the States, 2007, www.ecs.org).

Most charter schools were new schools serving a K–8 population. High school charter schools are less common. The average enrollment in a charter school is 292. The student population of these schools averaged 53.6% minority, 50.5% male, and 49.5% female (Education Commission of the States, 2007). By law, charter schools must have fair and open admissions policies that include all sectors of the community they serve.

Proponents of charter schools claim that the freedom to operate without excessive regulation allows them to stimulate innovation and change and to be more sensitive to local needs. For example, because of this exemption from many state regulations, about half of the charter schools are free to hire teachers who lack a teaching certificate and are free from contractual obligations that local districts have with teacher associations. Some critics see the charter school movement as a method for diminishing the power of local teacher associations.

Charter-school proponents make some of the same arguments as those favoring voucher plans. They contend that providing competition and freeing charter schools from regulatory burdens will allow them to develop innovate instructional programs that will become models for other schools to emulate.

Proponents argue that charter schools are cost-effective. They claim this is so because charter schools do not have to tolerate the bureaucratic inefficiencies characterizing typical public schools. Supporters contend that absence of excessive regulations lures outstanding teachers to charter schools who are unhappy with paperwork and other administrative constraints imposed by state and school-district regulations. In charter schools, these teachers face few limits on their abilities to introduce exciting and innovative instructional approaches. The proponents say that because of fewer restrictions charter schools are better able to meet the needs of at-risk students (Wohlstetter & Smith, 2006).

Opponents point to negatives associated with this approach. They claim that charter schools have the potential to divert money away from public schools. Charter schools draw money from the same sources as existing schools. When charter schools are created, unless there are unusual infusions of additional money to support operation of all publicly funded schools, the charter schools will consume dollars that will decrease amounts available to other schools. Hence, any improvements in education achieved at a charter school may come at the expense of a decrease in quality at other schools.

Other charter-school opponents argue that supporters of these schools exaggerate problems that bureaucratic constraints create for traditional public schools. They contend that, in spite of governmental and school-district regulations, numerous public schools have developed highly innovative programs and instructional practices. These schools have done so without having to ask for the regulatory relief that has been given to charter schools.

In recent years, education management organizations have sprung up that operate a number of charter schools. Some of these organizations are nationwide. Skeptics point out that these organizations are using the charter schools as a method for making a profit and decisions are made far from the local region. In some instances management organizations have received approval from one school board for charter schools and they have used that approval to open schools all across the state in other school districts. Local school boards often oppose these arrangements because they view these schools as lacking in accountability to the local community and operating with inadequate oversight.

Some critics of charter schools acknowledge that, at times, state and school-district regulations can inhibit schools' abilities to develop more-effective programs. However, they doubt that establishing regulations-free charter schools is the answer. They argue that if regulations are undesirable, efforts should be directed to changing the regulations for all schools, not just charter schools. Changes of this kind would open the door for widespread innovation and improvement.

Because many charter schools have been operating for over a decade, studies are beginning to provide information regarding their effectiveness. On the positive side, parents and guardians, learners, and teachers involved with charter schools rate these schools higher than parents and guardians, learners, and teachers involved with traditional public schools. However, the charter-school participants have been found to be somewhat less satisfied with facilities and support than are those associated with regular public schools (Bulkey & Fisler, 2002).

The data on the academic achievement of charter schools are mixed. Some studies have found improvements in the achievement of charter school students when compared to students in regular public schools and some have not. In general, charter schools have not proven to be a "panacea" or a beacon of educational reform. There are some good charter schools and there are some poor charter schools.

Researchers have identified several concerns about the operation of charter schools (Good & Braden, 2000). One hope of charter-school supporters has been that these schools will serve as models for innovation and change, and that new approaches established in these schools will spread to other public schools. To date, there is little evidence that charter schools are serving as important educational-innovation centers. Researchers Good and Braden found that (1) in California, 85% of charter schools were using a traditional approach to instruction; (2) in Michigan, studies revealed virtually no innovation in that state's charter schools; and (3) in Arizona, little was occurring in the charter schools that could be classified as new or powerful.

Have charter schools reduced administrative bureaucracies and devoted more resources to support teaching? Critics point out that many have not done so (Good & Braden, 2000). Some charter schools spend more money on administration, maintenance, and operations and less per student on instruction than noncharter public schools. Indeed, some charter schools may be overfunded when compared with traditional public schools (Nelson, 1997). This situation can occur because charter schools do not have the same high costs as traditional schools that enroll many more at-risk and special-needs learners.

One issue related to charter schools is that because they are subject to market forces, they may close. For example, in the region where one of the authors resides, a charter high school for at-risk students closed in January of the school year. This threatened the continuity of education for these students, and the intermediate school district stepped in to try to provide an education for these students for the rest of the year. Many charter schools have failed. In one large-scale study of the survival rate of charter schools, investigators found that, of an original total of 2,874 schools, 194 had closed and 77 others had been reconstituted as traditional schools within the host district (Looney, 2002). Most failures appear to have occurred because of mismanagement, fiscal instability, and bankruptcy rather than as a result of evidence relating to poor learner performance (Good & Braden, 2000).

In summary, after a decade of growth charter schools, as a whole, have not delivered on the promise to stimulate innovation and change. However, the charter-school movement continues to enjoy strong political support. Two key questions probably will remain central to the continuing debate about charter schools:

- Is the fundamental idea of charter schools flawed, and should this approach to educational reform and improvement be abandoned?
- Are problems associated with charter schools the result of poor implementation of an idea that basically is sound?

Web Extension 3–3

U.S. Charter Schools

The Center for Education Reform maintains this site. It includes excellent links to information focusing on topics such as (a) starting and running a charter school, (b) state information and contacts regarding charter schools, (c) profiles of individual charter schools, and (d) general resources and information sources regarding charter schools.

http://www.uscharterschools.org/

OPEN-ENROLLMENT PLANS

Open-enrollment plans vary from voucher plans in that they do not issue tax funds directly to parents or guardians. They also differ from charter schools in that they simply let parents or guardians choose an existing school for their child to attend. Most open-enrollment plans limit learners' choices to schools within a given school district. A few allow learners to cross district lines.

Sometimes open-enrollment plans are described as **controlled-choice plans.** Even though these plans are designed to honor parents' and guardians' preferences in assigning learners to individual schools, other factors are considered. School district administrators retain final control over assignment of learners to particular schools. Typically there are provisions that allow administrators to maintain acceptable racial balances in individual schools. In addition, most districts develop plans that allow people who live within the attendance boundaries of each school first choice. Thus, many excellent neighborhood schools have few slots available for learners who live outside the traditional attendance area.

Supporters believe that open-enrollment policies encourage parents and guardians to look carefully at the quality of academic programs in individual schools. The premise is that they will choose to send their children to those schools that they believe provide better learning experiences. Critics point out that, in districts with open-enrollment policies, parents and guardians often choose schools for reasons unrelated to the quality of educational programs. They contend that school-choice decisions are made for reasons such as the proximity of a school to the parents' or guardians' workplace or because prospects are higher for their child to play a varsity sport at school "A" as opposed to school "B."

Magnet Schools

Magnet schools represent another approach to school choice. Usually magnet schools have a specific theme for which they are especially well known. For example, there may be a magnet school specializing in the sciences or one specializing in the performing arts. In addition to serving the special interests of learners they enroll, magnet schools also provide urban school districts with a means of achieving acceptable levels of racial integration. Integration occurs because magnet schools, unlike schools that draw learners from neighborhoods that may not have racially mixed populations, enroll learners from all residential areas in a district. This feature has led many large cities to establish magnet schools. For example, Houston, Chicago, Boston, New York, and Philadelphia have had them for many years.

Magnet schools can provide interesting learning experiences for students, however, they do present certain problems. The issue of transportation is a particular concern. Some critics allege that lack of transportation for learners from economically impoverished families makes it easier for learners from more-affluent families to attend magnet schools. In response to this difficulty, many districts with magnet schools provide transportation subsidies of some kind to learners from low-income families.

Admission to many magnet schools usually requires learners to have established a record of excellent academic performance at the schools they previously attended. As a result, some opponents of magnet schools argue that these schools remove the best learners from other schools and, thereby, reduce the overall talent pool in these buildings. Some critics also allege that magnet schools receive higher levels of financial support than other schools. As a result, learners in non-magnet schools may receive a level of educational services that is lower than it would be in the absence of magnet schools.

What Do You Think?

- What do you think is the most compelling argument for school choice?
- What do you find as the most compelling argument against school choice?
- Which of the school-choice programs do you favor? Why?

COMPREHENSIVE SCHOOL REFORM DEMONSTRATION PROGRAMS

Traditionally, federal programs to improve education have been designed to support limited-purpose programs. For example, federal monies have been allocated to support special education programs, mathematics programs, certain literacy programs, and programs for learners in districts with high levels of poverty. These "add-on" programs have not sought simultaneous improvement of an entire school. Because of concerns that these narrowly focused agendas were not greatly affecting the overall quality of schools, Congress passed Public Law 105-78 (1997), which established the **Comprehensive School Reform Demonstration (CSRD)** program.

CSRD focuses on schoolwide reform. It is designed to help schools improve their entire operation. It calls for changes in basic academics, professional development of teachers, levels of involvement of parents and guardians, use of analyses of local needs, and use of research-based ideas for improvement. CSRD encourages school districts to develop programs that will allow all learners to meet challenging academic standards. Program funds flow from the federal governments to the states. State-level authorities pass on funds to individual school districts. In turn, local school districts allocate the money to eligible schools. States must meet certain criteria to qualify for the funds.

To be eligible for CSRD funds, a school must have a plan for comprehensive school reform that includes each of the following nine components:

- effective, research-based methods and strategies;
- comprehensive design with aligned components (with the intent of meeting the needs of *all* enrolled learners);
- professional development (for teachers and staff members);
- measurable goals and benchmarks;
- support within the school (to include a strong commitment of faculty, administrators, and staff);
- parental and community involvement;
- external technical support and assistance (available from an outside group with experience in supporting school reforms);
- evaluation strategies; and
- coordination of resources (suggestions for how money from various sources will be used to support the comprehensive improvement program). (Comprehensive School Reform Demonstration Program, 1998)

The intent of CSRD to pay for reforms that will benefit all learners in a school represents a shift in the nature of federal support for school-improvement initiatives. In the past, much federal money was targeted at specific subgroups within the total school population.

No Child Left Behind Act of 2001

In recent years, people concerned about making schools better have increasingly looked for improvements that would not only improve average levels of learner performance but would also ensure that learners in each subgroup of the school population is well served. As you know, an improved average by no means guarantees that all learners are doing better. Such a result is possible when sufficient numbers of learners score high enough on achievement tests to overcome scores of others who may be performing at about the same level (or even somewhat worse) than they were before. Critics of basing judgments related to school improvement on averages have been especially concerned that many proposed changes may not well serve young people from racial, language, and cultural minorities.

Certain provisions of an important piece of federal legislation, the **No Child Left Behind Act of 2001** (Public Law 107-110, 2002), reflect this concern. School districts now are required to measure more than "average" learner achievement. The law requires additional documentation that adequate progress is being made by learners from ethnic minorities, from homes in which English is not the first language, from economically impoverished backgrounds, and by learners with disabilities.

The No Child Left Behind Act features *accountability* as a basic principle. It requires every state to adopt standards that describe what students should learn at each grade level. Each school district and school is expected to make adequate yearly progress toward meeting state standards, and yearly "report cards" must be issued for individual schools. Within 12 years, all learners must reach the level of proficiency as defined by their state. Districts and schools that do not make progress will be required to take corrective actions and may face negative consequences if problems persist.

One of the purposes of stringent accountability is to provide data that parents and guardians can use to make choices and exercise their options. If a school does not meet its academic growth target for two consecutive years, parents and guardians have the right to transfer their child to a successful public school. School districts must pay for learners' transportation to the new school. If a school fails to meet adequate yearly progress goals for three consecutive years, parents and guardians of disadvantaged learners have the right to supplemental educational services at the expense of the school district.

Some provisions of the No Child Left Behind Act have important implications for you and your teaching colleagues. The law requires school districts to assign a "highly qualified" teacher in every classroom in which an academic core subject is taught. Academic core subjects are defined as English, reading or language arts, mathematics, science, foreign languages, civics and government, economics, the arts, history, and geography. A "highly qualified" teacher is defined as a person who has obtained full state certification or has passed the state teacher licensing examination, holds the minimum of a bachelor's degree, and has demonstrated subject-area competence in each of the academic areas in which he or she teaches.

This provision has created problems for some school districts. For example, there are several areas of the secondary curriculum where smaller schools often do not offer enough course sections to hire a teacher to teach only one subject. In the past, a person who had a valid teaching certificate in a related area, such as history, and who had some background in geography might be asked to teach one or two geography classes. This creates a serious problem for school administrators trying to offer a comprehensive curriculum.

This discussion has introduced only a few changes you may encounter in the schools as a result of passage of the No Child Left Behind Act. As you progress through your preparation program, you will want to find out how your state has defined a highly qualified teacher and what you will need to do to be designated as one. Your course instructor should be able to help you obtain this information.

No Child Left Behind is due to be reauthorized. Debates have started in Congress during 2007 regarding changes. You will want to monitor those changes and understand how they will impact education. Explore and learn more about No Child Left Behind in the *Video Viewpoint* feature.

Video Viewpoints 3–2   *No Child Left Behind*

WATCH: In this video segment of *ABC World News* some of the problems associated with No Child Left Behind are discussed. In this segment Elizabeth Vargas talks with the principal of a high-achieving school in Utah that was labeled "in need of improvement."

THINK: Discuss with your classmates or write in your reflective journal your responses to the following questions:

1. Do you think a school should be labeled because of the performance of as few as three students?
2. Is it realistic to expect that all students in a school will reach a minimum level of proficiency?
3. Should there be relief from laws if the government does not fund the legislation?

LINK: Should it be the role of the federal government to label schools or should that be left to the local community?

 To view this video, go to the Video Viewpoints DVD and click on this chapter's video: "No Child Left Behind."

School–Business Partnership Programs

Because our entire society benefits when learners have productive experiences in school, many outside our profession have a keen interest in what goes on in the schools. This interest has led to efforts to establish partnerships of various kinds between public schools and other agencies and organizations. For example, many colleges and universities around the country now link with specific schools for the purpose of helping them develop academic programs that will adequately prepare graduates for the demands of higher education. In some places, social agencies have established ties with schools that are designed to make their services more readily available to learners. (More information about this kind of cooperative activity is introduced in the next section, which focuses on full-service schools.) In recent years, corporations and businesses of all kinds have actively sought to establish formal **school–business partnerships.**

Establishment of **tech-prep programs** throughout the country has been one important effect of businesses' interest in the schools. Tech-prep programs developed in response to fears that many efforts to reform schools were promoting academic experiences having little practical value to students once they graduate. Tech-prep programs for the most part are 2 + 2 models, which means that they focus on the last two years of high school and two additional years of training, most often in community and junior colleges.

The intent of tech-prep programs is to provide rigorous, integrated experiences that will smooth the transition from school to the world of the contributing adult citizen. To this end, the **Carl D. Perkins Vocational and Applied Technology Act** of 1990 (http://www.ed.gov/offices/DVAE/CTE/legis.html) defines tech-prep as a program that:

- leads to an associate degree or two-year certificate;
- provides technical preparation in at least one field of engineering technology, applied science, mechanical, industrial, or practical art or trade, or agriculture, health, or business;
- builds student competence in mathematics, science, and communication (including applied academics) through a sequential course of study; and
- leads to placement in employment.

The U.S. Department of Education's Office of Vocational and Adult Education distributes money to support tech-prep initiatives through its Tech-Prep Demonstration Program. Applicants must be consortiums consisting of representatives of (1) grades K–12 schools, (2) colleges offering two-year associate degrees, and (3) businesses. Among other things, funded programs have to describe:

- how the proposed 2 + 2 program will be implemented,
- how the instruction will meet or exceed high-quality standards set by the state,
- the quality of the alignment between the first two and second two years of the four-year sequence, and
- the plan's ability to attract students. (Tech-Prep Demonstration Program, 2003)

Proliferation of programs designed to foster school programs that help students make a smooth transition to the workplace led to passage of the federal School-to-Work Opportunities Act in 1994 (http://www.ncrel.org/sdrs/areas/issues/envrnmnt/stw/sw3swopp.htm). This act provides grants to states and communities to develop systems and partnerships designed to better prepare young people for additional education and careers. The intent is for students to experience the workplace as an active learning environment and to ensure that they see relationships between what they experience in school and what they will need to know to earn a living. The focus is on working with learners throughout the entire span of their K–12 school years.

Business interest in school programs has taken many forms other than supporting legislation such as the Carl D. Perkins Act and the School-to-Work Opportunities Act. In some cases, schools have been helped in somewhat indirect ways. For example, companies have initiated child-care services and programs for employees, encouraging them to play active roles in their children's education. Often these initiatives have offered employees flexible work schedules to enable parents or guardians to visit schools during the day.

Other school–business partnerships have been much more ambitious and have encouraged partnerships as a way of improving entire school systems. One of the most notable efforts has occurred in Kentucky, where leaders of The Business Roundtable, which is a national group including chief executive officers of 200 of the nation's largest corporations, have encouraged their branches in individual states to join with local schools to improve instructional quality and to better prepare young people for the world of work. You can locate many examples of these school–business partnerships by using a search engine such as Google (http://www.google.com) and entering the terms "business roundtable" and "school-business partnerships."

In New York, the Long Island Works Coalition has established a school–business partnership for the purpose of ensuring a future workforce that possesses the educational background that local-area employers require. The program links employers, educators, parents, and learners. An important part of the program's agenda is identifying and closing gaps between business-skill needs and educational programs. Initiatives of this program include internship fairs that bring together local school students and employers that offer internship opportunities, an electronic-postcard system that provides information to school learners about career events and opportunities in the local area, "workforce summits" that bring together education and business leaders to discuss future workforce needs, and conferences for high school students that seek to encourage them to master important technology skills (Long Island Works Coalition, 2003).

In Wisconsin, learners of the Milwaukee Public Schools instituted a systemwide school-to-work emphasis. Elements of this approach are found in curricula at every grade from kindergarten through grade 12. For example, children in early childhood programs engage in activities that are designed to develop their problem-solving abilities. Elementary children receive basic training in various aspects of the world of work and have lessons involving classroom businesses. Middle school learners have out-of-school experiences with organizations and businesses in the city. High school students have opportunities to become involved in a variety of apprenticeship programs (*System-Wide School-to-Work Transition and Parental Choice*, 1999).

In New York City, the Chamber of Commerce has established a Department of Education and Workforce Development. The department's Partnership for Leadership program has established a way for school principals to seek out and receive assistance from experienced leaders in the business community. The Summer Jobs program provides opportunities for public-school students to gain work experience and learn skills that will help them obtain positions when they leave the school system (*Education and Workforce Development*, 1999).

In Alaska, the Anchorage School Business Partnership program has operated successfully since 1991. This sophisticated cooperative effort now involves almost 70% of the school district's schools and features nearly 200 separate partnership arrangements. The nature of business–school partnership varies greatly from activity to activity. In some cases, an individual business arranges for a single employee to work closely with a designated school. In others, large corporations have many employees working with large numbers of individual schools and their staffs. Some examples of collaborative activities include mentorships, internships for learners, on-the-job training opportunities, and donations of various kinds from participating businesses to support particular school projects (Anchorage School District, 2002).

Interest in business–school partnerships is increasing. However, as you continue to learn about these programs, you will find that they have critics as well as supporters. Some people who are skeptical about school–business partnerships fear that some businesses are not as interested in helping children as they are in promoting their own products. Supporters counter that schools can develop guidelines to prevent this sort of thing from happening and that it is in the interest of educators to encourage an interest in public education among people outside of the profession. Discussions about this issue continue.

FULL-SERVICE SCHOOLS

Individual **human-support-service professions** that serve our nation's education, health, legal, and social-support needs have developed huge bodies of sophisticated knowledge over the past half-century. Training of specialists in these professions has never been better. What has not happened, however, is the coordination of these professions in ways that build on the strengths of each and that bring their diverse understandings to bear on common problems. This is particularly true in public education. Difficulties children face cannot neatly be sorted into categories labeled educational problems, health problems, legal problems, and social problems. What children experience as individuals are difficulties that cross all of these lines.

Full-service schools are beginning to emerge. These schools attempt to bring all human-support activities together under one roof. The need to do this was recognized over 20 years ago when the Bicentennial Commission of the American Association of Colleges of Teacher Education devoted fully 40 pages to the need to link education and human services (Howsam, Corrigan, Denemark, & Nash, 1976). In the middle 1990s, the Children's Defense Fund in its publication *The State of America's Children Yearbook* (1994) highlighted the intractability of problems facing our young people and the need to engage multiple human-services professions in the effort to solve them.

Many full-service schools have been established to help learners from economically or educationally impoverished backgrounds. There is evidence that some families in these circumstances are unable to take advantage of some of the support services various social agencies provide. When these services are gathered together in one place—the school—access becomes more user-friendly. Full-service schools are in operation in many parts of the country. Their programs vary, but they always feature the provision of services to learners and their families that go beyond schools' traditional obligation to provide curriculum-related services. They often feature collaborations with professionals from specialties outside of education and from community agencies to provide support services that may include:

- after-school care for learners,
- medical and dental examinations conducted at the school,
- adult education for parents and guardians,
- family-support services provided by social workers,
- legal services,
- drug- and -alcohol-abuse prevention programs,

- counseling services for learners and their families, and
- emergency-treatment and crisis-reaction services. (Warger, 2000)

Some critics of full-service schools argue that they represent an attempt to charge the schools with solving every social ill. Opponents add that, although the efforts are well intentioned, expecting schools to deliver counseling, medical, and other kinds of support services to learners and their families has the potential to divert resources from schools' important instructional function. Other opponents argue that full-service schools irresponsibly take responsibilities that properly belong to families and put them in the hands of outsiders.

Supporters of full-service schools say that services provided at full-service schools by noneducators often are not paid for out of the education budget. Governments already pay for social workers, health specialists, and other specialists to work with families who need these services and who cannot pay for them with their own funds. Full-service schools simply move some of these professionals to school buildings, where learners and their families can easily access their expertise.

Proponents of full-service schools argue that such plans do not diminish the importance of families in learners' lives. Families play important roles in determining what goes on in full-service schools. Learners who are enrolled often would not be able to access many provided services if they were not available at the school site.

At the present time, many national organizations representing the interests of different human-support services advocate expanding the number of full-service schools. Any growth in their numbers will have implications for training of future social service professionals.

If your own preparation program is typical, when you begin teaching, you will have been introduced to information about such issues as learning styles, instructional design, psychological development of young people, classroom management, assessment of learners, and administrative arrangements of schools. You may have had little exposure to content related to public health, social work, law enforcement, and other areas that have always been discharged by social service professionals working in other settings. More attention to this kind of preparation will be needed if full-service schools become more common.

TEACHING IN A WORLD OF CHANGE

How do you cope with change? It is clear that the status quo in education is no longer acceptable. There are proposals for changing every aspect of education. It is likely that the schools in the near future will be very different from those of the past. This offers some exciting opportunities for those who like new challenges and who want to be involved in solving important educational problems. However, this change can be threatening to those who are comfortable with the current educational system.

Changes offer both opportunities and threats. Although some of the proposed changes offer interesting approaches to persistent problems, they may have consequences that threaten some of the basic principles of a free society. In their zeal to address one problem, proponents of a particular change may overlook some important negative consequences. What is needed are individuals who can review proposals and identify both the benefits and the challenges. This requires individuals with a thorough understanding of education. For those of you who choose to enter education, this is the challenge you will be accepting.

Profession Knowledge
To develop some more insight into the types of professional knowledge required of teachers, go to MyEducationLab and select the topic "Professional Development" and watch the video "Types of Professional Knowledge." View the video and respond to the questions. Some of the questions have been designed to prepare you for your licensure examination.

Key Ideas in Summary

- Change is afoot in education. As a prospective teacher, you need to become familiar with school-reform initiatives and join the national discussion related to these issues. By becoming involved, you can influence the direction of changes. If you do not, people whose views you do not share may influence the nature of your work environment in ways that dismay you.
- Because problems of schools are so complex, many critics of present practices are convinced that the only successful reforms will be those that will attack many variables at the same time. This effort is known as *systemic reform*. Many systemic-reform efforts emphasize outcomes of education rather than inputs, school choice, and redesigned teacher-compensation schemes.
- *School choice* implies that parents or guardians and learners should be able to select a school from among a number of alternatives. This approach represents a change from usual arrangements that assign learners to specific schools based on their home addresses.
- One approach to school choice is represented in *voucher plans*. When a voucher plan is in operation, parents and guardians essentially receive a voucher (a kind of check) from state authorities representing the total number of dollars required to support instruction for each child in the family. The voucher can be "spent" only at a school. Parents or guardians select the school they wish their child to attend and give the voucher to administrators at this school. School authorities add the value of the voucher to the funds they have available to support their educational programs.
- The *charter school* represents another approach to school choice. Charter schools are semiautonomous public schools that are freed from many state regulations. A charter school can be established at an existing public school or established as a new school. Individuals interested in establishing such a school provide a plan to an authorized chartering agency. The plan spells out what the school will do and how success will be measured.
- *Magnet schools* and *open-enrollment plans* are examples of other attempts to provide parents and guardians with school choice. Magnet schools typically have a theme (e.g., science education) where programs are especially strong. Parents and guardians from across an entire school district seek entry to magnet schools for their children regardless of where they live. Open-enrollment plans are arrangements that allow parents and guardians to disregard traditional school-attendance boundaries and enroll their children in any school in the school district. Ordinarily, some restrictions are set to prevent too many learners from crowding into just a few schools.
- The *No Child Left Behind Act of 2001* requires public schools in all states to make important changes. This legislation requires annual testing of all learners in several subjects in grades 3 through 8. It also requires schools to give annual report cards that detail each learner's progress, and it allows parents to move their child to another school if a school fails to meet achievement targets. In addition, the law requires a

"qualified teacher" in every classroom. A qualified teacher is someone who has passed a rigorous subject-matter examination and who has met all state certification requirements.

- Many businesses and corporations wish to play a part in improving the quality of public education. Private-sector support has been an important factor helping the spread of *tech-prep* programs that seek to integrate training during the last two years of high school and the first two years in a post-high school institution—typically a community or junior college. In addition to their support of tech-prep programs, many businesses have joined with schools in *school–business partnership* programs. These range from efforts to improve the quality of education within an entire state to efforts centered on a single school.

- Individuals from many professions are involved in important human-support-service activities. In addition to education, these include professionals trained in health care, social welfare, law, and law enforcement. There is a trend to bring these professional services together in schools. Interest in this approach has led to the establishment of *full-service schools*. In these schools, people from a variety of human-service professions are available to provide comprehensive support services for learners and their families.

For Your Initial-Development Portfolio

1. What materials and ideas from this chapter about *challenges of school reform* will you include as "evidence" in your portfolio? Select up to three separate items of information. Number them 1, 2, and 3.
2. Think about why you selected these materials. As you do so, consider these issues:
   - Specific uses you might make of this information as you plan, deliver, and assess the impact of your teaching
   - The compatibility of the information with your own priorities and values
   - Any contributions this information can make to your development as a teacher
   - Factors that led you to include this information, as opposed to some alternatives you considered but rejected
3. Place a check in the chart below to indicate the INTASC standard(s) to which each of your items of information relates. (You may wish to refer to Chapter 1 for more detailed information about INTASC.)

INTASC Standard Number										
ITEM OF EVIDENCE NUMBER	S1	S2	S3	S4	S5	S6	S7	S8	S9	S10
1										
2										
3										

4. Prepare a written reflection in which you analyze the decision-making process you followed. In your comments, mention the INTASC standard(s) to which your selected material relates.

Reflections

1. Supporters of *systemic reform* argue that, to achieve meaningful school improvement, multiple variables must be attacked simultaneously. Others argue that making multiple changes at the same time is so difficult that, in the end, no modifications to present practices will occur. They contend that incremental improvement that is achieved by addressing one problem at a time, in the long run, has more potential to improve schools than do all-encompassing systemic-reform initiatives. What are your own reactions to these arguments, and why do you take your position?

2. Suppose all school districts in the United States adopted *voucher plans.* What changes would there be in how schools operate? What problems might you and your teaching colleagues face? What challenges would confront your school's administrators? What positives do you see associated with this policy? What negatives? Would such a policy improve our schools? Why or why not?

3. Suppose you and a group of colleagues decided to establish a *charter school.* What problems of traditional public schools would you attempt to overcome? How might your freedom to ignore certain requirements your state imposes on most schools allow you to serve your learners well? You would have to present a plan to a chartering agency and win this agency's support for your ideas. Among other things, you would have to include a description of variables you would consider and procedures you would use to determine your school's effectiveness. What are some ideas you might include in your plan?

4. *Full-service schools* attempt to bring together at one place a range of educational, health, legal, and social-welfare services. Professionals from these human-support-service organizations work cooperatively to help learners and their families. Supporters argue that making these services available at a school site allows learners and families to access them easily. Detractors contend that providing noninstructional services at schools diverts schools from their primary mission of teaching. Opponents also argue that full-service-school staffing costs may divert funds to support services that are unrelated to instructing young people. What are your own reactions to full-service schools, and why do you feel this way?

Field Experiences, Projects, and Enrichment

1. In a few places around the country, local citizens have lost so much faith in the abilities of public-school officials to manage local school programs that they have turned over the operation of their schools to private corporations or to a local university. The term *contract school* sometimes is applied to a school that has been placed under the authority of this kind of external contracting agency. In essence, the private corporation or university contracts with the local citizens to improve the quality of educational services. Read about how successful these arrangements have been. Prepare a report to share with others in your class.

2. Most states have legislation allowing the establishment of charter schools. If your state has or is considering such legislation, find out what requirements must be met to establish a charter school. If your state legislature has not considered this issue, gather information about the situation in a neighboring state. Prepare a short paper in which you make reference to such issues as (1) the kinds of groups that can request authority to establish a charter school, (2) the limitations on the numbers of

charter schools that can be established, and (3) the provisions relating to funding of charter schools.

3. Though there are important national trends related to educational change, you will also find that some calls for modifications in schools and school programs center around issues that may loom large in some communities while being virtually nonexistent in others. An interesting example involves the theory of evolution. In many parts of the country, this issue is never raised. In others, it is an issue that only occasionally prompts local interest. In still others, it is a subject of great concern, and school board meetings often are punctuated by comments of school patrons who have conflicting views on this issue. You may be interested in learning more about the nature of this debate. Using a search engine such as Google (http://www.google.com), conduct several searches. Enter these terms as you seek links to relevant information: "evolution debate" and "intelligent design." Prepare a report for your class based on your findings.

4. The *No Child Left Behind Act of 2001* imposes important obligations on local schools and school districts. Interview an administrator from a local school district. Ask about changes the school district has made in response to this legislation and about any difficulties the district has faced in doing so. Share your findings with others in your class.

5. The activities that various *school–business partnerships* support vary greatly from place to place. To gain some idea of the scope of these activities, use a search engine such as Google (http://www.google.com) and enter the term "school–business partnership." Go to a selection of the identified links, and look for information related to the nature of activities that various partnerships support. Prepare a bulleted list of these activities, and make copies to share with others in your class.

References

Anchorage School District. (2002). *School business partnership report, 2001–2002.* ASD Memorandum No. 15 (2002–2003). Anchorage, AK: Author.

Bulkey, K., & Fisler, J. (2002). A decade of charter schools: From theory to practice. *Consortium for Policy Research in Education Policy Briefs.* Philadelphia: University of Pennsylvania (RB-35).

Cancoy, O, & Tut, M. A. (2005). High-stakes testing and mathematics performance of fourth graders in North Cyrus. *The Journal of Education Research 98*(4), 234–244.

Carnoy, M. (2000). School choice or is it privatization? *Educational Researcher, 79*(7), 15–20.

Children's Defense Fund. (1994). *The state of America's children yearbook 1994: Leave no child behind.* Washington, DC: Author.

Comprehensive School Reform Demonstration Program. (1998). *Guidance on the comprehensive school reform demonstration program.* U.S. Department of Education. http://www.nwrel.org/csrdp/about.html

Education and workforce development. (1999). http://www.publicpolicy.com/educat.html

Education Commission of the States. (2007). *Charter schools.* http://www.ecs.org/html/IssuesSection.asp?issueid=20&s=Quick+Facts

Good, T. L., & Braden, J. S. (2000). Charter schools: Another reform failure or a worthwhile investment? *Phi Delta Kappan, 81*(10), 745–750.

Howsam, R. B., Corrigan, D. C., Denemark, G. W., & Nash, R. J. (1976). *Educating a profession: Relating to human services education.* Washington, DC: American Association of Colleges for Teacher Education.

Levin, H. M. (2002). A comprehensive framework for evaluating educational vouchers. *Educational Evaluation and Policy Analysis, 24*(3), 159–174.

Long Island Works Coalition. (2003). *Long Island works coalition.* Long Island, NY: Author. http://www.liworks.org/about.cfm

Looney, M. (2002). *Charter schools today: Changing the face of American education.* Washington, DC: Center for Education Reform.

McCarthy, M., & Kuh, G. D. (2006). Are students ready for college: What student engagement data say. *Phi Delta Kappan, 87*(9), 664–669.

Moss, J., & Faison, C. L. (2006). Integrating and assessing critical thinking across the curriculum. In K. T. Henson, *Curriculum planning: Integrating multiculturalism, constructivism, and education reform* (3rd ed.). Long Grove, IL: Waveland Press.

National Commission on Excellence in Education. (1983). *A nation at risk: The imperative for educational reform.* Washington, DC: U.S. Department of Education.

Nelson, F. H. (1997). *How much thirty thousand charter schools cost.* Paper presented at the annual meeting of the American Educational Finance Association, Jacksonville, FL.

Palmer, L. B., & Gau, R. (2005). Charter school authorizing: Policy implications from a national study. *Phi Delta Kappan, 86*(5), 352–357.

Popham, W. J. (2003). The seductive allure of data. *Educational Leadership, 60*(5), 48–51.

Public Law 105-78. (1997, November 13). An act making appropriations for the Departments of Labor, Health and Human Services, and Education, and related agencies for the fiscal year ending September 30, 1998, and for other purposes. *Statutes at Large* (111 Stat. 1467).

Public Law 107-110. (2002, January 8). No Child Left Behind Act of 2001. *Statutes at Large* (115 Stat. 1425).

Spady, W. G. (1994). Choosing outcomes of significance. *Educational Leadership, 51*(6), 18–22.

System-Wide School-to-Work Transition and Parental Choice. (1999). http://www.aypf.org/tripreports/1995/tr101995.htm

Tech-Prep Demonstration Program. (2003, January 24). *Federal Register, 68*(16), 3517–3520.

Warger, C. (2000). *Research on full-service schools and students with disabilities.* (ERIC Document Reproduction Service No. ED182465).

Wells, A. S. (1990, March). *Public school choice: Issues and concerns for urban educators (ERIC/CUE Digest,* No. 63). (ERIC Clearinghouse on Urban Education No. ED322275).

Wiggins, G. (1989). A true test: Toward more authentic and equitable measurement. *Phi Delta Kappan, 70*(9), 703–713.

Wohlstetter, P., & Smith, J. (2006). Improving schools through partnerships: Learning from charter schools. *Phi Delta Kappan, 87*(6), 464–467.

CHAPTER 4

WHO ARE THE STUDENTS?

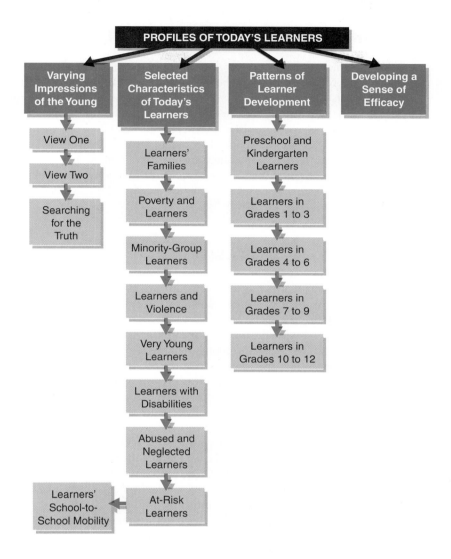

PROFILES OF TODAY'S LEARNERS

Varying Impressions of the Young
- View One
- View Two
- Searching for the Truth

Selected Characteristics of Today's Learners
- Learners' Families
- Poverty and Learners
- Minority-Group Learners
- Learners and Violence
- Very Young Learners
- Learners with Disabilities
- Abused and Neglected Learners
- At-Risk Learners
- Learners' School-to-School Mobility

Patterns of Learner Development
- Preschool and Kindergarten Learners
- Learners in Grades 1 to 3
- Learners in Grades 4 to 6
- Learners in Grades 7 to 9
- Learners in Grades 10 to 12

Developing a Sense of Efficacy

OBJECTIVES

This chapter will help you to

- explain that young people in the schools reflect great diversity and, at the same time, share certain common characteristics.

- identify selected characteristics of learners likely to be present in many elementary, middle, and high school classrooms.

- describe how your teaching practices may be influenced by the diversity reflected in your classes.

- cite examples of age- and development-related characteristics of young people that you might expect to see at different grade levels.

- describe some teacher characteristics that seem to be associated with learner success at different grade levels.

- explain why it is important for you to help learners develop a sense of self-efficacy.

VARYING IMPRESSIONS OF THE YOUNG

It is common to hear the remark from experienced teachers that contemporary students are different. There is no doubt that as society changes, as innovation changes the way individuals perceive the world and view reality, that there will be changes in the values, aspirations, and attitudes of the young. Although some of these changes may lead to problems, others pose opportunities that were not available to other generations.

How do you see the youth of today? To be an effective teacher you need to have an understanding of the youth, their attitudes and beliefs, and how they perceive school. At least two images of the youth emerge when individuals respond to this question. Their responses reflect patterns such as those included in these two views.

View One

The youth of today are overindulged, undersupervised, self-centered, and out-of-control. Many of them come from dysfunctional families and are familiar with crime, drugs, and violence. Alcohol and drug abuse are rampant as these undisciplined brats refuse to consider the consequences of their behavior. They are allowed access to movies and Web sites that are blatantly pornographic. Their preferred television programs reflect an emphasis on violence, sexual content, and disrespectful behavior. Those programs where people are humiliated and degraded are among the most popular.

Because of their preoccupation with instant gratification, they are disinterested in school. One bit of evidence is their eagerness to accept part-time employment so they can have what they want right now. The result is too many students in high school working an excessive number of hours while they are going to school and neglecting their education.

Important societal institutions that hold society together are little prized by young people. They generally have little use for organized religion or a rigorous education. Few of them bother to be informed or even participate in the political process when they are able to do so. On the other hand, young people accept what they find on the Internet or on television with no critical discernment.

Traditional role models, such as parents and teachers, are not held in particularly high regard. Heroes of young people tend to be overpaid, spoiled athletes and celebrities who demonstrate rude, antisocial, and boorish behavior.

View Two

The youth face challenges that were simply not present for past generations. However, claims that this is leading to dysfunctional youth is overblown. There is evidence that the numbers of children and young people who report using tobacco and drugs are going down. In recent years, the percentage of young people who have used marijuana is much lower than it was in the middle 1970s and there has been a downward trend in young people's illicit use of cocaine. The percentage of teenage pregnancies has declined significantly in the past 20 years.

Many young people in high school have part-time jobs. However, the number of students who work 20 or more hours a week has gone down over the past 20 years. The 20-hours-per-week figure is important because young people who work more than 20 hours a week tend to experience fatigue that negatively affects their performance at school.

Institutions viewed as important by children and young people are not greatly different from those prized by adults. For example, they hold organized religion and public schools in high esteem, and they don't hold television in particularly high regard.

Children and young people, when asked to identify role models who are important to them, cite parents and teachers as people they particularly admire, not rock musicians. When asked to comment on the importance of various groups to maintaining a "good society," young people rate school teachers and scientists high and rock musicians low.

Searching for the Truth

Did you find one of these views to be more credible than the other? If you chose View One, your selection would have been consistent with impressions that many members of the general public have about young people today. This view is consistent with much of what we see on television and read in the newspapers. The emphasis on problems of young people helps focus proper attention on issues that deserve public attention. On the other hand, it can also give people a distorted picture of the characteristics of typical learners in today's schools.

Research evidence often fails to confirm widely held popular attitudes. Though many people you ask might believe otherwise, the picture of children and young people provided in View Two is more consistent with the best evidence we now have (Carskadon, 1999; National Center for Education Statistics, 2006a; Naylor, 1999; & U.S. Department of Health and Human Services, 2001).

It is also interesting to note that student aspirations have changed. This is revealed in student expectations for postsecondary education. The proportion of students expecting to attain a bachelor's degree increased from 19% in 1981 to 34% in 2003. Those who expected to attend graduate school increased from 16% to 35%. The percentages did vary according to socioeconomic status (SES). Students in high SES families had a slightly higher expectation of attaining a bachelor's degree. However, high SES students were more than twice as likely to expect to attend graduate school. About 53% of the high-income students expected to attend graduate school, while 22% of the low-income students expected to do so (National Center for Education Statistics, 2006a).

Figure 4–1 provides some information about how secondary-level students view some selected dimensions of their school environment. You might reflect on how the data compare to general public perceptions.

Though the attitudes of young people on many key issues do not seem to deviate markedly from those of many adults, we need to keep in mind that the data represent averages of a huge group. With about 50 million young people in the schools (National Center for Education Statistics, 2002b), there is a variety of perspectives in the total population. This is a particularly critical point for those of us who work in the public schools.

As a teacher, you will fulfill your responsibilities at a workplace that brings together a cross section of our entire population. Many attitudes and perspectives that characterize the general population are sure to be represented in your classroom. This diversity will add spice (and challenge) to your teaching days.

SELECTED CHARACTERISTICS OF TODAY'S LEARNERS

The diversity of learners always impresses visitors who have not been in a school for a long time. As a teacher, you will be challenged to recognize and respond to common

Figure 4–1   Student perceptions of their school environment.

This figure shows the percentage of 10th grade students who agreed or disagreed with selected statements about their school environment.

Selected Statements	Agree	Disagree
Students make friends with students of other racial/ethnic groups	89.6	10.4
High-Minority School	89.9	10.1
Medium-Minority School	90.6	9.4
Low-Minority School	89.1	11.0
In class, I often feel "put down" by other students	16.7	83.3
High-Minority Schools	18.2	81.8
Medium-Minority Schools	14.3	85.7
Low-Minority Schools	16.8	83.2
Fights often occur between different racial/ethnic groups	28.0	72.0
High-Minority Schools	34.9	65.1
Meduim-Minority Schools	36.2	63.8
Low-Minority Schools	19.7	80.3
I dont feel safe at this school	12.6	87.4
High-Minority Schools	18.5	81.5
Medium-Minority Schools	11.1	8.9
Low-Minority Schools	9.3	90.7

Source: National Center for Education Statistics. (2005). Contexts of Elementary and Secondary Education, Table 29-2. Washington, DC: NCES.

characteristics of young people. At the same time, you will have to adjust your instruction to meet unique needs of individual learners.

Learners' Families

Television programs sometimes promote an image of a "typical" American family that includes a father who is employed, a mother who stays in the family's well-appointed suburban home, and two well-scrubbed children who romp endlessly with the family's shaggy dog. This image, in all its dimensions, never was typical. However, it is far from the picture revealed by current data. For example, there has been a decline in two-parent households in the past 25 years from about 83% in 1976 to about 68% in 2001 (National Center for Education Statistics, 2003).

Another change that has significant impact on education has been the number of school-aged youth who speak English as a second language. Between 1979 and 2003 the number of children who spoke a language other than English at home increased from 3.8 million to 9.9 million. There was an increase in the school population of 18% over this time period, but there was also an increase of 162% in the number of children who spoke a language other than English at home (National Center for Education Statisitcs, 2006d).

Families vary greatly in terms of their active involvement in young people's educational experiences. Parents and guardians from higher-income households are more likely to have some active contact with their children's schools. Educational levels of parents and guardians tend to influence their interest in education. There has been an increase in the educational level of parents over the past couple of decades. In 1979, the percentage of school-aged children who had parents who had graduated from high school rose from about 76% to about 88% in 2001. The percentage of parents with at least a bachelor's degree increased from 19% to 31% (National Center for Education Stastitics, 2003). Figure 4–2 reflects the increasing level of parent education by indicating the percentage of 25 to 29-year-olds who completed high school.

Because adults with more education are generally more involved with their children's schools, this is a positive sign that teachers can expect more interest from parents. As Figure 4–3 shows, family members tend to be more involved (1) in activities that require relatively modest commitments of their time and (2) when their children are in the elementary rather than the middle school or high school grades.

Current family and employment statistics indicate that large numbers of schoolchildren spend many hours with babysitters and at day-care centers. The kind of generation-to-generation communication that went on in traditional families happens less frequently today. As a result, we in the schools often provide social and personal information to learners that, in years gone by, was passed on by parents. Increasingly, the dividing line separating responsibilities of the home and the school is blurring.

Figure 4–2   **Increasing educational attainment.**

This figure shows the change in the educational attainment of 25- to 29-year-olds over time.

Year	Total	Male	Female
1971	77.7	79.0	76.5
2005	86.1	84.9	87.3

Source: National Center for Education Statistics. (2006). *Student Effort and Educational Progress*, Table 31-1. Washington, DC: NCES.

Figure 4–3   **Differences in percentages of parent/guardian involvement in school-related activities by grade level of their children.**

	Attended a General School Meeting	Attended Scheduled Meeting with Teacher	Attended a School Event	Acted as a Volunteer or Served on a Committee
Child in Grades K–5	84.6%	87.5%	70.4%	47.6%
Child in Grades 6–8	79.6%	70.4%	65.7%	29.1%
Child in Grades 9–12	67.3%	51.3%	57.3%	24.6%

Source: The Condition of Education, 2001 (p. 175), by the National Center for Education Statistics, 2001. Washington DC: NCES.

Poverty and Learners

Poverty continues to be a depressing national problem. Approximately one-fourth of our nation's children live in poverty (Futrell, Gomez, & Bedden, 2003). Yet, in most communities socioeconomic factors change slowly (Toutkoushidian & Curtis, 2005). This poverty rate is among the highest in all developed nations (Thomas & Bainbridge, 2002). During the first year of the new millennium, the number of poor increased by 1.3 million to 32.9 million (National Center for Education Statistics, 2001). Rates of poverty vary greatly from ethnic group to ethnic group. Households that include minority children of high school age that are headed by a female and in which no male is present are especially likely to be economically impoverished. Percentages of Americans younger than 18 living in poverty have generally increased over the past 25 years.

For many reasons, children from economically deprived homes often do not do well in school. Disadvantaged learners have difficulty with cognitive development, vocabulary, and reading (Thomas & Bainbridge, 2002; Frey et al., 2005). Too many of these learners are assigned to special education classes because of cognitive and developmental deficiencies. Many of these problems result because of mothers' inability to pay for quality prenatal care. Also, poor children often do not receive adequate diets, which may affect their performance in school. This is reflected in the dropout rate of students. The dropout rate for high school students living in low-income homes is about six times that of their peers residing in high-income homes. The rate was about an 11% dropout rate for the students living in low-income familes, 5% for students living in a middle-income family, and 2% from students living in high-income families (National Center for Education Statistics, 2004).

Many of the economically impoverished learners you teach will come from homes that lack personal computers. Large numbers of poor families cannot afford newspaper and magazine subscriptions. Poor children are not nearly as likely to observe their parents reading as are children from more-affluent homes. Because these learners seldom see their parents or guardians reading, you may find that some of them fail to understand the importance you attach to helping them acquire sophisticated reading skills. Failure of these learners to develop good reading proficiencies in the early grades often begins a cycle of failure that leads to poor academic performance in later school years.

Present trends suggest that you will be dealing with significant numbers of students from economically impoverished backgrounds during your years in the profession (Doorey & Harter, 2003). Helping these learners succeed requires you to plan instructional programs that take into account their special needs.

What Do You Think?

- What do you see as the opportunities and challenges of teaching diverse populations?
- What do you think you need to know in order to teach in a classrooom of diverse students?

Students Today

Go to MyEducationLab and select the topic "Students Today: Urban/Suburban/Rural." Read the article by J. Landsman, "Bearers of Hope." Answer the questions that accompany the article. Some of the questions have been designed to prepare you for your licensure examination.

Minority-Group Learners

Minority-group children are becoming a larger proportion of the total school population. At the beginning of the 21st century, they accounted for nearly 40% of all young people in school, an increase of 17% since 1972 (National Center for Education Statistics, 2002a). About 17% of the nation's schoolchildren are African American, and about 17% are of Latino heritage. Latinos are the fastest growing minority group in the schools today. Learners from Asian or Pacific Islander, Native American, and other racial and ethnic groups comprise about 5% of the total school enrollment (National Center for Education Statistics, 2002a).

Distribution of students from minority groups is not uniform across the country. In the South, African Americans account for 26% of the total school enrollment, whereas in the West, Latinos comprise about 32% of the total (National Center for Education Statistics, 2002a).

Minority-group students, with the exception of some of Asian heritage, often have not adapted well to school programs. Latino, African American, and American Indian students generally study less, are less likely to be enrolled in college-prep or honors courses, and are less likely to participate in extracurricular activities than their white and Asian classmates (McCarthy & Kuh, 2006). This pattern is especially pronounced among Latinos. For example, data published in 2002 revealed that nearly 28% of Latinos between the ages of 16 and 24 had dropped out of school before high school graduation. Though this percentage has declined in recent years, it still is well above the 2002 figures for African Americans (about 13%) and whites (about 7%) (National Center for Education Statistics, 2002a).

Educators today are concerned about the **achievement gap** between white students and those from many minority groups, including African Americans and Latinos. Scores of these minorities have lagged behind those of whites, though the gap between white and African American learners has narrowed in recent years (National Center for Education Statistics, 2002a). Educators today are working hard to understand factors that contribute to these achievement differences and to develop responses that will better serve the needs of African Americans and Latinos. Given (1) our profession's commitment to serve all learners well and (2) the reality that students from minority backgrounds are a growing percentage of the school population, you probably will be involved in efforts to design programs to reduce the achievement gap.

Learners and Violence

If young people you teach do not feel safe, their ability to learn will be impaired. In recent years, incidents such as that at Columbine High School in Colorado and others have raised serious questions about learners' safety at school. Although school violence continues to be a problem, you need to keep the issue in perspective. In general, schools are quite safe places. A student is almost twice as likely to be a victim of a serious crime away from school than at school (DeVoe et al., 2002).

Efforts to reduce the violent incidents in schools seem to be having a positive effect. From 1992 to 2003 there was a decline in the rate of violent crime at school. The rate declined by 53% for theft and 42% for all violent crime. The rates for all crime were higher when students were away from school than when they were in school (National Center for Educational Statistics, 2006b). Despite this positive trend, school violence continues to be a matter of great concern that educators, community leaders, law enforcement officials, and members of other groups continue to address.

Involvement in a physical fight without a weapon is the most common kind of physical violence young people experience at school. In 2001, U.S. schools reported nearly 188,000 such incidents. Middle school and high school students are much more likely to experience this problem than are elementary school students (National Center for Education Statistics, 2002a).

Although violence has occurred in a variety of schools, there are profiles of schools where students have a greater likelihood of being victimized. For example, more schools in the West report serious crimes occurring in and around their buildings than schools in the Northeast, Southeast, or Central United States. Schools in inner cities experience more problems than schools in suburban areas, small towns, or rural areas. Interestingly, poverty does *not* seem to be a variable associated with incidents of serious school violence. High-poverty and low-poverty schools report about the same percentage of episodes of violence on students (DeVoe et al., 2002). See Figure 4–1 for additional information about schools with varying characteristics and their reported violence.

Certain characteristics associated with a school's climate and culture have been found to be associated with violence and antisocial behavior. Among them are:

- overcrowding;
- poor design and use of school space;
- lack of firm, yet caring, disciplinary procedures;
- learner alienation;
- multicultural insensitivity;
- teacher and peer rejection of at-risk learners; and
- student resentment of school routines. (*How Can We Prevent Violence in Our Schools?* 2000)

Web Extension 4-1

National Center for Children Exposed to Violence

• •

The National Center for Children Exposed to Violence brings together a vast array of information related to the general issue of violence and children. At this site, you will find statistical information, a comprehensive online library, lists of publications, examples of programs that have been established to deal with this problem, and links to a large number of useful Web sites.

http://www.nccev.org/

Teacher practices may have unwittingly reinforced stereotypical constructs of boys as being aggressive (DeCorby et al., 2005). To learn about one school's experiences on helping to improve student attitudes and achievement, read this chapter's *Video Viewpoints* feature.

Video Viewpoints 4–1

Home Room: One Last Chance

WATCH: This *Nightline* special focuses on the Seed Charter School in Washington, D.C. The founders of this charter school believed that it would take more than choice, the elimination of red tape, and a change of curriculum to improve student performance. They believed that nothing short of changing the environment would work. They established a public boarding school for 40 students coming from troubled schools and difficult neighborhoods.

This segment details the experiences of several of the students and illustrates the challenges of improving student attitudes and achievement.

THINK: Discuss with your classmates or write in your reflective journal your responses to the following questions:

1. What do you see as the critical variables that need to be addressed if fundamental change is to occur?
2. What do you see as the implications of this program for reform efforts focused on improving student achievement?
3. What do you think can be done if it is impossible to change the environment?

LINK: How might reform efforts focus on cooperation between schools and other social agencies?

 To view this video, go to the Video Viewpoints DVD and click on this chapter's video: "Home Room: One Last Chance"

Very Young Learners

As you drive around neighborhoods today, you are likely to see a number of day-care facilities. Their growth is a reflection in the tremendous increase over the past 30 years in the number of female parents and guardians who have or who are actively looking for full-time employment outside the home. A side effect of this trend has been an increasing interest in enrolling young children in educational programs. Because of the expense and uneven quality of private day-care operations, public schools have been under pressure to expand programs available to 3- and 4-year-old children.

Growth of these programs has been dramatic. In 1970, for example, only about 13% of 3-year-olds and about 28% of 4-year-olds were in formal educational programs. In 1970, almost three times as many of the enrolled 3- and 4-year-olds attended private nursery schools as attended public nursery schools. By 2005, about 43% of 3-year-olds and about 69% of 4-year-olds participated in early childhood education programs (National Center for Education Statistics, 2006c). Figure 4–4 provides a breakdown of those enrolled in early childhood education programs.

Expansion of school programs for young learners has prompted much debate. Supporters cite research suggesting that early childhood programs can help young children to develop positive self-images and abilities to work productively and harmoniously with others. Critics argue that expansion of early childhood programs imposes obligations on schools that properly should be discharged in the home by parents and guardians. Forces supporting expansion of school

Preschool children have great curiosity and high energy.

Figure 4–4   Percentage of prekindergarten children enrolled in early childhood education programs.

	1991	2005
Age		
3	42%	43%
4	60%	69%
Gender		
Male	52%	60%
Female	53%	55%
Race/Ethnicity		
White	54%	59%
Black	58%	66%
Hispanic	39%	43%
Poverty Status		
Poor	44%	47%
Nonpoor	56%	60%

Source: National Center for Education Statistics (2006). *Participation in Education*, Table 2-1, Washington DC: NCES.

programs seem to be carrying the day, as economic pressures continue to encourage female heads of families with young children to seek out-of-the-home employment. The years ahead probably will witness an even greater expansion of school programs for very young learners.

What Do You Think?

- What is your position on the expansion of programs for young children?
- Where is the dividing line between the responsibility of parents and the needs of society for a highly educated citizenry?

Learners With Disabilities

In the past, learners with disabilities were isolated in special education classrooms. This practice was justified by the claim that such students needed training and assistance that was unavailable to them in the regular classroom. Since the mid-1970s, however, this situation has changed. The **Education for All Handicapped Children Act (Public Law 94-142)** of 1975 (renamed in 1990 the **Individuals with Disabilities Education Act [IDEA]**) required schools, to the extent possible, to teach learners with disabilities in traditional, mainstream classrooms. This has had an enormous impact on education. In 1976 about 3.7 million youth were receiving special education services. In 2003, about 6.6 million youth or about 14% of the total school population were receiving special education services (National Center for Education Statisics, 2006e).

In part, this federal legislation was the result of concerns that the past practice of isolating learners with disabilities stigmatized them. They did not get experience working with students without disabilities, and students without disabilities were harmed because they did not have the opportunity to learn about them. In addition, there was some indication that the curriculum presented to special education students was less challenging and did not allow them to develop to their fullest potential. Now, during a typical day, you will have students with a variety of disabilities in your classroom.

The National Center for Education Statistics (2002b) reports that programs for the disabled are directed at learners who comprise about 13% of the total school population. By far the largest group in this category, representing about 46% of the total, are young people classified as having "specific learning disabilities." Other major groups within this total and the percentages they represent are the following:

- Learners with speech impairments: 17.4%
- Learners with some degree of mental retardation: 9.7%
- Learners suffering from severe emotional disturbance: 7.6% (National Center for Education Statistics, 2002b, p. 66)

Abused and Neglected Learners

You may be surprised to learn that more children aged 4 and younger die each year from child abuse and neglect than from any other single cause (Childabuse.com, 2001). Problems of abused and neglected children have attracted public interest for years. As a teacher, you will have a legal obligation to report any injury to a learner that appears to be nonaccidental. You will not be doing anything unusual. Responsible governmental agencies receive around 3 million child abuse reports each year, many of them from teachers (Childabuse.com, 2001).

Suspected abuse is handled in most communities by **Child Protective Services (CPS).** This organization usually operates within a state or county agency, which might be known as the Department of Social Services, the Department of Human Resources, the Department of Social Welfare, the Department of Public Welfare, or some other name. Here are the types of abuse and typical behaviors of victims.

- *Physical abuse.* Signs of physical abuse may include bruises, welts, burns, bite marks, and other unusual marks on the body; or the learner may be having what seem to be too many accidental injuries at home. Some behavioral indicators of physical abuse include:
    - Learner is hard to get along with and may frequently be in trouble.
    - Learner has bruises, abrasions, lacerations, or swellings that appear not to have been caused accidentally.
    - Learner is unusually shy or too eager to please.
    - Learner is frequently late or absent or comes to school too early and seems reluctant to go home.
    - Learner's body shows evidence of bite marks or pinches.
    - Learner shies away from physical contact with adults.
    - Learner seems frightened of parents.
    - Learner may seek affection from any adult.
- *Neglect.* Learners who have been neglected at home may show up at school dirty. They may not have any lunch money. They may need glasses and dental care. Their clothing may be unkempt, or they may wear clothes that are inappropriate for the prevailing weather conditions. Some of these young people may beg food from their classmates. Examples of other indicators include:
    - Learner has a behavior pattern reflecting poor supervision at home.
    - Learner frequently falls asleep in class.
    - Learner has a medical condition that is not receiving attention.
- *Emotional abuse.* Emotional abuse is often reflected in extreme or excessive behavior patterns. Emotionally abused young people may be too compliant and passive; on the other hand, they may be very aggressive. Some other behavioral indicators of possible emotional abuse include:
    - Behavior is either too adult-like or too immature, given the learner's age.
    - Learner is behind in physical, emotional, and intellectual development.
- *Sexual abuse.* One indicator of this condition is that a learner's underclothing is torn, stained, or bloody. Or, the learner may experience pain or itching in the genital area. Other behavioral indicators of sexual abuse include:
    - Learner is very withdrawn, or learner engages in fantasy-like or baby-like behavior.
    - Learner has poor relationships with other children.
    - Learner engages in delinquent acts or runs away from home.
    - Learner says he or she has been sexually assaulted.

Many groups in our society are interested in doing something to reduce child abuse and neglect. They recognize that teachers can play an important part by recognizing potential abuse and reporting it to authorities.

Web Extension 4-2

National Clearinghouse on Child Abuse and Neglect Information

· ·

The National Clearinghouse on Child Abuse and Neglect is a service of the Children's Bureau, a program that is part of the U.S. Department of Health and Human Services' Administration for Children and Families. At this site, you will find numerous useful links to information about child abuse and neglect. These links give you access to materials that include those that focus on (1) relevant statistics, (2) preventative measures, (3) applicable laws, and (4) publications.

http://www.calib.com/nccanch

At-Risk Learners

Particular personal and situational backgrounds of some young people inhibit their success at school and place them at risk of failure. Experts have identified a number of **risk factors.** These include:

- living with only one parent,
- being a child of a single parent,
- having parents who failed to complete high school,
- living in a low-income household,
- living in high-growth states,
- having poorly developed academic skills (not necessarily low intelligence),
- having low self-esteem, and
- speaking English as a second language. (Druian & Butler, 2001)

Recent research reveals that schools that will serve at-risk students have important characteristics associated with (1) school leadership, (2) **school climate** (i.e., the general school atmosphere within which instruction, learning, and person-to-person interactions occur), and (3) classroom instructional and management practices (Druian & Butler, 2001). Principals in these schools work to focus the entire school on the importance of providing high-quality instructional services to *all* learners. The climate features an expectation that all enrolled young people will learn; a safe, orderly environment; and well-established and fairly administered rules that govern learners' conduct. Teachers use clear objectives to focus their instruction, deliver information using a variety of methods, and frequently monitor and evaluate learner progress toward mastery of the established objectives (Druian & Butler, 2001).

Learners' School-to-School Mobility

How probable is it that you will be teaching exactly the same learners at the end of the school year as at the beginning? Perhaps not as much as you might suppose. More than half of all learners make at least one school change (from one elementary school to another elementary school, from one middle school to another middle school, or from one high school to another high school) during their K–12 school years. From 15% to 18% of all school-age children move from one school to another during a given school year (Rumberger, 2002).

A surprisingly large number—30% to 40%—of these school-to-school moves are not caused by a change in residence by parents or guardians. Other reasons include:

- overcrowding in a learner's previous school,
- legislation related to class-size reduction that may force a learner to change schools,
- an expulsion policy that may require a learner to leave a former school, and
- legislation that, under certain conditions, allows parents and guardians to move their child from one school to another. (Rumberger, 2002)

Many studies report that learners who move from school to school more than three times do not perform as well academically and tend to have more behavior problems in school than less-frequent school changers (Rumberger, 2002). Young people who change schools frequently have lower rates of high school graduation than learners who change schools rarely or not at all.

As an educator, you have a professional interest in promoting the development of individual learners by encouraging them to remain in school. As a classroom teacher, you must be prepared to deal with class rosters that will not remain stable throughout the school year. You must develop ways to smooth the transition of new learners into the general flow of your classroom activity. In addition to taking steps to introduce these young people to other class members and to otherwise make them welcome, you have to ascertain their levels of understanding of the topics and subjects you teach.

To the extent possible, you should try to learn about newcomers' past enrollment history. It will be especially useful to find out what these young people were studying in their previous schools. In addition to checking records that may have come to your school from the learners' previous buildings, you may find it useful to conduct personal interviews with learners and, if possible, with their parents or guardians. When you have gathered this background information, you may find it necessary to develop learning materials for each transfer student that vary from those you are using with others in your class to provide information needed for success.

◆ ◆

Student Mobility

Go to MyEducationLab and select the topic "Family and Community." Read the article by C. Hartman "Students on the Move." Respond to the questions that are included. Some of the questions have been designed to prepare you for your licensure examination.

◆ ◆

PATTERNS OF LEARNER DEVELOPMENT

Ideas about how children develop shape ideas about how they should be educated. To be responsible, you need to base your instructional procedures on up-to-date knowledge about human development, not on outdated views. As you think about this issue, you might be interested in knowing that some perspectives that were very much in vogue at one time seem bizarre to us today.

According to one early view, children were mindless creatures who were incapable of feeling or knowing anything. Interesting ideas about education flowed logically from this idea. For example, supporters of this view tended to dismiss proposals to spend money on early childhood education because they saw formal education for very young children as pointless. Adults' roles were limited to meeting children's physical needs and to keeping them out of mischief.

In the past, others saw children as essentially miniature adults. Aside from their small size, children were believed to have adult characteristics, lacking only knowledge and experience. If these could be provided, it was assumed that children would be able to discharge adult roles at a very early age. Learning materials designed for use by adults were seen as perfectly appropriate for children. If children failed to learn, this failure was attributed to their laziness. The tradition of punishing children for failing to learn comes out of this view of childhood.

Still another historical perspective maintained that children came into the world totally lacking any personalities of their own. They were simply animated clay or putty awaiting appropriate "modeling" by adults. There was an assumption that young people, when appropriately guided, would turn into good citizens. In the schools, this view resulted in educational practices that were planned and delivered exclusively by adults. Children's interests were considered to be of little importance.

Most of these views from history have not stood up well to the rigors of modern scholarship. Today, we know that each child has unique qualities and that these qualities affect how individual children react to school. Though teaching might be simpler if young people were so many "lumps of clay," that is just not how it is. As a professional educator, your success in large measure depends on your recognition of diversity as an expected feature of your workplace.

Web Extension 4-3

Society for the History of Children and Youth

The Society for the History of Children and Youth maintains this Web site. On this page, click on a link titled "H-Childhood." This will take you to a page titled "H-Childhood: History of Children and Youth." Here you will find a useful link to reviews of recent publications that focus on the history of children. You will also be able to access discussion logs that focus on topics dealing with historical perspectives on children and adolescents.

http://academic.mu.edu/shcy/

As you think about this reality, consider the physical characteristics of young people in a typical eighth-grade classroom. On a visit, you might be struck by the differences in the appearances of the young people. Some of them are small and immature; others are as large and as physically well-developed as juniors and seniors in high school. Some of the boys may even sport mustaches (much to the envy of their less physically mature classmates). Differences in learners' rates of physical development present problems related not only to their ability to perform physical tasks, but also to their psychological development.

Preschool and Kindergarten Learners

Preschool- and kindergarten-age children are extremely active. They have quite good control of their bodies, and they seem to enjoy activity for its own sake. Because of their frequent bursts of activity, these children need regular rest periods. When rest periods are not provided, they may become irritable. Emotional outbursts often result when overtired children in this age group encounter even minor frustrations.

At this age, children's large-muscle coordination is better developed than their small-muscle coordination. As a result, tasks that require small-muscle control can be frustrating. Many children in this group have trouble managing shoestrings, buttons, and other fine-motor tasks that older children find easy. Some children in this age group may not yet have fully developed eyes and eye muscles. They may experience difficulty in focusing on small objects and in completing tasks that require good hand–eye coordination.

Boys in this age group tend to be slightly larger in size than girls, but girls are more advanced by almost any other measure that is applied. This is particularly true in the area of fine-motor-skill development. At this age, girls tend to display much better coordination than boys.

If you teach this age group, you have to be patient and able to tolerate a lot of activity in the classroom. You must understand that there are certain things these children simply cannot do. Be prepared to spend time tying shoes, mopping up paint spills, and buttoning coats, and learn to do these things with a smile. Children need a lot of affection at this time of their lives.

Learners in Grades 1 to 3

The high need for physical activity that characterizes kindergarten children carries through the first year or two of the primary grades. The large muscles still tend to be more fully developed than the small muscles. This large-muscle development gives these children a tremendous confidence in their ability to accomplish certain physical tasks. Many youngsters in this age group develop more confidence in their physical abilities than is warranted. The accident rate among primary-grades children is very high.

The early primary grades are difficult for many young people. Large numbers of them have a high need for activity. This need persists at a time when school programs begin to expect more "in-seat" learning, a clear break from the almost nonstop activity routine of many kindergarten classrooms. When there is too much forced sitting, youngsters in this age group may develop nervous habits such as pencil chewing, fingernail biting, and general fidgeting. These behaviors represent attempts of the body to compensate for the lack of the physical activity that it needs.

Typically, handwriting is introduced during this period. Learning how to perform this task can be a trying experience for late-maturing children, who may still have very poor control over their small muscles. If you are teaching in the primary grades, you need to be very sensitive in your comments to children regarding their first efforts at cursive writing. If small-muscle development is inadequate, no amount of admonishment from you will lead to improved writing skills.

Children's eyes do not fully develop until they are about 8 years old. Hence, many children in the primary grades experience difficulty when asked to focus on small print or small objects. This situation has important implications because serious reading instruction ordinarily begins in grade 1. You need to understand that difficulties experienced by some of your charges may be due to inadequate eye development. Some class members may not yet be able to maintain a focus on objects as small as printed words.

When teachers are sensitive to their needs, slow-developing children generally have little difficulty in catching up to their classmates as their physical development accelerates. However, if you are insensitive to differences in rates of individual development and attribute problems of physically slow-developing learners to laziness, these children may conclude that they cannot succeed. When learners develop this kind of self-image, they often stop trying. A pattern of failure established early in learners' education can follow them through their remaining years in school.

Primary-grades children have a high need for praise and recognition. They want to please the teacher and do well in school. When you give them positive recognition, they tend to blossom. A positive adjustment to school during these years often sets a pattern for success that persists as they continue their education.

Learners in Grades 4 to 6

In grades 4 to 6, most girls and a few boys experience a tremendous growth spurt. It is not uncommon for 11-year-old girls to be taller and heavier than 11-year-old boys. Many girls reach puberty during this period and, especially toward the end of this time, they tend to become very interested in boys. In contrast, many boys, even at the end of this period of their lives, have little interest in girls.

Friendships tend to divide along sex lines: Boys tend to associate with boys, and girls tend to associate with girls. There is considerable competition between boys and girls. Insults are a common feature of interactions between groups of boys and groups of girls.

Learners' fine-motor control is generally quite good by this time. Many of them develop an interest in applying their new abilities to "make their fingers do what they're supposed to do" by getting involved in crafts, model building, piano playing, and other activities demanding fine-muscle control.

Youngsters in grades 4 through 6 pose different challenges for teachers than primary-grade children. There is an especially acute need for you to pay attention to your role as motivator. You also must be prepared to deal with these learners' emerging sense of independence.

Many young people in this age group tend to be perfectionists. Frequently, they set unrealistically high standards for themselves. When they fail to perform up to these

Anthony Magnacca/Merrill

Students in the middle grades want to belong to a group.

standards, they may suffer extreme feelings of guilt. You need to be sensitive to these feelings and devise ways of letting these children know that they are developing in a satisfactory way.

Many teachers of this age group derive great pleasure observing their students' increased sophistication. Learners' interests broaden tremendously during these years. Some of them become voracious readers, some develop a great deal of technical expertise about computers, and others develop a surprising depth of knowledge about a wide range of additional topics. At the same time, these children still retain an engaging air of innocence and trust. They tend to be extremely loyal to teachers they like.

However, misbehavior problems are more prevalent here than in the primary grades. At this time of life, young people increasingly begin to look to their **peer group** (individuals who are similar in age and interests) rather than to adults for guidance regarding what is appropriate behavior. This tendency may occasionally challenge you. For example, you may come to school one day and discover that the peer group has decreed that "reading is boring." Given this dictum, you will face a difficult challenge motivating class members during the reading period. You have to become an expert in group dynamics and a keen observer of individual friendships within your classroom. Armed with such insights, you can often act to prevent the peer group from taking a negative position on important academic issues.

You need a healthy dose of patience when working with this age group. These children often find some school assignments to be frustrating and difficult, and you need to provide them with positive support. Learners make many mistakes. You need to be sympathetic and allow students the freedom to make and learn from their errors. At the same time, you have to maintain a reasonable and firm set of expectations. In this kind of atmosphere, children can make tremendous personal strides during these years.

Learners in Grades 7 to 9

Many educators consider young people in grades 7 to 9 to be difficult to teach, and there is evidence that a certain kind of teacher is needed to be successful. If you work with this age group, one of your challenges is to respond appropriately to these learners' incredible diversity. You will encounter variations in their maturity levels and often great day-to-day differences in the patterns of behavior of a single student. A particular eighth grader at one moment may be the very image of sophistication and at the next display a pattern of behavior that differs little from that of a fourth grader. Learners at this time of their lives swing crazily back and forth between adult and very childish behavior.

During these years, most girls complete their growth spurt. For boys, growth may continue to the end of this age range or even later. Nearly all individuals of both sexes attain puberty by the end of this period, and these young people often worry about the physical and psychological changes they are experiencing. Many wonder whether they are developing properly. Some young people become extremely self-conscious during this time of their lives, sometimes feeling as though their every action is being observed and evaluated. For many young people, their middle school/junior high school years are a highly uncomfortable time.

If you work with this age group, your prospects for success will increase if you are sensitive to the psychological changes that these young people are experiencing. You need to develop some tolerance for these students' occasionally loud, emotional outbursts. The range of development reflected among individual learners is huge, and developmental changes often are stressful. Indeed, this is the least stable period in a young person's life. In general, you need to be flexible and to develop the ability to respond appropriately to the sometimes wildly varying emotional, intellectual, and behavioral patterns you will observe in your classroom. If you are a person who likes variety and who can cope eagerly with young people whose day-to-day behaviors may be unpredictable, you may be among the middle school teachers who find work with these youngsters to be satisfying and stimulating (Henson, 2004). Teachers with these traits come to school looking forward to new, unexpected adventures every day that they teach.

Web Extension 4-4

National Middle School Association

The National Middle School Association (NMSA) is the nation's leading professional association for educators and others who are interested in promoting high-quality educational services for young adolescents. Click on the link labeled "Services/Resources." You will be taken to a list of links that include (1) the home page of *Middle School Journal*, NMSA's official publication; (2) information related to school curricula for early adolescents; and (3) an extensive listing of additional Web links to sites featuring information related to working with early adolescents.

http://www.nmsa.org/

Learners in Grades 10 to 12

One important issue for young people during their high school years is their search for personal identity (Erikson, 1982). They are trying to find personal selves that are distinct from those of their parents. They ask themselves questions such as "Who am I?" "Will I be successful?" and "Will I be accepted?" In their attempts to establish their personal identities, these students often experiment with behaviors that they believe will show the world that they are independent. They seek to become rulers of their environment. At the same time, they desperately look for evidence that others are accepting them as individuals.

David Elkind (1981), a leading developmental-learning theorist, suggests that young people may experience problems as they begin to develop the ability to engage in thinking processes involving abstract reasoning. With their newfound ability to think in more sophisticated ways, a number of adolescents concern themselves with abstract notions of self and personal identity. It may be that some adolescents who have developed the ability to view their own identities as an abstract idea are unable to distinguish between what they think about themselves and what others think about them. Elkind proposes that this view sometimes takes the form of either (1) an **imaginary audience** or (2) a **personal fable.**

Adolescent behavior in response to an *imaginary audience* results when adolescents fail to distinguish between their own thoughts about themselves and those others hold. When this happens, they tend to view themselves as perpetually "on stage." They are certain that everybody is carefully scrutinizing their every move. The imaginary-audience concept explains much about the behavior of young people in this age group. Shyness, for example, is a logical result of their feeling that any mistake made in public will be noticed and

Learners in grades 10–12 are often dealing with many issues in their lives and the challenge for teachers is to keep them focused on academic tasks.

Anthony Magnacca/Merrill

criticized. The slavish attention to fashion trends results from an expectation that deviations from the expected norm will be noticed and commented on negatively.

In explaining the *personal fable*, Elkind (1981) notes that adolescents often become disoriented by the many physical and emotional changes they experience. At the same time, many of them find these changes to be utterly fascinating. Some of them believe that their new feelings are so unusual that no one else has ever experienced them before, especially not parents or teachers. They may believe that they are living out a one-of-a-kind life story. Sometimes they keep diaries that are written out of a conviction that future generations will be intensely interested in their unique feelings and experiences.

As students in this age group have more and more life experiences, they test the validity of the imaginary audience and the personal fable against reality. In time, the imaginary audience gives way to the real audience, and the personal fable is adjusted as young people's interactions with others reveal that many others have experienced similar feelings and have had similar opinions.

If you teach in a high school, you will find that your students are capable of quite abstract thinking. At the same time, you will notice that young people in your classes have characteristics that separate them from college and university students and from older adult learners. For example, you are likely to observe that some students have emotional needs that require your attention. You need to strike a balance between your concern for students' psychological development and your commitment to provide them with a respectable grounding in the academic subject(s) you teach.

The task of motivating this group of learners has become increasingly challenging. Since 1983, the percentage of 12th graders who consider their schoolwork as meaningful has decreased from 40% to 21% (Scherer, 2002). One-third of 12th graders skip at least one day of class each week, and about half of the students say they spend three or fewer hours a week studying (McCarthy & Kuh, 2006). Although most American high school students do not give school their best efforts, a Public Agenda poll reported that 8 in 10 students are upbeat about their education (Public Agenda Online, 2002). This information suggests that you will find it helpful to learn individual interests of your students and use this information to prepare lessons that, to the extent possible, build on existing student enthusiasms.

What Do You Think?

- Which ages do you find most attractive as a teacher?
- What do you find most attractive about this age?
- What are your dispostions and skills that you think will help prepare you for this age?

DEVELOPING A SENSE OF EFFICACY

In this chapter, you have learned about a selection of learner characteristics. Though you need to be aware of these differences, you also should keep in mind that you will find some

**Video Viewpoints
4–2**

"Stinky": Robotics and Immigration

WATCH: This *Nightline* program focuses on a group of students in a Phoenix high school that entered a robotics competition with some of the best engineering universities in the nation. This involvement led to a change in their expectations and gave them an increased sense of efficacy. However, their expectations are being hindered by the political debate over illegal immigration.

THINK: Discuss with your classmates or write in your reflective journal your responses to the following questions:

1. What changed these students' sense of efficacy?
2. What are the lessons that could be taken from this example and applied elsewhere?
3. What is your response to the claims that children of illegal immigrants should be barred from public institutions such as schools?

LINK: What are some other examples of how political concerns interface with education of a particular group?

 To view this video, go to the Video Viewpoints DVD and click on this chapter's video: "'Stinky': Robotics and Immigration."

commonalities among the young people you teach. For example, all learners want to feel good about themselves. They want to believe that they are worthy human beings as well as capable learners. You want to help them develop a **sense of efficacy,** a belief that their existence "matters" and that they are capable of making important contributions to their world. To see an example of a student's sense of efficacy, go to this chapter's *Video View-points* feature.

In your effort to promote feelings of worth and competence, you also need to think about your own professional sense of efficacy (Phelps, 2006). As you continue professional preparation, you need to reflect on the actions you want to take to promote learners' development. Questions such as the following may help you think about your present strengths and weaknesses and about actions you might take to give you confidence and competence as you begin your career in the classroom:

- What are the special characteristics of learners I expect to teach?
- Which of these characteristics am I prepared to respond to in ways that will enhance students' personal growth and their mastery of important academic content?
- Is my knowledge of instructional approaches broad enough for me to respond to the needs of the learners I expect to teach? If not, how can I fill in any gaps?
- What is my level of comfort with day-to-day differences in learners' patterns of behavior? Are my ideas on this issue fixed? If so, what does this information tell me about the kinds of learners I would be best suited to teach?

Key Ideas in Summary

- Learners in today's schools are diverse. Abilities, attitudes, and perspectives characterizing our entire national population are represented in school classrooms. Though these differences are important, you will also find that young people from varying backgrounds share certain common characteristics.
- Families of typical learners by no means match the traditional family stereotype of an employed father, a mother who stayed at home, and two children. Many families are

headed by a single parent or guardian, often a female. Because so many parents and guardians work, many more children today spend much of their out-of-school time in day-care centers or with babysitters. Learners' parents and guardians are more likely to be involved with their children's school if (1) they have attained high levels of education, (2) they have higher incomes, and (3) they have children in elementary schools, as compared with middle or high schools.

- Large numbers of schoolchildren come from families with annual incomes below the federal poverty level. The poverty rate among schoolchildren's families in the United States is higher than that in other developed nations. More African American and Latino children come from poor families than do white children. Children from economically impoverished homes often do not perform well in school.

- With each passing year, minority-group children comprise a larger percentage of the total school population. African American and Latino children represent the largest minority groups in the schools. The makeup of the minority population of schools varies greatly from state to state and from school district to school district within individual states.

- Though violence in schools is an important problem, you need to keep in mind that learners are almost twice as likely to be victims of serious crimes at sites away from their school. The kind of violence a given learner is most likely to experience in school is involvement in a physical fight without a weapon. Middle school and high school learners are more likely to be the victims of violence at school than are elementary school learners. Serious crimes against learners are more common in schools with extremely large enrollments.

- Over the past quarter century, there has been a great increase in the numbers of 3- and 4-year-olds enrolled in school programs. In part, this trend has been spurred by the tendency for more and more mothers to hold down full-time jobs outside the home. There also have been concerns about the quality and the expense of programs offered by private day-care facilities. Today, about 40% of our nation's 3-year-olds and about 65% of our nation's 4-year-olds are enrolled in formal educational programs.

- About 14% of learners in the schools are eligible for programs directed toward the disabled. These learners have widely varied characteristics. In regular classes you teach, you are most likely to encounter learners classified as having "specific learning disabilities." Other large groups within this population are the speech-impaired and mentally retarded learners.

- Every state has laws requiring teachers to file reports with the appropriate authorities when they observe injuries to children that appear to be nonaccidental. Episodes of child abuse appear to be on the increase. Among categories of abuse are (1) physical abuse, (2) neglect, (3) emotional abuse, and (4) sexual abuse. Teachers are expected to know behavioral indicators of possible abuse.

- Many individuals who do not perform well at school have certain characteristics that place them *at risk*. Individual characteristics that often interfere with learners' adjustment to and success at school include (1) living with only one parent, (2) being a child of a single parent, (3) having parents who dropped out of high school, (4) living in a low-income household, (5) living in a high-growth state, (6) having poorly developed basic skills (but not necessarily low intelligence), (7) having low self-esteem, and (8) speaking English as a second language.

- Over half of all learners make at least one elementary to elementary, middle school to middle school, or high school to high school change during their K–12 school years. In any one year, 15% to 18% of school-age children change schools. There is evidence that learners who make three or more school changes do not do as well in school as learners making fewer school changes. Today, educators are working to develop ways to smooth the transition of school changers to their new schools.

- Children's general characteristics vary enormously as they progress through the school program. For example, preschool and kindergarten children tend to require high levels of physical activity. Learners in grades 1 to 3 still have underdeveloped fine-motor control, and they are often frustrated by tasks requiring them to manipulate small objects and do detailed work with their hands. In grades 4 to 6, girls are often physically larger than boys. For the most part, friendships among learners in these grade levels do not cross sex lines. There are tremendous differences in the physical development of individual learners in grades 7 to 9. These differences sometimes cause great personal anxieties on the part of these young people. During grades 10 to 12, many students are engaged in a search for personal identity. By this time in their development, many young people are able to deal with quite abstract levels of thinking.

- As a teacher, you will confront learners who have widely varying personal characteristics. One of your purposes is to help each learner you serve develop a *sense of efficacy*, a feeling that he or she is a worthy and capable human being. As an instructional leader, you also need to think about your own sense of efficacy. In pursuit of this purpose you should reflect on the kinds of expertise you need to help learners you teach, sources of information that may help you, and specific actions you can take to acquire the knowledge you will need to operate as a secure, confident, and competent professional.

For Your Initial-Development Portfolio

1. What materials and ideas that you learned in this chapter about *profiles of today's learners* will you include as "evidence" in your portfolio? Select up to three separate items of information. Number them 1, 2, and 3.
2. Think about why you selected these materials. As you do so, consider these issues:
   - Specific uses you might make of this information as you plan, deliver, and assess the impact of your teaching
   - The compatibility of the information with your own priorities and values
   - Any contributions this information can make to your development as a teacher
   - Factors that led you to include this information, as opposed to some alternatives you considered but rejected
3. Place a check in the chart here to indicate the INTASC standard(s) to which each item of information relates. (You may wish to refer to Chapter 1 for more detailed information about INTASC.)

ITEM OF EVIDENCE NUMBER	INTASC Standard Number									
	S1	S2	S3	S4	S5	S6	S7	S8	S9	S10
1										
2										
3										

4. Prepare a written reflection in which you analyze the decision-making process you followed. In your comments, mention the INTASC standard(s) to which your selected material relates.

Reflections

1. What are some popular ideas about what young people consider to be important? What are your own views? How do the opinions of others and those you hold square with studies that have been made of their attitudes? How do you account for any discrepancies?

2. You will find that large numbers of your learners' parents and guardians hold down full-time jobs, so many of the young people you teach may spend a considerable amount of each day in day-care centers. As a result of heavy work obligations, some of your parents and guardians may not have spent adequate time teaching their children about "appropriate" patterns of behavior. To what extent should you feel obligated to deal with this situation by spending time in your classes teaching basic social skills and acceptable behavior patterns to your students? How would you allocate time between this kind of teaching and the teaching of traditional academic content?

3. For the past quarter century, there has been an increase in the percentage of Americans under the age of 18 who live in poverty. What are your speculations regarding why this trend has developed? Based on your own understanding of present social trends, do you expect the poverty rate among children and young people to increase or decrease over the next decade? Why?

4. Review the general characteristics of learners in different grades. Did any of these descriptions surprise you? If so, which ones, and why? As you assess your own personality, which grade levels now most appeal to you as you think about your future as a classroom teacher? What led you to select your preferred group?

5. One of your major tasks as a teacher will be to promote a strong *sense of efficacy* in each of the young people you teach. You also need to develop your own professional sense of efficacy. As you assess your present level of development, how do you see your strengths and weaknesses? Specifically, what are some things you can do to turn these weaknesses into strengths and gain the confidence and competence you will need when you begin your teaching career?

Field Experiences, Projects, and Enrichment

1. Interview two or more teachers at a grade level you would like to teach or in your subject area(s) if you are interested in secondary-school teaching. Ask them to comment about the family life of learners in their classroom. In particular, seek information about economic status, family values, and the extent to which there is support in the home for what learners are expected to do at school. Also, inquire about problems associated with helping learners who transfer into the class in the middle of the school year. Share your findings with others in your class as part of a general discussion on the nature of learners in the schools.

2. Invite a school administrator to visit your class to speak about issues associated with (1) school violence and (2) abused and neglected children. Ask this person to comment on the frequency of problems. Inquire also about school-district regulations and applicable laws that require educators to take specific actions when problems occur.

3. Use a search engine such as Google (http://www.google.com) and resources in your library to identify articles that describe school programs that have proved to be particularly effective in helping learners from minority groups achieve academic

success. Prepare short synopses of four or five of these articles, and share this information with others in your class.

4. Invite a panel of three to five middle school and junior high school teachers to visit your class. Ask them to comment on some special challenges of working with learners in this age group and to identify aspects of working with these learners that they find particularly satisfying.

5. Interview a counselor who works in a school that serves the age group you hope to teach. Ask the counselor to describe issues that contribute to self-image problems of some of the young people in this school. Inquire about specific actions teachers can take to help these individuals develop a positive *sense of efficacy*. Share your findings with others in your class.

References

Carskadon, M. A. (1999). When worlds collide: Adolescent need for sleep versus societal demands. *Phi Delta Kappan, 80*(5), 348–353.

Childabuse.com. (2001). *Child abuse statistics.* http://www.childabuse.com/newsletter/stat0301.htm

DeCorby, K., Halas, J., Dixon, S., Wintrup, L., & Janzen, K. (2005). Classroom teachers and the challenges of delivering quality physical education. *The Journal of Educational Research, 98*(4), 208–220.

DeVoe, J. F., Peter, K., Kaufman, P., Ruddy, S. A., Miller, A. K., Planty, M., Snyder, T. D., Duhart, D. T., & Rand, M. R. (2002). *Indicators of school crime and safety.* Washington, DC: U.S. Departments of Education and Justice.

Doorey, N., & Harter, B. (2003). From court order to community commitment. *Educational Leadership, 60*(4), 22–25.

Druian, G., & Butler, J. A. (2001). *Effective schooling practices and at-risk youth: What the research shows* (School Improvement Research Series). Portland, OR: Northwest Regional Educational Laboratory.

Elkind, D. (1981). *Children and adolescents: Interpretive essays on Jean Piaget* (3rd ed.). New York: Oxford University Press.

Erikson, E. H. (1982). *The life cycle completed: A review.* New York: Norton.

Frey, B. B., Lee, S. W., Tollefson, N., Pass, L., & Massengill, D. (2005). Balanced literacy in an urban school district. *The Journal of Educational Research, 98*(5), 272–280.

Futrell, M., Gomez, J., & Bedden, D. (2003). Teaching the children of a new America: The challenge of diversity. *Phi Delta Kappan, 84*(5), 381–385.

Henson, K. T. (2004). *Constructivist methods for teaching in diverse middle level classrooms.* Boston: Allyn & Bacon.

How can we prevent violence in our schools? (2000). Educational Resources Information Center (Parent Brochure). http://www.eric.ed.gov/resources/parent/prevent.html

McCarthy, M., & Kuh, G. D. (2006). Are students ready for college: What student engagement data say. *Phi Delta Kappan, 87*(9), 664–669.

National Center for Education Statistics. (2001). *The condition of education 2001.* Washington, DC: Author.

National Center for Education Statistics. (2002a). *The condition of education 2002.* Washington, DC: Author.

National Center for Education Statistics. (2002b). *Digest of education statistics 2001.* Washington, DC: Author.

National Center for Education Statistics. (2003). *Participation in education, indicator 2.* Washington DC: Author.

National Center for Education Statistics. (2004). *Student effort and educational progress, indicator 16.* Washington, DC: Author.

National Center for Education Statistics. (2006a). *Contexts of elementary and secondary education, school attitudes and aspirations, indicator 23.* Washington DC: Author.

National Center for Education Statistics. (2006b). *Contexts of elementary and secondary education, school characteristics and climate, indicator 39.* Washington DC: Author.

National Center for Education Statistics. (2006c). *Participation in education, indicator 5.* Washington DC: Author.

National Center for Education Statistics. (2006d). *Participation in education, indicator 7.* Washington DC: Author.

National Center for Education Statistics. (2006e). *Participation in education, indicator 8.* Washington DC: Author.

Naylor, C. (1999). How does working part-time influence secondary students' achievement and impact on their overall well-being? *BCTF Research Report.* http://www.bctf.ca/ResearchReports/99ei02/report.html

Phelps, P. (2006). The three Rs of professionalism. *Kappa Delta Pi Record,42*(2), 69–71.

Public Agenda Online. (2002). Available at http://www.publicagenda.org/issues

Rumberger, R. W. (2002, June). *Student mobility and academic achievement.* Urbana–Champaign, IL: ERIC/EECE Publications—Digests. http://ericeece.org/pubs/digests/2002/rumberger02.html

Scherer, M. (2002). Perspectives: Who cares? And who wants to know? *Educational Leadership, 60*(1), 5.

Thomas, M. D., & Bainbridge, W. L. (2002). No child left behind: Facts and fallacies. *Phi Delta Kappan, 84*(5), 781–782.

Toutkoushidian, R. K., & Curtis, T. (2005). Effects of socioeconomic factors on public high school outcomes and rankings. *The Journal of Educational Research, 98*(5), 259–271.

U.S. Department of Health and Human Services. (2001). *Highlights—2001 National household survey on drug abuse (MHSDA).* Washington, DC: Author.

CHAPTER 5

HOW HAS DIVERSITY IMPACTED TEACHING?

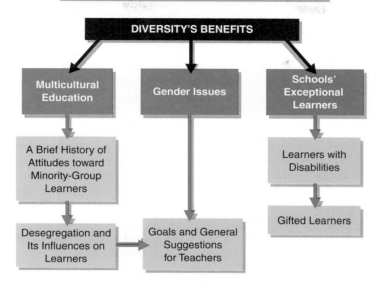

MEETING THE NEEDS OF DIVERSE AND SPECIAL STUDENTS

DIVERSITY'S BENEFITS

Multicultural Education

Gender Issues

Schools' Exceptional Learners

A Brief History of Attitudes toward Minority-Group Learners

Learners with Disabilities

Desegregation and Its Influences on Learners

Goals and General Suggestions for Teachers

Gifted Learners

OBJECTIVES

This chapter will help you to

- define multicultural education.
- state the implications of increased diversity for teachers.
- define a culturally responsive learning environment.
- identify the relationships between culture and learning.
- define historic views that were used to explain learning difficulties of different cultural groups.
- state how desegregation efforts impacted education.

- describe how within-school segregation can occur.
- state the challenges for teaching associated with the achievement gap.
- describe federal laws regarding learners with disabilities.
- explain how instruction might be altered to accommodate students with special needs.
- describe characteristics of gifted learners and differentiate between the *enrichment* and *acceleration* approaches.

DIVERSITY'S BENEFITS

Perhaps one of the most dramatic changes in education has been an increased diversity of students. This diversity includes ethnic diversity, language diversity, and ability diversity. In the ethnic and racial diversity category, the percentage of racial and ethnic minority students enrolled in school has increased significantly in the past 30 years. In 1972 about 22% of the public school students were from groups that were considered to be racial or ethnic minorities. In 2004, 43% of the students were from groups that were considered to be racial or ethnic minorities. The largest percentage of increase has been in the Hispanic enrollment because they represented 19% of the public school enrollment in 2004 compared to only 6% in 1972. At the same time, the percentage of students classified as white decreased from 78% to 57% (National Center for Education Statistics, 2006a). This has created what is often termed the "demographic divide." This refers to the vast differences that occur between schools and contributes to the view that there are "two Americas." For example, data indicate that there is a large discrepancy in the resources allocated to schools serving predominantly white, affluent students and those serving the poor and students of color. The ways schools are organized for teaching and learning, the qualifications of the teachers, the way students are assigned to teachers, the curriculum that is offered, access to technology, and the way families are involved all contribute to this demographic divide (Banks et al., 2005).

In addition to ethnic and racial diversity is language diversity. More than 1 million immigrants enter the United States every year and it is projected that by the year 2020 the foreign-born population of the United States will be 1 in 7 people. This compares with a ratio of 1 in 20 in 1950 (Garcia, 2002). In addition, today's immigrants come from many countries. In one recent year, most newcomers to the United States came from Mexico. The next four largest home countries were the Philippines, China, Vietnam, and India (Garcia, 2002). The children of these immigrants, most of them with English as a second language, are found in schools all across America. The number of school-age children who speak a language other than English at home increased from 3.8 to 9.9 million between 1979 and 2004 (National Center for Education Statistics, 2006). It is no longer just a few cities and states that have the responsibility for educating these children.

Ability diversity has increased as a result of legislation directed at the teaching of special populations. In the past, students who had special learning needs were generally segregated and taught in a special education classroom. However, this practice has changed and students with special needs are placed in the "least restrictive environment." This means that most students with special needs are now found in regular classrooms.

Those preparing for teaching in the 21st century need to understand that their responsibilities will be quite different from what they were in the past century. This poses both challenges and opportunities.

Some individuals view this increased diversity negatively. They wish for a simpler time when teachers did not worry about accommodating diversity. Those who did not fit simply dropped out. It was up to the children who did not speak English to learn to cope. Accommodating special needs was not seen as the responsibility of the teacher. However, that time is past. It is not an appropriate model for contemporary society and we do not think it was appropriate in the past.

We believe that diversity has a positive side. Throughout the history of this nation, diversity has provided the stimulus for innovation and change. It has contributed greatly to the strength of our nation. In the classroom, diversity provides the opportunity for a richer, more dynamic, and exciting learning environment. In this environment, new and relevant content can be learned by everyone, even the teacher. Rather than worrying about diversity, it ought to be embraced. You can enrich your classroom and yourself by establishing a classroom climate that helps students see diversity as a benefit. It will better prepare them for the realities of globalization. Finally, few things are more interesting than the variety of peoples and cultures across the face of the earth. This interest can be used to help create exciting classrooms.

What Do You Think?

- What is your view of the advantages and challenges of increased student diversity?
- What concerns you most about working with a diverse group of students?
- What do you need to do in order prepare for the diversity you will experience?

Special needs students also enrich classrooms. They often demonstrate remarkable attitudes and skills. They often demonstrate a commitment to learning and a task persistence that motivates everyone to strive to overcome obstacles. Educators increasingly understand that students have multiple strengths and abilities. Learning differences exist along a continuum and many individuals develop compensatory strengths (Banks et al., 2005).

Human capital is a precious resource. Maximizing human capital is important if our nation is to remain strong. When the abilities and talents of any one group is limited, we all suffer. A primary role of the teacher is to develop human capital. Your challenge is to work to develop the talents of females as well as males, students with disabilities, immigrants, children of the poor, and members of all ethnic and cultural minorities. Our society benefits each time a student graduates well prepared, confident, and ready to accept the challenges of a diverse world. To see how one teacher went above and beyond to ensure students at her school did not go hungry go to this chapter's *Video Viewpoints* feature.

MULTICULTURAL EDUCATION

Multicultural education means different things to different people (Gorski, 2000). James A. Banks and Cherry A. McGee Banks's (2001) definition is consistent with many: **Multicultural education** is education that promotes educational equity for all learners.

Fundamental to meeting the needs of a diverse student population is the development of **culturally appropriate practice.** Culturally appropriate practice requires that teachers have knowledge and skills that extend beyond knowledge of subject matter and how to teach. They need to know how to connect what is taught to the experiences, needs, atti-

**Video Viewpoints
5–1**

When Students Are Hungry: A Teacher's Mission

WATCH: View this *Nightline* video segment about a teacher who discovered children in her class who were hungry.

THINK: Discuss with your classmates or write in your reflective journal your responses to the following questions:

1. Have you looked for children who are hungry? How common do you think hunger is in the school population?
2. What steps could a teacher take to discover students who might be hungry?
3. What is the responsibility of a teacher and the school in addressing the issue of hunger in America?

LINK: What are some other variables associated with poverty that impact a student's ability to learn?

 To view this video, go to the Video Viewpoints DVD and click on this chapter's video: "When Students Are Hungry: A Teacher's Mission."

Scott Cunningham/Merrill

Today's schools enroll young people from diverse racial and cultural groups.

tudes, and expectations of those they teach (Banks et al., 2005).

Establishing Culturally Appropriate Practice

Today's teachers must establish a **culturally responsive environment,** giving all students equal opportunities to learn (Powell, McLaughlin, Savage, & Zehm, 2001). This includes:

- accepting learners' experience, values, and tastes;
- altering instruction and selecting texts, novels, and other reading materials that meet learners' academic needs;
- encouraging acceptance of students' native speech patterns;
- acknowledging the cultural heritages of all ethnic groups; and
- developing ethnic and cultural pride. (Brown, 2002)

Multiculturalism and Learning

What is the impact of culture on learning? Consider your own experience. As you matured, you developed certain expectations about learning such as how learners should behave in the classroom and what motivates them.

Cultures have different expectations. This can create a difference between teacher expectations and students' expectations. These differences can leave students torn between two sets of authority figures, forcing them to choose between pleasing their teachers or their family.

This potential disconnect between teachers' perspectives and learners' perspectives is growing. Although most teachers are white and middle class, students are more racially and linguistically diverse. For example, in the 1999–2000 school year, over 86% of the public- and private-school teachers and administrators were white but projections indicate that by 2026 the nonwhite, Latino K–12 enrollment will rise to 70% (Garcia, 2002).

The Need for Accurate Information

Planning instruction to meet the needs of all students requires knowing their backgrounds. Faulty assumptions can lead to failure. For example, a teacher who believes that boys are "just naturally" poor readers may hold lower expectations for boys on reading assignments. Like-wise, assuming that cultural groups have common experiences and even innate inadequacies can interfere with your ability to plan successful instruction and interact positively with students. This was illustrated in the movie *The Freedom Writers* when a teacher asked an African American student for the "black perspective." The student reacted angrily and asked to be re-moved from the class.

Teachers must learn from their students and the communities where they teach. You need to make connections with the students and the communities where you teach. Culturally appropriate practice requires that your knowledge grow and change as students and their social contexts change. There is no simple list of cultural differences that can be learned. What is required is an attitude of inquiry and openness to different cultural perspectives.

✦ ✦

Using the Experiences of Students
Go to MyEducationLab and select the topic "Diversity and Multiculturalism," and then watch all four parts of the video "Incorporating the Home Experiences of Culturally Diverse Student in the Classroom" and respond to the questions. Some of the questions are designed to prepare you for your licensure examination.

✦ ✦

A Brief History of Attitudes toward Minority-Group Learners

An understanding of past views of minority-group learners can help us understand why many minority learners have not done well in school. An early explanation was the **genetic-deficit view** (Savage, Savage, & Armstrong 2006), the idea that certain groups simply had a different genetic composition that predisposed them to be successful or unsuccessful in certain endeavors. Some groups were perceived as simply lacking the necessary intellectual tools to allow them to succeed in school. It was thought best to encourage them to pursue other paths so that they would not be discouraged and get frustrated.

By the 1960s, the genetic-deficit position had given way to a **cultural-deficit view** (Erickson, 1987), blaming poor performance on the homes for lack of intellectual stimulation and inadequately preparing their children for school. Even though there is evidence that children who are not prepared for school and who do not attend quality preschools have a more difficult time in school, it is not a cultural phenomenon. There is a tremendous variation within any culture, and individuals from all cultures can learn. This cultural-deficit notion ignores the responsibility of the school to accept the strengths of the culture and to build on those strengths.

Another explanation for their poor performance was the **communication-process position** (Erickson, 1987), which attributes poor academic performance to the differences between the language patterns of minority-group learners and those of majority-group learners. Again, communication is important and much of school does require good knowledge of English. However, it is not the only variable influencing achievement and should not be an excuse for not developing the abilities and talents of all students.

Recently, educators have downplayed these explanations that shift the blame away from the schools, arguing that schools have failed to plan for the success of all learners. This argument is that the schools must plan to accommodate students' needs rather than expecting students to accommodate to the school. Building programs that reflect the premise that "all students can learn" has become a hallmark of education reform (Henson, 2006).

Desegregation and Its Influences on Learners

Attempts to address the need for more diverse educational experiences have historically addressed three issues (Simon-McWilliams, 1989):

- Ending legal segregation and following court-ordered plans to achieve integration
- Within-school segregation of minority learners and females
- Achievement levels of minority-group learners and females

Corbis/Bettmann

Brown v. Board of Education led to significant protests. In some cases troops had to be called out to protect African-American students when they attended schools that had been all white.

Efforts to End Legal Segregation

The 1954 Supreme Court case *Brown v. Board of Education* began abolishment of segregated schools. However, the efforts to develop schools that reflect the cultural diversity of society have been only moderately successful.

Success has been limited by the attitudes and action of the general population. The tradition of school organization in the United States has been that of local control. Therefore, schools in a given state are usually organized into a number of local school districts. Each district only has authority within the boundaries of that district.

The result is a patchwork of school districts. As people move and purchase homes, the school system is one of the most important variables they consider. In a response to past integration efforts, such as busing students to achieve a racial balance, families who did not want their children riding on school buses or attending a school outside the local community simply moved to another district. This left some districts with primarily a minority population. This flight also removed many of the students who were most likely to succeed in school. This further created the image that the school districts with large minority populations were of lower quality. The result has been one where communities, and therefore school districts, become largely segregated according to ethnicity and socioeconomic status. This has been called "de facto segregation."

One court case attempted to address this de facto segregation by seeking busing across school district boundaries. However, a key 1974 Supreme Court decision (*Milliken v. Bradley*) denied courts authority to order busing between districts to meet this goal, making busing an option only inside each district. As a result, many inner-city schools became overwhelmingly African American, Latino, or both. Similarly, many suburban schools became primarily white.

Some school districts tried creating high-quality "magnet schools" as a method to attract a diverse population back into school districts with large minority populations. The idea was that if a school could be created with a high-quality program in a specific content area, such as science, a variety of parents would choose to live in the school district. Some school districts created high-quality magnet schools with themes such as environmental science, engineering, performing arts, and the health professions. These schools did achieve some success in attracting a diverse student population.

Within-Individual-School Segregation

Another common problem is that of within-school segregation. This occurs when students from different groups end up in different "tracks." Placement in these tracks may be based more on variables such as gender, ethnicity, or socioeconomic status than on ability. Within-school segregation can take subtle forms in the elementary school such as grouping certain students together in particular classrooms or more obvious tracking in secondary schools. Research has suggested that race and socioeconomic status can play important roles in assigning students to tracks even when grades and test scores are contolled (Banks et al., 2005). For example, one individual who later received a Ph.D. and became a college professor recounts his experience waiting to be grouped the first day of school in junior high school.

> Names were called out and students began leaving the auditorium. . . . I kept waiting for my name to be called, but my anxiety continued to grow. . . . I was in the last group of names to be called, which meant that I was in the lowest academic ability group in the school. I looked at the other students in my group, and many of them were my peers from elementary school. . . . Being the last called in junior high school, which corresponded with the view I had of myself that I was a less-capable learner than my peers, was a seriously debilitating experience for me. . . . (Powell et al., 2001, p.55)

What Do You Think?

- Some teachers argue that grouping students according to ability allows them to focus more on the needs of students. How would you respond to this argument?
- Have you experienced grouping in your education? What was the impact on you and on others?

Attempts have been made to counter within-school segregation by eliminating tracks, opening class enrollment to any who wish to enroll, improving counseling and advisement, changing teacher attitudes and expectations, and focusing on heterogeneous grouping of students. However, within-school segregation is still all too common.

Profound Multicultural Questions

Go to MyEducationLab and select the topic "Diversity and Multiculturalism." Read the article by Sonia Nieto, "Profoundly Multicultural Questions" for an interesting discussion about multicultural education and the concern for achievement. Respond to the questions that accompany the article. Some of the questions are designed to prepare you for your licensure examination.

GENDER ISSUES

Gender discrimination is another area that has received considerable attention in recent years. The original focus was on the inequities experienced by females. They, like some minority and low socioeconomic status children, were not encouraged to pursue some academic tracks and they were hindered by low expectations. Girls were not expected or encouraged to enter demanding professions.

Much of this has changed, although some evidence indicates that some of these attitudes persist. Although more females attend college than males, fewer females pursue advanced degrees in science and mathematics (Sheldon & Epstein, 2005). One reason why some women avoid these majors is because they were not advised to take classes that would prepare them for success in these areas.

One of the challenges in addressing this issue is a view concerning the aptitude of females. For example, relatively recently the president of Harvard tried to explain away the achievement gap for females in math and science by suggesting that they lack the required aptitude to achieve success in these fields.

One issue focuses on different expectations and treatment of males and females in the classroom. Girls often perform poorly in coeducation classes. For example, they do not participate as frequently as boys unless their class has both a female majority and a female teacher.

More recently, gender inequities have focused on males. National news magazines have carried articles claiming that the recent emphasis on standardized tests and more passive approaches to learning are detrimental to the education of males. They claim that boys are now the ones being shortchanged and an achievement gap between males and females is beginning to appear.

Some parents have sought support for single-gender schools. In New York City, for example, many private girls' schools have been established (Lewin, 1999). In addition, there has been an especially high level of interest in all-girl kindergartens.

What Do You Think?

- How would you have faired in a single-gender school?
- What advantages and disadvantages do single-gender schools offer?
- Will single-gender schools detract from efforts to ensure that female learners are appropriately supported and challenged in coeducational schools? Why or why not?

GOALS AND GENERAL SUGGESTIONS FOR TEACHERS

Although policy decisions need to be made at the state and national levels to address the needs of diverse students, in the final analysis it is the teacher who makes the difference. The beginning point is that of teachers' beliefs about their schools and students' diversity (Lawrence, 2006). Many recommendations for responding to multicultural and equity needs have been made (Brown, 2002; Savage, Savage & Armstrong, 2006; Sleeter & Grant, 2002). Those suggestions include the following.

Committing to the Idea That All Can Learn

Maximum success for all students requires high expectations. Inadequately challenged learners usually achieve below their abilities and many drop out of school. Successful teachers need to believe that all students can learn. This requires posing the issue in a constructive manner. Rather than concluding "These students can't learn," the statement needs to be phrased as "They did not learn; why not?" This question helps you problem solve and design instruction that would be more appropriate for the specific group of students you are teaching. Your belief in your students' ability to learn is a prerequisite for the students to develop the self-confidence they need to succeed.

Modifying Grouping Practices

In many schools, grouping practices may place ethnic, racial, and socioeconomic students at a disadvantage, which is because the basis for the grouping is often on variables other than ability. Those shunted into a low-ability group early in their school years often stay in those same groupings throughout their school years, falling further behind each year.

Within-class groups do better when there is no attempt to standardize the ability levels of members within each group and when learners in each group constitute a representative racial, cultural, and gender sample of the entire class.

Accommodating Learning-Style Differences

Individuals' **learning styles** vary. The term *learning style* refers to a person's preferred way of learning. Cultural backgrounds influence learners' style preferences (Sleeter & Grant, 2002). This suggests that lessons should allow individuals to approach content differently. Some need opportunities to manipulate objects. Some handle reading assignments well. Still others benefit from working with photographs, tables, and charts. Periodically, teachers' assumptions about their students' learning styles should be reassessed because some students change their learning-style preference as they mature (Sternberg, 1994). Matching instructional strategies with learners' style preferences improves both achievement and interest levels (Lovelace, 2005).

Accommodating diversity requires that teachers use different methods to accommodate different learning styles.

> ### Web Extension 5–1
>
> ### Educating Teachers for Diversity
> ◆
> This site lists contacts for meeting the needs of diverse classrooms including postal addresses, telephone numbers, and Web addresses.
>
> http://www.nea.org/webresources/diversitylinks.html

Becoming Aware of Your Own Perspectives

All ethnic and cultural groups have certain established assumptions about "how the world is" and about what constitutes proper behavior. Don't assume that everybody shares your basic views. This kind of thinking can create problems when you work with learners from ethnic and cultural backgrounds whose fundamental perspectives may differ from your own. Realize that you will be teaching all of the children from all of the homes. Their prior experiences will vary tremendously and their expectations about appropriate behavior and how to achieve success in school may vary tremendously.

What Do You Think?

- What are your assumptions and expectations about the students that you expect to teach?
- What are your assumptions about students from different ethnic groups?
- What assumptions do you make about male and female students?
- How can you check the validity of your assumptions?

Relying Less on Standardized Tests

To say the least, in recent years, the producers of **standardized tests** have prospered. By summarizing tremendous amounts of data, these tests allow easy school-to-school comparisons. But, at best, standardized tests give a limited view of learners' capabilities, and pressures for teachers to "teach to the test" can narrow the curriculum and reduce teaching to a formula. In fact, some curriculum programs prescribe exactly how teachers are to teach and what they are to say. This "one-size-fits-all" approach to education does not accommodate diverse students and diverse learning styles and will harm many children, particularly minorities and children of the poor (Garan, 2004).

Standardized tests pose particular problems for ethnic and cultural minorities. Critics contend that standardized tests discourage many learners from even finishing high school. This is especially true for high-stakes tests that must be passed as a condition for graduation. Several factors might account for this. First, students who have a primary language other than English have more difficulty comprehending the test and knowing how to respond. Second, minority and poor students often attend schools with the fewest resources and the least qualified teachers. Therefore, they have not been given an adequate opportunity to learn what is tested. Finally, a lack of opportunities outside of school needs to be considered. (For example, how many poor inner-city children have computers at home? How many books can be found in their homes? How many have traveled extensively? How many have role models who can help them learn how to learn?) The whole issue of assessment must be addressed if policies and practices are to be designed that best meet the needs of the tremendously diverse student population found in the schools. More discussion on the issues in assessment will be presented in Chapter 7, "How Do We Know Students Have Learned?"

Teacher Favoritism in the Classroom

It is only natural for teachers to develop better relationships with some learners than others. However, a professional educator must make sure that this natural tendency does not lead to prejudicial classroom practices that may interfere with the opportunity for all students to receive a quality education. What is the basis for your favoritism? Is it based on racial, ethnic, and gender issues? How does it impact your behavior in the classroom? Often the impact of favoritism from our behavior is very subtle.

Favoritism in the classroom can lead to the development of a social environment that interferes with the ability of all students to learn. This is often demonstrated by the way you interpret similar behavior. What might be viewed as "cute" or "clever" coming from one student might be interpreted as insolence coming from another. Instances of misbehavior might be overlooked when demonstrated by one student, but a heavy-handed approach used when demonstrated by another. Some students may receive praise for their contributions, but the contributions of others may be overlooked. This teacher action affects students in the classroom and they become more likely to behave in expected ways (Good & Brophy, 2003). Your credibility and high achievement in your classes require that your students know that they will be treated fairly. You need to be conscious of your expectations and actions so that you can create a learning climate that supports all students.

Providing Good Teachers

The central ingredient in good schools is good teachers; yet, the learners who most need quality teachers are the least likely to get them. Teachers in predominantly minority schools tend to be less experienced, teaching out of their field, and holding **emergency teaching certificates,** in lieu of normal qualifications. For example, in California students in predominantly minority schools were five times more likely to have teachers with substandard credentials than those schools serving mostly white students (Banks et al., 2005).

Individuals seeking a teaching career often realize that teaching in schools in poorer communities offers more challenges. They often do not have the resources or the support of teachers in more affluent communities. In addition, the recent emphasis on accountability has led some to suggest that teacher evaluations should take into account student test scores. Although it may seem logical that teachers should be responsible for student learning, research suggests that many other factors, such as socioeconomic status, have a powerful impact on student performance. Therefore, teachers seeking teaching positions may be discouraged from seeking jobs in poorer communities. When they recognize that part of their performance evaluation will be based on their students' test scores, they may naturally seek schools where students do well. Currently, there are few incentives for teachers to work in poor, diverse schools.

In summary, schools in America have become more culturally diverse. This diversity is going to continue. Even though there have been some exciting improvements in the way schools accommodate and respond to diversity, many challenges remain. As a professional educator dedicated to developing the potential of all students, you need to prepare yourself so you can attain the rewards and the excitement that come from working with diversity.

SCHOOLS' EXCEPTIONAL LEARNERS

There are great differences among **exceptional learners.** Generally they are individuals who deviate markedly from the norm. This means that exceptional learners include gifted and talented students as well as those with learning disabilities, physical problems, and emotional or behavioral difficulties; however, they share many characteristics of other schoolchildren. Some are extremely bright, and some find learning difficult. Some are positive about school, and some dislike being at school. As much diversity exists among these learners as among all students.

The remainder of this chapter introduces some of these characteristics and describes approaches for working with each group.

Learners with Disabilities

As noted in Chapter 4, the separation of students with disabilities into separate classrooms was common until the late 1970s. However, this approach was largely unsuccessful. For example, in the late 1970s, one million children with disabilities did not attend school at all (National Education Association, 1999). The current situation is different; the law requires that they be educated in regular classrooms to the maximum extent possible (Plata, Glasgow, & Trusty, 2005). The fact that about 95% of classrooms enroll one or more learners with disabilities means that you are certain to have students with special needs in the classrooms where you teach (National Center for Education Statistics, 2002). See Figure 5–1 for the likelihood of students with certain disabilities to spend time in different instructional settings. You will need to understand how to work with these students and their parents in order to help them achieve their potential.

Figure 5–1   Likelihood of students with certain disabilities to spend time in different instructional settings.

Instructional Setting	Speech and Language Impairment	Visual Impairment	Orthopedic Impairment	ADD and Specific Learning Disability	Hearing Impairment	Serious Emotional Disturbance
In regular classroom 79–100% of school day	87.8%	48.1%	46.6%	43.8%	38.8%	24.9%
In regular classroom 40–78% of school day	7.3%	20.1%	21.3%	39.3%	19.9%	23.3%
In setting outside of regular classroom from 60% or more of school day	4.9%	31.8%	32.1%	16.9%	42.2%	51.8%

Source: Table 54. Digest of Educational Statistics, 2001 (p. 67). Washington DC: National Center for Education Statistics

Federal Legislation

Recognizing that separating these students from their peers was not serving them well, prompted passage of important federal legislations. In addition to the educational issues related to the education of students with disabilities, it also became a civil rights issue. The separation of students into special classrooms was seen as a form of discrimination that harmed not only the students with disabilities but also the regular education students. As noted in Chapter 4, this situation began to change with the passage in 1975 of Public Law 94-142, the Education for All Handicapped Children Act. In 1990, Congress modified the law, renaming it Individuals with Disabilities Education Act (IDEA). This law is regularly updated. For example, a recent update requires schools to use new assistive technologies.

Other relevant federal legislation includes the 1992 **Americans with Disabilities Act.** Patterned after the Vocational Rehabilitation Act, this act extends the civil rights of individuals with disabilities to include (a) private-sector employment, (b) all public services, (c) transportation, and (d) telecommunications. The access ramps found in businesses, on city street corners, and on school campuses are one clear result of this legislation.

Collectively, recent federal legislation requires schools to observe seven key principles:

- The adoption of a policy of **zero rejects.** This means that schools must enroll every child, regardless of how disabled.
- A commitment to **nondiscriminatory testing.** Schools must use multiple indicators to determine whether a learner has a disability and whether special services are needed.

- The provision of an **appropriate education,** requiring schools to devise and implement an **Individualized Education Program (IEP),** for each learner with a disability. You will be required to help develop IEPs for your special students.
- An agreement to teach each learner with a disability in the **least restrictive environment**, enabling learners with disabilities to have school experiences provided to others.
- The protection of learners' rights by recognizing **due process** rights of students and their parents/guardians.
- IEPs must be made with **parent/guardian participation,** allowing them substantive decisions in planning activities.
- Public schools must go beyond **mainstreaming** and adopt inclusion. *Mainstreaming* requires special learners to spend part of the school day in a regular classroom and part (sometimes a majority) in a separate, self-contained special education classroom. *Inclusion* ensures these

> **Web Extension 5–2**
>
> ## Office of Special Education Programs (OSEP)
>
> The U.S. Department of Education's Office of Special Education Programs (OSEP) helps states and local school districts provide appropriate educational services to individuals with disabilities who are between ages 3 and 31. The following Web site offers information about legislation, special projects, research, statistics, and links to additional resources.
>
> http://www.ed.gov/about/offices/list/osers/osep/index.html

students an education within a regular classroom where special aids, supports, and teaching accommodations are provided to meet their needs.

Varieties of Educational Settings

Several alternative settings can be used to meet the requirements of the "least restrictive environment." In some instances, these students may spend part of the day in your classroom and part of the day in another educational environment. Seven distinct environments are used with learners with disabilities. One of the common settings for students when they are not in your class is a "resource room" where specialists provide educational services uniquely suited to their needs.

Nationally, about one-fourth of the special needs students spend all day as members of a **special class** taught by a special education teacher. Those students with needs that cannot be met in the regular classroom may be educated in **separate public-school facilities** (facilities operated by a school district away from a regular school), **separate private-school facilities** (facilities operated by private entities that are away from a regular school), **publicly supported residential facilities** (school district facilities away from regular schools where learners live and are taught), **private residential settings** (facilities away from a regular school that are operated by private entities where learners live and are taught), or **homebound or hospital settings** (homes or medical facilities where learners live and are taught) (National Center for Education Statistics, 2001).

Classroom teachers are more likely to have learners with some disabilities, such as speech and language impairments, than others. In contrast, learners with serious emotional disturbances typically spend most of their school days in other educational settings (National Center for Education Statistics, 2001). Many public schools are beginning to work with parents who home-school their special needs students, even permitting home-based students to attend certain classes and even participate in extracurricular activities (Anderson, 2006).

Preparation of Individualized Education Programs

Federal regulations require that an Individualized Education Program (IEP) be established for each child with disabilities. An IEP must be developed soon after the learner's condition is verified. Participants must include the learner's regular teacher, one or both parents/guardians, and a nonteacher (usually a counselor). The child may be present, when appropriate.

Discussion during the first meeting centers on examination and development of the following information:

- The learner's present educational attainment level
- Special services/modifications needed to facilitate the learner's educational development
- Goals the learner is expected to achieve in one year
- Objectives, benchmarks, and evaluation procedures to be used to measure the learner's progress toward established goals
- Identification of the least restrictive environment

Each IEP team meets at least once annually to discuss progress. At these meetings, members can set new goals and revise their services. Parents/guardians who disagree with decisions have the right to additional testing and an impartial hearing.

Altering Instruction

Special needs identified during IEP meetings may require you to change some of your instructional practices. These changes will be of two basic types. Sometimes your response

Federal legislation has influenced the classroom. Special assistance is to be provided for those students who need it.

will take the form of an **accommodation,** a change that allows a learner to complete the same assigned tasks as others in your class by changing such variables as

- the time allowed for the work to be completed,
- the setting where the work is accomplished,
- the nature of presentations or responses you accept from the learner at various points during the learning process, and
- the nature of evidence you will accept to verify that learning has occurred.

Other changes will take the form of a **modification,** which involves substituting a different task for these learners. Changes may involve changing standards or assigning a task that corresponds to their unique educational needs.

The **Office of Special Education Programs (OSEP)** is the component of the U.S. Department of Education that oversees programs for learners with disabilities. OSEP funds several groups that promote high-quality school programs for these learners. One of these is **Family Partnership for Education (FAPE).** See Figure 5–2 for examples of ideas adapted from those FAPE has developed.

Figure 5–2   Ideas for altering practices to serve needs of learners with disabilities.

Assessment Procedures	• Give directions orally. • Remove time limits and provide as much time as needed. • Provide alternatives to paper-and-pencil tests such as projects, oral exams, etc. • Provide tests that are typed rather than handwritten. • Teach study skills and test-taking skills. • Review key vocabulary.
Making Assignments	• Break lengthy assignments into several parts. • Shorten assignments to focus on key elements. • Consider performance tasks (models, collections, etc.) in place of written assignments. • Specify and list what the student will need to do in very specific terms. • Modify assignments based on the needs of the student (oral reports rather than written reports, several smaller projects rather than one complex one, etc.).
Providing Directions	• Use both oral and written directions. • Give directions in small steps. • Number and sequence directions in logical order. • Ask student to repeat directions to check comprehension. • Provide visual organizers and prompts. • Provide a model. • Stand near students when giving directions or presenting a lesson.
Grading	• Mark correct answers rather than incorrect answers. • Use pass-fail or alternative grading. • Provide grades for individual progress. • Permit opportunities to redo assignments or projects. • Provide numerous data sources in grading rather than high-stakes tests.

Source: Adapted from *School Accommodations and Modifications* (October 31, 2001). FAPE Coordinating Office PACER Center, Inc. 8161 Normandale Blvd. Minneapolis, MN 55437.

Public Reporting of Learner Performance

In times past, many school districts either excused special students from taking standardized tests or did not report their test scores. The current practice of forcing schools to administer and report these test scores encourages schools to expose these students to the same curriculum as their non-challenged peers.

The No Child Left Behind Act of 2001 added important legislative support to improving the learning of students with disabilities. This law requires school districts to provide information each year on the performance of subgroups within the general school population, including learners with disabilities. It was made to ensure that low achievements of learners in certain subgroups (e.g., ethnic and racial minorities, economically disadvantaged learners) were not hidden among scores of a school's entire student population. This makes you as accountable for the progress of special learners as you are for all other learners in your classroom.

Inclusion Issues

The practice of including special needs students in regular classrooms was first called "mainstreaming." However, a more commonly used term now is "inclusion." This change in terminology from "mainstreaming" to "inclusion" signals a change in attitude. Mainstreaming is generally viewed as a *requirement* for schools to serve individuals with disabilities in regular classrooms. However, "inclusion" carries the connotation that the inclusion of special needs students is done so because their presence there is desired.

Supporters of inclusion support the notion that regular classrooms can provide all, or nearly all, of the instructional services for learners with disabilities. The Individuals with Disabilities Education Act and follow-up legislation strongly endorsed this idea. Proponents believe that, when learners with disabilities are taught in regular classrooms, their academic achievement improves and their classmates without disabilities also benefit. The idea is that, in a highly diverse society, individuals gain from coming into contact with others whose personal characteristics differ from their own. This perspective underlies the National Institute for Urban School Improvement's sponsorship of National Inclusive Schools Week. This annual event gives schools, classrooms, families, and communities opportunities to celebrate how the diversity associated with special needs individuals enriches our lives.

Does the recent trend favoring inclusion suggest that you no longer will find people who challenge this approach? Indeed not. Proponents and skeptics continue to argue the pros and cons. In addition, educational researchers continue to study inclusion.

Examples of Arguments Supporting Inclusion

Special education once was considered a separate place or a separate program. It is

The presence of students with special needs in the regular classroom can benefit all students.

Richard Haynes/Prentice Hall School Division

neither. Special education is a collection of services designed to meet the unique needs of individuals with disabilities. Regular classroom teachers, with appropriate support equipment, instructional materials, and knowledge about the needs of individual learners, can provide high-quality services to the special learners in their classes. Evidence is strong enough to support **full inclusion** programs, which place learners with disabilities in regular classrooms at all times regardless of the nature or severity of their disabilities. Initially, there was concern that nonchallenged learners, especially high performers, would object to having special students, afraid that it would lower achievement levels, but a recent study (Plata, Glasgow, & Trusty, 2005) found that high achievers accept having challenged students in their classes.

Inclusion helps learners with disabilities see themselves as part of the total student population, not as individuals who have been labeled as "different." In addition, their classmates learn about the diversity of the general population—a reality of life.

Examples of Arguments Opposing Inclusion

Opponents of inclusion say that advocates of inclusion have an unrealistic view of the difficulties regular classroom teachers face when working with learners with disabilities. The time required to manage special equipment, rearrange furniture, and teach students who may have multiple disabilities takes time from instruction, possibly lowering the achievement levels of all class members.

Critics say that most teachers lack the kind of training, support equipment, and teaching materials needed to help learners with disabilities; consequently, both learners with and learners without disabilities are being shortchanged.

What Do You Think?

- Which arguments for and against inclusion do you find most persuasive?
- What are your concerns about including students with special needs in your classroom?

What Research Says

Inclusion is too new to have extensive research on its long-term effects. Some have reported that learners *with* disabilities taught in inclusive classrooms have:

- Performed better on standardized tests (*Long-Term Effects of Inclusion*, 2003). Plata, Glasgow, and Trusty (2005) concluded that "Supporting students with and without LD, their teachers and other caretakers ensure that inclusion is not a utopian strategy but one in which experiences are positive and productive for all concerned." (p. 142)
- Left these experiences with improved social and communication skills (*Long-Term Effects of Inclusion*, 2003)
- Increased their personal knowledge of the world (*Long-Term Effects of Inclusion*, 2003).

Learners *without* disabilities taught in inclusive classrooms have:

- Developed attitudes associated with valuing individual differences (*Long-Term Effects of Inclusion*, 2003)
- Left this experience with enhanced self-esteem (*Long-Term Effects of Inclusion*, 2003)

An interesting additional finding is that low-achieving students without disabilities have benefited from being in inclusive classrooms. These positive results seem to result from

Web Extension 5–3

Council for Exceptional Children

This is the home page for the Council for Exceptional Children, which is the leading professional organization for educators with particular interests in the education of learners with disabilities. It offers links to a variety of topics associated with the education of exceptional children, including many that deal with inclusion.

http://www.cec.sped.org/

their exposure to the review, practice, instructional clarity, and feedback their teachers have provided for students with disabilities (*Long-Term Effects of Inclusion*, 2003). Read about Pat's experience with inclusion and teaching a diverse classroom in this chapter's *A Day in the Life* feature.

Characteristics of Learners with Specific Disabilities

The inclusion principle places an obligation on you to welcome learners with disabilities as regular class members and to provide them with the help they will need to succeed. This requires knowing how to help those who are challenged. You should devote part of your personal professional-development work toward preparing yourself to help these special learners.

Perhaps the best way to make all class members feel they belong is to promote the idea that learners with disabilities are no different than other learners. This attitude causes classmates to ignore their classmates' disabilities and accept them as members of their classroom community (Williams, 1998).

General characteristics of learners with disabilities are just that—*general*. Great diversity exists among learners in each category. Many learners fall into several categories simultaneously.

The following subsections identify conditions that will characterize some learners with disabilities.

Speech Impairments

Learners with speech impairments are individuals whose speech differs in significant ways from that of others in their age groups. They experience difficulties associated with making certain sounds, stuttering, and maintaining an appropriate vocal quality. Many have low self-images. Consequently, many students with speech impediments drop out of school.

Visual Impairments

With your help, visually impaired or blind students can compete well with their classmates if their communications skills are well developed. For example, you need to give assignments orally to visually impaired learners, sometimes making audio recordings of assignments and lesson-related information.

Many blind learners use personal computers to communicate in writing with their teachers. Blind learners also use **Braille**. Braille is a touch reading system developed for blind people.

Blind students may require time to master the new room arrangements and learn how to move from place to place.

Hearing Impairments

Hearing-impaired learners have difficulty producing speech and acquiring language skills. They fall into two basic categories. Deaf learners have a hearing loss so serious that their

A DAY IN THE LIFE . . . Working with Parents

Pat Taylor sat exhausted at the end of another school day. This had been an especially busy and stressful day. On the top of the desk was a stack of papers to be graded. They would have to wait as attention needed to be directed toward tomorrow. Pat was stressed because the time normally spent getting ready for the next day had been taken up with an IEP meeting.

Immediately after school, Pat, the resource teacher, and the school principal had met with the parents of a student with Down Syndrome. The meeting had been stressful because the meeting included not only the parents but also an attorney.

In this particular case, the parents were not sure that the school was doing all that was required by law. They wanted their child to be fully included in the regular classroom whereas the school felt like the student needed some time working in a separate classroom with the resource teacher. Pat could understand their frustrations and felt like their suspicions were based on prior experiences. Pat actually enjoyed having the student in class because he brought an enthusiasm for all tasks that was contagious. Other students in the class benefited by having him in the class and they bent over backward to help him. However, Pat saw how emotional involvement might interfere with doing what was best for the student. Pat did see that the student benefited from the more individualized attention the resource teacher could give.

The conference had been tense and every recommendation challenged. Everyone had to be careful about what was said and a lot of work had gone into the preparation for the conference. After the meeting, Pat had met with the resource teacher to discuss the implications of what had been decided in the meeting. Pat was trying to unwind a bit but now it was time to begin getting ready for tomorrow.

As Pat began thinking about tomorrow, planning had to take into consideration not just the needs of the special needs students, but, also, the needs of several limited English proficient students. What this meant was that the students could not just be given an assignment out of the textbook. Special care had to be taken to make sure that they understood what was said in the classroom and that instruction took into account their reading levels. Cooperative learning and group work had proven to be quite effective but some extra time and effort were required to prepare group tasks and gather the needed material. Some graphics needed to be developed that could be used to help these students follow the oral portions of the lesson.

Then there were the academically talented students. What could be done to keep them challenged and engaged?

So much to do, so little time. However, just sitting here would not get it done.

✓ Disposition Check

Clearly Pat has had a trying day. Parent conferences, especially those in which parents are questioning school practices, are among the most stressful parts of teaching. The stress level reaches a peak when an attorney is introduced into the equation. However, times of stress are times when teacher dispositions become of paramount importance.

How will you respond to parents who let you know that what you are doing is not good enough? Not only can this happen; it probably will. Parents of students with special needs want no less than other parents. They want teachers who are sensitive to the needs of their children and who will help them succeed. They often face considerable stress and frustration as they attempt to deal with the regulations and the bureaucracy. Teachers must understand this and keep a focus on the student rather than taking a personal affront to actions or comments that could be perceived as negative.

This scenario also indicates that Pat needed more time. Lack of time to address all of the needs present in the classroom may be one of the greatest challenges facing teachers. This is especially stressful for conscientious teachers who want to do their best for all students.

Reflect on this situation.

1. What dispositions are of critical importance in high-stress situations?
2. What dispositions are reflected in Pat's actions?

ability to acquire normal use of language is greatly impaired. Hard-of-hearing learners have significant hearing loss, but are still able to acquire normal speech patterns.

Some learners with hearing impairments use hearing aids. By knowing how to replace the batteries and keeping a supply on hand, you can prevent a learner from losing a day's instruction.

Attention Deficit Disorder and Other Specific Learning Disabilities

Attention deficit disorder (ADD) and other specific learning disabilities include disorders characterized by impairments to one or more of the psychological processes associated with understanding and using language. These learners have problems in listening, thinking, speaking, writing, spelling, and calculating. Such labels as *perceptual handicap*, *dyslexia*, or *minimal brain dysfunction* refer to these kinds of learning disabilities.

Class members with learning disabilities often find it hard to follow directions and start assignments. Some have a low tolerance for frustration. More than one-half of all who receive federally sponsored services fall within this category (U.S. Department of Education, 2000, p. 20).

Orthopedic Impairments

Generalizing about learners who are orthopedically impaired is difficult because they may suffer from one (or more) of several conditions that interfere with their motor control. You must learn the nature of each disability and its implications for the instructional process before you can pinpoint the learner's specific needs. For example, some may lack the ability to tap keys on a computer keyboard. Think about ways to help them access computer-based information and ways they can show that they have mastered assigned content. For example, some of them may not be able to complete written exams or to stand up in front of a group to make an oral presentation.

Emotional Disturbance

Behaviors of emotionally disturbed learners interfere with their development and with their ability to establish and maintain harmonious relationships with others. Characteristics of learners in this group vary. Some learners may be outspoken, defiant, and rude seekers of attention. Others may be withdrawn, quiet, and even fearful.

Some emotionally challenged students cannot make independent decisions. Their peers may refuse their request for help, causing them to have low self-concepts and perform poorly in school.

Mental Retardation

Mental retardation applies to people (1) whose intellectual development lags significantly behind that of their age mates and (2) whose potential for academic achievement is markedly lower than that of their classmates. Mental retardation has three general categories: *educable*, *trainable*, and *profoundly retarded*. Most who spend all or part of their school day in regular classrooms are in the educable category. They deviate the least from the normal range of mental functioning.

Huge differences exist among educable learners but all can benefit from the school program. Their IEPs and your teaching should reflect their characteristics. Because of excessive failure, many have low self-confidence. When given a new assignment, they may feel defeated before they begin. Figure 5–3 suggests several methods for teaching students with various disabilities.

Figure 5–3   **Instructional ideas for helping learners with various disabilities.**

Learner Disability	Suggested Approach
Speech Impairment	• Call on student only when they volunteer. • Praise student when a contribution is made. • Provide opportunities for students to speak one-on-one with you so that a "safe" environment free of ridicule is provided.
Visual Impairment	• Communicate instructions that are given to others in written form slowly and clearly. • Provide an audio recording of complex and important information they need. • Have students come to classrooms when other students are not present so they can explore the classroom and learn about the placement of furniture and important objects.
Hearing Impairment	• Always face student when giving directions so they have an opportunity to read lips. • Do not move around classroom when speaking. • Write key points on a transparency so that student has a visual representation of the important points. • Provide a printed outline of the lesson.
Attention Deficit Disorder and Other Specific Learning Disabilities	• Keep noise and other possible distractions to a minimum. • Provide self-paced instructional opportunities. • Attempt to include high motivational appeal lessons. • Provide a great deal of structure in the lessons. • Direct instruction and small-group activities often work well.
Orthopedic Impairment	• Allow more time for students to complete assignments. • Arrange classroom furniture so that those who need assistance in walking can easily get to important places in the classroom. • Provide students with extra time when moving from one classroom to another.
Emotional Disturbance	• Provide lessons in a manner so that students believe they have a chance of success if they put forth effort. • Reduce distractions as students work. • Take extra care in giving directions and make sure the students know the procedure that will be followed and that they are to follow directions. • Help students see the connection between their behaviors and the consequences that follow. They need to know they determine the consequences and consequences are not because of chance or luck.
Mental Retardation	• Keep lessons short, direct, and to the point. • Introduce new material in short, sequential steps. • Avoid placing students in highly competitive situations. • Build confidence by reducing the number of tasks and ensure that they complete the tasks they start.

Source: To Assure the Free Appropriate Public Education of All Children with Disabilities. Twenty-Third Annual Report to Congress on the Implementation of the Individuals with Disabilities Education Act (pp. 11–27), 2001. Washington, DC: U.S. Department of Education.

Assistive Technology

Using multiple approaches increases the probability of success. As you plan to meet each learner's needs, welcome help from others. Learn to use **assistive technologies**—individual pieces of equipment or complex systems of equipment designed to maintain or improve the functional capabilities of learners with disabilities (National Council on Disability, 2000a). Assistive technologies help them organize their work, take notes, prepare written responses to assignments, access reference materials, and change information formats to meet their special learning needs. Some assistive technologies are low-tech; others are high-tech.

Examples of low-tech technologies are pencils with special grips, writing paper with raised lines, and sign language. High-tech assistive technologies include devices that convert speech into writing and electronic gear that enables students to use a single switch to move a computer cursor or to input data into a computer program.

Recent developments allow individuals with serious physical and health limitations to use single-switch systems and other new devices to work with computers. IEP planning groups are now required to consider how adaptive technologies might be incorporated into their IEPs.

Web Extension 5–4

Computer and Web Resources for People with Disabilities

◆ ◆

The Alliance for Technology Access is an organization dedicated to helping people with disabilities take advantage of new technologies. This site tells about the group's book, *Computer and Web Resources for People with Disabilities*. The book provides (1) true-life stories of individuals who are extending their capacity through the use of special technologies, (2) extensive descriptions of many newly available assistive technologies, and (3) provides lists of organizations, publishers, and online sources of additional background materials.

On the left side of the page you will see the major heading "ATA Resources," and under this, the subordinate heading "Read Book." Clicking on Read Book will take you to a table of contents and clickable links that will allow you to read the entire book online. Part II, "The Technology Toolbox," contains descriptions of assistive technologies that are currently available.

http://www.ataccess.org/resources/atabook/default.html

Overrepresentation of Certain Minorities

For many years, educators have worried about the overrepresentation of certain minority groups among schoolchildren designated as learners with disabilities, especially African Americans. Recently, African Americans accounted for 14.5% of the national school population, but made up 20.3% of the population of learners with disabilities. See Figure 5–4 for more statistics related to this issue.

This shows some startling differences between the likelihoods that African Americans and white (non-Latino) learners will be identified as having certain disabilities. For example, in 1998–1999, African American learners were:

- 2.9 times as likely as white students to be labeled mentally retarded,
- 1.9 times as likely to be labeled emotionally disturbed, and
- 1.3 times as likely to be labeled as having a learning disability. (U.S. Department of Education, 2000)

Some educators suspect that many African American learners have been erroneously identified as candidates for special education services. To determine why such mistakes occur, educators have begun to examine the characteristics of schools with the same percent of specific groups within the total school population and the percentages of these groups who have been designated as learners with disabilities. One finding is that there is no overrepresentation of African Americans in the learners-with-disabilities populations of

Figure 5–4   Comparison of percentages of minorities ages 6 through 21 in the learners with disabilities population and the general population.

	American Indian/Alaska Native	Asian/ Pacific Islander	African American (Non-Latino)	Latino	White (Non-Latino)
Percentage of total population of individuals identified with disabilities ages 6 through 21	1.3	1.8	20.3	13.7	62.9
Percentage of general population ages 6 through 21	1.0	3.8	14.5	16.2	64.5

Source: To Assure the Free Appropriate Public Education of All Children with Disabilities. Twenty-Third Annual Report to Congress on the Implementation of the Individuals with Disabilities Education Act (pp. 11–27), 2001. Washington, DC: U.S. Department of Education.

schools in which the entire school community—teachers, principals, parents/guardians, and others— holds high expectations for *all* students, regardless of the particular ethnic, racial, social, or economic groups to which they belong (*Addressing Over-Representation of African American Students in Special Education*, 2002).

In schools where these conditions are lacking, teachers and administrators may be failing to differentiate their instruction in ways that promote success among all groups. Frustrations about their inability to help learners from certain groups may lead some teachers to conclude that these learners themselves are flawed, not their instruction. These attitudes may cause mistakes in recommending learners for specially designed programs.

To combat this possibility, organizations such as the Council for Special Education and the National Alliance of Black School Educators recommend that schools adopt a **pre-referral intervention process** (*Addressing Over-Representation of African American Students in Special Education*, 2002). Instead of immediately referring "problem" learners to groups that will conduct formal screening to determine their eligibility for services for learning disabled learners, the pre-referral intervention process first seeks to determine whether something might be done to improve the nature and quality of instruction they are receiving. The hope is that the pre-referral process will help regular classroom teachers provide instruction more responsive to the needs of individual learners and, as a result, decrease their desire to refer so many members of certain minority groups to screening for classification as learners with disabilities.

GIFTED LEARNERS

For almost four decades the federal government has been interested in programs for gifted learners. As early as 1972, Congress established the **Office of Gifted and Talented**. Public Law 91-230 (*United States Statutes at Large*, 1971, p. 153) defined **gifted learners** as "children who have outstanding intellectual ability or creative talent, the development of which requires special activities or services not ordinarily provided by local education agencies." In 1974, the passage of Public Law 93-380 drew more federal attention to gifted learners by allocating federal funds to local and state agencies to improve gifted-and-talented programs. The **Jacob K. Javits Gifted and Talented Students Education Act**

of 1994 provided additional federal support for these programs by authorizing the U.S. Department of Education to award grants, provide leadership, and sponsor a national research center focusing on the educational needs of gifted and talented learners.

The Gifted Student Stereotype
Go to MyEducationLab and select the topic "Diversity and Multiculturalism." Read the article "Beyond the Gifted stereotype" to get some perspectives on overcoming stereotypes about gifted students and suggestions on how to work with them in the classroom. Respond to the questions included with the article. Some of the questions are designed to prepare you for your licensure examination.

THE SELECTION ISSUE

Identifying gifted students is difficult for most teachers; "lacking awareness of the characteristics and instructional requirements of high ability students (places) teachers at a disadvantage" (Manning, 2006, p. 65). In years past, educators relied almost exclusively on standardized-test scores, especially IQ test scores, to identify gifted learners. Today, much broader criteria are used, including information about applicants' psychomotor skills and creative talents.

In the 1970s, when federal legislation encouraged many schools to offer special programs for gifted learners, some authorities thought these programs should not accept more than about 3% of the total school population (Mitchell & Erickson, 1978). Over the years, political pressures have caused an increase in the number of eligible participants.

Special school programs such as those designed for gifted students channel money away from programs for all other learners. School boards are reluctant to allocate funds to programs that serve only a few learners, creating an incentive for expanding enrollments in programs for gifted learners. Currently, programs for gifted learners in only a few states serve fewer than 6% of enrolled learners. Some states' programs enroll more than 14% of the total student population (National Center for Education Statistics, 2001, p. 67).

Pressures Facing Gifted Learners

Sometimes, classmates encourage their gifted peers to "do less." Succumbing to these pressures, gifted learners may ask you to ease up on assignments. You should remind all students that your rigorous expectations are not designed as punishment but, instead, represent learning opportunities that are, in the long-term, the best interests of all.

Parents, guardians, and, regrettably, some teachers may pressure gifted learners to perform flawlessly. This can lead to unrealistic self-expectations and frustration, which can damage gifted learners. Help them focus on their strengths and their accomplishments, not their shortcomings. These bright students must understand that everyone has strengths and weaknesses and that being less than perfect is no sign of failure.

Enrichment Programs

Enrichment programs represent one of the two basic approaches schools use to serve gifted learners. These programs provide

---

Web Extension 5–5

The National Research Center on the Gifted and Talented

This is the home page of The National Research Center on the Gifted and Talented (NRCG/T). At this site you will find highly useful lists of downloadable online resources that focus on school programs and instruction for gifted learners.

http://www.gifted.uconn.edu/nrcgt.html

learning experiences that go beyond those given other learners, challenging gifted students to reach their potentials. Yet, enrichment programs try to maintain continuous contact between gifted and non-gifted learners by keeping them together in regular classes and by moving them through the K–12 instructional program at the same rate. This means, for example, that gifted learners will take U.S. history at the same time as their non-gifted peers. But it also means that the specific learning experiences provided for them in the context of the U.S. history course will be different and more challenging than those to which non-gifted learners are exposed.

When involved in an enrichment program, be sure that you require gifted learners to perform tasks that differ from tasks required of other learners. Avoid asking gifted students to do *more* of the same because it sends a message that giftedness is a burden rather than a blessing. Your gifted students may believe that they are being punished for having special abilities.

Enrichment is the most popular approach for responding to the needs of gifted learners. It has wide support from parents, guardians, and administrators and parallels a view of the school as a place where all kinds of learners come together.

Acceleration Programs

Acceleration programs, a second category of responses to the needs of gifted learners, increase the pace at which gifted learners complete their schooling. For example, in an accelerated program, a gifted learner might complete the entire high school program in just two years. Supporters of these programs believe that giftedness is best developed when bright learners are as intellectually challenged as possible, including moving them into classes with older learners, where more-advanced content is taught. Web quests and blogs let gifted students move even faster (Renard, 2005).

There are two types of acceleration: *subject-matter acceleration* and *grade-level acceleration*. Subject-matter acceleration allows gifted learners to take courses earlier. For example, a sixth grader might enroll in a ninth-grade algebra class. Grade-level acceleration occurs when a learner is allowed to skip an entire grade and enroll in a class of older learners. This leads some critics of acceleration to claim that it may interfere with the social adjustment of gifted learners.

The percentage of gifted learners who are in accelerated programs is small compared with the percentage enrolled in enrichment programs. Enrichment programs have been much easier to sell to education policymakers because they are more consistent with traditional patterns.

Developing Learners' Potential

Robert J. Sternberg and Todd I. Lubart (1991) say that you can encourage creativity among gifted learners by providing opportunities for them to engage in responsible risk taking.

For example, consider the results of awarding a low grade to a learner who submits a drawing rather than an essay when asked to describe a short story. A bright student soon "learns" that risk taking, particularly creative risk taking, doesn't pay. But, by rewarding creativity, you can create a safe, encouraging environment that tells them that risk taking has some value. Explain how new information is important to them personally and how they can use it to perform innovative and creative tasks.

By organizing your class into groups of three to five learners each, according to their ability levels, you can assign them work that differs in sophistication and intensity from work you give to others. This arrangement also allows you to differentiate assignments for the rest of the class.

Helping gifted learners see ways that assignments are relevant to their own interests and personal lives can stimulate their creative powers. By helping identify problems and goals, they will develop a stronger sense of purpose. This commitment, in turn, can stimulate responses that fully use their intellectual and creative resources.

Key Ideas in Summary

- The learner population is becoming increasingly diverse, challenging teachers to provide instruction that appropriately fits each child's background.
- Diversity is one of our national strengths. The varied experiences and backgrounds of our people enable them to bring multiple perspectives to bear on vexing problems. You must help all students develop pride in their backgrounds and a commitment to democratic decision making.
- Multicultural education seeks to provide equity for all learners by drawing on insights from history and the social and behavioral sciences, and especially from ethnic studies and women's studies. Establishing a *culturally responsive environment* in your classroom creates an important zone of comfort for both you and your students.
- Today, most new teachers are white and middle class, in sharp contrast to today's diverse student bodies. As a result, today's teachers and students may have different views on what constitutes appropriate behavior. By taking time to learn about the backgrounds of all your students, you can respond logically to these learners' backgrounds.
- Never assume that all youths from a particular racial, ethnic, or home-language group share similar views and values. Perspectives of African Americans living in rural areas often vary greatly from African Americans living in central cities. Many people of Latino heritage do not speak Spanish as their first language; therefore, we must focus on characteristics of individuals, not on reputed (and often incorrect) characteristics of the large groups to which they belong.
- The *cultural-deficit* view of the first half of the 20th century attributing poor school performance to failure of the learner's home environment to support school learning is now generally rejected. Now we think that the failure of many minority-group children is the lack of programs responsive to their needs.
- Many college-preparatory programs in high schools enroll higher percentages of white students than are represented in the overall student body, whereas learners from ethnic and cultural minorities are overrepresented in special-education classes. Segregation by gender has also been observed. For example, by far, most learners in high school physical science classes are male.
- Recommendations to improve educational services for ethnic- and cultural-minority learners include (1) committing to the idea that everyone can learn, (2) modifying grouping practices, (3) accommodating learning-style differences, (4) making teachers aware of their perspectives, (5) relying less on standardized tests, (6) ensuring that teachers avoid favoritism, and (7) assigning good teachers to work with minority-group learners.
- *Exceptional learners* are different from the norm in some significant way. Gifted students are among groups of exceptional learners in today's schools. Differences among exceptional learners are as great as those among the total student population of the school.
- Traditionally, teachers had little daily contact with exceptional learners. Now, the Individuals with Disabilities Education Act (IDEA) requires schools, to the extent possible, to provide services to these learners in regular classrooms.
- Federal legislation requires teams of individuals, including the student's regular teacher, one or more parents/guardians, and representatives of the school district to develop an *Individualized Education Program (IEP)* for each disabled learner.
- Teachers of learners with disabilities must modify their instructions in two basic ways. They make accommodations, such as: special work deadlines, the work place, and the

types of acceptable responses. *Modifications* involve assigning tasks that differ from the tasks assigned to other learners.

- Today, legislation such as the *No Child Left Behind Act* requires schools to report achievement levels of subgroups, including learners with disabilities.
- *Inclusion* is the idea that learners with disabilities, to the extent possible, should receive instructional services in regular classrooms. It carries the connotation that inclusion is beneficial for all students. Debates about its appropriateness continue.
- Learners have many kinds of disabilities. Some have multiple disabilities including speech, visual, and hearing impairments; attention deficit disorder (ADD) and other specific learning disabilities; orthopedic impairments; emotional disturbance; and mental retardation.
- Recent developments in *assistive technology* are helping learners with disabilities to cope better with school environments.
- Educators question the high percentage of minority students who are being labeled as learning disabled.
- Gifted learners have outstanding intellectual or creative abilities that require nurturing by special school programs.
- Programs for gifted learners are of two basic types. The most popular type, *enrichment programs*, keeps them in their regular age-group classes and courses, providing special learning experiences. *Acceleration programs* allow them to skip grades.
- Teachers unintentionally punish gifted learners by assigning them to do more work than that required of non-gifted learners. Letting gifted learners help plan their own programs ensures opportunities to engage in risk taking and creativity.

For Your Initial-Development Portfolio

1. What materials and ideas in this chapter about diversity will you include as "evidence" in your portfolio? Select up to three separate items of information. Number them 1, 2, and 3.
2. Think about why you selected these materials. As you do so, consider these issues:
   - Specific uses you might make of this information as you plan, deliver, and assess the impact of your teaching
   - The compatibility of the information with your own priorities and values
   - Contributions this information can make to your development
   - Factors that led you to include this information
3. Place a check in the chart below to indicate to which INTASC standard(s) each of your items of information relates. (You may wish to refer to Chapter 1 for more detailed information about INTASC.)

INTASC Standard Number										
ITEM OF EVIDENCE NUMBER	S1	S2	S3	S4	S5	S6	S7	S8	S9	S10
1										
2										
3										

4. Prepare a written reflection in which you analyze the decision-making process you followed. Mention the INTASC standard(s) to which your selected material relates.

Reflections

1. You learned that individuals' backgrounds affect their attitudes. Who influenced your views? How will they affect your treatment of future students?
2. How will you help students with varied cultural, ethnic, social, and economic backgrounds develop positive self-concepts while promoting a common commitment to democratic values?
3. How should school district leaders deal with pressures to fund certain categories of learners when they are also responsible for providing a high-quality education to all school learners?
4. In this chapter, you learned about many kinds of disabilities. How might you learn more about less familiar conditions?
5. How will you respond to critics who argue that gifted learners are already "advantaged" and do not need further support?

Field Experiences, Projects, and Enrichment

1. Visit some diverse classes and note how many members of each group ask questions and how many are asked questions.
2. Organize a panel discussion focusing on this question: "Do school programs today do a good job of serving female learners?" Use relevant data from Web sites and journal articles.
3. Invite to your class a director of programs for learners with disabilities. Ask about the kinds of federal and state regulations that must be observed and ask to see a copy of an IEP.
4. Ask two or more teachers of a grade level you intend to teach how they provide instruction for exceptional learners. What kind of special training do they get from the district?
5. Prepare a list of Web sites that provide enrichment experiences for gifted learners. For each site, give a title, its URL, and a brief description of contents.

References

Addressing Over-Representation of African American Students in Special Education. (2002). Arlington, VA: Council for Exceptional Children, and Washington, DC: National Alliance of Black Educators.

Anderson, J. J. (2006). Bearing olive branches: A case for school-based and home educator dialogue. *Phi Delta Kappan, 87*(6), 468–473.

Banks, J. A., & Banks, C. A. M. (Eds.). (2001). *Handbook of research on multicultural education.* San Francisco: Jossey-Bass.

Banks, J.A., Cochran-Smith, M., Moll, L., Richert, A., Zeichner, K., LePage, P., Darling-Hammond, L., Duffy, H., & McDonald, M. (2005). Teaching diverse learners. In L. Darling-Hammond and J. Bransford (Eds.), *Preparing teaching for a changing world.* San Francisco: Jossey-Bass.

Brown, D. F. (2002). *Becoming a successful urban teacher.* Portsmouth, NH: Heinemann.

Brown v. Board of Education, 347 U.S. 483 (1954).

Erickson, F. (1987). Transformation and school success: The politics and culture of educational achievement. *Anthropology and Education Quarterly, 18*(4), 335–356.

Garan, E. M. (2004). *In defense of our children: When politics, profit and education collide.* Portsmouth, NH: Heinemann.

Garcia, E. (2002). *Student cultural diversity* (3rd ed.). Boston: Houghton Mifflin.

Good, T. L., and Brophy, J. E. (2003). *Looking in classrooms* (9th ed.). Boston: Allyn and Bacon.

Gorski, P. (2000). *The challenge of defining a single "multicultural education."* http://www.mhhe.com/socscience/education/multi/define.html 1-15-2004

Henson, K. T. (2001). *Curriculum planning: Integrating multiculturalism, and motivism, and education reform* (3rd ed.). Long Grove, IL: Waveland Press.

Lawrence, S. M. (2006). Contextual matters: Teachers' perceptions of the success of antiracist classroom practice. *The Journal of Educational Research, 98*(6), 350–358.

Lewin, T. (1999, April 11). Amid concerns about equity, parents are turning to girls' schools. *New York Times.* http://www.nytimes.com/library/_national/regional/041199ny-girls-schools.html 1-15-2004

Long-term effects of inclusion. (2003, November). Arlington, VA: ERIC Clearinghouse on Disabilities and Gifted Education. http://ericec. org/faq/i-long.html 2-20-2007

Lovelace, M. K. (2005). Meta-analysis of experimental research based on the Dunn and Dunn Model. *The Journal of Educational Research, 98*(3), 176–183.

Manning, S. (2006). Recognizing gifted students: A practical guide for teachers. *Kappa Delta Pi Record, 42*(2), 64–65.

Milliken v. Bradley, 418 U.S. 717 (1974).

Mitchell, P. B., & Erickson, D. K. (1978). The education of gifted and talented children: A status report. *Exceptional Children, 45*(1), 12–16.

National Center for Education Statistics. (2001). *Digest of education statistics, 2001.* Washington, DC: Author.

National Center for Education Statistics. (2002). *Percent of public schools with students with various disabilities, and of those, percent with special hardware and special software for these students, by type of disability and by school characteristics: 2001.* Washington, DC: Author. http://nces.ed.gov/pubs2002/internet/table12.asp 2-20-2007

National Center for Education Statistics. (2006a). *Participation in education, Indicator 5, Racial/ethnic distribution of public school students.* http://nces,ed,gov/programs/coe/2006/section1/indicator05.asp 2-20-2007

National Center for Education Statistics. (2006b). *Participation in education, Indicator 8, Children with disabilities in public schools.* http://nces.ed.gov/programs/coe/2006/section1/indicator08.asp

National Council on Disability. (2000a). *Federal policy barriers to assistive technology.* Washington, DC: Author.

National Education Association. (1999, May). Inclusion confusion. *NEAToday Online.* http://www.nea.org/neatoday/9905/cover.html

Nieto, S. (1999). *The light in their eyes: Creating multicultural learning communities.* New York: Teachers College Press.

No Child Left Behind Act of 2001, Public Law 107-110, 115 Stat. 1425 (2002).

Plata, M., Glasgow, D., & Trusty, J. (2005). Adolescents with learning disabilities: Are they allowed to participate in activities? *The Journal of Educational Research, 98*(3), 136–143.

Powell, R. R., McLaughlin, H. J., Savage, T. V., & Zehm, S. (2001). *Classroom management: Perspectives on the social curriculum.* Upper Saddle River, NJ: Merrill/Prentice Hall.

Renard, L. (2005). Teaching the DIG generation. *Educational Leadership, 62*(7), 44–47.

Savage, T. V., Savage, M. K., and Armstrong, D. G. (2006). *Teaching in the secondary school* (6th ed.). Upper Saddle River, NJ: Merrill/Prentice Hall.

Sheldon, S. B., & Epstein, J. L. (2005). Involvement counts: Family and community partnerships and mathematics achievement. *The Journal of Educational Research, 98,* 196–206.

Simon-McWilliams, E. (Ed.). (1989). *Resegregation of public schools: The third generation.* Portland, OR: Network of Regional Desegregation Assistance Centers and Northwest Regional Educational Laboratory.

Sleeter, C. E., & Grant, C. A. (2002). *Making choices for multicultural education: Five approaches to race, class, and gender* (4th ed.). New York: John Wiley & Sons.

Sternberg, R. J. (1994). Allowing for thinking styles. *Educational Leadership, 52*(3), 36–40.

Sternberg, R. J., & Lubart, T. I. (1991). Creating creative minds. *Phi Delta Kappan, 72*(8), 608–614.

United States Statutes at Large. (1971). 91st Congress, 1970–1971 (Vol. 84, Part 1). Washington, DC: U.S. Government Printing Office.

U.S. Department of Education. (2000). *To assure the free appropriate public education of all children with disabilities: Twenty-second annual report to Congress on the implementation of the Individuals with Disabilities Education Act.* Washington, DC: Author.

U.S. Department of Education. (2001). *To assure the free appropriate public education of all children with disabilities: Twenty-third annual report to Congress on the implementation of the Individuals with Disabilities Education Act.* Washington, DC: Author.

Williams, L. J. (1998). *Membership in inclusive classrooms: Middle school students' perceptions.* Unpublished doctoral dissertation, University of Arizona, Tucson.

CHAPTER 6

WHAT IS TAUGHT AND HOW IS IT TAUGHT?

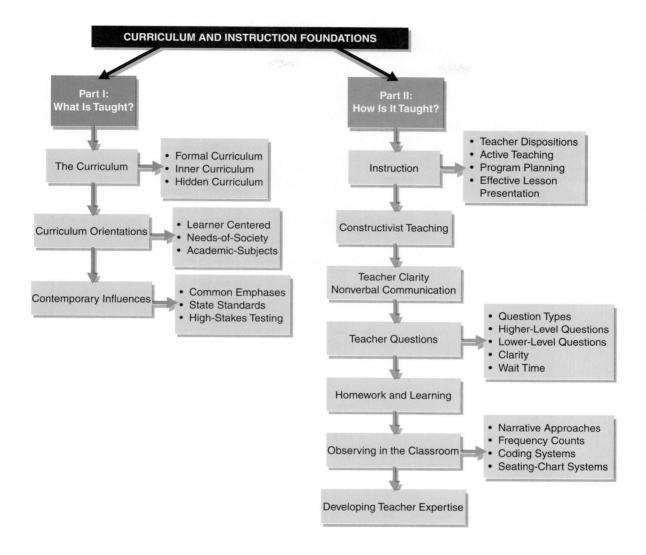

CURRICULUM AND INSTRUCTION FOUNDATIONS

**Part I:
What Is Taught?**

The Curriculum
- Formal Curriculum
- Inner Curriculum
- Hidden Curriculum

Curriculum Orientations
- Learner Centered
- Needs-of-Society
- Academic-Subjects

Contemporary Influences
- Common Emphases
- State Standards
- High-Stakes Testing

**Part II:
How Is It Taught?**

Instruction
- Teacher Dispositions
- Active Teaching
- Program Planning
- Effective Lesson Presentation

Constructivist Teaching

Teacher Clarity
Nonverbal Communication

Teacher Questions
- Question Types
- Higher-Level Questions
- Lower-Level Questions
- Clarity
- Wait Time

Homework and Learning

Observing in the Classroom
- Narrative Approaches
- Frequency Counts
- Coding Systems
- Seating-Chart Systems

Developing Teacher Expertise

OBJECTIVES

This chapter will help you to

- distinguish among *learner-centered*, *needs-of-society*, and *academic-subjects* curricula.
- suggest ways the *hidden curriculum* sends messages to learners.

- explain how *teachers' dispositions* influence their teaching.
- list qualities of *active teaching* and *constructivist teaching*.
- describe classroom observation techniques.

Teacher enthusiasm helps motivate students.

Anne Vega/Merrill

INTRODUCTION

What is worth knowing? How can this knowledge be taught? These are key questions that form the heart of education. They are the questions that are usually of most interest to those preparing to become teachers. However, there is not universal agreement about the answers to these questions. For example, does the knowledge needed for individuals to enter the world of work define what is worth knowing? Do requirements for what is needed to enter higher education define what is worth knowing? What about values, character, and ethical behavior? Do the schools have any responsibility to teach these important areas of knowledge? Should the knowledge that is taught be primarily that focusing on the experiences and the values of our society or should it include that of other cultures? How should these important areas be taught? Is the responsibility of the teacher to tell the students and the responsibility of the students to accept what they are told? Should the students be confronted with problems and then be assisted in solving them? In short, there are many competing claims about what is worth knowing.

The answers to questions related to what is worth knowing are influenced by the view you have of the role of school in society, your philosophy of education (Warner, 2006), your understanding of how individuals learn, and the traditions and history of education. First, we will consider the question of what is worth knowing. This refers to what is identified as the "curriculum."

PART I

THE CURRICULUM

Curriculum is a Latin word meaning the course to be run (Eisner, 2002). Over the years, the term has come to mean a sequence of learning experiences, or the course that is to be followed to reach educational goals.

Curriculum can be defined several ways. It is often defined as the planned or formal specification of content and skills to be taught. Others define the curriculum as all of the experiences, both formal and informal, of students in an educational setting. This means that there are several types of curriculum that might operate in the schools.

The Formal Curriculum

The *formal curriculum* refers to the explicit or the planned curriculum. These are the goals, objectives, and content that are clearly identified as the responsibility of the school. This usually includes the sequence of the content, and the books, curriculum guides, and materials that are used. Eisner (2002) defines the formal curriculum in education as a series of planned events that are intended to have educational consequences.

However, if there is anything we have learned about human behavior, it is that individuals do not learn information exactly as it is presented to them. Learners discover meaning by making connections with previous experiences (Protheroe, 2007). Our brains try to "make sense" out of what is provided and relate new information to prior experiences. Thus, in some sense, each individual experiences the curriculum differently from all others. This is what some have termed the "inner curriculum."

Inner Curriculum

The term *inner curriculum* describes learning that occurs within learners as they process new information (Thomas & Brubaker, 2000). Because contemporary students come from diverse language, cultural, ethnic, and economic backgrounds, it can be expected that they will interpret information differently.

Those who have conceptualized the inner curriculum believe that the formal curriculum (the planned experiences) acts as a framework, a structure, or a scaffold that helps individuals developing their unique understandings. This framework, if properly developed, can help students interpret content in light of their own experiences.

However, in all groups of learners, some conclusions may be misconceptions or at least are unexpected. As a teacher you need to monitor student learning so that you can better determine the extent to which the inner curriculum learned by a given student matches the formal or the planned curriculum. Learning about the personal background of each student can help you understand how the formal curriculum can best be used as a scaffold to help individuals "make sense of" what you teach.

The Hidden Curriculum

At school, students learn more than the specified content. They also learn from the "hidden curriculum." The hidden curriculum is what is taught implicitly (Henson, 2006). For example, the content we choose to teach, the rules we implement, the way we organize the classroom, and the methods we use to teach the content all send messages to students. It sends messages about what is appropriate, what is important, and what students should do and even how they should think.

Gail McCutcheon (1988) states that hidden curriculum messages are "transmitted through the everyday, normal goings-on in schools" (p. 191). These messages and patterns vary from school to school and are influenced by administrators, teachers, parents, and guardians.

What is omitted from the curriculum can send strong messages. For example, at a time when the world is rapidly becoming more diverse, almost one-forth of students polled in one study said that their school does little to encourage contact among students from different backgrounds (McCarthy & Kuh, 2006). The fact that this information is omitted sends a message to the students regarding the importance of diversity and cultural contact.

Your everyday behavior will help shape your school's hidden curriculum and will tell your students what you consider important, sometimes even sending unintended messages. For example, suppose you are emphasizing the importance of reading. However, if your students never see you reading or if they overhear you stating that you don't like to read, they will receive mixed messages and may question your motivations in urging them to become better readers. The "lesson" these students take away from this experience is part of the hidden curriculum.

What Do You Think?

- What were some of the hidden messages you learned when you were a student?
- How can teachers guard against sending unwanted hidden messages?

When you are planning your curriculum, you need to start with the formal or the planned curriculum. However, you need to consider the inner curriculum and how the students are making sense out of what they are encountering. Then you need to think about the hidden messages that you might be sending by what you choose to omit and by how you plan on running the classroom. The next section will focus primarily on the formal or the planned curriculum.

Curriculum Orientations

One of the most important questions in planning the formal curriculum is "How do we decide what content is important?" Tradition plays a major role in this decision. For example, American history is generally taught at the fifth grade in nearly every region of the United States. The reasons why this content has been placed at the fifth grade have been largely forgotten. However, whenever people are employed to teach fifth grade, they can expect that their social studies curriculum will focus on American history. Furthermore, because this has become to some a prevalent pattern, schools are reluctant to change this sequence because of student mobility. They worry that not following a traditional curriculum sequence will be harmful to those students who might move in or out of different school districts. A large part of the school curriculum is in place because of tradition and particular topics or subjects have come to be identified with certain grade levels.

Tradition, however, can be a poor reason for deciding the curriculum. What it identifies as worth knowing should have some deeper basis than "We've always done it that way."

Several orientations are generally used to identify what is deemed important. Some people favor a **learner-centered orientation**. This orientation begins with the premise that what is important to teach is what meets the needs and the interests of the student. These individuals point out that the purpose of education is to develop individuals to their fullest potential. Therefore, education should begin by considering the needs of individuals. This approach emphasizes individual interests and needs more than subject-matter content. They see personal development as the most important obligation of the school. For further discussion of learner-centered education, see Henson (2004).

Others contend that schools are an important social institution that prepares individuals to take their place in society. Therefore, they believe that schools should use a **needs-of-society orientation** that identifies what is important by what society needs. If, for example, society needs highly skilled engineers, then the curriculum should have a heavy math and science component.

Another group points out that education is charged with transmitting bodies of knowledge. The needs of students and the needs of society change frequently; so these programs may lack intellectual rigor and may be poor foundations for identifying what is important for everyone to know. These individuals contend that what is important to know should stand the test of time and focus on knowledge contained in organized bodies of knowledge. These individuals favor a curriculum built around an **academic-subjects orientation** emphasizing traditional school subjects such as English, history, mathematics, and science.

Learner-Centered Curricula

One of the historic roots of the learner-centered curriculum is the work of the 18th-century philosopher Jean-Jacques Rousseau. Rousseau argued that children are born good and that whatever evil faults they develop later in life are caused by society's negative influences. He wanted schools that would protect youth from society and allow their naturally good instincts to unfold. Therefore, he felt that identifying what is important for students to know based on the needs of society was inappropriate and would only perpetuate corruption and injustice.

According to Rousseau, people pass through four distinct growth phases. From birth to age 5, perceptual skills and muscle coordination develop. At this stage, Rousseau recommended that educators protect children from social restraints and allow them to experience directly the consequences of their own actions.

During the next stage, ages 5 through 12, Rousseau recommended no formal education. For this age group, he believed that personal experience alone was a sufficient teacher.

Rousseau argued that education should be formal at ages 12 to 15, exposing children to teachers who would go light on instruction and provide activities to stimulate learners' curiosity.

Rousseau saw the final stage of development occurring between the ages of 15 and 20 when individuals develop refined human-relations skills, an appreciation of beauty, and a sense of personal and religious values. He thought this age group should be encouraged, but not forced, to study religion and ethics. Rousseau's ideas influenced curricula designed to "humanize" school programs.

Perhaps the best-known American advocate of learner-centered education was the eminent American educational philosopher John Dewey. Dewey advocated building the curriculum around the experience and curiosity of the child. This does not mean he did not believe in rigorous academic content. He believed that rigorous academic content was best taught and learned when organized in such a way that it related to learners' life experiences. Therefore, teachers had to have in-depth knowledge of many subjects, not so they could lecture the students on the knowledge, but so they could relate the knowledge to individual interests and assist the student in gaining deeper understanding of that knowledge and how it related to other bodies of knowledge. Present-day supporters of needs-of-learner education often argue that the need for this orientation is increasing as students become more ethnically, linguistically, and culturally diverse (Polakow, 1999).

The Case for Learner-Centered Curricula.   An important strength of these curricula is their concern for individual learners as the heart of the planning process. This reminds educators of their responsibility to serve young people and provide experiences that will help them develop their own unique talents and abilities to their fullest.

Learning experiences associated with this orientation can break down artificial barriers among subject areas. Individuals do not experience life as a sequence of subjects. Rather, decisions that are made in life usually cross subject-matter boundaries. Using student interests as the basis for planning and organizing courses helps provide the basis for drawing information from a wide selection of academic specialties.

In addition, because the curriculum is based on student needs and interests, learner-centered curricula are highly motivating. Students have a "need to know" the information and are more likely to see school as important than if they are encountering content that they will not be expected to use until sometime far in the future.

The Case Against Learner-Centered Curricula.   Critics of curricula based on learners' needs often focus on the issue of efficiency. Diagnosing and responding to students' special needs require excessive time and therefore are not cost-effective. Doubters also believe that all learners should master some common content, regardless of their levels of initial interest. Furthermore, learners may be poor judges of their own needs and will choose shallow academic experiences. Pandering to poor decisions of immature learners may produce graduates who are ill equipped for the demands of living in a complex, technological society.

Web Extension 6–1

Sudbury Education Resource Network (SERN)

Sudbury model schools base their philosophy and practices on the learner-centered orientation developed at the Sudbury Valley School in Massachusetts. Core ideas include freedom, democracy, trust, and responsibility. Here, learners direct their own educational experiences. The following site gives support for practices in Sudbury schools and links to pages maintained by individual schools that are committed to this mode of education.

http://www.sudburynetwork.org/modelIntroduction.htm

Finally, some critics argue that it is unrealistic to believe that teachers can have the breadth of knowledge necessary to assist students in learning interdisciplinary content in some organized and meaningful manner.

Needs-of-Society Curricula

Those supporting the needs-of-society approach to defining what is important to learn point out that the schools are one of the most important institutions in society. If individuals do not exit the schools prepared to contribute to society in some productive ways, the society will certainly experience a myriad of problems and will decline. Those approaching the development of curriculum based on the needs of society look at issues such as enduring social issues, citizenship knowledge and participation rates, and the need for an informed and productive work force. One curriculum pattern that emerges out of the needs-of-society approach is that of a problems approach.

School programs that emphasize the problems approach are designed to help learners develop skills and insights relevant to solving pressing social problems. Supporters contend that to ensure social survival, schools should address enduring social issues that threaten the fabric of society. These might involve identifying a series of problems and the knowledge that individuals need to know in order to address these problems. A major part of the curriculum would be to teach problem-solving and critical-thinking skills.

The needs-of-society approach often includes an emphasis on vocational or career and technical education. This is often supported by business and corporate interests to emphasize that well-prepared individuals are necessary if the nation is to remain competitive in the world. Frequently, attacks on so-called frills in school programs are made by people who want schools to be more career-oriented.

Another major emphasis in the needs-of-society approach is an emphasis on citizenship development. This approach has a long history and dates back to the founding of the nation. The early founders of the nation saw education as critical for the preservation of a democratic society.

The Case for Needs-of-Society Curricula.   The needs-of-society advocates argue that education should be meaningful. If students see the relationship to what they are learning in school to real issues or to what they need to know to seek meaningful employment, they will be more motivated and will take school much more seriously. Those supporting the needs-of-society orientation also contend that the schools need to be accountable to society. Education must address the need for individuals to have a basis of important knowledge and useful skills. In essence, schools exist because of resources provided by society and therefore, the curriculum must address the needs of society.

Supporters point to magnet schools as one example of how they apply the needs of society. Magnet schools are based around themes such as "The Medical Profession," "Performing Arts," or "Space and Aviation." Students interested in aviation will be more interested in mastering a subject such as mathematics if it is taught in the context of something that interests them such as becoming a pilot rather than by plodding through a traditional mathematics textbook.

The Case Against Needs-of-Society Curricula. A major problem of the needs-of-society emphasis is the difficulty in identifying which needs to address. Hasty decisions lead to programs that are excessively narrow in scope and shallow in content.

The rate of change is also a problem. A student who chooses a particular path might be preparing for a career that by graduation will be obsolete. For example, change in the technology sector is so rapid that school programs cannot be expected to keep up. In addition, the cost of new technology is more than can be supported by typical educational budgets.

Those who advocate an emphasis on citizenship face issues relating to values and beliefs. It is not possible for the school to be values neutral. Who will decide what issues to address and which values of perspective to adopt in confronting enduring social issues or citizenship responsibilities? What does citizenship mean and what content should be taught? Is citizenship the preservation of tradition or is it informed social criticism? These two perspectives would lead to very different curriculum designs.

Working with other teachers in planning the curriculum can be a professionally and personally rewarding activity.

Academic-Subjects Curricula

Since the time of ancient Rome, a common way to organize the curriculum has been the use of subjects, assuming that there are disciplines (or bodies of knowledge) that group together elements of content that are related in some natural way. Advocates believe that organizing knowledge into academic subjects such as mathematics or music makes it easier to learn. Often state laws mandate inclusion of certain subject content in K–12 programs. Organizing the curriculum around academic subjects is the most prevalent pattern of curriculum design. It answers the question of what is most important by looking at what the experts in key subject areas have defined as important.

However, this does not fully settle the issue. There is not enough time in the school year to cover everything. Some selection is needed. Some states have designated that certain subjects are "core" or "essential" subjects, whereas others are considered to be "supplemental" or even frivolous. For example, science and mathematics are defined as "essential," but music and art usually are not. However, some research indicates that learning art and music results in improved achievement in the "essential" subjects. Some subjects, such as health and physical education that have been somewhat pushed aside in favor of more "academic" subjects, are now taking on more importance as societal concerns over fitness and childhood obesity have received more attention.

Those individuals who agree with the academic-subjects orientation may disagree over what content within a subject should be emphasized. For example, in recent years there have been several individuals who have defined specific content knowledge that they think everyone should know. One popular series of books is titled "What Every _____ Should Know." However, others emphasize that what students should learn from the various subjects is not a body of facts and unrelated pieces of information, but the key concepts and principles of the subject area. These individuals support the **structure-of-the-disciplines approach.** This approach to subject-matter knowledge advocates students learn how each discipline is organized and how specialists in each discipline ask and answer questions. The goal is to develop an understanding of the key ideas or principles of a subject and the inquiry and the problem-solving procedures used by experts.

The Case for the Academic-Subjects Orientation.   The experts in subject areas have developed and defined a coherent body of knowledge. The most effective way to facilitate learning is to present this content in a logical, systematic manner. For example, it is unrealistic to expect individuals to develop a clear understanding of a complex subject like mathematics on their own by pursuing their own interests. Each generation does not need to reinvent what is already known. There is a logical structure and sequence and this is what should be taught.

Another advantage is that society and those interested in the accomplishments of the young find academic-subjects curricula familiar and respectable, making it easily presented to them. This facilitates keeping schools accountable because there are bodies of knowledge to be learned that can be measured. This helps society make important resource allocation decisions and allows for more productive discussion with parents and guardians. Discussing the student's curriculum with parents and guardians is an important element that tends to enhance achievement (Sheldon & Epstein, 2005).

Most textbooks are organized to be used in academic-subjects curricula. For example, there are separate books for classes in mathematics, English, and biology. Textbooks that represent a fusion of content from several academic disciplines are less common. The continuing wide use of textbooks provides support for an academic-subject-matter orientation across grade levels.

The Case Against the Academic-Subjects Orientation.   Because life is not organized into separate subjects, some critics suggest that the school curriculum should be more interdisciplinary, allowing content to be drawn from many sources. A look at the faculty of academic departments in universities reveals that most of the "experts" need extensive interdisciplinary knowledge in order to address their research agenda. Schools are not just preparation for the future; they should emphasize the present. The justification that "someday you will need to know this" simply does not motivate most students. They have to have a "need" or a reason to learn. Teaching students a body of knowledge that they may need at some point in the future is simply ineffective and inefficient.

Even subject-matter specialists do not agree on what content is most important. A survey of subject-matter specialists, such as professors of science, history, or English, reveals a wide range of content that they think students need to know. In addition, the body of knowledge that everyone needs to know often has a cultural or ethnic bias. The ideas and contributions of cultures and societies outside the Western tradition are often ignored. Even setting aside the usual ethnic identity and cultural pride arguments, the case can be made to strip away the "cultural blinders." Looking at knowledge from a multicultural perspective can open up new and exciting innovations.

In summary, identifying what is important to know is not as simple and straightforward as it might appear. There are several different perspectives that lead to different curriculum patterns. Parents may have very different views about what should be taught. You need to be prepared to face challenges to what you are teaching in the classroom.

What Do You Think?

- What curriculum orientation is the one that seems to be closest to your views?
- Can elements of the different orientations be combined?
- What do you see as the current curriculum emphasis?

Contemporary Influences on the Curriculum

Because responsibility for education has been delegated to the various states, ultimately each state has the responsibility for defining what is to be included in its curriculum. In the past, the state would usually provide broad guidelines or curriculum frameworks and delegate the actual curriculum responsibility to local school districts. Therefore, a common overall sequence of topics would be found within a given state, but specific emphases would vary from district to district. With an increased mobility of students between states, over time the state frameworks became quite similar.

Common Curriculum Emphases

Guidelines on what should be taught are usually included in state regulations governing education, especially in state curriculum standards. A review of these guidelines reveals the following general patterns.

The content defined to be taught in elementary school programs include instruction in reading and language arts, mathematics, social studies, science, health, physical education, and fine arts. State guidelines often specify the priorities given to each of these subjects by designating the amount of time that should be devoted to each subject.

The amount of time designated for each subject in elementary schools varies from place to place. Some states mandate minimum amounts of time be devoted each day or week to certain high-priority topics or subjects. In other subjects, time-allocation decisions are left to local districts, principals, and individual teachers.

For the most part, elementary schools are charged with developing the "basics." Because proficiency in reading is key to academic success in so many other areas, it is one of the basics that is given priority.

The influence of the needs-of-society orientation can also be noted in the emphasis placed on subjects in the elementary curriculum. International comparisons have indicated that the average mathematic scores of students in other nations are higher than those of the students in the United States. Therefore, mathematics has been given high priority. In fact, some elementary teachers report that they spend the majority of the school day teaching reading and mathematics and that other subjects, such as science and social studies, are included "only if there is time."

Middle school and junior high school programs generally continue to emphasize the same subjects as those in elementary schools. However, particularly in grades 7 and 8, options for students with different interests and abilities begin to appear. For example, several mathematics courses may be offered. Some students may take algebra, others may choose a less rigorous course, and still others may enroll in a more challenging class.

In senior high school, state and local high school graduation requirements largely drive the programs. These requirements vary from place to place, but most prescribe a minimum number of semesters of instruction in English/language arts, mathematics, science, and physical education. Many places now require specified levels of computer literacy. However, electives have generally been a prominent feature of secondary schools.

Many school-reform reports have recommended requiring more work for high school graduation in certain so-called basic subjects such as English, mathematics, social studies, and science. Over the past 20 years, larger numbers of students have been enrolling in these courses. However, this trend does not reveal much about the nature of the content that learners encounter in these courses. At best, curricular programs provide a sketchy outline of what goes on in schools. The real school program is the one shaped by teachers as they work with students.

Today's explosion of knowledge, ready access to information via technology, and improved understandings of how individuals learn require continuous curriculum evaluation and revision. Content once considered indispensable is being replaced with newer content. Some of the curriculum patterns you remember from your own school days may have given way to new priorities.

Such changes will not come easily. Tradition exerts a powerful force, and schools have proved to be among the most change-resistant of our institutions (Armstrong, 2003). However, despite these difficulties, pressures on schools to modify programs in light of new conditions continue to mount. Read this chapter's *Critical Incident* feature to learn about one teacher's plan to change her curriculum pattern.

Critical Incident

A Curriculum-Change Proposal Confronts Practical Realities

Tradition is a powerful force, often constraining teachers' attempts to better serve learners' needs and interests. This profile shows some challenges you might confront should you decide to change the content in your instructional program.

As you read this profile, think about these questions:

- What values lie behind Sondra McPhee's proposal?
- What values lie behind Dr. Gutierrez's reaction?
- How might Sondra and Dr. Gutierrez overcome the resistance to changes to the eighth-grade U.S. history program?

Some Forces That Shape Curricula

Searching the Web for ways to motivate her eighth-grade history students, Sondra McPhee discovered oral history, which would allow her to focus on content that was more immediate to her students' own lives. After several weeks of planning, she sent a memo to her principal, Dr. Viola Gutierrez, explaining some changes she planned to implement.

In her memo, Ms. McPhee said she would include much more about the lives of youths in early America, including clothing styles and the games they played. This would replace such topics as profiles of national leaders, elections, economic developments, and foreign affairs. Dr. Gutierrez eventually sent Sondra a note asking her to come in to discuss her oral-history proposal.

Dr. Gutierrez complimented Sondra for her professionalism in searching out research to support her case. However, she rejected the proposal because it lacked several topics covered on the state U.S. history test for eighth graders. She also feared that some influential parents might think it would "water down" the history program.

Finally, Dr. Gutierrez pointed out that the administrators at the district's high school were concerned about the lack of subject-matter preparation junior high students had when they entered grade 9. An oral-history program would make students appear to be even less prepared for high school.

State Standards

One of the significant changes that has taken place in recent years is the establishment of state standards. Because of pressures to make schools more accountable for student learning, many states have moved beyond just the specification of curriculum frameworks. They have defined specific content standards that they expect all of the students in the state to master.

State curriculum standards specify required content and experiences in certain subjects in elementary schools and in individual courses in middle schools and high schools. By the early 1990s, many content-specialty organizations developed curriculum standards that specified content to be included in each elementary grade and in middle and high school courses, sometimes suggesting methods for teaching these topics. In 1995, Diane Ravitch, a former U.S. assistant secretary of education, published *National Standards in American Education: A Citizen's Guide*, saying that standards improve the activity of life (p. 89).

Ravitch's book prompted several states to establish state curriculum standards. These standards are usually developed by a committee of individuals within the state. Generally this committee represents a cross section of individuals. Subject-matter specialists, teachers, parents, and representatives of the business community are usually included. The result is that standards are usually the result of political compromise and do vary from state to state.

Some of these standards reflect the work of content-specialty organizations such as the National Council of Teachers of Mathematics, the National Science Teachers Association, the National Council of Teachers of English, and the National Council for the Social Studies. Enthusiasm for state curriculum standards is still quite high. The movement to state standards was provided with additional momentum by the No Child Left Behind Act (2002). This act requires every state to develop and assess performance on a rigorous set of standards.

State standards have been used as the basis for state-level testing. As a result, they have had a major impact in the classroom.

The Case for State Curriculum Standards.   Defenders of state curriculum standards contend that they will improve education. Some research supports this assertion (Suter, 2000), noting that standards:

- facilitate school-to-school comparisons,
- help ensure that required content is actually taught,
- make it easier for learners to move from school to school by requiring all schools in a state to emphasize similar kinds of content at each grade level, and
- promote educational equity by ensuring that all children will experience their stated rigorous content.

The Case Against State Curriculum Standards.   Some people question the value of standards, saying the following:

- Standards remove local control of academic programs, preventing teachers from meeting the needs of their students.
- Standards are heavily influenced by academic specialists who assume all students will attend higher education and become academic specialists.
- Standards-based content is influenced by pressure groups and, therefore, the standards may become distorted and not reflect the needs and desires of mainstream society.

State Curriculum Standards and Teachers

State standards have had a major impact on teachers. In some cases, school districts and school administrators rigidly specify what each teacher is to teach every day and there has been much closer monitoring of what is taught in individual classrooms. Spending time on content that is not a part of the state standard is discouraged. The net result has been a loss of teacher choice in establishing the curriculum for their classroom. As a teacher, you need to remember that you are responsible for addressing state standards and your teaching evaluations may be based on how well you do this.

High-Stakes Testing

High-stakes tests are those tests that have serious consequences associated with the outcomes. For example, No Child Left Behind has mandated frequently testing at specified grade levels. Associated with this testing are specific test scores that must be attained. If those scores are not met, schools must notify the public of their shortcomings, parents and guardians have a right to remove their children, and the school can be placed under state control. Many states have also developed exit examinations that students must pass before they can be promoted or receive their diploma.

These high-stakes tests are usually standardized tests developed by companies that specialize in test development. The result is that most of the tests include a large number of easily scored test items such as multiple choice. These items are usually tested on a sample population and norms are developed.

The Impact on Teachers

Because the tests have some important impacts on schools and teachers, they have become an important force in the curriculum. Teachers realize that their schools, and in some cases the individual teacher, will be evaluated using the outcomes of high-stakes testing, so they focus the curriculum on what they expect to be on the test. This has led to a "narrowing" of the curriculum. This means that those parts of the curriculum less likely to be tested will be omitted. Much time will be spent on those areas likely to be tested. Because many higher-level outcomes are more difficult to test, the danger is that some of the more important outcomes will be ignored. Those parts of the curriculum that are not tested may be ignored.

Web Extension 6-2

Fair Test •••

The National Center for Fair & Open Testing maintains this site. This group is particularly concerned about biases in standardized tests that may disadvantage certain racial, cultural, and income groups. Many links challenge the overuse of standardized tests.

http://www.fairtest.org

The Case for High-Stakes Tests

Supporters of high-stakes tests claim that their use will do the following:

- High-stakes tests will help the public compare schools and school districts, and this increased competition will improve all schools.
- High-stakes tests will hold teachers and administrators accountable and, therefore, will improve teaching.
- High-stakes tests help school districts and administrators focus resources in areas of need.
- High-stakes tests help to identify teachers who need help.

The Case Against High-Stakes Tests

Much controversy swirls around high-stakes testing. Critics claim the following:

- Standardized tests only gauge performance on the day (or days) and times that a test is given (Armstrong, 2003).
- Variables such as family income and parents' levels of education may influence scores more than teaching, making the use of standardized-test scores to compare schools and teachers unfair.
- Many variables affect learning, including the availability of learning resources and physical facilities.
- Many standardized tests use multiple-choice, matching, and true–false questions, which ignore higher thinking levels.

In summary, state curriculum standards and testing have taken some of the curriculum decisions out of the hands of teachers and local educators. However, district leaders still have much discretion over programs, making place-to-place variations in (1) content selection, (2) priorities in program components, and (3) sequences of learning experiences.

Within school districts, spirited faculty discussions still focus on which curriculum orientation is preferable. There has been an added benefit because addressing state standards in order to improve school scores often requires teacher collaboration.

What Do You Think?

- Do you think there is too much emphasis on high-stakes testing?
- Should the results of high-stakes testing be used as a measure of teacher-effectiveness?

In some instances, the focus on high-stakes graduation standards has led to legal challenges relating to adequate funding required in order to make sure students have the opportunity to learn what is required on the tests. This has led to estimates of substantial increases in educational funding. This could prove to be beneficial to education or it might cause states to back off of strict rules relating to graduation competency tests.

Many object to using standardized testing as the sole criterion for evaluating schools and teachers. Considerable emphasis on developing alternative evaluation approaches is likely. Learn more about high-stakes testing by reading the *Video Viewpoints* feature.

Video Viewpoints 6–1

The Test

WATCH: This *Nightline* video segment discusses both sides of the issue of high-stakes testing, showing the need for high standards and discussing whether graduation or promotion should rest solely on the scores from only one test.

THINK: Discuss with your classmates or write in your reflective journal your responses to the following questions:

1. Should promotions and graduations hinge on single test scores?
2. These tests are shaping school curricula. Is this a problem?
3. What are some additional issues of high-stakes testing?

LINK: How does high-stakes testing affect equal educational opportunities and labeling of students?

 To view this video, go to the Video Viewpoints DVD and click on this chapter's video: "The Test."

PART II

INSTRUCTION

Instructional Expertise and Teachers' Dispositions

The second question "How can important knowledge be taught to the young?" is a primary concern of novice teachers. This question is important to you because research indicates that the teacher is the most significant variable that influences academic performance. A growing body of evidence suggests that effective teaching requires expertise in instructional design and delivery (Good & Brophy, 2004).

Teaching is a complex act because it deals with a complex organism, human beings. Not only will you be trying to facilitate learning for one of these complex organisms, you will be doing so with groups of thirty or so at a time. In addition, the students in your class will come with varying needs, abilities, motivations, and prior experiences. Many things compete for their attention as they try to identify who they are and how they fit into this world. This is, indeed, a daunting task!

There has been considerable study of teaching and learning and some general principles have emerged that can assist you in this complex task. However, there is still a great deal we do not know. New research in areas such as neuroscience and brain development is providing new insights that have implications for teaching. This means that teachers must be lifelong learners (Phelps, 2006).

In addition to facilitating the learning of academic content in the cognitive domain of learning, teachers must also attend to attitudes and beliefs, or the affective domain, because these two domains are inseparable. Ideally, you need to create a classroom learning community in which you and your students not only become excited about learning new content, but where they also learn how to relate to others and consider the moral and ethical application of knowledge.

Individuals involved in teacher preparation increasingly are focusing on the issue of **teachers' dispositions**. Teachers' dispositions are the perceptions and attitudes that shape their behavior (Combs, 1962). Perceptions are influenced by the values and attitudes of the individual. In schools, much student behavior is ambiguous and open to a variety of interpretations. For example, an individual who believes that individuals are basically good may arrive at a very different interpretation of a student's action or statement than an individual who believes that students are not to be trusted. Therefore, the dispositions held by a teacher may be at least as important as the teaching skills. Teacher dispositions will influence how and when teachers decide to utilize their teaching skills.

For example, if you view teaching as a "technical act," then teaching is nothing more than learning the "right" response to predictable issues and problems. However, if you view teaching as

Treating students with dignity and respect is an important part of a teacher's disposition.

Scott Cunningham/Merrill

a complex interpersonal act involving human desires and motivations, then teaching becomes a matter of applying professional judgment to unique situations rather than applying predetermined "right" responses. In fact, the fatal flaw of some educational reform proposals is that they view teaching as a technical act that can be packaged and delivered by anyone to all students in the same way. In essence these proposals seek to make teaching "teacher proof" by removing the dispositions of the teacher as an important variable.

Another important dimension of teacher dispositions involves how you view teaching. Do you view teaching as an activity that requires "putting knowledge into students" or helping students "discover knowledge"? Your dispositions toward teaching will exert a profound influence on how you choose to teach. For example, one of the authors recently worked with a math student in the teacher-preparation program who insisted that teaching mathematics required "putting math into students." No amount of discussion convinced this student that alternative approaches to teaching mathematics could be valuable. A year after starting teaching, this individual was not rehired by the school district because the new teacher was unable to adapt to the needs of the students.

What are your attitudes and how do they impact your choices? Some of the important beliefs that influence teacher perceptions and behavior include the following:

- All students are worthy individuals.
- Diversity strengthens education and society.
- All students and teachers must be lifelong learners.
- Learners must feel competent and worthy.
- All students are able to succeed, and you can ensure that they do.
- Lessons should encourage learners to become actively involved in creating their own knowledge. (Shechtman, Levy, & Leichtentritt, 2005)

A theme that runs through these examples of desirable dispositions is that learners are individuals who need to be treated with dignity and respect. You must respond to your students' differences in ways that help everyone grow in self-esteem while developing academically and socially. In preparing to meet individual learners' needs, you may wish to consult teacher-effectiveness research. The following section offers some general principles and conclusions that have been drawn from teacher-effectiveness research.

Active Teaching

Some research suggests that **active teaching** is associated with enhanced learner achievement (Good & Brophy, 2004). The term *active teaching* refers to teachers who believe their responsibility is teaching, and they take a direct role in leading the class. This role includes organizing content, motivating students, presenting information, monitoring progress, and assessing student learning. Active teachers accept responsibility for teaching students rather than expecting them to learn from curriculum materials. They demonstrate, explain, monitor progress, and allocate most of the available time to activities related to learning the objectives of the lesson (Good & Brophy, 2004).

Program Planning

In order to provide a quality learning experience for all students, lessons must be well planned. Good planning is related to fewer behavior problems and more successful lessons. One of your professional duties as a teacher involves planning appropriate lessons and learning experiences for your students. Twenty-first-century educators advocate a collaborative approach to curriculum planning (Tubbs, Terry, & Chan, 2006). These responsibilities include: (1) matching instruction to learners' characteristics, (2) conducting task analyses to identify an appropriate beginning point and a logical sequence for instruction, (3) specifying learning intentions, and (4) matching programs to learner characteristics.

Preparing instruction that is well suited to your learners requires considering the difficulty level of the new material in light of your learners' capabilities (Teddlie & Reynolds, 2000) and interests. Your lessons must stimulate learners to want to learn the new information. This requires knowing your learners well. Your strategy for each lesson should be right for the content selected for that lesson (Acheson & Gall, 1992), right for the learners, and right for you (Walker & Chance, 1994/1995).

Task Analysis

As you plan for a given group of learners, you need to engage in task-analysis activities. **Task analysis** requires that you take the content that is to be taught to students and (1) identify the desired results from their learning of the content, (2) break the content into smaller components or subtasks that logically build toward the desired results, and (3) define an appropriate teaching approach for each of these components.

This enables you to determine what prerequisite knowledge and skills are needed in order for students to succeed.

Specifying Learning Intentions

After you determine how to break down and organize the content, the next task is to specify **learning intentions** for each block of content. A learning intention, sometimes called a **lesson objective**, identifies what learners should be able to do as a result of learning the content. Usually one or more learning intentions are developed for each of the subtasks identified during the task-analysis phase. Their attainment of these objectives lets you know whether your students have mastered the new material so that they can move to the next subtask. This facilitates reteaching and prevents wasting time covering content for which the students are not prepared.

Effective Lesson Presentation

Once the task analysis is performed and the lesson intentions identified, then the content needs to be presented in a comprehensible manner. Comprehensible means presenting the new material at a level that is appropriate for the developmental level and prior knowledge of the students. Keep in mind that what might be comprehensible for one group of students might not be comprehensible for another group of students. This means that just because a lesson was appropriate for one group of students does not mean it would be appropriate for another group of students. Comprehensible and effective lesson presentation has several key elements.

Stimulating and Maintaining Interest.   As you select content, you need to know what interests and motivates learners. Because interests of individual learners vary, you will need to use a variety of approaches to motivate them. Variety is essential because each learner's needs are unique (Lovelace, 2005). During the presentation-of-instruction phase, three distinct periods of motivation to be considered are

- motivation at the beginning of the learning sequence,
- motivation during the learning sequence, and
- motivation at the conclusion of the learning sequence.

The purpose of initial motivation is to capture learners' interest. At this stage, you should build on learners' general curiosity by introducing something novel or puzzling. Explain or show how the new material connects to the students' own lives.

Within-the-lesson motivation helps sustain learners' interest levels. Because learners are motivated by success, praise them when they accomplish parts of a larger assignment. Maintain a positive, threat-free classroom climate that tells students they have your support as they struggle with new content.

End-of-the-instructional-sequence motivation efforts help learners to consolidate new information, reinforcing their interest. At this phase of a lesson, pointing out to class members how much they have accomplished gives them a sense of achievement.

Web Extension 6–3

Project-Based Education

At this Web site you will find a useful discussion of an approach to teaching that motivates by requiring students to apply new knowledge as they complete assignments. You will find interesting descriptions of (1) class-motivated projects, (2) team-motivated projects, and (3) self-motivated projects.

http://www.motivation-tools.com/youth/project_education.html

Sequencing Lessons.   Over the years, many approaches to lesson sequencing have been developed. The essential element in effective lesson sequencing is that it follows a logical sequence. One such sequence begins by first communicating what is to be learned. The teacher indicates how this new knowledge relates to previously learned knowledge, presents information in an organized manner in a series of logical steps, includes frequent checks for understanding, provides an opportunity for students to practice the skill or apply the knowledge, gives feedback to students regarding their understanding, and brings the lesson to a close by quickly reviewing the main points of the lesson.

Relating new knowledge to previously learned knowledge is facilitated by the use of advance organizers. An advance organizer presents students with a familiar or known organizing scheme that helps them organize or scaffold the new learning. For example, a teacher might state "As you are encountering this new information about the different parts of government, you might relate it to a baseball team." This organizer provides a way for the students to learn that there are specific roles that different parts of government fulfill just as there are specific roles that the team members, coaches, and umpires must fill in order for the team to succeed. If baseball is not something that fits a particular group of students or helps explain the content in a way that they understand, then a different advance organizer is needed.

Stating the learning intention can also be used as an advance organizer. This specifies what learners should be able to grasp or do as a result of a particular lesson. For example, you might say "When we've finished this lesson, you should be able to identify at least four main parts of a short story."

During the lesson sequence **connected discourse** needs to be maintained. This kind of verbal communication features smooth, point-by-point development of the content you are introducing. The verbal points made by the teacher are logical and connected with few digressions off the topic comments. Building lessons around themes (Protheroe, 2007) and giving **internal summaries** throughout your lessons, pausing to reflect upon what has been

Allowing students to work together and select their own material to read is an example of learner-centered curriculum.

learned so far, also add to the logical flow and help students understand the lesson sequence.

Pacing. Pacing refers to the rate at which you proceed through a lesson. Although students need time to absorb the material (Richards, 2006), good active teaching moves at a brisk pace while maintaining a smooth, continuous developmental flow, avoiding dwelling on matters outside the lesson. Asking questions throughout the lesson helps to ensure that the content is being learned.

Constructivist Teaching

A growing body of research supports a philosophical orientation known as **constructivism** (Henson, 2004). According to this view, learning does not occur simply by the brain taking a "picture" of something and filing it away somewhere in the brain to be retrieved later. Rather, learning is constructed by the brain as it seeks to relate new knowledge to prior knowledge. Therefore, the brain "constructs" the meaning or understanding. Each student will have a unique construction. Sometimes these constructions might be "misconceptions."

One way of testing these constructions is through group-based problem solving. As students work with each other, they test and modify their understandings. Active engagement in the learning process and with content is a hallmark of these approaches (Parsley & Corcoran, 2003). Many constructivists use **cooperative learning**, a structured way of involving small groups of learners working together to complete a given task (Protheroe, 2007; Siegel, 2006).

When using constructivist methods, teachers (1) emphasize concepts and main ideas rather than small bits of information (Cankoy & Tut, 2005) and (2) use mastery goals rather than performance goals. **Performance goals** are goals that students strive to reach in order to compete with classmates. **Mastery goals** are noncompetitive goals that students pursue when mastering content. Shih (2005, p. 316) reported that because their use involves fewer handicapping strategies, "Mastery goals remain the most adaptive type of goals for evoking beneficial patterns of learning."

Group based problem solving is an important aspect of constructivist learning.

◆ ◆

Constructivist Teaching
Go to MyEducationLab and select the topic "Curriculum and Instruction." Read the article "Guiding the Innate Constructivist." Identify how the examples given in the article apply constructivist principles. Respond to the questions that accompany the article. Some of the questions are designed to prepare you for your licensure examination.

◆ ◆

What your students take away from your lessons will depend as much on how they interact with the new content as on the content itself. You want students to learn how to control their own behavior, take responsibility for their own learning, and construct their own knowledge and understanding.

> ### Web Extension 6–4
>
> ## ASCD Tutorials: Constructivism
>
> The Association for Supervision and Curriculum Development (ASCD), a large professional organization for school administrators and university professors, sponsors this site. It has an extensive tutorial that defines *constructivism*, introduces examples of classroom applications of constructivist teaching, explores the relationship between constructivist teaching and assessment practices, and introduces other topics and issues with ties to the constructivist perspective.
>
> http://webserver2.ascd.org/tutorials/tutorial2.cfm?
> ID=27&TITLE=Constructivism

Teacher Clarity

Clarity is a defining characteristic of effective teachers. As with any communication, if it is not clear, little can be comprehended or learned. One of the more important dimensions of teacher clarity is the verbal and nonverbal teacher behavior. The verbal behavior (the spoken words) is relatively easy to capture and discuss. The nonverbal behavior is somewhat more difficult. However, the nonverbal behavior of the teacher frames and influences the verbal message. Communication experts claim that the largest part of communication is the nonverbal dimension.

Elements of Nonverbal Communication

One element of nonverbal communication is **paralanguage**. Paralanguage is not the words themselves but voice intonation, precision, articulation, and the rate of speaking. It influences what we hear and how we interpret it.

Paralanguage comes from family, community, region, and culture. Differences between speaker's and listener's paralanguage patterns cause misunderstanding. For example, if you were brought up in a part of the country where speech rates, patterns, and vowel sounds differ dramatically from those where you are now teaching, your students may have difficulty grasping what you say.

Nonverbal behaviors involve gestures and other behaviors that do not require voice. Mixed signals can block communication. For example, suppose you scowled and said "I'm really proud of you." What is the impact of such a mixed message? In fact, when there is a conflict between the verbal and the nonverbal channels of communication, students tend to pay more attention to the nonverbal. Nonverbal behaviors basically come from an "unaware" sender to very "aware" receivers. This means that although teachers are often unaware of the verbal signals they are sending, the students are quick to pick them up. As teachers, we must attend to the nonverbal messages we are sending. Observers can sometimes help identify nonverbal messages. Videos of our teacher behaviors can also be useful in revealing to us those "unaware" messages.

Teachers' Questions

Over one hundred years ago an educational researcher claimed that "to teach well is to question well"(DeGarmo, 1903). Effective teachers ask more questions than less-effective teachers. In one study, effective junior high school mathematics teachers were found to ask an average of 24 questions per class period, whereas their less-effective counterparts asked an average of only 8.6 questions (Rosenshine & Stevens, 1986). Questions are important in keeping the students engaged and alert in the classroom and for checking their understanding.

However, there is more to questioning that just the number of questions asked. You can improve the effect of your questioning by attending to such issues as: (1) the levels of the questions, (2) the kinds of questions, (3) the clarity of questions, and (4) the time given for a response.

Lower-Level Questions

Lower-level questions refer to those that require little more than recall of information. They are appropriate for checking understanding of basic information. A productive sequence is: (1) ask a question, (2) wait for a response, and (3) react.

Asking questions briskly allows for many questions in a short time (Good & Brophy, 2004) and for more students to respond. A brisk pace keeps learners alert and reveals misunderstandings.

Higher-Level Questions

Higher-level questions require students to engage in more sophisticated thought processes such as application or analysis of the material. Redfield and Rousseau's review of research (1981) found that teachers' use of higher-level questions increases achievement. However, more recent summaries of research reveal more inconsistent results (Good & Brophy, 2004). For questioning to ensure academic success, students must be capable of complex thinking. Some suggestions for asking questions are:

- use many open-ended, probing questions;
- give learners time to think before they answer;
- consistently model the responses you expect by the way you answer students' questions; and
- define and use words that have been shown to trip at-risk students on standardized tests. (Bell, 2003)

The goals for a specific lesson indicate the type and level of questions that you should use (Good & Brophy, 2004).

Clarity of Questions

Avoid asking questions that can be responded to in many ways. For example, a learner could logically answer the question, "Who was the first president of the United States?" with any of the following responses: (a) a man, (b) a Virginian, (c) a general, (d) George Washington.

You could ask, "What was the first U.S. president's name?" Cazden (1986) and Henson (2004) say that giving some background information before asking questions solicits better answers.

Long, complex questions confuse learners. Shorter questions are preferred (Good & Brophy, 2004). Avoid terms that students might not understand.

Wait Time

The interval between when you ask a question and a learner responds is called **wait time**. Teachers have been found to wait an astonishingly short period before answering their own questions, rephrasing their questions, or calling on different learners to respond. Rowe (1986) reported that, on average, teachers wait less than one second for learners to respond, yet students score higher on tests demanding higher-level thinking when teachers wait at least three seconds (Tobin, 1987). Increasing wait time enables students to continue interacting with the information (Wormeli, 2002).

Increasing wait time has interesting results: Teachers ask fewer questions but more higher-level questions, make greater use of answers, and increase their confidence in their students (Rowe, 1986).

> **Web Extension 6–5**
>
> ### Effective Classroom Questioning
>
> This University of Illinois site has information about questioning. Topics included relate to (1) levels and kinds of questions, (2) planning questions, (3) teacher-learner interactions when a questioning technique is being used, and (4) assessing teachers' questioning skills.
>
> http://www.oir.uiuc.edu/Did/docs/questioning.htm

Homework and Learning

The amount of homework teachers assign is a topic of considerable debate. There appears to be cycles in the attention given to homework. Parents' desire for more homework seems to grow for 15 years and then calls for less homework dominate for the next 15 years (Cooper, 2001b). We seem to be at the end of a cycle that has been calling for more homework. Parents are now questioning the value of great amounts of homework that have accompanied the increased emphasis on testing and accountability. They are worried that too much homework is taking away time for students to engage in other worthwhile out-of-school activities and is placing too much pressure on students.

Homework does have benefits if used appropriately. It is more likely to improve achievement when teachers take time to explain the purposes of the assignment (Cooper, 2001b). The benefits of homework also depend on the age groups (Cooper, 2001b); it benefits high school students most, middle and junior high school students only about half as much, and elementary students only marginally.

In general it appears that in middle school and junior high, homework influences achievement until students' total assignments reach about two hours a night. Senior high students profit from longer assignments. Cooper (2001a) offers the following guidelines:

- Use the 10-minute rule. Limit your students' total homework assignments to 10 minutes multiplied by their grade level.
- Know your purposes and don't limit homework to academics.
- Use homework as one of several instructional strategies.

How much homework is enough? Learn more about this topic in the *Video Viewpoints* feature.

Observing in the Classroom

As you begin your preparation to be a teacher, you will be required to observe in classrooms. However, profiting from observation requires more than merely visiting

**Video Viewpoints
6–2**

Homework

WATCH: This *Good Morning America* segment focuses on the debate over how much homework should be assigned to young children, citing a University of Michigan study that found that the amount of time young children spend on homework has increased dramatically. Some parents worry that homework is replacing other activities, lowering students' motivation levels.

THINK: Discuss with your classmates or write in your reflective journal your responses to the following questions:

1. What is the role of homework in learning?
2. Can too much homework be detrimental to learning? How?
3. How can you determine how much homework to assign?
4. How can you gain support from parents for homework policies?

LINK: Should homework policies be based on other community activities or only on what is educationally sound?

 To view this video, go to the Video Viewpoints DVD and click on this chapter's video: "Homework."

classrooms. Observers need to focus on important elements of teaching that might be easily missed by a casual observer. As one colleague once complained about students in the observation phase of their preparation, "They look but don't see."

To profit from observations, you need to know what to observe and how to gather information. Two tools you can use to gather information are **event sampling** and **time sampling**.

In event sampling, an observer identifies specific classroom events such as motivation, classroom questions, and discipline techniques and records information about those events as they occur in the classroom.

In time sampling, an observer records events at selected time intervals. For example, an observer might note what is happening in a classroom every 15 seconds. If you are observing a classroom using a 15-second interval, then if the teacher were giving directions during the first 15-second interval you are observing, you would record "1—lecturing." If the direction-giving continued through the next 15-second interval, you would record "2—lecturing." If the teacher is asking a question at the end of the third 15-second interval, you would record "3—teacher question." This scheme captures the pace and the flow of the lesson. At the conclusion of the observation, it is possible to identify how long it took to give directions and how much time was spent on activities such as asking questions and handling classroom management and discipline problems.

Many different kinds of observational tools can be made using event sampling, time sampling, or a combination of the two. Some examples are introduced in the following subsections.

Narrative Approach

The narrative approach is often called **scripting.** The attempt is to record events by writing down everything observed. Because verbal behavior dominates most classrooms, this approach focuses on what teachers and learners say.

A limit of this approach is that so many events occur so rapidly that recording everything is impossible, providing only a partial picture of what happened. To avoid this limitation, some observers use a system called **selective verbatim.**

In selective verbatim, an observer identifies a particular event that is of interest and records everything said that relates to this event. Events might be "teacher questions," "motivational statements," "classroom-control statements," and "praise statements." An observer interested in the types of praise statements made during a lesson would write down every praising comment made by the teacher. Sometimes observers make an audio recording of the lesson so they can recheck the accuracy of their written comments. Figure 6–1 provides an example of a selective verbatim record that focuses specifically on how the teacher gave praise to students.

Frequency Counts

Frequency counts record the number of occurrences of events during a lesson. For example, an observer might be interested in the number of times that students make contributions to the classroom discussion. Each time a student makes a contribution, this would be marked on the observation form. Other events that might be of interest could be: (1) teacher praise statements, (2) high-level questions, (3) low-level questions, (4) classroom disruptions, or (5) correct (or incorrect) responses to teacher questions. Tally marks are often used to indicate each occurrence. The frequency counts might also be categorized according to the gender of the student.

Figure 6–1   Example of a selective verbatim observation record.

Observation Focus: Teacher Praise Statements

Topic: Reviewing Math Homework at the Beginning of the Lesson

Directions: Each time the teacher makes a statement intended to provide praise to students regarding their work or behavior, write down the time of the occurrence and the exact statement.

Time	Statement
9:02	Thank you for sitting down.
9:02	I like the way John has his paper ready.
9:03	I'm pleased that the class got ready so quickly.
9:05	Good question.
9:06	Okay.
9:07	Good answer.
9:07	Right!
9:08	Good.
9:08	Juan, that's a good way to solve that problem.
9:10	Thank you for putting the book away.
9:11	Okay.
9:12	Good.
9:13	Good job class.

Points of Analysis:
How many praise statements were directed to individuals?
How many were general praise statements?
How many statements were in response to behavior?
How many praise statements focused specifically on the action being praised?
How many praise statements were general and unspecific?

An example of a frequency-count system is shown in Figure 6–2. Because these systems require little writing, tallies can capture many behaviors.

Coding Systems

Coding systems use codes or symbols that represent behaviors. A system may be simple checks, minuses, and pluses or it may be a complex scheme that assigns numbers to a wide array of behaviors. Usually, a coded record is made after a preestablished interval of time, for example, once every 20 seconds.

New codes can be added during the observation as interesting behaviors are noticed. For example, suppose an observer began an observation with a very simple coding scheme that used only these two codes: (1) a learner who is working on the assigned task and (2) a learner who is not working on the assigned task.

During the observation, noticing that some learners were out of their seats, talking, or doing schoolwork other than the assigned task, the observer might decide to add specific codes to indicate these behaviors. (One way to do this would be to designate code 2a for "out of seat," code 2b for "talking," and code 2c for "other schoolwork." Code 2 would be reserved for all additional examples of learners who were not working on assigned tasks.) See Figure 6–3 for an example of an observation system using coding.

Figure 6–2   Example of a frequency-count observation.

Observation focus: Frequency of Occurrence of Selected Teacher and Student Behavior Identified By Gender

Directions: Each time one of the specified behaviors occur, place a tally mark under male or female if the action is directed toward them or if they respond.

	Students	
Teacher Behaviors	**Male**	**Female**
Asks low-level question		
Asks high-level question		
Praises a student contribution		
Expands on a student contribution		
Criticizes a student response		
Corrects a student behavior		
Student Behaviors	**Male**	**Female**
Answers question correctly		
Answers question incorrectly		
Does not answer		
Asks questions or make a contribution about lesson topic		

Points of analysis
Were more high- or low-level questions directed to one gender?
Did the teacher expand on the contributions of one gender differently than the other?
How many praise statements?
How many criticisms?
What is the percentage of correct answers and incorrect answers?

Figure 6–3   **Example of a coding observation system using time sampling.**

Observation Focus: Motivational Strategies

Directions: During each five-minute lesson segment identify the motivational strategy used by the teacher using the letter corresponding to the strategy.

Motivation Strategy Codes

a. Appeals to curiosity
b. Uses novelty
c. Relates content to student interests
d. Provides praise or encouragement
e. State importance of the material to be learned
f. Demonstrates enthusiasm
g. Predicts success or enjoyment
h. Warns about test or grades
i. Threatens punishment for noncompletion

Time observation started_____

First 5 min.	Second 5 min.	Third 5 min.	Fourth 5 min.

Points of Analysis:
How many different strategies were used?
When did most of the motivational statements occur?

Seating-Chart Systems

Seating charts can be helpful. A system could be devised to show which learners you worked with or to show your location during different parts of the period. Begin developing a seating-chart system by making a sketch of the classroom, including the locations of each seat. Gender may be designated by using a small "f" or "m."

Next, develop a set of symbols to represent the teacher behavior to be observed. For example, a simple arrow pointing to a seat might indicate a teacher question to a particular learner, and an arrow pointing away from the seat might indicate a comment from the learner to the teacher. Numerals or letters can be designated to represent learner behaviors at selected time intervals. The location of the teacher at different times could be indicated by a sequence of circled numbers (1 indicating the first location, 2 indicating the second, and so forth). Any symbols that work for the observer are fine. Study the sample information provided in the chart featured in Figure 6–4.

Many questions can be answered by examining data gathered from a completed chart such as depicted in Figure 6–4:

- How many learners were involved in the discussion?
- Were more males or females called on?
- Were learners seated on one side of the room called on more frequently?
- Were more questions directed to students up front?
- How many volunteers did the teacher fail to call on?

Figure 6–4   Example of a seating-chart-related observation.

Observation Focus: Identifying Discussion Participants

Lesson Topic: Review for a Test

Directions: Each space in the chart below represents a learner seat. Sex of learners should be indicated by an *m* for males and an *f* for females. The following symbols are drawn in the box denoting the learner's seat and are used to indicate the first time the particular behavior is noted:

- A learner raises a hand to volunteer (indicated by a vertical line).

- A learner is recognized and makes a contribution (indicated by an arrow pointed away from the learner).

- The teacher calls on a learner (indicated by a down-pointing arrow).

- A learner is called but fails to respond (indicated by a zero drawn immediately below the down-pointing arrow indicating a teacher question).

- Repetitions of the same behavior are indicated by horizontal marks across the vertical ones. Note examples below:

This learner volunteered four times but was not called on.

This learner was called on and made a contribution twice.

This learner was called on three times.

Seating Chart with Sample Data

m ≢ 1	m ↑ 2	f ↓↑ 3	m 4	f 5
m ↓↑ 6	f ↑ 7	m ≢↓○ 8	f 9	m 10
f ↑ 11	m ↓○ 12	f 13	m 14	f ↑ 15
f ↓○ 16	m ≢ 17	m 18	f 19	m 20
m 21	f 22	f 23	f ⌗ 24	m ⌗ 25
f ⌗ 26	f 27	m 28	f 29	f 30

Developing Teaching Expertise

Beginners often fail to realize that there are developmental stages for teachers. You should not expect to demonstrate the skill of an experienced teacher your first year. Good teachers improve, progressing through a series of developmental stages—from novice to expert (Steffy & Wolfe, 1997). Do not be too self-critical, and give yourself time to grow. Allow more experienced and skilled teachers to help you grow (Halford, 1998). Many school districts have developed "induction" or "mentoring" programs designed to pair new teachers with more experienced teachers.

In summary, knowing what to teach (the curriculum) and how to teach it (instruction) are the central elements of teaching. However, there is no consensus on what should be taught. Most states have curriculum guidelines that delimit what should be taught. It is common today for states to have specific standards that must be addressed. Because standards are often the focus for state testing, this has taken some of the teacher discretion out of the decision of what to teach.

Teaching is a complex act. It takes place in an environment where unpredictable events often occur. Many things can be taking place simultaneously. In this chapter, we have identified a few elements of effective teaching and given some suggestions on how to observe so that you can learn from others.

You must realize that learning to teach is a growth process and you should not expect to be an "expert" immediately upon entering the classroom.

Key Ideas in Summary

- The term *curriculum* refers to the selection and organization of content and learning experiences. It differs from *instruction,* which deals with specific means of achieving the general plan described in a particular curriculum.
- *Standardized tests* are used to compare scores of students in a given classroom or school with norms (expected scores of students with similar characteristics). U.S. schools administer more standardized tests each year than do schools in any other country. Citizens use the scores to judge school districts, schools, teachers, and administrators—pressuring teachers to cover content found in standardized tests.
- *State curriculum standards* specify kinds of content, and sometimes particular learning experiences, required in elementary school grades and in courses in middle and high schools. Standards developed by content-specialty organizations in English, social studies, science, and mathematics have influenced some state standards. Increasingly, standardized tests are being developed that tie to information referenced in state standards.
- *Learner-centered curricula* are based on the idea that learner interests and needs should drive the curriculum. Jean-Jacques Rousseau was an early proponent of this perspective. These curricula are said to motivate learners by preventing content fragmentation. Critics argue that preparing separate academic experiences for each learner's needs and interests is impractical because learners are poor judges of their needs.
- *Needs-of-society curricula* seek to produce learners capable of maintaining and extending broad social goals. These curricula have two basic types: a *problems approach* to help learners recognize and respond to important issues, and a *citizenship development approach* providing students with skills needed to make a living. Needs-of-society curricula motivate learners because the content is highly relevant to

their lives. Critics suggest that identification of so-called *problems* may cause conflicts with parents and others who have different perspectives. Critics say that vocationally oriented programs may not keep up with the rapid changes in the job market, and therefore may provide obsolete experiences.

- *Academic-subjects curricula* organize programs into academic disciplines such as mathematics, history, and English. Advocates of this approach say that material within a discipline has similarities, facilitating its mastery. Critics say that the real world is not divided into separate disciplines, and that academic-subjects curricula fragment learning, making the transfer of knowledge difficult.

- Academic-subjects curricula can be prepared in two ways: (1) those designed to teach the findings of *subject-matter specialists* and (2) the *structure of the disciplines*, designed to introduce the processes professionals use in the disciplines.

- *Broad-fields curricula* combine two or more traditional subjects into a single broad area or theme to remove boundaries between and among individual subjects. Critics point to the lack of interdisciplinary teaching materials and to the lack of teachers who have depth of knowledge in several disciplines.

- The *inner curriculum* is the learning that results when a learner's past experiences meld with the classroom information.

- The *hidden curriculum* includes teachers' behaviors and other aspects of the school settings that suggest what students should be doing and even about what they should be thinking.

- Most elementary schools teach reading and language arts, mathematics, social studies, science, health, physical education, and the use of computers. Most high schools offer some electives, while requiring a minimum number of courses in English, social studies, mathematics, science, and physical education. Curricula are heavily influenced by state curriculum standards.

- Your instructional effectiveness will be influenced by your *dispositions*. Dispositions are attitudes and perceptions that affect your behavior. Desirable dispositions promote behaviors that help learners grow: academically, in self-esteem, and socially.

- When you engage in *active teaching*, you will (1) present new information, (2) monitor progress, (3) plan opportunities for learners to apply what they have learned, and (4) reteach content to those who need additional help mastering material.

- Effective lessons feature actions you take to (1) stimulate and maintain learner interest, (2) present material systematically, (3) model expected behaviors and expected products of learning, (4) maintain an appropriate lesson pace, (5) ask questions skillfully, (6) provide opportunities for learners to practice what they have learned, and (7) monitor learners' progress.

- *Constructivist teaching* assumes that young people are driven to interpret information they encounter. What they learn results from their engagement in new experiences and their personal interpretations of these experiences.

- Teacher clarity is associated with student achievement. You need to consider your (1) verbal style, (2) nonverbal style, (3) lesson-presentation style, and (4) ability to provide cogent explanations.

- Sometimes homework affects learners' levels of achievement, and sometimes it does not. It benefits high school students more than middle school students and high school students and middle school students more than elementary students.

- Many observation systems help detect what happens in classrooms. Some use time sampling, some use event sampling, and others use a combination of the two.

For Your Initial-Development Portfolio

1. What materials and ideas in this chapter will you include as "evidence" in your portfolio? Select up to three separate items of information. Number them 1, 2, and 3.
2. Focusing on these ideas, consider these issues:
   - Specific ways you can use this information to plan, deliver, and assess the impact of your teaching
   - The degree to which these ideas reflect your own values
   - Ways this information can aid your development as a teacher
3. Place a check in the chart below to indicate the INTASC standard(s) to which each of your items of information relates. (You may wish to refer to Chapter 1 for more detailed information about INTASC.)

INTASC Standard Number										
ITEM OF EVIDENCE NUMBER	S1	S2	S3	S4	S5	S6	S7	S8	S9	S10
1										
2										
3										

4. Prepare a written reflection in which you analyze the decision-making process you followed. In your comments, mention the INTASC standard(s) to which your selected material relates.

Reflections

1. Review materials in the chapter that deal with state curriculum standards. Do you think they will: (a) improve education; (b) have little impact, negative or positive, on education; or (c) produce generally negative results?
2. Can you think of some examples of "learning" you took away from the *hidden curriculum* in a school you attended? What are some precautions you might take to protect students?
3. In this chapter, you learned to select content that is right for: (1) the subject matter you are teaching, (2) the particular group of learners in your class, and (3) you. What challenges might you face? How might you go about overcoming them?
4. Think about homework assignments you faced when you were a learner at the grade level you would like to teach. Did your teachers give you time to complete any of the work during the school day? Did they make the purposes clear?
5. Today, observers have many tools for gathering information about a teacher's behavior during an observation period.

Field Experiences, Projects, and Enrichment

1. Locate in your library a list of subjects taught at two or more grade levels within a given school. From titles and descriptions of these subjects, decide whether they are based on a needs-of-learner orientation, an academic-subject-matter orientation, a needs-of-society orientation, or a combination of two or even all three of these perspectives. Prepare a written report that summarizes your findings.

2. Through your library or your state department of education's Web site, locate a copy of your state's curriculum and examine requirements related to either (a) a specific elementary school subject or grade level you would like to teach or (b) a specific middle school or high school course you would like to teach. What are some things you can be doing during your teacher-preparation program to make lessons comply to your state's curriculum standards? Respond to these questions in a paper titled: *Reactions to State Curriculum Standards and a Personal Plan for Preparing to Meet Them.*

3. Review ideas for gathering observational data. Select one teaching behavior. Visit a classroom and use an observation instrument to gather data on this behavior. You may wish to consider a scheme based on a narrative approach, frequency count, coding system, or seating chart.

4. Interview an experienced teacher in your content area and grade level. Ask this teacher to comment on his or her homework practices. Ask questions related to (1) the frequency of homework assignments; (2) the approximate amount of time, on average, learners must commit to complete the typical assignment; (3) learners' attitudes toward homework assignments; and (4) what school policies, if any, relate to the issue of making regular homework assignments. Share this teacher's comments with others in your class.

References

Acheson, K. A., & Gall, M. (1992). Technologies in Clinical Supervisers of Teachers. White Plains, NY: Longman.

Armstrong, D. G. (2003). *Curriculum today.* Upper Saddle River, NJ: Merrill/Prentice Hall.

Bell, L. I. (2003). Strategies that close the gap. *Educational Leadership, 60*(4), 32–34.

Cankoy, O., & Tut, M. A. (2005). High-stakes testing and mathematics performance of fourth graders in North Cyprus. *The Journal of Educational Research, 198*(4), 234–244.

Cazden, C. (1986). Classroom discourse. In M. Wittrock (Ed.), *Handbook of research on teaching* (3rd ed., pp. 432–463). New York: Macmillan.

Combs, A. (Ed.). (1962). *Perceiving, behaving, becoming.* Washington, DC: Association for Supervision and Curriculum Development.

Cooper, H. (2001a). *The battle over homework: Common ground for administrators, teachers, and parents.* Newbury Park, CA: Corwin Press.

Cooper, H. (2001b). Homework for all: In moderation. *Educational Leadership, 58*(7), 34–38.

DeGarmo, C. (1903). *Interest in education: The doctrine of interest and its concrete applications.* New York: Macmillan.

Eisner, E. (2002). *The educational imagination: On the design and evaluation of school programs* (3rd ed.). Upper Saddle River, NJ: Merrill Prentice Hall.

Good, T. L., & Brophy, J. E. (2004). *Looking in classrooms* (9th ed.). New York: Longman.

Halford, J. M. (1998). Easing the way for new teachers. *Educational Leadership, 55*(5), 33–36.

Henson, K. T. (2004). *Constructivist teaching strategies for diverse middle-level classrooms.* Boston: Allyn & Bacon.

Henson, K.T. (2006). *Curriculum planning: Integrating multiculturalism, constructivism, and education reform.* Long Grove, IL: Waveland Press.

Lovelace, M. K. (2005). Meta-analysis of experimental research on the Dunn and Dunn Model. *Journal of Educational Research, 98*(3), 176–183.

McCarthy, M., & Kuh, G. D. (2006). "Are students ready for college: What student engagement data say." *Phi Delta Kappan, 87*(9), 664–669.

McCutcheon, G. (1988). Curriculum and the work of teachers. In L. E. Beyer & M. W. Apple (Eds.), *The curriculum: Problems, politics, and possibilities* (pp. 191–203). Albany: State University of New York Press.

No Child Left Behind Act of 2001, Public Law 107-110, 115 Stat. 1425 (2002).

Parsley, K., & Corcoran, C. A. (2003). The classroom teacher's role in preventing school failure. *Kappa Delta Pi Record, 39*(2),84–87.

Phelps, P.H. (2006), "The three. t's of professionalism." *Kappa Delta Pi Record, 42*(2), 69–71.

Polakow, V. (1999). A view from the field. In K. T. Henson & B. F. Eller (Eds.), *Educational psychology for effective teaching.* Belmont, CA: Wadsworth.

Protheroe, N. (2007). "How children learn." *Principal, 86*(5), 41–44.

Ravitch, D. (1995). *National standards in American education: A citizen's guide.* Washington, DC: Brookings Institution.

Redfield D., & Rosseaa, E. (1981). A meta-analysis of experimental research on teacher questioning behavior. Review of educational research, 18(2), 237–245.

Richards, J. (2006). Setting the stage for student engagement. *Kapp Delta Pi Record,42*(2), 92–94.

Rosenshine, B., & Stevens, R. (1986). Teaching functions. In M. Wittrock (Ed.), *Handbook of research on teaching* (3rd ed., pp. 376–391). New York: Macmillan.

Rowe, M. B. (1986). Wait time: Slowing down may be a way of speeding up. *Journal of Teacher Education, 37*(1), 43–50.

Shechtman, Z., Levy, M., & Leichtentritt, J. (2005). Impact of life skills training on teachers' perceived environment and self-efficacy. *Journal of Educational Research,98*(3), 144–152.

Sheldon, S. B., & Epstein, J. L. (2005). Involvement counts: Family and community partnerships and mathematics achievement. *The Journal of Educational Research, 98*(4), 196–207.

Shih, S. (2005). Role of achievement goals in children's learning in Taiwan. *The Journal of Educational Research, 98*(5), 310–319.

Siegel, C. (2006). Implementing a research-based model of cooperative learning. *The Journal of Educational Research, 98*(6), 339–349.

Steffy, B. E., & Wolfe, M. P. (1997). *The life cycle of the career teacher: Maintaining excellence for a lifetime.* West Lafayette, IN: Kappa Delta Pi Publications.

Suter, L. E. (2000). Is student achievement immutable? Evidence from international studies on schooling and student achievement. *Review of Educational Research, 70*(4), 529–545.

Teddlie, C., & Reynolds, D. (2000). *The international handbook of school effectiveness research.* New York: Falmer Press.

Thomas, R. M., & Brubaker, D. L. (2000). *Theses and dissertations: A guide to planning, research, and writing.* Westport, CT: Bergin & Garvey.

Tobin, K. (1987). The role of wait time in higher cognitive learning. *Review of Educational Research, 24*(1), 69–95.

Tubbs, J. E., Terry, D., & Chan, T. C. (2006). "As the crow flies." A case study in K. T. Henson (Ed.), *Curriculum planning: Integrating multiculturalism, constructivism, and educational reform,* 3rd., ed. Long Grove, IL.: Waveland Press.

Walker, V. N. & Chance, E.W. (1994/1995). National Award Winning Teachers, exemplary instructional techniques and activities. *National Forum of Teacher Education Journal* 5(1), 11–24.

Wormeli, R. (2002). Beating a path to the brain. *Middle Ground, 5*(5), 23–25.

Warner, A. R. (2006). Philosophies in conflict. In K. T. Henson (Ed.), *Curriculum Planning: Integrating multiculturalism constructivism, and education reform,* 3rd. ed. Long Grove, IL.: Waveland Press.

CHAPTER 7

HOW DO WE KNOW
STUDENTS HAVE LEARNED?

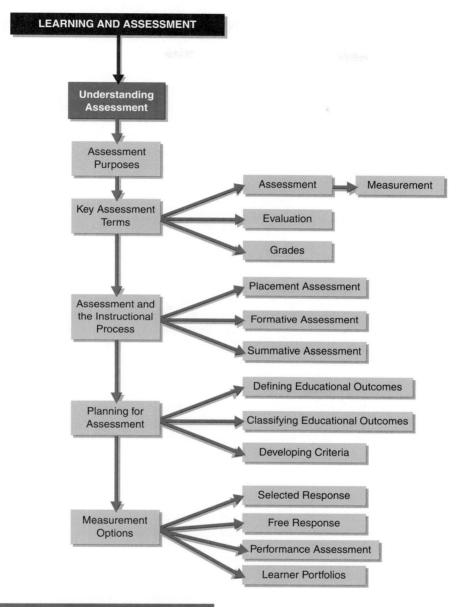

LEARNING AND ASSESSMENT

Understanding
Assessment

Assessment
Purposes

Key Assessment
Terms

Assessment → Measurement

Evaluation

Grades

Assessment and
the Instructional
Process

Placement Assessment

Formative Assessment

Summative Assessment

Planning for
Assessment

Defining Educational Outcomes

Classifying Educational Outcomes

Developing Criteria

Measurement
Options

Selected Response

Free Response

Performance Assessment

Learner Portfolios

OBJECTIVES

This chapter will help you to

- explain the multiple roles of assessment in education.

- define commonly used assessment terms.

- point out the functions of *placement assessment, formative assessment,* and *summative assessment.*

- describe steps you might take as you plan a high-quality assessment program.

- describe characteristics of measurement options, including *selected-response measures, free-response measures, performance assessment,* and *portfolios.*

THE NEED TO UNDERSTAND ASSESSMENT

When you teach, you make daily decisions about the progress of your learners and about the effectiveness of your instruction. Making good decisions requires sound evidence. In addition, you have a professional stake in assessment because student achievement scores are often used to inform the public about the quality of individual schools and the relative excellence of those who teach in particular schools. Therefore, your performance evaluations and possibly your right to keep your job may depend on good assessment. These realities strongly underscore the importance you should attach to becoming a sophisticated planner, interpreter, and user of assessment data.

THE PURPOSES OF ASSESSMENT

Assessment has a variety of uses. One of the most common uses is that of determining if students have learned. This is defined as assessment of learning. However, Stiggins, Arter, Chappuis, and Chappuis (2004) point out that assessment is an important dimension of the learning process and should also be defined as assessment for learning. Sound assessment procedures become a learning experience.

Other reasons for good assessment are that it helps you evaluate the effectiveness of your teaching, helps identify individuals who might be having difficulty learning, can help determine the value of instructional materials, informs other interested parties in the progress of a given student or a group of students, helps make decisions about the allocation of scarce resources, and forms the basis for grading and student evaluation.

With accountability now a major thrust in education, sound assessment has taken on increased importance. Results of assessment are increasingly provided to the public as indicators of the relative quality of teachers and instruction. However, assessments can produce accurate or inaccurate information about student learning and they correctly or incorrectly represent learning (Stiggins et al., 2004). Therefore, questions about the assessment procedures and the resultant data must be asked. Are sound assessment procedures being used to generate the data? Are the data a valid measure of the quality of instruction? What do the data actually indicate? There is a problem of assessment illiteracy among educators and the public that can interfere with efforts to improve education (Popham, 2001).

It has become increasingly important for teachers to have a clear understanding of assessment in order to address misconceptions and to make sure that the data are useful for making important decisions. Just conducting an assessment does not mean that the data gathered are of value in making these important decisions. In fact, poorly gathered data can result in flawed conclusions that can lead to the waste of important time and resources.

Assessment information also has an impact on the students and their attitudes toward school. From the time learners first arrive at school, they desire indications of success. Data gathered from fair and appropriate assessment procedures can provide these affirmations. Evidence of success motivates learners to continue working and creates an expectation of future success (Stiggins, 1997).

Students who are uncertain about their success may begin to doubt the value of their school experiences. These students may devalue what they do at school because they do not have a sense of accomplishment. Because of its potential to promote a negative view of schooling among learners, you need to view assessment as a component of the instructional process that you can use to reshape programs in ways that will enable students to succeed.

Good assessment is also useful for professional growth. When you think about teaching a given lesson, a variety of instructional approaches are available. Over time, attention to assessment data can help you decide techniques that are more effective with the kinds of young people you teach. As you seek to identify these successful instructional approaches, you need to keep track of how well individual techniques helped members of your class to learn material. If they have done well, you can logically conclude that your instructional approaches have been effective. On the other hand, if many people in your class have not performed adequately, you should consider alternative approaches to helping them master the content.

KEY ASSESSMENT TERMS

In casual conversations, several key assessment terms are used interchangeably. As a professional, you need to understand differences among them. A sound understanding of the meanings of these terms can help you identify sources of error, clarify issues, and make informed choices.

Assessment

Assessment refers to the purposeful collection of data from a variety of sources for the purpose of rendering a judgment (Gallagher, 1998). In order to ensure that the assessment procedures used are appropriate and that the evidence of student learning you need is gathered, an assessment plan needs to be developed. An assessment plan involves the identification of data sources that are relevant to a specified set of learning outcomes. Useful information sources may include measurement tools such as tests, or they may draw on your observations of learners' in-class performances, abilities to complete projects according to specified guidelines, and abilities to succeed on tasks associated with daily assignments. Sometimes members of your class will know that they are being assessed. On other occasions, for example, when you are watching groups of learners work on an in-class project, they may be less aware that you are assessing their work.

When developing an assessment plan, you should decide whether your plan is consistent with what you want learners to achieve. The first step in this plan is to identify your learning targets. What do you want students to know and be able to do as a result of your teaching? These targets are usually written as learning objectives. These targets may focus on different intellectual levels or tasks. Different intellectual levels or tasks usually require different types of assessments. For example, simply knowing a lot of facts doesn't mean that the student can apply the information or skill in a new situation. Figure 7–1 is an example of the beginning of an assessment plan for a unit of instruction. This unit has some basic terms to be learned. The learning of these terms might be best measured using a teacher-developed test with multiple-choice and matching items. However, this teacher also wants students to apply what they have learned. This will be assessed by looking at student work samples and entries in the student portfolios.

Learning how to critique and evaluate something can be assessed by asking the students to evaluate something using an essay type of an assessment item. Students will also be given a performance task for which they will be required to create a new product. This requires students to analyze and synthesize what they have learned. By identifying the types of learning targets at the planning phase, the teacher can make sure that important learning outcomes are assessed.

Figure 7–1   **An assessment plan example.**

Learning Target (Objectives)	Learning Level	Type of Assessment
Defines basic terms	Recall	Multiple-choice, matching items
Applies principles	Application	Student work, portfolio entries
Critiques a communication	Evaluation	Essay item
Creates a project	Analysis	Performance-assessment task

This plan also indicates what the teachers will need to do. They will need to write some multiple-choice and matching test items, develop an essay test item for which they will need to use some criteria to evaluate what someone else has proposed, design a performance task and a rubric they can use to evaluate the performance, and inform the students about things they need to include in their portfolio.

When implementing the assessment plan, the teacher will want to make sure the assessments are based on an adequate and fair sampling of behaviors that are of interest. For example, the person using this plan will want to consider what samples of student work will be collected and how many multiple-choice and essay test items need to be constructed.

Measurement

Measurement involves quantifying the presence or absence of a quality, trait, or attribute (Gallagher, 1998). For example, if you want to determine the height, width, or weight of an object, you measure it. Of course, the accuracy of this value depends on your using the right measurement tool. If you want to measure the length of something, you do not use an instrument designed to measure its weight. In addition, if you are interested in the size of a large object such as a football field, then you need a long tape measure rather than a ruler. If precision is needed, you need a tool more exact than a ruler or a yardstick.

Unfortunately, when you are faced with a need to choose the right measurement tool for use in school, the decision often is not as obvious as when you are choosing something used to measure size or weight. In education, two types of measurement tools are normally used. One of those is the standardized test constructed by testing companies and administered to a large number of students. The other general type is the teacher-constructed assessment that is designed for a specific unit of study and a specific group of students. Either of these types can be appropriately or inappropriately used. When you teach, you want to use assessment procedures that provide you with useful information.

Standardized tests are often selected by the school district or the state. You may not have a choice about which standardized tests are used. However, you do need to know what they are measuring and the uses and limitations of the data they generate. To read about standardized tests as a college admission requirement go to this chapter's *Video Viewpoints* feature.

A large percentage of the assessments that occur in your classroom will be teacher generated. When using teacher-developed assessment procedures, you need to understand the choices available to you and the principles of sound assessment. Poorly constructed teacher-generated assessments often fail to measure important objectives, focus on too narrow of a sample of what learners have been taught, and are poorly constructed so that they do not give a clear indication of which students have learned and which students have

Video Viewpoints 7–1

Uses and Misuses of Standardized Tests

WATCH: This *Nightline* segment focuses on the issue of the uses of the SAT as a college admission requirement. The segment discusses some history of the SAT and points out that the current impact might be the opposite of what was originally intended. Much of the discussion centers on the recommendation of the chancellor of the University of California to eliminate the SAT as an admission requirement. He made this recommendation after visiting an upscale private school that was preparing 12-year-old students for the SAT. Further investigation revealed a variation in scores based on ethnicity and a lack of data indicating that high SAT scores actually predicted college success.

THINK: Discuss with your classmates or write in your reflective journal your responses to the following questions:

1. What is the value of a standardized test such as the SAT?
2. Do you think that important and high-stakes decisions should be based on performance on a single test?
3. What evidence do you think would be appropriate for indicating that a person is ready for college?

LINK: What do you see as the social implications of basing admission decisions on a test that seems to be at least partly related to socioeconomic status?

 To view this video, go to the Video Viewpoints DVD and click on this chapter's video: "Uses and Misuses of Standardized Tests."

not. They often include poorly worded or even "trick" questions. When this happens, learners' scores are not good indicators of what they know or have learned.

Evaluation

Up to this point, we have discussed the process of gathering data. Evaluation is the next step, interpreting the meaning of the data. Evaluation is the intellectual process of making a judgment about the worth or value of something. For example, a physician may measure the height and weight of a child. The importance of this information is realized only when the physician makes judgments about whether the child is developing satisfactorily.

Your learners' scores on a test tell you little until you interpret them. To answer the question of whether achievement is satisfactory, you must make an evaluative judgment. To do so, you need clear criteria. The two common ways to establish criteria are norm referencing and criterion referencing.

> ### Web Extension 7–1
>
> #### American Evaluation Association
>
> Here at the home page of the American Evaluation Association you will find a wide range of information on the general area of evaluation. There are lists of useful publications, notices about professional meetings focusing on evaluation-related issues, discussions of key issues confronting professional evaluators, and numerous links to additional information about evaluation.
>
> http://www.eval.org/

Norm-Referenced Evaluation

In norm-referenced evaluation, judgments about an individual learner's level of performance are made by comparing the individual's scores to scores of the appropriate reference group. A common way of establishing these norms, or expected scores, is by reference to scores that are distributed along a **bell-shaped curve**. This is a symmetrical curve derived from a mathematical formula. It is based on the assumption that any given trait or ability is found in the total population in a distribution that is similar to the bell curve. Most scores will be grouped near the mean, or the average, and will decrease in frequency as one moves away from the mean in either direction. In other words, there will be a few people on each end of the distribution, with the numbers increasing toward the middle, or the mean.

Standardized tests usually use norm-referenced evaluation. Developers of standardized tests first administer an initial version to a sample group. They plot these **raw scores** (scores based on the number of correct answers that have not been subjected to any kind of mathematical adjustment) on a distribution and apply the mathematical formula to establish what are commonly called norms, or **derived scores.** Good test developers know that they need to choose a reference group that is representative of the total population of the intended target group so the norms or derived scores will approximate what one could expect if the test were actually given to the entire population.

For example, if it is reported that a given learner's score places him or her at the 50th percentile, this means that 50% of the comparison population performed at or below the score of this individual on this test. If the learner's score were at the 90th percentile, 90% of the comparison population would have test results at or below this person's score. Usually when standardized tests are returned, both the raw score, which is the number the person actually got right, and the derived (standardized) score are given.

When you look at scores of class members on a standardized test, you need to ask several questions. How was the norm group selected? How should individuals' scores be interpreted? When were the norms established (Gronlund, 1998)? If you are to have confidence in the results, what you must determine is whether the group used to standardize the test has characteristics that are similar to your own learners. If curricula and learning conditions of the **norming group**—the group whose scores are used to establish expected scores for individuals who take a standardized test—vary markedly from those of the tested group, the conclusions or the evaluation of performance will be flawed.

Criterion-Referenced Evaluation

When you use criterion-referenced evaluation, the judgments are made based on how the performance of each person compares to a standard or a set of criteria rather than on how their scores compare to those of others (Gallagher, 1998). The standard established is set at a level appropriate to the type of knowledge or skill being assessed.

For example, if a company needs a worker who can carry 70-pound bags, the hiring officials are interested in whether people who apply for the job can carry this mandatory load. They are not interested in how this individual's load-carrying ability compares to some group of individuals. It may well be that the reference group is composed of physically unfit individuals, none of whom can carry a 70-pound bag. Even the top person in the group would be satisfactory. What this company needs is a criterion-referenced evaluation to determine that all of the individuals they interview have met the minimum criteria. So it is with many areas of life. For example, we are not interested in how the pilot of a plane on which we are traveling compares to some reference group. We really want to know that the pilot has demonstrated competency in all of the tasks required in flying a plane against very rigorous standards.

Both norm-referenced and criterion-referenced evaluation can be applied to the same assessment (Gronlund, 1998). Many standardized-testing companies report the norms and also learner performance in skill areas. For example, a math test may include how many addition, subtraction, multiplication, division, and word problems the learner scored correctly. In the classroom, this kind of information informs you that a particular learner, for example, did better than 90% of the learners in the class on the entire test (a norm-referenced conclusion) but failed to meet the minimum criterion for solving word problems (a criterion-referenced conclusion).

Two issues merit attention when you use criterion-referenced evaluation. First, you need to consider the appropriateness of what is being measured. It is sometimes tempting to focus only on what is easy to observe or measure. This is true because you may find it difficult to decide what to measure when your focus is on more complex content. For example, if you are teaching geography, you will find it easier to construct tests focusing on use of latitude and longitude than on a more complex geographic concept such as *diffusion of innovations*. Giving in to the temptation to use ease of measurement as a basis for constructing criterion-referenced tests can result in an inappropriate focus on less important, even trivial, content.

Another issue relates to setting the criterion. What should be the level of acceptable performance? If you set your standard too low, people in your class who have not really mastered the material may be incorrectly judged to have done so. On the other hand, if you set too high a standard, those who have mastered a great deal of new content may be judged to have failed.

Setting the criterion level in the classroom is largely a matter of professional judgment. You need to decide what is acceptable minimal performance, a determination that will vary depending on the nature of the intended learning. Some tasks such as basic reading and mathematics skills are so important for the future success of learners that a high standard of expected performance makes good sense. However, other types of outcomes will be much less critical for future success. In these situations, you will be justified in setting a lower criterion level.

What Do You Think?

- Which evaluation approach is most appealing to you?
- What are the strengths and the weaknesses of each approach?

Grades

The purpose of grades is to communicate the evaluation conclusions. A good grading system clearly communicates to other interested parties the conclusions of the evaluation so that they will have a clear understanding of the performance of the individual on the assessment. Grades are of interest to learners, parents and guardians, employers, and higher-education admissions officers. Because of their importance as a communication tool, you need to consider what your grading system communicates to these other interested parties and whether or not it is accurate and fair.

A system commonly used in the United States awards letter grades. A grade of A is supposed to indicate excellence, a grade of C is supposed to indicate average, and a grade of F is supposed to indicate failing. The letter-grading system sometimes is used in conjunction with a norm-referenced system.

> **Web Extension 7–2**
>
> ## CRESST
>
> At this site you will find the home page of the National Center for Research on Evaluation, Standards, and Student Testing (CRESST). This group, an affiliate of the Graduate School of Education and Information Studies at UCLA, sponsors research on a variety of topics related to assessment. Here you will find links to research reports, monographs, newsletters, and other resources that focus on CRESST's areas of concern.
>
> http://www.cresst.org

When this system is used, a large group of learners clustered around the midpoint are given Cs, a smaller number of learners are given Bs or Ds, and a few learners at each end of the distribution are awarded As or Fs.

You can also base grades on a criterion-referenced system. When this is done, you establish a separate standard that learners must meet to qualify for each grade. For example, you might indicate that all learners who accomplish 90% of the objectives of the course will get an A, those who master 80% will get a B, and so forth. Another criterion-referenced approach ties mastery of specific tasks to specific letter grades. In such an arrangement, you might define *C-level* performance as completion of certain critical tasks. To qualify for higher grades, members of your class would have to complete additional tasks successfully. You might develop separate lists of tasks that learners would need to complete for grades of A or B. This scheme would allow your learners to identify the level of mastery required for each grade and make decisions about which grade to work for. One interesting feature of criterion-referenced grading schemes is that they make it possible for all students to receive *any* grade; there is no mandatory distribution of As, Bs, Cs, Ds, and Fs.

In general, you should judge the worth of a letter-grading system or any alternative for reporting information related to learner performance on how well it communicates evaluation information to learners and to other interested parties. Critics of letter grades claim that they do not provide enough details and, therefore, are of limited value. For example, a letter grade may be an average or summary of several isolated performances and may mask the more typical strengths and weaknesses of a learner. In addition, a grade may be based on elements of behavior bearing only a tenuous connection to learning of academic content. Some teachers consider variables such as behavior, work habits, and effort. In such cases, a learner who does well on academic tasks may receive a lower grade because of discipline problems.

◆ ◆

Grading and Communication

Go to MyEducationLab and select the topic "Assessment." Read the following article: "Grading to Communicate" by Tony Winger. Then go to the topic "Standards and Accountability" and read the article "Grading in a Standards-based System" by Susan Colby. Answer the questions accompanying the articles. Some of the questions are designed to prepare you for your licensure examination.

◆ ◆

Some critics argue that grading systems place too little emphasis on the individual learner. They say that a better scheme would begin with assessment of each learner's abilities. According to this view, an individual learner's progress, as evidenced by grades, should be based on how much measurable growth is demonstrated by the learner between the beginning and the end of the grading period. Such a system would have the desirable effect of focusing teachers' attention on the individual characteristics of their students (Tomlinson, 2001).

Although this perspective appeals strongly to people who want school

This teacher is explaining grading criteria to members of the class.

programs to place a strong emphasis on serving special needs of individual learners, present-day interest in accountability testing presents difficulties for teachers and schools who might be interested in adopting this kind of approach. Opponents argue that grading individuals only against themselves denies the public an understanding of how well individual learners are doing when compared with their age mates within individual classes and schools and between schools and school districts.

One alternative to letter grades that has been tried is extensive written comments prepared by the teacher. The idea is that written evaluations can communicate strengths and weaknesses of learners with more clarity than letter grades. Important constraints limit the practicality of this approach. Good written evaluations require long commitments of teacher time, and opponents of this approach argue that this time is better spent planning lessons and interacting with learners. In addition, the validity of a written evaluation, like a letter grade, depends on the quality of information that supports it. The worth of a written evaluation based on an inappropriate or excessively limited sample of learner behavior has no more value than a letter grade based on a similarly inadequate set of information.

What Do You Think?

- What are the principles that influence how you will grade student performance?
- What type of grading system do you favor?
- What do you find attractive about that system?

ASSESSMENT AND THE INSTRUCTIONAL PROCESS

Assessment plays multiple roles in the instructional process. These include:

- placement assessment,
- formative assessment, and
- summative assessment. (Gronlund, 1998)

Placement Assessment

Placement assessment addresses the question "Where do I begin?" The purpose is to identify whether the students have the necessary prerequisite knowledge and skill to be successful in a given unit of study. It is performed prior to beginning a new unit or course of study. Often it takes the form of a **pretest**, a test designed to provide information about what the learner may already know or think about content that is to be learned.

Understanding the entry-level knowledge of the students you are teaching is important in making decisions about where to start. If students do not have the necessary prerequisite knowledge and skill, they are

Anthony Magnacca/Merrill

Placement assessment often involves individual assessment of student ability.

unlikely to be successful and you are likely to have motivation and classroom management problems. In addition, placement information provides a baseline you can use to determine what value has been added to learners' stores of understanding as a result of your teaching.

Sometimes you will also want to use placement assessment to help you understand learners' attitudes toward content you are about to introduce. This information can give you insight into the kinds of motivational challenges you may face when you begin teaching the new material.

Placement assessment need not be an extensive or time-consuming process. It should be kept relatively quick and short. All you need to determine is an approximate understanding of what the students already know or can do.

Formative Assessment

Formative assessment takes place while an instructional sequence is occurring. The basic question addressed in formative assessment is "Are the students learning the material?" You use it to determine whether they are making satisfactory progress and whether you need to modify your instructional approaches and possibly reteach some of the material. Your formative-assessment procedures may include short quizzes covering limited amounts of content that you give at frequent intervals during your instructional sequence. You can also use daily or weekly work samples as sources of formative-assessment information.

You use formative assessment to make instructional adjustments that will improve the prospects that your students will learn (Gronlund, 1998; Tanner, 2001). You do not use formative assessment to award grades. Information you get from formative assessment provides you with a kind of status-check on student learning and the quality of your teaching. If your formative assessments show that your learners are experiencing a high rate of success, you have some assurance that you are appropriately organizing and pacing your instruction. On the other hand, if you find a high rate of failure, this can signal a need to alter your teaching approaches in ways that are better suited to the particular needs of your learners.

If persistent problems occur and reteaching a subject seems to have little impact, you might want to consider a type of formative assessment called **diagnostic assessment** (Gronlund, 1998). The purpose of diagnostic assessment is to probe for specific causes of a failure. For example, if learners are making mistakes in responding to math problems, you might want to find out whether there is a consistent error pattern that reveals their lack of understanding of one of the basic computational procedures.

Summative Assessment

Summative assessment takes place at the conclusion of an instructional unit or sequence. The purposes are to determine which learners have accomplished the objectives and to provide you with information you can use to communicate to others what your students have learned. The results of summative assessment form the basis for assigning grades.

You need to plan your summative-assessment procedures at the same time as you plan your instructional units. The first step in planning a unit of instruction should be to clearly identify those "enduring understandings" or skills that you expect students to learn during your unit of instruction. The second step is to identify the type of evidence you would find acceptable in determining if the students have learned what you expect them to learn. Each learning outcome or expectation needs to be accompanied by a description of the evidence you will use for assessing learner performance.

When assessment is clearly tied to important learning outcomes, summative assessment becomes a valuable component in the learning process. If you do not engage in careful planning for summative evaluation, there is a danger that your tests and other adopted assessment procedures will not measure important outcomes and any judgments you make about student learning or the effectiveness of your teaching will be flawed.

The consequences of poor learner performance on summative assessments are serious and can mean failure of a course or even failure of an entire grade. Because of the importance of summative evaluations, you have a professional and ethical obligation to make sure they are appropriate and valid. In addition, the high-stakes nature of these assessments emphasizes the importance of developing good formative-evaluation procedures. Formative-evaluation results can provide an early alert to learning problems, and they occur when there is still time for you to salvage an instructional situation that is not working. Corrective action in light of formative-assessment information can lead to instructional modifications that will help your learners master material and do well on your summative assessments.

PLANNING FOR ASSESSMENT

High-quality assessment requires considerable planning. You will experience problems if you ignore placement and formative assessment and wait until the end of the unit to develop tests and other summative-assessment procedures.

Defining Educational Outcomes

As stated above, for assessment to be valid, it needs to have a clear relationship to important instructional outcomes. Failure to spend the time needed to tie assessments clearly to the important learning outcomes you have identified may lead to focusing on tasks that are easy to measure rather than ones that are important. If this happens, students may conclude that they need to concentrate on the trivial and unimportant dimensions of a learning task.

Suppose you are teaching a high school social studies class and design a unit on the Civil War featuring learning outcomes that ask learners to give serious thought to causes and effects of the conflict. However, you do not consider what evidence you will need to determine whether they have learned this important content and you are now at the end of the unit. You determine you need to give a test. The tendency in this situation is to develop test items that measure relatively low-level learning outcomes. Tests constructed in this hasty manner often do little more than assess low levels of outcomes such as naming selected Civil War generals and identifying significant battles. Although there might be some value in having some of this knowledge, it does not indicate how well the students understand the causes and effects of this important national event. Members of your class will quickly conclude that the large "cause-and-effect" issues are unimportant and that, despite what you say in class, your real interest is having them memorize isolated facts.

Classifying Educational Outcomes

What is useful in designing educational assessment is to have some framework for helping to identify educational outcomes at different levels of complexity and sophistication. Some outcomes require your learners to do little more than recall names, dates, or other facts. Even though it is important to have a factual base, a sound instructional program also includes more complex outcomes such as those that challenge learners to interpret, apply, and create.

Identifying the level of complexity of educational outcomes provides you with guidance as you develop your assessment program. Some assessment procedures are useful when measuring less complex outcomes, and others are better suited to measuring more complex outcomes.

The term **taxonomy** refers to a classification scheme. Several taxonomies that focus on educational outcomes have been developed (Bloom, Englehart, Furst, Hill, & Krathwohl, 1956; Krathwohl, Bloom, & Masia, 1964; Marzano, 2001). Taxonomies can be useful as you plan instructional programs. They provide you with a framework for addressing a wide range of educational outcomes. Educational taxonomies generally emphasize three main domains of learning: the **cognitive domain**, the **affective domain**, and the **psychomotor domain**.

The cognitive domain includes a category of thinking associated with remembering and processing information. The affective domain includes attitudes, feelings, interests, and values. The psychomotor domain focuses on muscular coordination, manipulation, and motor skills.

A team of researchers headed by Benjamin Bloom developed the most popular cognitive taxonomy (Bloom et al., 1956). Though it is popularly known as **Bloom's Taxonomy**, the full title is *Taxonomy of Educational Objectives: Handbook 1, Cognitive Domain*.

Bloom's Taxonomy is organized into six categories that are scaled according to their complexity. It begins with the relatively simple cognitive process of recall of factual information and moves to the more complex cognitive processes of applying, analyzing, synthesizing, and evaluating. The six levels are as follows:

1. *Knowledge.* This category refers to the recall of specific items of information, such as recall of facts, procedures, methods, or even theories and principles. Many refer to this category as the "memory level" because it demands only the recall of information from stored memory.
2. *Comprehension.* This category requires a cognitive process that is a step beyond recall. It requires that learners not only recall specific items of information, but that they also reflect on their grasp of its meaning by interpreting, translating, or extrapolating. Many refer to this category when they say they want learners to "understand" the material.
3. *Application.* This category refers to the ability not only to understand material, but also to know how and when to apply the information to solve problems. Thus, when confronted with a problem, the learner is able to identify the needed information or principles and apply that information without being told what to do.
4. *Analysis.* This category refers to the ability to break complex information down into parts and to understand how the parts are related or organized. This level involves having learners understand the structure of complex information. It involves cognitive processes such as comparing and contrasting.
5. *Synthesis.* This category refers to the cognitive processes that we usually associate with creativity. Synthesis is the reverse of analysis. It requires putting parts together in some new or unique way and might involve such tasks as writing a composition or designing a science experiment to test a theory.
6. *Evaluation.* This category refers to judging something against a set of criteria. This means that one is not simply making a value judgment about the worth of something. Evaluation requires that judgments be based on specified criteria that might be provided by the teacher or, alternatively, be developed by the learner.

In using Bloom's Taxonomy to plan your assessment procedures, you start by looking at your knowledge-level learning outcomes. Next, you choose measurement approaches that can provide information about learners' abilities to store and recall specific bits of information. For example, you might choose true–false or matching tests because they are useful in measuring this kind of thinking and they are relatively easy to construct. For more sophisticated kinds of learning outcomes (e.g., those at the levels of application, analysis, and synthesis), you would need to choose different kinds of measurement tools because true–false and matching tests are not capable of assessing learners' abilities at these higher cognitive levels. For these learning outcomes, you might choose essay tests, learner-developed projects, or other suitable procedures.

Cognitive learning is only one dimension of education. Schools also seek to engender positive attitudes and values. You probably would feel terribly disappointed if young people at the end of the year scored well on tests of reading proficiency but left the school vowing "never to pick up another book." Learning in school should not focus exclusively on cognitive learning.

We want students to develop positive attitudes toward the subject, themselves, and others. We also expect that they will develop values and prosocial behaviors that will help them become contributing members of society. This does not happen just from learning information or intellectual processes. These important outcomes fall into the affective domain. Because this domain includes the more subjective area of attitudes and interests, the categories are not quite as precise as those in the cognitive domain. However, they are helpful as guides for developing plans for instruction and assessment.

A team of researchers headed by David Krathwohl developed a taxonomy for the affective domain titled *Taxonomy of Educational Objectives: The Classification of Educational Goals. Handbook II: Affective Domain* (Krathwohl, Bloom, & Masia, 1964). This taxonomy, sometimes known as **Krathwohl's Taxonomy**, is organized into five categories on the basis of increased internalization of an attitude, interest, or value. The categories are as follows:

1. *Receiving.* The lowest level of internalization is that of showing an awareness of or being willing to receive other information or stimuli. This category indicates that little change can occur if an individual is unwilling to even attend to information. For example, a learner is not likely to develop a more positive attitude toward reading if that person is unwilling to even listen to information about books.
2. *Responding.* The next level moves a step beyond the passive reception of information or stimuli and requires that the person make some sort of a response. It might be a willingness to ask questions, seek more information, or participate in an activity. Following our reading example, a person at this level might ask questions about a book or a reading selection or even seek out other titles by the same author.
3. *Valuing.* At this level the individual has begun to internalize the attitude, value, or interest so that he or she expresses an interest in or commitment to activities or positions. A person at this level might demonstrate a commitment by choosing an activity when given a free choice. For example, he or she would actually choose to read a book. Another indicator of valuing would be a willingness to take a stand or try to persuade others of the value of the book that was read.
4. *Organization.* At this level individuals start to integrate personal beliefs and attitudes and to establish a hierarchy. They begin to demonstrate priorities and use those priorities to make choices when confronted with decisions that involve conflicts between two or more of their values, beliefs, or commitments. At this level a person who is coming to value reading would choose that activity over others when faced with a choice. For example, this person might choose to read rather than watch television or play a video game.

5. **Characterization.** At this level the attitudes, beliefs, and values have become so internalized that they become a way of life. Others can see the commitment of a person without being told because of the consistent choices and actions of the individual. Individuals who have reached this level would be recognized by others as people who enjoy reading. They would not have to make this declaration. Their choice of activities and their action would clearly indicate that they enjoy reading.

Assessments of behaviors in the affective domain is difficult using traditional tools such as paper-and-pencil tests. If you are interested in gathering information about affective behaviors of learners, you need to place them in situations that give them opportunities to receive new information and opportunities to begin internalizing an attitude or value. For example, to assess individuals' attitudes toward reading, a teacher would need to observe the choices students made when presented with a variety of choices, one of which was reading. It also needs to be noted that internalization is a long-term growth process that requires measurement over time.

The psychomotor domain has not been as clearly defined as the cognitive and affective domains. Several attempts have been made to develop psychomotor taxonomies, but none has become as well entrenched as the Bloom and Krathwohl taxonomies. Generally, the framework that has been used in attempting to construct a psychomotor taxonomy has the progression from learning a psychomotor skill with assistance and guidance to almost automatic performance at a high level. For example, students learning to use a computer keyboard would move from learning how to hold their hands and receive assistance in finding the right keys to a place where they can type quickly without even giving much thought to the location of specific keys. Skilled athletes develop an almost automatic performance of demanding psychomotor skills. They don't have to stop and think about all of the small components of the performance; they just do it.

Developing Criteria

Some things need to be considered either when you are in the process of designing an assessment plan or when you are evaluating an already existing assessment. The following questions suggest criteria or guidelines that will help you plan useful assessments.

- **Are the important outcomes assessed?** This question relates to the previous discussion. You need to make sure that what you assess is important and that every key learning outcome is included. You want to avoid making judgments about your learners or your instruction based on data that bear little or no relationship to what is important. You can avoid this problem by establishing close links between your intended learning outcomes and your assessment procedures.
- **Are the assessment procedures appropriate for the nature of the outcomes?** This guideline focuses on the issue of validity. **Validity** is concerned with the degree to which a measurement tool measures what it is supposed to measure. For example, a ruler is not a valid measurement tool for determining weight. A valid measurement tool will elicit the type of performance or behavior specified by the learning outcome. Any single measurement tool, such as a single paper-and-pencil test, will unlikely be valid for measuring all learning outcomes. Good assessment plans include a variety of measurement tools.
- **Are there sufficient samples of behavior to allow for a fair judgment?** The major issue posed by this question concerns the inappropriate judgments that sometimes result when only a limited sample of learner behavior is considered. The remedy is

to provide learners with several opportunities to demonstrate their levels of mastery of individual learning outcomes.

- *Do the measurement tools meet adequate technical standards?* This guideline focuses attention on the need to establish assessment procedures that are clear and of a high quality. Tests should be free from trick questions, and test items should be appropriately formatted and error-free. Does the material meet an appropriate **reliability** standard? To meet this criterion, assessment tools must be designed in such a way that different evaluators will arrive at similar conclusions when making judgments about the performance of the same individual.

- *Is the assessment appropriate for the developmental level of the learners?* Assessment devices that are appropriate for secondary-level students often are not appropriate for primary-level learners. Some assessment procedures are not well suited for use with learners who have special needs. For example, a written examination that features complex instructions may cause severe problems for poor or slow readers. Their scores may be more a reflection of their inadequate reading skills than of their mastery of the content.

- *Are the assessment procedures free of bias?* Care needs to be taken to ensure that the assessment procedures do not conflict with cultural norms and beliefs. For example, timed tests may not be appropriate for those cultural groups that do not emphasize time or speed. When learner-produced projects are used as evidence that learning has occurred, young people from affluent homes with computers and other resources may be greatly advantaged compared with learners who have fewer resources at their disposal.

- *How are the results of the assessment interpreted and used?* Clear criteria for evaluating the results of the assessment plan are essential. You should be able to use results to pinpoint specific strengths and weaknesses of individual learners. A good assessment plan will allow you to make detailed analyses of the performances of all your students. You want to be able to go beyond the ability to say "Bobby is good in geography." If you have designed your assessment procedures well, you should be able to make statements such as "Bobby can identify places on flat maps and globes using lines of latitude and longitude. He also has shown that he can identify names and locations of major ocean currents. He still needs to work on his ability to make analyses that require putting several kinds of information together at the same time. For example, he finds it difficult to predict what the climate at a given location on the globe might be when given its elevation, location on the continent, latitude, position relative to major bodies of water and mountain ranges, and situation with respect to prevailing winds."

MEASUREMENT OPTIONS

You can select from among numerous measurement tools as you gather data about learners' performance. You should select specific tools based on the type of learning you wish to assess and your intended uses of the gathered information.

Traditional measurement options sort into two broad categories: (1) standardized tests and (2) teacher-made assessment procedures of various kinds, including the traditional paper-and-pencil tests that have long been a feature of classroom life. Standardized tests have the advantage of being written by test-construction experts. Thus, they usually are free from serious design flaws. Individual test items typically have been carefully field-tested and, if needed, revised.

Web Extension 7–3

The National Center for Fair and Open Testing
•••

The fairness of school testing processes is a widely debated issue. An advocacy group that is committed to eliminating abuses that sometimes have been associated with standardized testing maintains this site. You will find links to materials focusing on eliminating test biases that might negatively influence test takers because of their gender, race, class, and cultural characteristics.

http://www.fairtest.org/

Strengths of standardized tests are counterbalanced by several problems. The issue of fairness, particularly as such tests relate to minority-group learners, continues to be debated (Armstrong, 2003; Ferguson, 1998). Such tests typically assess learner performance at a single point in time. Critics of standardized tests contend that a one-time-only snapshot of a learner's ability represents an inadequate measure of what that student knows. In addition, content emphasized in a standardized test may not match well with what you have been teaching, a circumstance that raises serious validity questions. Without a tight connection between the content covered in the standardized tests and the content of your lessons, results simply are not a valid measure of what learners have taken away from your instructional program.

On the other hand, tests you prepare yourself can be tightly aligned to what you have emphasized in class. The possibility of establishing congruence between what has been taught and what is tested is an advantage of teacher-made tests. The negative side concerns the fact that teacher-designed test items may be of poor quality. This poor quality introduces an element of chance or error so that wrong conclusions are drawn concerning what an individual student knows or can do. Teacher-designed tests do not get the kind of careful review to which new standardized tests are routinely subjected. This implication is that, as a teacher, you have to assume a lot of responsibility for designing test procedures carefully. When you do, you can get valid results that should allow you to draw confident conclusions both about performance levels of individual learners and about the effectiveness of the instructional approaches you have been using.

When you prepare traditional classroom tests, you can select from options that fall into one of the two basic categories of "selected-response measures" and "free-response measures."

Selected-Response Measures

Selected-response measures include those tests that require individuals to choose, or select, a response from those provided. They are not free to provide answers other than those represented on the test. Examples of test items in this category include two-response items, multiple-choice, and matching. Advantages of selected-response measurement tools include flexibility and efficiency (Stiggins, 1997). You will also find that they represent time-efficient choices because they are objectively and easily scored.

Two-Response Test Items

Selected-response measures that allow members of your class to select from two possible answers, one of which is correct, are called **two-response tests**. The most common assessment device of this type is the true–false test. Other choices in this category are yes–no, agree–disagree, supported–unsupported, cause-effect, and fact–opinion items. You can use two-response tests to measure cognitive as well as affective outcomes. For example, agree–disagree items are useful in measuring attitudes and opinions.

Two-response assessments are popular because they are easy to construct. However, this ease of construction can create problems. If you prepare a true–false test in a hurry, the result may be a set of questions that focuses on trivial material with little connection to your priority learning outcomes. Creation of good two-response tests requires commitment of thought and time.

Because two-response items are easy to write and do not require a large response time, you can include a large number of items on a test. As a result, tests of this type permit you to sample a broad range of content. Generally speaking, more items and a broader sampling of content make for a more valid measurement.

A disadvantage of two-response items is that they emphasize absolutes. For example, true–false responses indicate that something is always true or always false. This makes it more difficult to construct good items, can confuse learners, and can result in some heated arguments concerning correct responses.

Two-response items that measure complex outcomes are difficult to construct. You may prefer to use essays or other kinds of assessment approaches when seeking to evaluate learners' higher-level thinking skills. Some critics also dislike two-response items because they provide a good opportunity for learners to guess at answers they do not know. For example, individuals responding to a two-response item have a 50% chance of getting it right even if they do not know the correct response. Some attempts have been made to compensate for uneducated guessing by adding a correction space where learners must correct "incorrect" items.

Multiple-Choice Items

Multiple-choice tests are the most widely used type of test item (Gallagher, 1998). They require test takers to select an answer from among three or more alternatives. Individual test items include a **stem** that is often in the form of a question and three or more answer choices. One of the options is the correct or best choice, and the others are called **distractors**.

Multiple-choice items can be used to measure a variety of simple-to-complex outcomes. Multiple-choice items that are well constructed do have the capability to assess higher-level thinking abilities. This can be done by creating such good distractors that the respondent must engage in some problem solving in order to select the correct response from the alternatives. For example, one of the authors once took a multiple-choice exam in a research class that required the application of statistical procedures in order to identify the correct response. Another example was a multiple-choice test item on a social studies test that required the student to examine a political cartoon in detail in order to identify inferences and biases of the artist. However, constructing good quality multiple-choice test items that can measure higher-level outcomes takes considerable time and skill.

One of the attractions of multiple-choice items is that, like two-response items, you can score them easily. Multiple-choice tests also are less susceptible to guessing than two-response items because learners must select from among several answer choices.

When writing multiple-choice items, your objective should be to provide distractors that are plausible choices that would be chosen by an individual who does not know the material. If this condition is not met, learners will easily eliminate the implausible distractors and select the correct answer, even if they really do not know the material.

As compared with two-response tests, multiple-choice tests can assess learners' abilities to deal with degrees of correctness or incorrectness. These tests allow you to tell your class to choose the "best answer." When constructing multiple-choice tests, include a number of alternative answers, several of which might be partially correct, but only one of which represents the "best" response.

Multiple-choice tests can measure a broad range of content in a relatively short period of time. In addition, if you develop your distractors carefully and pay close attention to kinds of mistaken choices specific learners make, you can get good information about the nature of particular students' misconceptions.

Using multiple-choice tests has some disadvantages. First of all, as mentioned earlier, preparation of good items is difficult and time-consuming. Time saved in scoring multiple-choice tests may be more than counterbalanced by the time required to construct good items. Like two-response tests, multiple-choice tests do provide some opportunity for guessing. However, the development of good distractors can reduce the influence of guessing.

Matching Items

The matching item is a variety of the multiple-choice test that has several special features. Individual items relate to a single topic. Further, all items in the set serve as distractors. For example, you might develop a matching item that asks members of your class to match selections of literature with their authors. The distractors would include all items in the long list of authors that you provide as part of the test. Matching tests usually consist of two lists. One list is the stimuli or the questions; the second list includes possible responses.

A couple of formats can be used to prepare matching items. One places the numbers or letters for items on the answer next to the stimulus. Another option includes instructions that direct learners to draw a line connecting each stimulus item with the correct response on the answer list. This design often is used with young children who have not learned to form letters.

Similar to other selected-response tests, matching items are easy to score, so you can include a large number of items on a single test. To avoid making the test too easy, all items should relate to the same theme or class of items. For example, a matching item should not mix matching authors with themes and artists with techniques. This arrangement makes it relatively simple for learners to eliminate some distractors (e.g., all of the names of authors, if the stimulus relates to an artistic technique) and mark correct responses even though, in fact, they may not have a good knowledge of the content.

One of the main disadvantages of matching tests is that they tend to focus on relationships. This restricts the range of content they can assess. In addition, matching tests are not well suited to assessing learners' abilities to perform tasks requiring the use of higher-level thinking skills.

Free-Response Measures

Free-response measures require learners to generate responses of their own rather than to select responses from a list of provided alternatives. The most common types of free-response measures are essay, short-answer, and fill-in-the-blank items. Free-response tests provide a stimulus that prompts the individual to produce or supply a response. For example, an item might ask for an explanation or interpretation, a solution to a problem, defense of a position, or a comparison and a contrast. These are supplied out of the individual's store of knowledge with few prompts other than the test item.

Free-response items have the potential for assessing a broad range of thinking. For example, an essay item might require that the individual evaluate a proposal or a written selection. For this reason, free-response items tend to be used most frequently to measure more sophisticated learning, focusing on the ability of an individual to demonstrate analysis, synthesis, and evaluation learning. However, free-response items are sometimes used as inefficient measures of low levels of learning. For example, if a student responds to an essay item and then the item is scored according to the inclusion of specific facts or bits of information, it does not indicate the ability of the individual to perform high-level tasks but is a knowledge-level test of what can be pulled from the memory bank.

As with selected-response items that are constructed at the last minute, free-response items can be poorly constructed and the conclusions about the level of student learning of questionable validity. It takes time and skill to construct good free-response items. Care needs to be taken to make sure that the item elicits the type of intellectual response that is desired. Questions need to be written with clarity and precision so that individuals understand exactly what they need to address, the approximate length of the response you are expecting, and general categories of information you hope to see in their answers. Poorly written items such as "explain the causes of the Civil War" are too broad and poorly defined. Entire volumes have been written on this topic, and historians have long debated the roots of the conflict. An improved version might read something like this:

> In a response not to exceed two pages in length, describe (a) at least two political causes, (b) at least two economic causes, and (c) at least two social causes of the Civil War.

In addition to writing free-response items with clarity and precision, you also need to pay attention to how the response will be evaluated. Your correction task will be easier if the question includes references to some specific categories of information you want to see included (such as in the previous example). To help you maintain a consistent correction pattern, consider preparing a model response or a checklist that includes information you hope to see in learners' answers (Gallagher, 1998). Even when you have prepared this kind of a correction guideline, you should be open to considering the appropriateness of alternative answers that, though varying a bit from your own expectations, represent reasonable responses to your question.

Free-response tests have some disadvantages. One problem concerns scoring. Because you need to read and analyze each response, scoring is time-consuming. Poor handwriting can slow down the correction process. Because a range of possible answers may be appropriate for many free-response questions, you sometimes have to make difficult decisions about when and when not to award credit for a given item. Generally, free-response items should be scored based on the ability of the student to demonstrate the intellectual process demanded of them rather than on whether they give the "answer" expected by the teacher. For example, if a student is asked to "analyze" something, did the response identify critical components and explain their relationships? Those are the critical components of analysis, not the presence of specific facts. Because free-response items have many possible answers, arguments over grading and scoring are common.

Another potential problem with scoring is that free-response items involve a number of different abilities such as writing, spelling, and handwriting. The tendency is to give more credit to those learners who have good writing or spelling skills. This is fine if your intended learning outcome refers to these skills. However, if you are interested in learners' thinking or problem-solving abilities, then your primary focus needs to remain on these abilities, not on writing and spelling.

Because scoring is somewhat subjective, your evaluation of individual responses can be influenced by such variables as (1) your mood or attitude when you score the answers, (2) your prior knowledge about individual learners' past levels of performance, and (3) the order in which you read the test papers. You need to make an effort to control the influence of these variables. For example, when possible, you might take time to read papers a second time and in a different order.

Another disadvantage of free-response items is that they sample a limited amount of material. This can lead to errors in judgment. For example, you might ask a question on a free-response test that happens to be one of the few things that the learner knows. You may mistakenly assume that this person has a good grasp of the entire range of content expectations based on good a response to the one test item. On the other hand, a single item may focus on one of the few areas that a particular student does not know and the conclusion is drawn that the student lacks knowledge.

The problem of placing too much emphasis on a learner's answer to one free-response question can be helped if you broaden the content sampled by providing a number of short-answer items. The downside of this approach is that you take away the opportunity to probe the depth of understanding that you can get by asking learners to provide extensive answers to just one or two questions.

Performance Assessment

Most traditional paper-and-pencil types of measurements serve as surrogates or symbolic representations of learning. When you give a test, you do so based on a belief that the resulting score will tell you something about whether the learner has mastered the content. This may not be a valid assumption for a couple of different reasons. First, any test is just a sample of material and a person might be able to pass a test but not have the full range of knowledge required for success. As a result, the score may be an invalid representation of mastery.

Second, tests take place in a controlled environment and may not indicate the ability of a person to apply what has been learned outside of the artificial testing environment. For example, some states have allowed individuals to take tests in the place of course work and student teaching in order to obtain a teaching credential. The type of skill required to pass a test is much different than the skill required to stand in front of 30 students and manage the environment so productive learning takes place.

In recent years, there has been a growing interest in assessing tasks in more realistic and relevant ways. This type of assessment has been called **performance assessment**, **authentic assessment**, or **alternative assessment**.

The basic characteristic of these forms of assessment is that they attempt to assess the performance of a student on a realistic or "authentic" task. One performance assessment that is familiar to most people is the assessment used to award a driver's license. Even though individuals usually take a traditional examination covering items such as rules of the road, this is not deemed sufficient to give a person permission to drive on public highways. To get a license, a person must actually drive a car while being observed and evaluated.

Many important educational objectives require performance assessment. Performance assessment is especially useful in evaluating learner behaviors associated with such tasks as working with others, giving oral presentations, participating in discussions, playing a musical instrument, demonstrating physical education skills, conducting experiments, setting up equipment, and using computers.

Several factors need to be considered when planning a performance assessment. For example, you need to develop a sound understanding of the purpose of the assessment. Do you intend to capture a learner's "typical" performance, or are you more interested in the learner's "best" performance (Gallagher, 1998)? Assessing for different purposes requires different procedures. In addition to identifying purposes, you need to identify the outcomes that you wish to evaluate. This information will help you develop appropriate criteria for making valid judgments.

Performance Evaluation
To view an example of a performance evaluation task and a scoring rubric, go to MyEducationLab and select the topic "Assessment" then view the following two artifacts: "Science Fiction Book Report" and "Colonial Economies." Both artifacts are examples of performance assessment tasks. "Colonial Economies" is an excellent example of a performance task for a group. It also includes a rubric that can be used for scoring the performance task.

Developing the criteria for judging learner performance is an important step in your planning process. The criteria fulfill two key functions. First, they make public the guidelines you will follow in making judgments about individual learners. Second, they communicate your expectations to members of your class (Gallagher, 1998). Failure to develop clear criteria risks compromising the validity of your assessment. Criteria often are organized into *scoring rubrics*. These are sets of guidelines that provide clear definitions for kinds of performances and evidence required for specific ratings to be awarded.

Checklists are one assessment tool that can be useful in performance assessment. Completed checklists provide you with information about the presence or absence of targeted behaviors. You gather information by using a sheet with a list of focus behaviors and place a check mark by each one that occurs during the time you observe learners.

Rating scales represent a somewhat more sophisticated version of checklists. They enable you to make judgments about the quality of observed behaviors by using descriptors of rating points such as "unacceptable," "acceptable," or "above average."

Rubrics or "behaviorally anchored rating scales" are assessment tools that identify specific levels of performance required for each level of the rating scale. These can be very useful in helping to make sure that different people are scoring the performance in a similar manner and in communicating to individuals what they must do in order to reach a given performance level.

Learner Portfolios

One means of attempting to make assessment more authentic has been the implementation of portfolios. A learner portfolio is a purposeful collection of artifacts and performances related to a learner's effort, progress, or achievement. These artifacts and performances are gathered over time and are usually related to specific guidelines concerning the types of items to include. One analogy that might be used is that of an architect or a landscaper. These individuals put together collections of their work that they can show others to demonstrate their knowledge and skill. Learner portfolios put together a selection of material to show other interested parties what the student can do. This has become a popular approach to evaluating student progress and learning.

When preparing to use learner portfolios, you need to develop guidelines that indicate:

- categories of information to be included,
- decision rules for selecting specific kinds of items,
- criteria for judging the material, and
- the learner's reflections on what he or she has experienced and learned. (Stiggins, 1997)

A learner portfolio may include results of performances on traditional selected-response and free-response tests

This learner discusses contents of his portfolio with his teacher. Teachers today often use learner portfolios as sources of evidence when they make judgments about the progress of individual members of their classes.

Anthony Magnacca/Merrill

and also photos, sketches, visual displays, self-assessments, work samples, reflections on dis-cussions, and other relevant materials. Ideally, each learner portfolio will provide as complete a picture or story as possible about the individual's development.

You can use learner portfolios to document growth of individuals over time. A sample of learner work products over a semester or a school year has the potential to provide much useful information to interested parties such as parents and guardians. Good learner portfolios yield a much more comprehensive picture of an individual's development than a report that focuses only on performance on traditional tests.

Because they can capture a rich array of material, learner portfolios can provide insight into areas that are normally overlooked, such as interests, abilities to persist when confronted with complex tasks, and self-concepts. In addition, you can involve members of your class directly in gathering information for their portfolios. This kind of activity helps them to develop their organizational skills and encourages them to reflect on what they have learned.

There are good learner portfolios, and there are poor portfolios. Learner portfolios that have been put together in the absence of well-planned criteria may look nice, but the information they contain may be trivial, and inferences made on their contents are suspect. Some guidelines that can help you prepare high-quality learner portfolios follow:

- Identify the purpose of the learner portfolio. A portfolio is defined as a purposeful collection. It is not just a random storehouse. Keep in mind your purposes for your instruction. What is it that you are seeking to accomplish? Then consider the types of evidence you could use to reflect on the achievement of these important outcomes.

  Next consider whether you want the portfolio to be a working learner portfolio, a showcase learner portfolio, or a record-keeping learner portfolio (Gallagher, 1998). A working learner portfolio includes items that show the individual's growth over time and reveals both strengths and weaknesses. A *showcase learner portfolio* features only exhibits that reflect an individual's most notable accomplishments. A record-keeping learner portfolio is used to keep material that might be passed on to other teachers to help them understand the learner and design instruction to better meet the learner's needs.

- Decide on the contents. Because learner portfolios can contain a wide range of material, you need to exercise care to ensure that the portfolio's contents are useful. If this is not done, the end result may be examples that include much material that will be of little use when you attempt to evaluate learners' attainment of important outcomes. All items included in the learner portfolio should have a clear relationship to important outcomes.

  Stiggins (1997) suggests that the content should tell a story. A useful way to conceptualize a portfolio is to define a story line that you want to be able to follow. Guidelines can then be given to class members that will help them select representative material that best tells the story. It is important that enough items are included to enable you to make valid judgments.

- Prepare cover sheets describing categories of individual items. When students choose an item to include in their learner portfolios, they should be asked to assign the item to a particular category of information and to explain why they are including it. This helps evaluators and learners understand the importance and the meaning of the material. This is a useful step in making sure that learners reflect on their work and progress. If you provide students with cover sheets identifying categories of content to be included, they will have an easier time deciding what kinds of information to include and how to categorize individual materials.

- Identify criteria to be used in scoring a learner portfolio. Because so much material can be included in a portfolio and because items vary from portfolio to portfolio, evaluating a portfolio can be a challenge. To simplify this task and to avoid being influenced by extraneous variables such as attractiveness of presentation, you need to develop clear criteria to use as you review each portfolio. These criteria should be specific enough so that a group of individuals viewing a given learner portfolio will score it in the same way.

    As you consider scoring criteria, you should also think about how much weight you will give to specific entries. Some items will count more than others as you decide whether a learner has accomplished worthwhile learning outcomes. Deciding on how to weigh individual categories of information ahead of time will save you considerable frustration when it comes to actually reviewing learner portfolios and making decisions about the performances of members of your class.

In summary, portfolios can provide a rich array of information that will help you make sound judgments about individual learner performance. To be useful, they need to be carefully conceptualized and organized. If this is not the case, portfolios can become only a collection of items bearing little relationship to important learning outcomes. Read about one teacher's choice to incorporate portfolios as an assessment tool in this chapter's *Critical Incident* feature.

Critical Incident

The "Evils" of Portfolio Assessment

"Estelle, I need help." As he spoke these words, Garth Peterson, a second-year U.S. history teacher at Edison High School, grabbed a stool and pulled it up to the desk where Estelle Garza, head of the social studies department, busily organized some papers. The digital clock that just this year had replaced the venerable Waltham read 9:45 P.M. The open house had just ended, and the last parent was leaving the building.

Ms. Garza tucked a final set of materials into a file folder and slowly looked over to Garth. "Another preconception out the window, Garth? An unhappy parent? Someone with a lurking suspicion that you're spending 'all your time' with the kids who 'aren't motivated,' while denying your talents to their 'eminently qualified, dedicated, and hardworking' sons or daughters who are 'really going to amount to something'? So, what's up? I doubt you'll shock me."

"Estelle, it's about a parent, but the issue's not about my failure to give somebody a proper share of my time. It has to do with what I'm making the students do. To get to the point, Mrs. Hamlin, Stephanie's mom, is desperately anxious for Stephanie to get into an Ivy League school. She claims my evaluation procedures are insufficiently challenging and that I'm 'killing' Stephanie's chances to get the high SAT scores she'll need to impress the Ivy League admissions people."

Estelle gave Garth her noncommittal I'm-listening-and-keep-talking nod and said, "What's the nature of this precipitous fall from the heights of evaluative excellence we've all aspired to here at Edison? Come clean. What kinds of terrible things have you been up to?"

(continued)

(continued)

"Come on, Estelle, you know nobody's as concerned as I am that our people leave here with a solid grounding in history. The last thing I would do is back away from high academic standards. It's just that, what I see as a scheme to push the kids harder, Mrs. Hamlin sees as something fluffy, soft, and nonchallenging. It's depressing."

"Garth, *do* get to the point. Exactly what have you done?" Estelle looked wearily at her watch.

"I'm in trouble because of the 'p' word . . . *portfolios.* I'm having people in my class put a huge amount of effort into preparing portfolios. Incidentally these *do* include their grades on all the usual traditional kinds of tests. My people, including Stephanie, have done a great job putting materials together. They've written sophisticated reflections on what they have been doing and what they've learned. I think I'm pushing these students much harder than I did when my only evaluations were multiple-choice and essay tests."

"So what exactly is Mrs. Hamlin's worry?" asked Estelle, smiling and urging Garth to continue.

"I've had a hard time figuring that out. But sorting through everything she said, I think there are two or three things bothering her. First of all, she believes that taking traditional true-false, multiple-choice, and essay tests will be the best preparation for the SAT because those are the kinds of items Stephanie will encounter when she takes it. Her logic is that time spent doing the portfolios diverts Stephanie away from the task of developing good test-taking skills."

"OK, that's one concern. What else?"

"Here's another one," Garth replied. "Mrs. Hamlin worries about differences in portfolios prepared by individual students. She thinks this makes fair grading impossible because contents aren't the same. Stephanie has had good grades. These grades have come from her ability to score well on traditional tests. I think Mrs. Hamlin sees portfolio evaluation as a threat to Stephanie's final history grade . . . something that could lower her overall average and reduce the probability of her being admitted to a top university."

Estelle nodded. "Anything else?"

"One more thing. Mrs. Hamlin questions the value of having students spend time writing reflections on their own learning and including them in the portfolios. She says that high school students are too immature to engage in this kind of analysis. Again, I believe it comes back to her concern for SAT test scores. She's afraid that time spent on reflective writing takes time away from learning the 'facts' Stephanie should be working to master."

"Well, Garth," Estelle commented, "you seem to have a pretty good idea of what's bothering Mrs. Hamlin. What are you going to do now?"

1. *Should Garth be worried about Mrs. Hamlin's comments?*

2. *What do her concerns tell you about her values?*

3. *What do we learn about those of Garth?*

4. *Are differences in perspective between Garth and Mrs. Hamlin attributable to differences in their values?*

5. *If you were faced with this situation, what would be your next step?*

6. *Are there others who should be involved?*

7. *If so, who are they, and what roles should they play?*

Key Ideas in Summary

- Public concerns about the quality of the educational system require you to have a good understanding of assessment and assessment alternatives. A lack of knowledge about high-quality assessment procedures can lead you to collect flawed data and draw faulty conclusions about the performance of your learners. In addition, your teaching evaluations may be low if you fail to prepare your students for standardized tests.

- Assessment results provide information you can use to change your instructional practices in ways that lead to higher levels of learner motivation and achievement. You can make several important uses of assessment information. For example, you can use assessment results as the basis for adjusting instruction to learners' levels of readiness. You can also use this information as you plan an appropriate sequence of learning experiences for members of your class. As you teach, you can use periodic assessments as "reality checks" that will tell you if a lesson is appropriately designed or if you need to make some midcourse corrections. Finally, assessment results allow you to make summative evaluations at the conclusion of a block of instruction that will tell you what individual learners have taken away from their exposure to your instruction.

- *Assessment* refers to the broad process of collecting data from a variety of sources about what individuals have learned. *Measurement* refers to the process of quantifying the presence or absence of an attribute or quality. *Evaluation* is the process of making a judgment about what the data gathered through the various measurement and assessment processes means. *Grades* are communication devices you use to advise others of evaluation results.

- You typically will use one of two basic orientations as you make your evaluation decisions: (1) a *norm-referenced* approach or (2) a *criterion-referenced* approach. When you use a norm-referenced approach, you will compare the scores of individual learners against those of a group with similar characteristics. A criterion-referenced approach will enable you to compare scores of an individual learner against a standard or a set of criteria.

- Assessment activities comprise an integral part of your instructional responsibilities. You use *placement-assessment* information to help you determine an appropriate beginning point for instruction related to a new topic. For example, you may use a *pretest* as a means of determining learners' readiness for the new material. As instruction on a given topic goes forward, you will use *formative-assessment* techniques to periodically gather information that will tell you how well members of your class are learning the new material. You will use this information to modify your instructional program to accommodate class members' learning needs. You will use *summative assessments* to provide information about what knowledge and skills learners have acquired at the conclusion of a series of lessons or at the end of a school term.

- You need to make important decisions when you plan for assessment. Among other things, you need to (1) define your intended educational outcomes, (2) classify the educational outcomes you identify, and (3) develop criteria you will use as you make judgments related to the adequacy of learners' levels of achievement. Your plan should provide for adequate sampling of learner behavior or performance and include technically sound measurement tools that are appropriate for the outcomes being assessed. You also need to select fair and bias-free procedures.

- *Selected-response measures* are among the tools you may use to gather evaluation information about your learners. Measures of this type require your learners to choose answers from among several choices. Some examples are two-choice tests (e.g., true–false tests), multiple-choice tests, and matching tests.
- *Free-response measures* require students to generate their own responses rather than to select answers from a list of provided alternatives. Some examples include essay tests, short-answer tests, and oral tests.
- *Performance assessments* require members of your class to demonstrate new learning in contexts that closely parallel real-world settings. This approach to assessment is known by varying labels, including *authentic assessment, direct assessment,* and *product assessment.* Sometimes you will use tools such as checklists and rating scales to gather information related to assessments of this type.
- You may be interested in having your learners organize information about what they have learned in the form of a *learner portfolio.* A learner portfolio is a purposeful collection of products and performances that includes information related to the learner's effort, progress, or achievement. You can use portfolios to document learning and growth of individuals over time.

For Your Initial-Development Portfolio

1. What materials and ideas that you learned in this chapter about *assessing learners* will you include as "evidence" in your portfolio? Select up to three separate items of information. Number them 1, 2, and 3.
2. Think about why you selected these materials. As you do so, consider these issues:
   - Specific uses you might make of this information as you plan, deliver, and assess the impact of your teaching
   - The compatibility of the information with your own priorities and values
   - Any contributions this information can make to your development as a teacher
   - Factors that led you to include this information, as opposed to some alternatives you considered but rejected
3. Place a check in the chart below to indicate the INTASC standard(s) to which each of your items of information relates. (You may wish to refer to Chapter 1 for more detailed information about INTASC.)

ITEM OF EVIDENCE NUMBER	INTASC Standard Number									
	S1	S2	S3	S4	S5	S6	S7	S8	S9	S10
1										
2										
3										

4. Prepare a written reflection in which you analyze the decision-making process you followed. In your comments, mention the INTASC standard(s) to which your selected material relates.

Reflections

1. Today, assessment results that focus on learners' academic achievement often are used to compare schools (and sometimes teachers) to determine their effectiveness. Some critics of this use of assessment data argue that using learners' scores to make comparisons between schools and teachers tends to drive teachers away from schools that most need their help. This result occurs because teachers naturally seek employment in schools where learners traditionally have done well on standardized tests. The net effect is to decrease the quality of educational services delivered to learners in schools where test scores traditionally have been low. What are your reactions to this argument? If you believe learner scores on achievement tests should not be used as a basis for making comparisons among schools and teachers, what approach should be used to make these judgments?

2. An editorialist in a local newspaper recently made these comments:
   Despite additional money that has gone into the primary grades' reading program over the past five years, local pupils' scores continue to be unacceptably low. Fully 40% of our third graders scored below the national average. This simply is unacceptable. Community concern about reading was expressed to the school board five years ago when the issue of increased funding to improve reading instruction was debated. As a result, thousands of additional dollars were committed to fix the problem. The dismal test results are a painful disappointment given the actions, it had been hoped, this new money would support.

   • Under what circumstances would it be appropriate to regard these tests results as "dismal"?
   • Under what circumstances would it be appropriate to consider these tests as being "good" or even "excellent"?
   • If you were to write a letter to the editor in response to these comments, what would you say?

3. *Placement assessment* involves steps designed to help you determine an appropriate beginning point for your instruction. You need to learn something about learners' prior levels of understanding and attitudes to get an appropriate answer to the where-do-I-start question. When you have worked for a time with a given class, your observation of individual learners and records of their past performance will be good sources of placement-assessment information. You face a somewhat different situation at the beginning of the school year when you decide how to begin your initial lessons. What approaches might you take then to determine the appropriate instructional level?

4. The issue of grades and grading has long been a subject of debate within the education profession. Norm-referenced grading assumes that learners in your class have characteristics that are similar to the test group used to establish performance expectations. Criterion-referenced grading assumes that you have identified a preestablished standard of performance that has some grounding in reality. Grading based on individual improvement carries within it the possibility that you may give a high grade to a learner who has improved tremendously relative to where he or she began but who, even with this improvement, knows much less than others in your class.

   Preparing written comments about individual students instead of grades requires you to invest a huge block of time, particularly if you are teaching in a middle school or high school where you may teach more than 100 students each day. Think about the subjects and learners you will be teaching. What approach to grading will you take, and why?

5. *Selected-response measures* allow you to assess a wide range of content on a single test. However, these assessment measures generally are not well suited to providing information about learners' abilities to engage in higher-level thinking. *Free-response measures* require learners to prepare fairly lengthy responses to individual questions. As a result, a single free-response test ordinarily cannot cover a wide range of content. On the other hand, tests of this type do allow you to engage learners' higher-level thinking skills. In preparing a large examination that might include a mixture of selected-response items and free-response items, how will you decide which elements of content will be assessed by each type?

Field Experiences, Projects, and Enrichment

1. Make a collection of newspaper and magazine articles that relate to assessment of learner achievement. What types of measures are mentioned? How are the results being used? Are any criticisms of these procedures mentioned? If so, what are they, and who are the people who are making them? What consequences, if any, are reported for schools and teachers with learners whose scores are low?

2. Visit a local school. Identify the standardized tests that are used to measure learner achievement in the district. Interview teachers who must administer these tests. Ask them to describe strengths and weaknesses of these assessments. Gather information related to how these tests influence these teachers' instructional programs. Ask them whether they sense any pressure to improve learners' performances on these tests. If such pressure exists, does this represent a change from conditions in past years?

3. Identify some learning outcomes for a subject that interests you. Identify some examples of appropriate measurement tools for each of the outcomes. Describe your reasons for your selection of these approaches.

4. Gather some tests that either have been used or are suggested for use in the classroom (they may even be tests you have taken). Look at the included items. Do they provide an adequate sample of the content? Which outcomes are measured? Are the items clearly written? How might you improve these tests?

5. Enter the term *portfolio* into a search engine such as Google (http://www.google.com). Gather information about how portfolios for elementary, middle school, and senior high school learners are formatted. Prepare a report for your class in which you share some examples, paying particular attention to categories of information that are used and criteria that are employed to assess overall portfolio quality.

References

Armstrong, D. G. (2003). *Curriculum today*. Upper Saddle River, NJ: Merrill/Prentice Hall.

Bloom, B. S., Englehart, M. D., Furst, E. J., Hill, W. H., & Krathwohl, D. R. (1956). *Taxonomy of educational objectives: Handbook 1, Cognitive domain*. New York: Mckay.

Ferguson, R. F. (1998). Can schools narrow the black–white test gap? In C. Jenks & M. Phillips (Eds.), *The black–white test core gap* (pp. 318–374). Washington, DC: Brookings Institution.

Gallagher, J. D. (1998). *Classroom assessment for teachers*. Upper Saddle River, NJ: Merrill.

Gronlund, N. E. (1998). *Assessment of student achievement* (6th ed.). Boston: Allyn & Bacon.

Krathwohl, D. R., Bloom, B. S., & Masia, B. B. (1964). *Taxonomy of educational objectives: Handbook II: Affective domain*. New York: Mckay.

Marzano, R. J. (2001). *Designing a new taxonomy of educational objectives.* Thousand Oaks, CA: Corwin Press.

Popham, J. (2001). The Truth About Testing! An educator's call to action. Alexandria, VA: Association supervision and curriculum development.

Stiggins, R. J. (1997). *Student-centered classroom assessment* (2nd ed.). Upper Saddle River, NJ: Merrill.

Stiggins, R. J., Arter, J. A., Chappuis, J., and Chappuis, S. (2004). *Classroom assessment and student learning.* Portland, OR: Assessment Training Institute, Inc.

Tanner, D. E. (2001). *Assessing academic achievement.* Boston: Allyn & Bacon.

Tomlinson, C. A. (2001). Grading for success. *Educational Leadership, 58*(6), 12–15.

FORCES SHAPING EDUCATIONAL POLICIES AND PRACTICES

CHAPTER 8

HOW DID WE GET HERE?

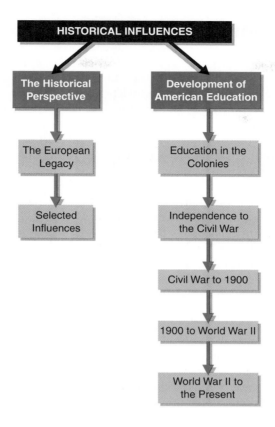

HISTORICAL INFLUENCES

- The Historical Perspective
  - The European Legacy
  - Selected Influences
- Development of American Education
  - Education in the Colonies
  - Independence to the Civil War
  - Civil War to 1900
  - 1900 to World War II
  - World War II to the Present

OBJECTIVES

This chapter will help you to

- recognize that historians' perspectives affect written history.
- explain why some critics argue that American education has not always developed in ways that have advantaged *all* learners.
- cite examples of practices in today's schools derived from European precedents.
- identify patterns of American education as they developed in the colonial period and years of the early republic.

- summarize key 19th-century developments that helped shape today's American education.
- describe important developments in the evolution of 20th-century American education.
- explain that personal histories of learners coming from certain cultural traditions can affect their attitudes toward school.

◆   ◆   ◆   ◆

INTRODUCTION

No matter where you go in the United States, from the snowy mountains of Colorado to the warm paradise of Hawaii, you will find public schools. In spite of the socioeconomic and ethnic composition of the student populations, you will find great similarities. Adlai Stevenson, a politician and one-time candidate for president, once proclaimed the free common school system as the most American thing about America (Tyack, 2001). Over time, the citizens of the United States have developed the most universal and popular system of education. They have come to view education as a public good that is essential to the health of the nation (Tyack, 2001).

How did this happen? Many choices had to be made. The educational system of the United States could have developed in a very different direction. Many varied controversies and choices could have been made. And so it is today. Several pathways can be chosen and some critics claim that the contemporary educational system is broken and needs fundamental change. Tyack (2001) claims that the politics of education is more complicated than it has ever been. He contends that some critics are placing a new spin on the concept of democracy through the application of market principles such as choice and competition. He asks the question: "Is education primarily a consumer good or a common good?" (p. 8).

Has education lost its way? Are proposed reforms challenging basic principles and leading education in a dangerous direction? Some critics complain that educational change is much like a swinging pendulum that moves from one pole to another rather than moving forward. If it is true that we have lost our way and that educational change is little more than a swinging pendulum influenced by the rhetoric of whatever group is currently in power, perhaps it is because we have forgotten the past. Some who defend the study of history contend that those who do not know history will repeat the mistakes of the past. This certainly can be applied to education.

The study of the history of education can help us understand why certain practices have evolved over time. It can help us understand the controversies that have faced educational leaders in the past and the choices they made. This understanding can help us understand current controversies, which can help us choose among competing proposals. The study of history can help us uncover practices that have been successful and those that have not. This does not mean simply because something was successful in the past that it should be continued or that because something was unsuccessful in the past that it should be permanently discarded.

Some educational practices and traditions have developed in response to a specific need or issue that is no longer relevant. For example, the school calendar was developed around the needs of rural America and an agrarian society. Another example is that past definitions of the curriculum and a definition of "the basics" were based on the needs of society at that time. The current needs of society are quite different so the definition of "the basics" might be quite different.

What Do You Think?

- What might be some educational practices and traditions that are no longer responsive to the needs of society?
- How would you define what is "basic" for the 21st century?

The history of education is complex and does not offer simple answers to contemporary issues. However, it does provide a context and case studies that can help us evaluate current educational practices and proposals for change. When reviewing history, we need to consider why a particular educational practice was established. Does that practice still meet a need? As proposals for change are put forward, we need to consider if that proposal meets new needs or if it is something that will take us in directions that are inconsistent with our deeply held values. A basic purpose for the study of the history of education is that it provides a rich understanding of the issues we need to consider as we make decisions about change and the future.

THE HISTORICAL PERSPECTIVE

Beginning the study of the history of American education requires that you have an understanding about historical perspective. The usefulness of history in understanding issues is often limited by an inadequate understanding of history. What is history? History is frequently defined as everything that has happened in the past. Although this may be technically true, it is of limited usefulness. The amount of information about even relatively small events in history is so vast that trying to learn "everything that happened in the past" is impossible.

The histories we read are written by historians. Historians must sort through data and select what they view as significant as they attempt to put together the "story" of the past. Thus, the purposes and the biases of historians influence the information they select and the conclusions they draw. What this means is that there is not just one story but many. There is not just one historical story but many. There are many stories about education that can be told and alternative conclusions that can be drawn. Therefore, it is the responsibility of the reader to question the assumptions and the data of the historian. Readers should critically analyze what is included in the story and why. This is certainly the case as you review the history of education in the United States.

One example that many current advocates of change have claimed is that educational quality has seriously declined in recent years and drastic change is necessary. As evidence, they may present examples of sophisticated passages drawn from old reading books or present examples of well-crafted student writing. Comparing these early examples of student performance to the "average" student in the contemporary classroom certainly seems to indicate that performance has declined.

But what data are overlooked? First, we should determine if the students who used these books and wrote these passages were typical of their age. A century ago less than half of the age-eligible students were actually enrolled in schools and most left by the eighth grade. Whole segments of the population, such as Native Americans, African Americans, women, and individuals with disabilities, were denied educational opportunities. There is a very real possibility that the examples chosen were not typical of the education level of the students at that time.

A second question that should be addressed is what data might have been omitted in drawing the conclusion of decline? For example, what are we to make of information indicating that average IQ scores have steadily risen over the century? How do we account for the fact that even young students today are engaged in sophisticated computer applications that only a decade or so ago were reserved for a few university students? How do we explain data indicating that, even with a much more diverse student population, average student scores on comparable tests are at least as high, or higher, than those of students just a generation ago?

When studying the history of education, we might keep in mind the program of popular radio personality Paul Harvey entitled, "And, now, for the rest of the story." Those who seek to make education their profession and who wish to respond to current controversies must be prepared to search for and relate the rest of the story.

We need to remember that some stories have not have been fully told. Although we read about education for one segment of the population, what stories have not been told? What were the stories of Native Americans, African Americans, Latinos, women, immigrants, and those with special needs? When you read historical accounts, focus on more than a simple recitation of past events. Look for the untold or even distorted accounts by looking at the purposes and the biases of those telling the story.

Many of the stories of American education tell the story of the dominant group. You are getting a perspective that reflects many of the biases of the majority of Americans, who are white and of European descent. People with this point of view accept both the general "goodness" of the basic organization of education in this country and the legitimacy of the majority political power that has developed and maintained many long-standing school practices.

You will find analysis of this issue to be tricky. It is not that American educators for many years have failed to embrace the idea of serving all children. Rather, it is a question of how much their practices have benefited young people from different groups. In general, school practices have provided more benefits to learners when they have been consistent with the priorities and values learners bring with them from home. Children from the majority white culture often have found the school world to be a logical extension of the values and perspectives prized in their own families. On the other hand, young people from ethnic and cultural minorities have sometimes found a jarring discontinuity between the expectations of their parents and families and the expectations of the school.

What Do You Think?

- What is your response to the assertion that schools are failing?
- Do you think schools have been responsive to the needs of all groups in society?

Even though today you will find schools more sensitive to this problem than they have been in the past, many learners from ethnic and cultural minorities still do not do as well in school as their white-majority classmates. Increasingly, educators are coming to understand that "no child should have to go through the painful dilemma of choosing between family and school and of what inevitably becomes a choice between belonging and succeeding" (Nieto, 1992, p. xxv). For example, think about how Native American youngsters must have felt not many years ago when the only textbook references to them mentioned "savages" who were obstacles to development and progress.

Educational historians point out that sensitivity to ethnic and cultural differences is new. Throughout the 19th century and well into the 20th, individuals responsible for schools and school programs largely supported the idea that the white-majority European-based culture was the "true" American culture; it was the task of all learners to conform to its perspectives. "Good" schools were not designed to respond to cultural differences. They were supposed to root them out and turn children from minority groups into "real" Americans (Coleman, 1993).

As an example of this point of view, consider this statement from the 1888 annual report for a special residential school for Native Americans in which the school's superintendent lamented the negative influences on the school's children when, occasionally, they had to be allowed to go home to visit their families:

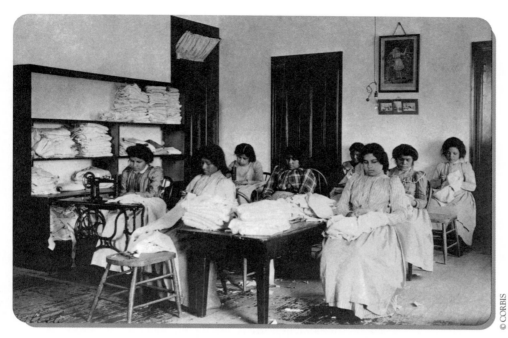

© CORBIS

Attempts to "Americanize" Native American students led to the creation of boarding schools far away from their homes.

Children leaving even the best training schools for their homes, like the swine, return to their wallowing filth and barbarism. (Commissioner of Indian Affairs, 1888)

As you might imagine, when such attitudes prevailed, there was little support for the idea that school programs should be responsive to learners' ethnic and cultural differences. Schools *could* have modified some practices to accommodate cultural and ethnic differences years ago. For example, public schools could have adapted some existing educational models that were well suited to serving children from Native American groups. There were also educational legacies from Africa, Asia, and the Hispanic world that might have been considered. Such models *were* known. Regrettably, for decades educational leaders considered them irrelevant. As a result, for many years American education developed under the assumption that "proper" and "correct" education derived from European practices (Reagan, 2000).

The sections of this chapter that follow are not intended to suggest that modeling American education on European practices was the only course that could have been taken or even that it was the most appropriate. The reality simply is that the structure of today's educational enterprise finds its roots in traditions from Europe.

As you may know, school populations today are more ethnically and culturally diverse than they have ever been (Armstrong, 2003). As a result, educators are working hard to develop school programs that are responsive to the needs of all. These reforms are being inserted into an American school system that historically did not hold responding to cultural diversity as a high priority. You can better understand challenges that accompany these change efforts if you are familiar with the historical developments that have shaped the American system.

The European Legacy

Few deny that our schools derive many practices from Europe. There is more debate today about how well these traditional models have served all learners. In particular, you will find that contemporary historical scholarship increasingly questions whether schools have adequately responded to the special needs of young people from ethnic and cultural minorities.

Many school practices are so familiar that you may find it hard to imagine different ways of doing things. Many of your assumptions about schools and schooling reflect long-standing cultural choices. For example, chances are you've never worried excessively about any of the following characteristics of American education:

- The idea that content should be organized under major categories or headings
- The idea that knowledge should be divided among individual subjects
- The idea that teaching should occur in a setting that brings young people together in groups for instructional purposes
- The idea that schools should be organized into a sequence of grades
- The idea that as many people as possible should be educated
- The idea that teachers should consider individual differences when planning instruction
- The idea that schools should help learners develop rational thinking processes
- The idea that teachers should have some kind of specialized training
- The idea that schooling should be a preparation for responsible citizenship
- The idea that schooling should provide young people with some understandings and skills needed in the adult workplace

Where did these ideas come from? For the most part, they evolved over the centuries from educational practices in Europe. The thinkers of ancient Greece, for example, developed the idea that knowledge could be organized into categories and that logical, rational thinking processes were important. The emphasis on education for citizenship likewise has roots in the concern of the ancient Athenians about producing adult citizens who could participate in democratic decision making.

Origins of Selected Influences

The ancient Romans wanted young people to receive a practical education that would provide them with "useful" knowledge. This perspective is one that many present-day Americans share. The Romans, too, argued about whether students should be harshly punished or whether gentler, more sensitive approaches made better sense.

The Middle Ages witnessed the development of important work that divided knowledge into individual subject areas. The tradition of churches taking responsibility for secular education also traces to this period. American parochial schools continue this legacy.

Today's concern for universal education is a continuation of a trend that

---

Web Extension 8–1

What Every Schoolboy Knows

At this site you will find topics dealing with education in Elizabethan England. There is information about differences in education for girls and boys and for children from different classes in English society. There is an interesting description of subjects a son of a noble might have been taught during each hour of the instructional day.

http://renaissance.dm.net/compendium/54.html

became pronounced during the Reformation. Many church leaders believed that the Bible was the repository of all wisdom; hence, it was desirable for all to learn to read so they might have access to its truths. Later, during the Renaissance, a growing emphasis on the worth and the importance of the individual evolved. Our schools' concern for meeting individual differences developed from this perspective.

In the early 17th century, the work of Francis Bacon (1561–1626) helped to establish the idea that truth could be challenged and modified through observation and careful weighing of evidence. This provided the foundation for the modern scientific method, something that continues to be enormously important in today's schools. Another person who had a great influence on the development of education in Europe and, later, the United States, was John Amos Comenius (1592–1670). Comenius promoted the ideas of organizing learning into sequential, graded schools and of viewing education as something that should prepare people for happy lives.

The famous 18th-century educator Johann Heinrich Pestalozzi (1746–1827) suggested that education should take place in a caring atmosphere and should function as an agent to improve society. The view that education could promote social improvement was considered radical in Pestalozzi's time; today it has become an article of faith among many Americans. No matter what intractable social problem is garnering headlines at a given moment, one predictable response to the problem is that more education is needed. Pestalozzi would have agreed. Pestalozzi also introduced the idea that teachers should be provided with special training.

During the 19th century, a wave of interest in many aspects of education swept across Europe. One result was that, by the end of the century, mandatory public schooling had been adopted as public policy throughout much of the continent. Friedrich Froebel (1782–1852), who is regarded as the "father of the kindergarten," worked hard to convince people that they should support efforts to provide young children with well-planned educational experiences. The 19th-century educator Johann Friedrich Herbart (1776–1841) developed a standardized format for lesson planning. Lesson plans you will use probably will include many features initially introduced in Herbart's design. The 19th century also witnessed a tremendous growth of interest in the importance of the psychology of learning.

DEVELOPMENT OF AMERICAN EDUCATION

If you review American educational history, you will discover that, at different times, people have had a range of expectations regarding what schools should emphasize. Varying expectations have led to divergent views regarding the characteristics of a good school. Educational policymakers have responded in different ways to these key questions:

- What is the most important purpose of education?
- Who is to be educated?
- What are learners expected to take away from their educational experiences?
- How are learners to be educated?

An understanding of how responses to these questions have changed over time will help you better understand conflicting views represented in today's debates about educational policies and practices.

Education in the Colonies

Several stories can be told about education in early America. Among those are the stories of Native Americans, New England Colonies, the Middle Colonies, and the Southern Colonies. Each of these stories gives a different perspective on the development of education in America.

Native Americans

One story of education that is seldom told is that of Native American education. As noted earlier, the European view of Native Americans was often that of barbaric and uneducated savages. However, this generalization is not an accurate depiction of reality.

There were diverse and rich Native American cultures in existence at the time of the arrival of the first European settlers. It is estimated that there were about 2,000 different languages spoken by Native Americans (Altenbaugh, 2002). There were relatively sophisticated economic and cultural systems such as the Hopis and Zunis in the Southwest, the Iroquois Federation in the Northeast, and the Cherokees in the Southeast. These cultures had to have some sort of an educational process in order to survive.

Although there was great diversity between tribes, there were some common educational elements. They had some clear educational goals and practices. Tribes emphasized values such as courage, generosity, obedience, cooperation, diligence, and respect. They had a deep respect for childhood and usually avoided harshness and physical punishment. A common method of disciplining children was through public humiliation. Others, such as the Hopis and their use of the Ogre Kachina, used stories of supernatural creatures carrying away naughty children as a discipline tool (Altenbaugh, 2002).

The educational process was generally informal but systematic. It emphasized learning through experience and imitation and used the tradition of storytelling to convey values and beliefs. Education was a community responsibility as well as that of the nuclear family (Altenbaugh, 2002).

Some Native American groups adopted the educational traditions of the colonists. For example, between 1778 and 1871, the United States government signed almost 400 treaties with Native American groups. Most of these contained educational provisions and the promise of education was used to persuade many tribes to give up land. One Cherokee noted they supported education because "We want our children to learn English so the white man cannot cheat us" (Cremin, 1980, pp. 234–237).

Three types of Native American schools emerged. There were tribal neighborhood schools, tribal boarding schools, and schools that were operated by religious organizations or private individuals. In fact, the "Five Civilized Tribes" that were removed to Indian Territory by President Andrew Jackson developed successful education systems. For example, it is reported that the Cherokee Nation had a better school system than the neighboring states of Arkansas and Missouri. The Chickasaw Nation was reported by observers to have the best school system west of the Mississippi (Peavy & Smith, 1999, p. 16).

However, control of Native American schools was turned over to the Bureau of Indian Affairs in 1870. The purpose of this change of control was to eradicate Native American religion, language, and heritage. It was predicted that this process of assimilation would take about 20 years (Altenbaugh, 2002).

One of the patterns of Native American education that emerged was the off-reservation boarding school for secondary education. There were reservation day schools for elementary education that became feeder schools for the boarding schools. The commissioner of education noted that the boarding schools were the first stage of the assimilation process because it separated the students from the influences of their family. One commissioner stated that boarding schools "will exterminate the Indian but develop the man" (Altenbaugh, 2002).

The practice of off-reservation boarding schools proved to be a failure. Parents who supported education resisted the concept of acculturation and the cruelty that students often experienced at boarding schools. For example, children on the Navajo reservation were hunted by posses and were roped like cattle and taken away from their parents (Adams, 1995).

Conditions at the boarding school were often poor with several students occupying a single bed. There was poor sanitation and poor nutrition. Children often resisted the efforts of the schools and often ran away. Graduation rates were low and it was acknowledged after 1900 that the schools were a failure.

In summary, the story of Native American education is not a positive one. The dropout rate of Native American students continues to be higher than for any other group. Underachievement and absenteeism continue to be persistent problems. Perhaps this situation might have been different if different choices had been made and the first successful models of education had been allowed to continue and flourish.

What Do You Think?

- Do you think that different responses to Native Americans would have prevented some of the current problems?
- How would you characterize the story of Native American education?

The New England Colonies

Another story that can be told from the history of early American education is that of the New England Colonies. This story is deeply influenced by the prior experience of Puritans and their values and beliefs. The educational story of the New England Colonies indicates that it developed into the most formal system of education.

Some familiarity with conditions in 16th- and 17th-century England will help you understand the nature of American education as it developed in New England during the colonial period. In England during this period, there was little room for open discussion of alternatives to the established church, the Church of England. Because it was the official church of the English government, governmental officials considered people who espoused religious views in opposition to those of the Church of England to be disloyal not only to the church, but also to the state. In effect, the Church of England was seen as the religious arm of the government. Religious dissenters received harsh treatment. Governmental officials saw such people as potential threats to the power of the crown.

Political problems in England for groups such as the Puritans, who wanted to reform the policies of the Church of England, led them to consider moving to the New World. They also feared remaining in England and exposing their children to what they considered to be the religious errors of the Church of England. The Puritans who settled in New England sought to establish a church and government different from those they had left behind. Their belief that their own church and government were more consistent with the Bible's teachings had important educational implications. Because of their suspicion of centralized government, the family was the fundamental unit in Puritan society. The commandment to "honor thy father and mother" was taken quite seriously and in 1649 the Massachusetts General Court issued a law that condemned to death any son over sixteen who was "stubborn or rebellious" (Altenbaugh, 2002).

The Puritans saw the Bible as the source of all wisdom. As a result, they placed a high priority on literacy so that believers could seek the wisdom of "God's Holy Word." This focus established a clear educational relationship between education, the family, and the church. These beliefs helped establish the tradition of local control.

However, all was not well. Puritan families did not always fulfill their educational responsibilities. This concern was addressed in the **Massachusetts School Law of 1642**. This law charged local magistrates with the responsibility of ensuring that parents would not neglect the education of their children. Although the law itself did not provide for the establishment of schools, it did establish education as an endeavor that had important consequences for the whole community and gave power to local officials to levy fines on those who neglected the education of their children (Altenbaugh, 2002).

However, giving families this responsibility did not work well. Five years later, the famous "Old Deluder Satan Act" of 1647 extended educational requirements of the Massachusetts School Law of 1642. The name by which the law is popularly known derives from wording in the act that promoted education as a buffer against Satan's wiles. The law required every town of 50 or more families to hire a teacher of reading or writing. The teacher was to be paid by either the community or parents of the learners. This act signaled a move for the community to assume more responsibility for the education of the young.

Dame Schools.   One organization that began to assume responsibility for the education of the young were "dame schools." These were schools that were operated by a local woman, often a widow, who cared for children as young as two and taught them basic literacy. The dame schools had a basic curriculum that stressed the alphabet, some simple spelling, and some religious training. The boys might be taught some simple arithmetic and the girls learned how to knit and sew (Altenbaugh, 2002).

This type of education seemed to work well in a largely rural society where modest levels of education were required in the world of work. However, as history indicates, change is constant. As cities began to grow, immigration increased, and economic power began to shift toward cities, this largely informal educational system was insufficient. As political and economic tensions between the colonies and England began to increase, newspapers and political pamphlets encouraged higher levels of literacy for a broader spectrum of the population (Kaestle, 2001).

During the 17th century, concern for publicly supported education referred only to the very basic education of young children; few learners attended secondary schools. However, small numbers of secondary schools did come into being during this time. One of the most famous was the **Boston Latin Grammar School,** founded in 1635. This school had a specific purpose: preparation of boys for Harvard. The curriculum consisted of difficult academic subjects, including Latin, Greek, and theology.

The Middle Colonies

Another story is that of the Middle Colonies. The settlers who came to this region of the Atlantic Coast came from a very different tradition than that of the Puritans. People who settled the Middle Colonies of New York, New Jersey, Delaware, and Pennsylvania, however, came from different parts of England than the Puritans, and they were a more diverse group. These immigrants came mostly from the northern Midlands of England and Wales. Some of these settlers were descendants of the Dutch and Swedes who originally occupied parts of New York. Many English Quakers came to the New World between 1675 and 1725, and a majority of them settled in Pennsylvania. People originally from the north of England, Scotland, and Ireland settled western and frontier areas of the Middle Colonies during a period extending approximately from 1717 to 1775 (Fischer, 1989).

Not surprisingly, given the mixed origins of the population, patterns of schooling in the Middle Colonies were varied. For example, merchants in New York sponsored private schools that emphasized commercial subjects thought necessary for young people who would pursue business and trade. In contrast, the Pennsylvania Quakers maintained schools that were open to all children. These Quaker schools were notable for their willingness to recognize the educational needs and rights of African Americans, Native Americans, and other groups who usually were not encouraged (and often not allowed) to go to school.

Benjamin Franklin was among the first to give American education a practical orientation. In his 1749 work, **Proposals Relating to the Youth of Pennsylvania,** Franklin proposed a new kind of school, oriented to the "real" world, that would be free of all religious ties. Two years later, he established the **Franklin Academy,** an institution that was nonsectarian and offered such practical subjects as mathematics, astronomy, navigation, and bookkeeping. By the end of the Revolutionary War, the Franklin Academy had replaced the Boston Latin Grammar School as the most important secondary school in America. Students at the Franklin Academy had the right to make some choices about their courses of study, thus setting the pattern of elective courses common in high schools today.

For all its strengths, relatively few learners attended the Franklin Academy. It was a private school, and tuition was beyond the means of most families. However, the establishment of the Franklin Academy directed a great deal of attention to the importance of secondary education. This interest was reflected in the subsequent establishment of many other private **academies.**

The private academies popularized the idea that secondary education had something important to offer, and they laid the foundation for public support of secondary schools. Collectively, the academies helped establish the following important precedents for American education:

- American education would have a strong orientation toward the practical rather than the purely intellectual or theoretical.
- American education would be nonsectarian.
- American education would feature diverse course offerings.

The Southern Colonies

Yet another story of education is that of the Southern Colonies. A revolution in England in the late 1640s resulted in victory for the side supporting Parliament and the Puritans against the king and the established Church of England. King Charles I was executed. For a dozen years England existed as a Puritan-controlled commonwealth, governed for much of this time by Oliver Cromwell as Lord Protector. This was an especially dangerous period for large landowners, members of the nobility, and others who had supported King Charles and wanted the monarchy restored (something that was finally achieved in 1660, when Charles II assumed the throne).

Because of dangers in England, many supporters of the king's cause migrated to the New World, often settling in the Southern Colonies of Maryland, Virginia, North Carolina, South Carolina, and Georgia. Large numbers of these settlers came from the southwestern part of England, an area different from both the East Anglican homeland of the Puritans and the northern Midland, northern English, Scottish, and Irish homelands of most of those who settled the Middle Colonies (Fischer, 1989). As can be predicted, the values and beliefs of the settlers in this part of the Atlantic Coast were far different from those of the Puritans in New England.

Settlements in the Southern Colonies were distributed along rivers. There were few towns, and most families were separated by considerable distances. Under these conditions, it was difficult to gather sufficient numbers of children in one place to establish schools. Wealthy families hired tutors for their children. People in these colonies continued to identify strongly with upper-class English values. Many sent their sons to England to be educated in English schools. Education in these colonies was generally restricted to children of wealthy landowners; little schooling was available for children from less-affluent families.

What Do You Think?

- What patterns established in the early years of our nation still persist?
- How do you account for the differences in the way different colonies responded to education?

Independence to the Civil War

For the first years of the United States' existence as an independent country, few educational innovations were introduced. The nation faced challenges such as defending its independent status from outside threats, settling the nation, and providing workers for growing industries. There was more interest in getting young people into the workforce than in providing them with extensive education. Schooling beyond rudimentary elementary instruction was generally available only to children of families who were able to pay for this privilege and who did not need the income that a young person could generate. Proposals for an educational system that was universal and free were just beginning to be discussed. Neglect of education for the slaves and African Americans developed a heritage that continues to influence education.

Web Extension 8–2

Colonial Period

At this site you will find numerous links to topics associated with education during colonial times, including Puritan theology and its influences on education, hornbooks, the dame school, the *New England Primer*, the role of apprenticeship in education, the Latin Grammar School, and educational practices in the three major groupings of colonies (New England, Middle, and Southern). Included also are photographs and other visual depictions of selected items of interest.

http://www.nd.edu/%7Erbarger/www7/colonial.html

Developments in Secondary Education

In the early 19th century, only a few students attended secondary schools. The most popular secondary school continued to be the academy, which responded well to an American educational bias in favor of preparing learners for practical problem solving and work rather than for a life of scholarship. Many new academies were established during the first half of the century. By 1850, when the number of academies reached its peak, over 6,000 were in operation (Barry, 1961).

Although the academies had good reputations, they had an important drawback. Overwhelmingly, they were private tuition-charging institutions. This limited their enrollment because only young people from relatively well-off families could attend. Gradually, people became convinced that larger numbers of young people than were being accommodated by the private academies could profit from secondary-level education. This recognition led to support for a new institution: the public high school.

The first public high school, the **Boston English Classical School,** was established in 1821. The school's courses closely paralleled the practical curriculum of most academies. The idea of public high schools did not catch on quickly, however. In 1860, there were only 40 public high schools in the entire country (Barry, 1961), but by 1900 they outnumbered the academies.

The Work of Horace Mann

During the 1820s, a leading figure in the development of American education, Horace Mann (1796–1859), began to make his views known. Mann, elected to the Massachusetts legislature in 1827, was an eloquent speaker who took up the cause of the **common school,** one for the average American. Mann's mission was to convince taxpayers that it was in their own interest to support the establishment of a system of public education. He pointed out that public schools would graduate students whose skills would ultimately improve living standards for all. In Mann's view, the school was a springboard for opportunity. It was an institution capable of equalizing differences among people from different social classes.

Mann's arguments were persuasive. In 1837, Massachusetts established a State Board of Education. Horace Mann gave up his career in politics to become its first secretary. In time, Mann's views attracted the attention of people throughout the entire country.

In addition to his interest in encouraging people to support public schools, Mann also recognized the importance of improving teachers' qualifications. In response to this concern, the nation's first **normal school** (an institution specifically designed to prepare people for careers as teachers) was established in 1839. In the beginning, normal schools provided only one or two years of formal education. Their importance is the precedent they set for formalizing the education of future teachers.

Prompted by Mann's work, public schools began to be established throughout the country. By 1860, 50.6% of the nation's children were enrolled in public school programs (U.S. Department of Commerce, 1975). A majority of states had formalized the development of free school systems, including elementary schools, secondary schools, and public universities. In 1867, a National Department of Education was established as part of the federal government.

Courtesy of the Library of Congress

Horace Mann helped convince American taxpayers that it was in their best interests to support public schools.

Courtesy of the Library of Congress

Interiors of many schools in the late 19th century were very plain. Note the total absence of decoration in this classroom.

By the late 1860s, many of the basic patterns of American education were in place. That these patterns continue is a tribute to the vision, patience, and political skills of Horace Mann.

What Do You Think?

- Today there seem to be challenges to some of the basic principles of public schools. Do you think there should be more invested in developing alternatives to the public schools?
- Do you think that Mann's contention that the public schools would be a great equalizer to overcome differences in social class has been validated?

Civil War to 1900

The post–Civil War years witnessed unparalleled industrial growth. Technological innovations reduced the need for unskilled labor. The resulting demand for workers with knowledge needed in the workplace intensified interest in vocational education.

Huge numbers of immigrants entered the United States during this period. These people required both useful work skills and an orientation to the values of their new country. These needs placed new demands on educators, and there was a great increase in the number of schools. The schools were eager to "Americanize" newcomers, and many immigrant learners were exposed to school programs that made light of their native cultures and languages. There can be no doubt that American public schools exacted a psychological toll on many immigrant children.

To finance public schools, the famous **Kalamazoo case** (*Stuart v. School District No. 1 of the Village of Kalamazoo*, 1874) ruled that the state legislature had the right to pass laws levying taxes for the support of *both* elementary and secondary schools. This ruling established a legal precedent for public funding of secondary schools. As a result, secondary school enrollments increased as school districts began building many more high schools. Because of a widespread desire to provide older learners with "useful" educational experiences, many secondary schools broadened their curricula to include more practical, work-related subjects.

Organizational activity among teachers increased during this period. Prior to 1900, organizations that were the forerunners of today's American Federation of Teachers and National Education Association were established (see Chapter 2 for more information about these groups). Reports of such groups as the NEA's Committee of Ten (1892) and the Committee on College Entrance Requirements (1900) began to influence public school curricula. In the

Schools of a century ago were often crowded and held in poor classrooms.

last decade of the 19th century, these groups acknowledged that schools should provide some services to learners with varied academic and career goals.

However, they continued to assert that the primary purpose of high schools was to prepare students for college and university study. This orientation represented a temporary reversal of a century-long trend to view secondary education as a provider of more practical kinds of learning experiences.

African American Education

Another story that is seldom told is that of African American education. During the slavery era, plantation owners had two goals. They wanted slaves to develop work skills while they exercised social control. They wanted slaves to have awe and respect for the plantation owner (Webber, 1978). To accomplish these purposes they relied on illiteracy and ignorance. Anti-literacy bills were passed by South Carolina and Georgia as early as 1740 and 1770. Local laws were also developed that sometimes made it a crime to sell writing material to slaves (Webber, 1978).

Education for African Americans in the north also left a lot to be desired. African American students were often excluded from the public schools, so separate schools were established for them. Legislation in many northern states established segregated schools. The rationalization was that African American students needed only the bare minimum of an education because they possessed limited intellectual ability. Horace Mann declared that the intellect of the blacks was inferior to that of the whites (Kaestle, 1983). Even some African American parents had concerns about an integrated education. Some felt like their students would be at a disadvantage in competing with wealthier, white children. Others questioned what kind of an education their children would receive from a white teacher (Kaestle, 2001).

In 1846 a group of African Americans petitioned the Boston School Committee to integrate the schools. The committee claimed that their "peculiar" mental and physical characteristics required a different education (Kaestle, 2001). This was turned into a court case that was unsuccessful in promoting integration. However, in 1855 a state law was passed that abolished segregation of Massachusetts schools. This chapter's *Video Viewpoints* feature introduces you to the pioneers of the school integration movement.

Video Viewpoints 8–1

The Reunion

WATCH: This *ABC News Special Report* from August 2004 is a reunion of individuals who started school in 1960 and were pioneers in the school integration movement. It includes both black and white students.

THINK: Discuss with your classmates or write in your reflective journal your responses to the following questions:

1. Would you judge this "social experiment" to have been successful?
2. What are the lessons you think can be learned from this experiment that can be transferred to other places?
3. What are some of the subtle ways that black students were discouraged from excelling?

LINK: What did you learn about integration from this segment that you can take with you into teaching?

 To view this video, go to the Video Viewpoints DVD and click on this chapter's video: "The Reunion."

After the Civil War, there was a great interest in the education of African-Americans students.

At the end of the Civil war in 1865, four million slaves were now free. Booker T. Washington described the situation as an entire race trying to go to school. Some exslaves opened Sabbath schools designed to provide an elementary education. However, in the post-Civil War period, the South was unreceptive to the education of African Americans and most of the northern states continued the practice of segregated education (Altenbaugh, 2002). In spite of barriers designed to discourage African American education, they retained their faith in education. In 1890 in St. Louis, a larger percentage of the African American population was attending school than the white population (Altenbaugh, 2002). In 1896 the *Plessy v. Ferguson* upheld the "separate but equal" doctrine that continued segregated schools as the dominant pattern of education until the famous *Brown v. Board of Education of Topeka* in 1954.

◆ ◆

Desegregation Today
Go to MyEducationLab and select the topic "History of Education." Read the article "Beyond *Brown*" to learn about contemporary issues and problems in implementing *Brown v. Board of Education*. Respond to the questions that accompany the article. Some of the questions are designed to prepare you for your licensure examination.

◆ ◆

The story of African American education is not a positive one. One might speculate how the story might be different if different choices had been made following the Civil War.

1900 to World War II

Toward the end of the 19th century, educators recognized that many learners who were entering high schools were having difficulty doing the required work. As numbers of high school students increased, this problem stimulated much discussion about what might be done to ease learners' transitions from elementary schools to high schools. A new kind of institution, the **junior high school,** was proposed as a solution.

The first junior high school was established in Berkeley, California, in 1909. The Berkeley school district developed a 6–3–3 plan of school organization that, in time, came to be widely copied elsewhere (Popper, 1967). The first six grades comprised the elementary program, the next three grades the junior high school program, and the final three years the senior high school program.

The number of public schools and of learners attending them increased tremendously during the first four decades of the 20th century. Schooling became almost universal during this period. In 1900, only 50.5% of young people ages to 20 were in school, but by 1940, 74.8% of this age group was enrolled (U.S. Department of Commerce, 1975). Given the tremendous growth in the total U.S. population between 1900 and 1940, these figures indicate that millions more children were served by schools in 1940 than in 1900. Teacher-preparation requirements also were evolving across the country. See Figure 12–1 for more information.

Contributions of John Dewey

An individual who had a tremendous influence on education during this period was **John Dewey** (1859–1952). Dewey viewed education as a process through which young people are brought to fully participate in society. He saw its primary goal to be the promotion of individual growth and development. Hence, schools should not set out to serve the goals of society (e.g., turning out electrical engineers if the society is short of them) at the cost of overlooking the unique needs of individual learners. Schools, Dewey contended, should produce secure human beings who are committed to their own continuing self-education.

Dewey believed that every learner actively attempts to explore and understand the environment. Because of this drive, learners need to be provided with intellectual tools they can use to make sound judgments when they encounter novel situations. For this reason, Dewey argued that it was more important for young people to master systematic thinking processes than to learn specific items of information. Thinking processes can be applied universally, but specific information often has little value beyond the context in which it is learned.

Dewey was especially concerned that learners master the scientific problem-solving method. This systematic approach features (1) identifying a problem, (2) gathering information relevant to its solution, (3) developing a tentative solution, and (4) testing the solution in light of additional evidence. Dewey believed that young people who become familiar with this method of dealing with novel situations gain confidence in their abilities to develop good responses to dilemmas they will face throughout their lives. Dewey's work continues to influence educational thought and practice. Interest in teaching problem-solving techniques and a commitment to responding to individual differences still feature prominently in American schools today.

What Do You Think?

- What are some current educational practices that reflect the influence of Dewey?
- The influence of Dewey has faded somewhat in recent decades. How do you account for this?

The Testing Movement

Present-day schools also continue to be influenced by an early 20th-century testing movement that was developed in France. Education in France became compulsory in 1904. At that time, a special commission was established there to identify young people who might benefit from regular instruction in public schools and those who would be better off in special classes. In 1905, to help with this identification, Alfred Binet and his associates developed a test, called the **intelligence quotient (IQ) test,** that was designed to predict learners' likelihood of success in regular-school classrooms. Soon educators from other countries, including the United States, were seeking information about ways to measure intelligence. You may find it interesting that a test designed to predict school success was viewed almost immediately as a test of intelligence. The presumption was that the school program had been designed so that the most intelligent would do the best. (Today, this idea is debated. Some people, for example, argue that some of the "most intelligent" learners question school practices and procedures and often do not do as well.)

The testing movement in the United States grew during World War I. The military needed a way to identify individuals well suited to a variety of necessary tasks. Intelligence tests were prepared to provide information that could be used to classify individuals by intelligence. At the time these tests were developed, few people doubted that the scores represented highly reliable measures of intelligence.

Some of the first intelligence tests were given to European immigrants. Immigrants from Western Europe did better than immigrants from Eastern Europe. (This was hardly a surprising development because most tests were developed by Western Europeans or Americans trained by Western Europeans.) There is some evidence that laws passed by Congress restricting the numbers of immigrants from Eastern Europe resulted from dissemination of these score differences. This might be one of the first examples of a **cultural bias** that can be embedded within tests of this sort. A test with a cultural bias is one that includes features that make it more likely for people from certain cultural groups to receive higher scores than people from other cultural groups.

During and after World War I, many educators embraced the testing movement. Educators began to counsel learners and direct them to individual courses on the basis of their IQ scores. There is evidence that some teachers' patterns of interaction with learners were affected by their perception of these learners' intelligence as defined by IQ scores.

In recent years, the use of intelligence tests, particularly paper-and-pencil group intelligence tests, has been challenged. African Americans, Latinos, and other minorities have objected to the cultural biases that are embedded in certain intelligence tests. Other critics have argued that a factor as broad and diffuse as intelligence cannot possibly be measured by a single test. The debate about intelligence testing continues. Although there is not a consensus on this issue, it is fair to say that educators increasingly hesitate to predict the educational futures of young people on the basis of a single measure such as an IQ score. Read this chapter's *A Day in the Life* feature to learn about Pat Taylor's experiences with a student and her intelligence test score.

The Cardinal Principles

As special circumstances and needs associated with the war expanded interest in the testing movement during World War I, people also became concerned about education's more general purposes. In particular, the last year of war, 1918, was a landmark one for education. In this year, the National Education Association's Commission on the Reorganization of Secondary Education identified seven specific goals. These seven goals came to be known as secondary education's **Cardinal Principles:**

- Health
- Command of fundamental processes
- Worthy home membership
- Vocational preparation

A DAY IN THE LIFE . . . Looking Beyond Test Scores

In many classes there are students who surprise you. Such was the case of Juana. Juana was a Hispanic girl whose parents did not speak English. At the beginning of the year, Pat Taylor noticed on Juana's cumulative records that her IQ score was listed as in the mid 80s. Pat had expected her to be one of those students who needed extra help and struggled with school work.

Such was not the case! Juana turned out to be an enthusiastic student who did everything well. On all of her assignments and tests she was near the top of the class. She was one of the classroom leaders who was quick to help other students who needed help. She was especially helpful in translating material for the two limited English-speaking students in the classroom. In short, she became one of Pat's favorite students.

As the year progressed, Pat wanted to make sure Juana's abilities were recognized and that she was encouraged to pursue education beyond high school. There was a special academic enrichment program in the school that was supposed to take the most talented students and provide them with some challenging and academically enriching experiences. Pat decided that Juana was a perfect candidate for the program and that it would provide her with experiences that would help her obtain a scholarship for college. Pat wrote the school counselor a glowing letter of recommendation for Juana.

Today the school counselor met with Pat. The counselor started by telling Pat how impressed she was with Pat's recommendation and the samples of Juana's work that had been submitted. "However," the counselor continued, "I don't think she is a good candidate for the enrichment program. I wouldn't want her to be placed in a program where she might have trouble keeping up with the other students." "Wait a minute," responded Pat, "She is motivated, enthusiastic and demonstrates good task persistence. She is doing just fine competing with the other students in my class." "Well, yes," said the counselor, "However, one of the criteria for admission is an above average IQ and her score is just in the 80s."

Pat was absolutely livid. Wasn't the real test of ability how a person performed rather than a score on a test given several years ago? What was education all about if it wasn't finding talent in students and encouraging them to excel?

However, the counselor was not moved. Rules were rules and Juana simply did not qualify.

✔ Disposition Check

Sometimes students are labeled and misjudged by criteria of questionable validity. Teachers have a responsibility to look beyond first impressions or isolated bits of data. Teachers who are committed to students and who do develop attachments to students are often frustrated by the inability of others to get beyond labels and strict rules.

1. As you review this situation consider what dispositions were being demonstrated by Pat?
2. What dispositions were being demonstrated by the school counselor?
3. How might your dispositions lead to conflict with others in the school?

- Citizenship
- Worthy use of leisure time
- Ethical character

These principles laid the groundwork for the **comprehensive high school.** People supporting comprehensive high schools believed that the high school program should feature educational experiences broad enough to promote student development in all seven areas delineated in the Cardinal Principles. This perspective represented a huge change from the traditional view of the high school as an institution designed to prepare students for colleges and universities. In time, publication of the Cardinal Principles led many high

Corbis/Bettmann

John Dewey, one of the giants of American educational thought, developed much of the intellectual foundation for progressivism.

schools to expand their course offerings. By no means, however, did all high schools give equal emphasis to each of the many subjects that came to be offered; in many, considerable attention (critics would say too much attention) continued to be given to college and university preparatory courses.

The Progressive Movement

Changes in the schools brought by both attention to the Cardinal Principles and actions taken by groups looking for a more practical emphasis in the curriculum suggested that more and more people had come to see education as a necessity for all young people. Compulsory-attendance laws became common during the first two decades of the 20th century. Increasingly, learners were being required to stay in school until they turned 16.

In the 1920s and 1930s, the influence of those who also wanted schools to respond humanely to the needs and interests of individual learners was strong. The term **progressive education movement** has been applied to the general program of people who sought these goals. Supporters of the progressive education movement drew inspiration from John Dewey's work. The installation of counseling programs in schools, for example, which developed at an especially rapid rate during the 1930s, represented a logical extension of Dewey's concern for individual development. Figure 8–1 identifies the basic principles of the Progressive Education Association.

World War II to the 21st Century

After World War II, the progressive education movement developed into a loosely knit group of people who supported school practices that came to be known as **life-adjustment education.** In some of its more extreme forms, life-adjustment education seemed to encourage learners to do whatever they pleased. Systematic attention to intellectual rigor or subject matter was avoided. Opponents of such programs suggested that schools that failed to provide young people with needed understandings and skills shortchanged learners. These critics attracted many supporters, and by the middle 1950s, support for life-adjustment education had greatly diminished.

Figure 8–1   Principles of the Progressive Education Association.

The Progressive Education Association sought to reform education in the early 1900s. They became a powerful force that still influences educational policy and practice. The principles they used to guide reform proposals were:

1. Children should be free to develop naturally.
2. The best motivation for learning is the natural interest of the child.
3. The role of the teacher should be that of a guide rather than that of a taskmaster.
4. Student growth and development must be measured scientifically rather than just by grades.
5. The physical growth and general health of the student require attention.
6. The needs of children are best met when the home and school work together.
7. The school should be a leader in trying new educational ideas.

Responding to International Challenges

Rarely can change in education (or, indeed, in other social institutions) be attributed to a single event. But in the fall of 1957, the former Soviet Union's launching of the first earth satellite, *Sputnik*, so changed the public's perception of education's role that many subsequent alterations in school curricula can be traced back to this single, seminal event. *Sputnik* shocked the nation by challenging America's presumed technological supremacy. People looking for an explanation of why the Soviet Union was first with such an accomplishment placed much blame on public education. Large audiences listened sympathetically to critics who told them that American schools had gone soft and that instruction in subject-matter content compared unfavorably with that provided to learners in other countries. Instruction in the sciences was identified as a particularly weak area of the curriculum.

Reacting to pressures to "do something" about the schools, the federal government passed the **National Defense Education Act** in 1958. This legislation provided federal funds to improve the quality of education. Large-scale curriculum-reform projects were launched, first in mathematics and the sciences and later in the social sciences. Special summer workshops designed to upgrade teachers' skills were held on college campuses across the nation. Massive effort was underway to improve the quality of textbooks and other instructional materials. People carried high hopes that this revolution in American school programming could be carried to a successful conclusion.

Although the curriculum-reform movement of the 1960s produced important changes, these modifications fell well short of the expectations of many supporters of the National Defense Education Act. Teachers who attended summer programs funded by this legislation became proficient in the use of new techniques and materials, but only a small minority of all teachers participated. Teachers who had not had training in the use of new programs and materials often were ill at ease with many of the new programs. A majority of teachers continued doing things much as they had always done them.

Another problem involved the new instructional materials themselves. Subject experts who had little experience working with learners in public schools developed many of them. Consequently, some of the new materials were written at reading levels that were too difficult for many learners. Also, the issue of motivation was ignored. Many young people simply were not interested in the content of the new programs.

Probably the changing national culture of the 1960s did more than anything else to subvert those changes being pushed by people who wanted to introduce more "intellectual rigor" into school programs. There was growing discontent over official governmental policies toward fighting in Vietnam and minorities were frustrated in the nation's large cities, so the ground was not fertile for changes that appeared to critics to be efforts to push "establishment" values on the young. Increasingly, young people questioned the relevance of school curricula that seemed to favor esoteric intellectual subjects rather than topics of more immediate personal concern.

Advent of the Middle School

After World War II, concerns increased about the junior high school. Many people had originally hoped that junior high schools would be particularly sensitive to the emotional and developmental needs of early adolescents. Over time, however, a majority of junior high schools became academic preparatory institutions for the high schools. In reaction to this trend the **middle school** has become tremendously popular.

The middle school movement first attracted large numbers of supporters during the 1960s. This interest continued throughout the 1970s, 1980s, and on into the 1990s.

Individual middle schools often have one of several different grade-level organizational patterns. Generally, a middle school has three to five grades, and it almost always includes grades 6 and 7 (Lounsbury & Vars, 1978). The National Middle School Association and other supporters of middle schools emphasize programs that are sensitive to the special characteristics of learners in the 10- to 15-year-old age group. For example, middle school proponents tend to (1) support interdisciplinary approaches to program organization and (2) favor motivational techniques that emphasize cooperation rather than competition (Henson, 2004). The view that young people in this age group need school programs uniquely suited to their needs has greatly increased middle schools' popularity. Today the middle school is the dominant school type for learners between the elementary and high school years.

The Evolution of the Middle School

To get more information about the middle school movement, go to MyEducationLab and select the topic "History of Education." Read the article "The Evolution of Middle Schools" to learn about the development of the middle school movement and the basic principles of middle school education. Answer the questions accompanying the article. Some of the questions are designed to prepare you for your licensure examination.

School-Improvement Initiatives

Beginning in the early 1980s, public worries about the quality of American education led to a period of intense scrutiny of school programs. There were concerns about the sophistication of thinking being developed by school programs, the readiness of graduates to assume jobs requiring ever-more-complex levels of technical proficiency, the general reading and writing abilities of learners, the scores on academic-achievement tests, and unfavorable comparisons between American learners and those in other nations.

A number of major themes appear regularly in recommendations to improve the schools that have been broadly circulated since the early 1980s. There has been a frequent call for school programs to become more rigorous. At the high school level, this recommendation has sometimes taken the form of a proposal to reduce the number of electives and to require all learners to take a common core of content drawn from the academic disciplines.

Recommendations have also addressed the issue of teacher quality. There have been suggestions of various ways to attract brighter, more committed people to teaching and to improve the quality of their preparation (Holmes Group, 1986). There also has been a recognition that quality people will not remain in the profession unless there are improvements in teachers' working conditions (e.g., improving salaries and empowering teachers to make more decisions about how they discharge their responsibilities).

The issue of school administrative organization also has been addressed. There have been recommendations to decrease sizes of schools to allow for more personal attention to learners. There have also been suggestions that principals spend more time in their roles as instructional leaders than in their roles as business managers. Additionally, there have been proposals to lengthen the school year to make it conform more to those in countries where learners are doing better on content-achievement tests than their U.S. counterparts.

For the past 15 years, discussion of educational improvement has been stimulated by reports of interested national groups and federal government action, as well as by increased local interest in providing parents with more choices regarding how and where their children are educated. National efforts have included the work of members of the Education Commission of the States and the National Governors' Association. They have focused attention on such issues as the kinds of school programming that should be provided for students not going on to colleges and universities, improvements needed in technological literacy of graduates of American schools, and enhancements in student learning of traditional academic subjects.

These efforts have spawned public interest in (1) various approaches to school choice, including voucher plans, open enrollment plans, magnet schools, and charter schools; (2) increased interest in school–business partnerships; and (3) recognition that it may be necessary to establish full-service schools to respond to the varied needs many learners bring with them to school. A theme running through all of these proposals is that reform needs to be systemic. As you will recall from Chapter 3, "What Are the Proposals for School Reform?" *systemic reform* presumes that the problems schools face are multiple and diverse and no single difficulty can be solved without careful attention to the entire spectrum of problems.

Testing and Curriculum Standards

You probably are very familiar with two key elements of systemic-reform initiatives: (1) the increased focus on the content learners are taught and (2) the reliance on test results to provide evidence about what learners have achieved. Over the past decade and a half, the general public has looked increasingly to standardized-test scores as measures of educational quality. As interest in making place-to-place comparisons has increased, there has been a greater tendency to use test scores to compare performance levels of learners who may not have been exposed to the same kinds of content. As a result, schools increasingly have been pressured not only to introduce learners to rigorous content but also to provide the same *kinds* of content to similar groups of learners in all schools (Armstrong, 2003). Actions of federal and state governments and of subject-matter specialty groups (organizations interested in promoting better teaching in English, mathematics, science, social studies, etc.) to identify **curriculum standards** accelerated during the 1990s. These standards identified specific content to be taught in individual grades and courses and often also identified expected levels of proficiency for learners.

At the federal level, much interest in promoting curriculum standards began in 1989, when President George H. Bush joined with the nation's governors to host an educational summit. Following this event, the National Educational Goals Panel and the National Council on Education Standards and Testing were formed. These two groups sought responses to questions about (1) what schools should teach, (2) kinds of testing that should be used, and (3) standards of student performance. In 1994, Congress passed the **Goals 2000—Educate America Act,** Public Law 103-227. This legislation called for massive efforts to improve the quality of the nation's schools. It provided for the establishment of a National Education Standards and Improvement Council, a group charged with overseeing the development of national content standards.

This development had two immediate effects. On the one hand, it stimulated a heated debate among conservative members of the U.S. Senate and the House of Representatives about the appropriateness of interfering with local control of education by imposing national curriculum standards on schools. The net result was a continuation of the idea that the federal government would support the idea of curriculum standards but that state and local officials should develop the standards.

A second result of discussions surrounding the Goals 2000 legislation was a great increase in subject-matter specialty groups' interest in developing curriculum standards related to their discipline areas. Beginning in the 1990s, many of these groups produced curriculum standards that featured content recommendations and, sometimes, teaching suggestions for individual elementary school grades and middle school and high school courses. (For more information about the work of these groups, see Chapter 6, "What is Taught and How is it Taught?") Interest in the importance of curriculum standards was reinforced by the passage of the No Child Left Behind Act of 2001 (2002). This legislation requires all states to have rigorous curriculum standards in place, to develop programs to assess learners' performance on tests related to these standards, and to provide interventions to help learners whose achievement levels fall below certain standards.

In summary, the school system we have today is the product of historical movements and choices in the past. It may well be that changes in society have led to the need to change these historical practices and to institute new ones. However, many of these practices have become so much a part of the "tradition" that there are many who resist the changes.

It is useful to look at current events and realize that these will be the "history" of tomorrow. You might consider what events are likely to bring about lasting change in education.

What Do You Think?

- What do you see as some educational practices that no longer address important educational and societal needs?
- What do you see as contemporary issues that are likely to lead to important educational changes?

Key Ideas in Summary

- The history of American education, as is the case with all history, reflects the values and biases of those who have written it. Because the majority of Americans are white and of European descent, it is not surprising that much educational history fails to question the appropriateness for *all* American children of educational practices rooted in traditions from Europe. In times past, some instruction in American schools failed to provide positive models for learners from minority cultures. Educators today are increasingly sensitive to this issue.
- Among educational practices and assumptions that trace their origins to Europe are (1) the idea that content should be organized under major headings, (2) the practice of dividing knowledge into separate subjects, (3) the tradition of dividing schools into an ordered sequence of grades, (4) the view that teachers should develop instructional plans that take learners' individual differences into account, (5) the idea that as many people as possible should be educated, (6) the practice of providing special training for teachers, and (7) the vision of schooling as a preparation for effective citizenship.
- In the American colonial period, practices in early New England were influenced heavily by views of Puritan leaders. Schools there developed a strong tradition of local control and placed heavy emphases on teaching children to read and learn from the Bible. Schools in the Middle Colonies, which were less tied to perspectives of religious leaders than those in New England, featured varied emphases. There was

special interest in developing schools that taught practical subjects to learners, and the first secondary-level *academies* appeared here. Great distances separated many families in the Southern Colonies. In many places no schools existed, and wealthy families hired resident tutors to teach their children. Sons of the upper classes often were sent to school in England.

- Settlers in the Middle Colonies came from more diverse backgrounds than early residents of New England. In New York, many early private schools sought to prepare young people for commercial careers. In Pennsylvania, Quakers established schools that were open to all children.

- The first high school was established in Boston in 1821. Unlike academies, which were mostly private institutions, most high schools were publicly supported. At first, the growth of high schools proceeded slowly. In 1860, for example, there were only 40 high schools in the entire country.

- Horace Mann championed the common school in the 1820s and 1830s. He believed that it was in the taxpayers' interest to support a strong system of public education. He saw schools as vehicles for equalizing differences among people from different social classes and as engines for the future economic growth of the nation. Mann also supported the development of normal schools—formal institutions dedicated to the preparation of teachers.

- The post–Civil War period witnessed many changes in education. The famous *Kalamazoo* case established a legal precedent for public support of secondary as well as elementary education. Teachers began to form professional organizations. The large number of immigrants entering the country challenged educators to develop programs responsive to their needs and to the needs of American employers. Toward the end of the 19th century, there was interest in narrowing the focus of the school curriculum to place more emphasis on knowledge students would need to succeed in colleges and universities.

- During the first 20 years of the 20th century, the conflict regarding the purpose of the American high school was resolved with the development of the *comprehensive high school*, an institution that had multiple objectives. Comprehensive high schools, in theory at least, offered programs designed to serve the *Cardinal Principles of Secondary Education*, which included (1) health, (2) command of fundamental processes, (3) worthy home membership, (4) vocational preparation, (5) citizenship, (6) worthy use of leisure time, and (7) ethical character.

- John Dewey had a significant influence on 20th-century American education. Dewey believed that education should focus primarily on the development of the individual. He was especially interested in providing learners with the kinds of problem-solving abilities they would need to successfully confront the challenges they would face throughout their lives.

- By the second and third decades of the 20th century the *testing movement*, which originated in France and developed rapidly during World War I, led to the extensive use of intelligence testing of learners in American schools. In recent years, much skepticism has been generated regarding the idea that an IQ score represents an accurate measure of something as complex and sophisticated as human intelligence.

- After World War II, there was interest in *life-adjustment education*. Critics felt that this view of education encouraged learners to do only what pleased them and that school programs lacked needed intellectual substance. By the 1950s, much enthusiasm for life-adjustment education had faded.

- In the late 1950s, following the launching of the earth satellite *Sputnik* and continuing into the very early 1960s, there was a push to place heavier emphasis in schools on challenging academic content. Particular efforts were made to strengthen programs in mathematics and the sciences. As public dissatisfaction with the nation's fight in Vietnam increased, suspicions began to be directed at leaders of many public institutions, including the schools. In time, these suspicions led to widespread rejection of narrow school programs with strong focuses on traditional academic subjects; increasingly, young people questioned the relevance of such programs.
- Beginning in the 1960s, concerns about junior high schools prompted a great deal of interest in middle schools. This interest continues to the present time. Supporters of middle schools believe that their programs tend to be more responsive than junior high school programs to the special needs of learners ages 10 to 15.
- Beginning in the 1980s, a large number of proposals to reform the schools were made. These were prompted by concerns about the intellectual levels of school graduates, unfavorable achievement comparisons between American and foreign learners, and perceived learner deficiencies in such key areas as reading and writing.
- In recent years, there has been a great expansion in the establishment of *state curriculum standards* that specify content to be covered in individual elementary school grades and in middle school and high school courses. Increasingly, standardized tests are tying to content referenced in these standards. Adoption of state curriculum standards has been supported and, in some cases, mandated by federal legislation. In addition, the movement has been encouraged by many subject-matter specialty organizations that have developed standards pertaining to their own disciplines.
- Learners who come to school bring personal cultural histories with them that act as filters when they take in experiences provided by the school. Legacies from such diverse sources as the culture of Africa, Islamic beliefs, traditional Chinese examination practices, and Hinduism often affect how learners with ties to these influences perceive and react to the school programs.

For Your Initial-Development Portfolio

1. What materials and ideas that you learned in this chapter about educational history will you include as "evidence" in your portfolio? Select up to three separate items of information. Number them 1, 2, and 3.
2. Think about why you selected these materials. As you do so, consider these issues:
   - Specific uses you might make of this information as you plan, deliver, and assess the impact of your teaching
   - The compatibility of the information with your own priorities and values
   - Any contributions this information can make to your development as a teacher
   - Factors that led you to include this information, as opposed to some alternatives you considered but rejected
3. Place a check in the following chart to indicate to which INTASC standard(s) each of your items of information relates. (You may wish to refer to Chapter 1 for more detailed information about INTASC.)

	INTASC Standard Number									
ITEM OF EVIDENCE NUMBER	S1	S2	S3	S4	S5	S6	S7	S8	S9	S10
1										
2										
3										

4. Prepare a written reflection in which you analyze the decision-making process you followed. In your comments, mention the INTASC standard(s) to which your selected material relates.

◆───

Reflections

1. Has American schooling been designed to benefit individuals of European descent more than others? What evidence do you have to support your views? Should schools try to develop both a common and shared set of values and an appreciation for values of individual cultural groups that might differ from those common and shared values? Why or why not?

2. Some people allege that certain school programs and instructional materials have demeaned learners from some groups. Do you think this continues to be a problem? What might you do in your own classroom to help each learner develop a positive self-concept?

3. You were introduced in this chapter to a number of commonplace educational practices that were adopted by American educators from European precedents. (Recall such things as the practice of dividing knowledge into separate subjects, division of schools into grades, and so forth.) Suppose early on we had decided not to do these things. How might our schools be different? Why do you think they might be more effective or less effective than they are today?

4. Today, some critics argue that curricula in our schools should place more emphasis on specific technical skills high school graduates will need when they enter the job market. How do you think John Dewey would have reacted to this proposal? What differences do you see between Dewey's values and those favoring more technical-skills training? What do you think about this issue, and how do your views reflect your personal values?

5. As a teacher, you have an obligation to help your learners make adjustments required for them to master certain content, get along with others, and prepare themselves for success either in a future academic environment or in the workplace. Some of your learners will come to you with personal histories tied to traditions that may have values and priorities that differ from your own. How will you discharge your responsibilities to help these learners develop competencies that, in your professional judgment, they should acquire while, at the same time, respecting the unique perspectives they bring to the classroom?

Field Experiences, Projects, and Enrichment

1. In the Middle Ages, many people in charge of teaching the young felt that certain kinds of information had to be kept secret. For example, information about the religious practices of the ancient Greeks and Romans was considered particularly dangerous. Do we face any similar situations in education today? Together with several other people from your class, organize a symposium on the topic "What Learners Should *Not* Be Taught in School."

2. Many lingering influences from European precedents remain in our schools today. As you look ahead to schools during the next two decades, which of these influences will weaken? Which will grow stronger? Who stands to benefit from any changes you foresee? Prepare a chart that summarizes your ideas, and share it with your class as you briefly summarize your position.

3. Some people argue that the comprehensive high school has outlived its usefulness. They suggest that it would be better to have separate schools for separate purposes. Organize a debate on this topic: "Has the Comprehensive High School Outlived Its Usefulness?"

4. This chapter includes some examples of how legacies from the histories of particular groups can affect their receptivity to certain kinds of content and particular instructional practices. Are there fairly large numbers of learners from certain ethnic, religious, or cultural minority groups in the schools in your local area (or in an area where you might like to teach)? Your professor may be able to provide you with this information. Select one of these groups as a focus. Then, use Google (http://www.google.com) or another Web search engine to locate links to articles containing information about this group. Follow some links that interest you, and take notes you will use as the basis for a brief oral presentation to your class. In your presentation, emphasize specific perspectives of this group that may affect how its younger members view their school experiences.

5. Interview several teachers in an area where you might seek employment as a teacher once you complete your university program. Ask these individuals to tell you how their professional lives have been affected by the increased interest in state curriculum standards and related tests. Do they think these changes have acted to improve education? Share their reactions with others in your class.

References

Adams, D. W. (1995). *Education for extinction: American Indians and the boarding school experience.* Lawrence, KS: University of Kansas Press.

Altenbaugh, F. J. (2002). *The American people and their education: A social history.* Upper Saddle River, NJ: Prentice Hall.

Armstrong, D. G. (2003). *Curriculum today.* Upper Saddle River, NJ: Merrill/Prentice Hall.

Barry, T. N. (1961). *Origin and development of the American public high school in the 19th century.* Unpublished doctoral dissertation, Stanford University.

Coleman, M. (1993). *American Indian children at school, 1850–1930.* Jackson: University of Mississippi Press.

Commissioner of Indian Affairs. (1888). *Annual report.* Washington, DC: U.S. Government Printing Office.

Cremin, L. A. (1980). *American education: The national experience.* New York: Harper and Row.

Fischer, D. H. (1989). *Albion's seed.* New York: Oxford University Press.

Goals 2000—Educate America Act, Public Law 103-227, 114 Stat. 2763 (1994).

Henson, K. T. (2004). *Constructivist teaching strategies for diverse middle level classrooms.* Boston: Allyn & Bacon.

Holmes Group. (1986). *Tomorrow's teachers.* East Lansing, MI: Author.

Kaestle, C. (1983). *Pillars of the republic: Common schools and American society: 1780–1860.* New York: Hill and Wang.

Kaestle, C. (2001). The common school: Introduction. In S. Mondale & S. Patton (Eds.), *School: The story of public education* (pp. 11–17). Boston: Beacon Press.

Lounsbury, J. H., & Vars, G. E. (1978). *Curriculum for the middle years.* New York: Harper and Row.

Nieto, S. (1992). *Affirming diversity: The sociopolitical context of multicultural education.* New York: Longman.

No Child Left Behind Act of 2001, Public Law 107-110, 115 Stat. 1425 (2002).

Peavy, L., & Smith, U. (1999). *Frontier children.* Norman, OK: University of Oklahoma Press.

Popper, S. H. (1967). *The American middle school.* Waltham, MA: Blaisdell.

Reagan, T. (2000). *Non-Western educational traditions: Alternative approaches to educational thought and practice* (2nd ed.). Mahwah, NJ: Lawrence Erlbaum Associates.

Stuart v. School District No. 1 of the Village of Kalamazoo, 30 Mich. 69 (1874).

Tyack, D. (2001). Introduction. In S. Mondale & S. Patton (Eds.), *School: The story of public education* (pp. 1–8). Boston: Beacon Press.

U.S. Department of Commerce. (1975). *Historical statistics of the United States, colonial times to 1970: Part I.* Washington, DC: Bureau of the Census.

Webber, T. L. (1978). *Deep like the rivers: Education in the slave quarter communities, 1831–1865.* New York: W.W. Norton and Co.

CHAPTER 9

WHAT IS THE ROLE
OF SCHOOL IN SOCIETY?

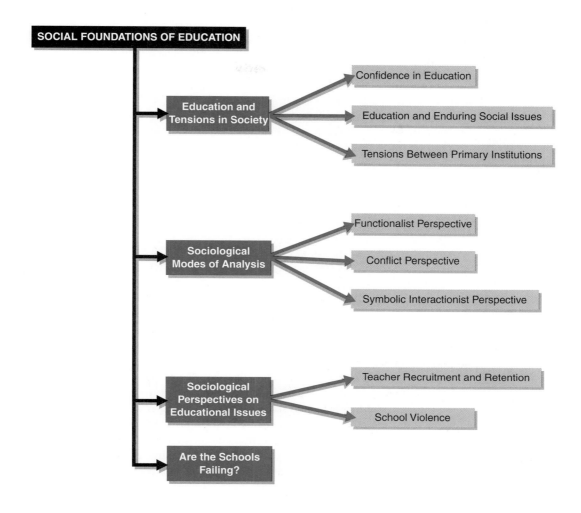

SOCIAL FOUNDATIONS OF EDUCATION

Education and Tensions in Society
- Confidence in Education
- Education and Enduring Social Issues
- Tensions Between Primary Institutions

Sociological Modes of Analysis
- Functionalist Perspective
- Conflict Perspective
- Symbolic Interactionist Perspective

Sociological Perspectives on Educational Issues
- Teacher Recruitment and Retention
- School Violence

Are the Schools Failing?

OBJECTIVES

This chapter will help you to:

- define the complex relationship between school and society.
- explain tensions between school and society in the United States.
- define three different modes of sociological analysis used to identify and evaluate the role of school in society.
- apply sociological modes of analysis to current educational issues.
- draw conclusions about the success of American schools.

INTRODUCTION

Education is one of the primary institutions in society because of its role in cultural transmission and societal development. In less-developed nations education is often informal and accomplished through kinship relationships (Curry, Jiobu, & Schwirian, 2005). In these places, education is viewed as a privilege that is available only to the few, and the adult literacy rate is about 50%. Many primary-age children are not in school, and the dropout rate at the primary level is as high as 100% (Ballantine, 2001).

In highly industrialized societies, informal approaches to education are viewed as inadequate. Education is viewed as vital for the nation's social, political, and economic development. Indeed, there is a relationship between a society's quality of education and economic development (Macionis, 2005). Therefore, the educational function is conducted by formal institutions called "schools."

Because of the importance of education, schools in an industrialized society have become highly integrated into the economic, political, and social systems. Groups from different political, economic, and ideological perspectives attempt to shape schools according to their own agendas (Altenbaugh, 2002). Those who control education control the political, social, and economic agendas of the nation. Therefore, the control of education is of major importance and has serious implications for the society's future.

In industrialized nations, the formal system of schools staffed by professionals creates some inevitable tensions. If education is conducted largely by the family, there is little concern about the values, beliefs, norms, and expectations passed on to the young. The family is in charge of and can control what is taught. However, if education is conducted by someone outside the family, uncertainty and suspicion are inevitable.

Other tensions emerge when schools are expected to accomplish conflicting societal purposes. For example, schools are expected to be a primary institution for socializing the young and integrating them into the immediate society. This socialization purpose is viewed as important for creating a unified society and perpetuating the status quo. However, in industrialized societies, schools are also expected to prepare individuals for innovation and cultural change. This challenges the status quo and existing norms.

Sociologists study the ways societies are maintained and how they change. They are interested in groups and the structure of society, especially the family, religion, education, politics, economics, and health (Ballantine, 2001). They investigate ways these institutions interact with each other and contribute to stability and change.

Because education is one of the primary institutions of society, education is an important field of study for sociologists. Therefore, viewing education through the sociology perspective can help us understand current practices, important issues, and proposals for change.

This chapter will highlight some of the tensions and issues relating to the role of education in the United States. To assist in the understanding of these issues, three modes of sociological analysis will be provided. Examples of how the sociological perspectives shed light on educational issues and the question of school failure will be addressed.

EDUCATION AND TENSIONS IN SOCIETY

Frequently tensions exist between institutions in society. This is especially true with education because education is dealing with impressionable students who will lead the society in the future. That is one of the reasons why dictators are quick to seize the school system when they take over a country.

Confidence in Education

Citizens of the United States have a strong faith in the value of education. As a result, the United States has developed the most comprehensive education system in the world (Curry, Jiobu, & Schwirian, 2005). Our schools are expected to accomplish many purposes.

The nation's founders proposed a mass educational system that would be free to most citizens because they believed that diffusion of knowledge to the general population was important for building a nation. They wanted a consistent and systematic education that would produce individuals with a strong sense of civic duty. A literate citizenry was viewed as necessary in order to produce loyal Americans, develop moral training, and promote social stability (Altenbaugh, 2002). Thus, public-supported mass education became a foundation for the educational system of the United States.

Following through on this early legacy, schools have come to be viewed as a key element in achieving the "American dream." Schools provide the "credentials" that open doors to high-income and high-status occupations. In addition, the schools have been perceived as a major institution for addressing injustice and helping individuals attain personal happiness (Curry, Jiobu, & Schwirian, 2005).

This faith in education has led to the assignment of a wide range of responsibilities to the schools, bringing both positive and negative elements. On the positive side, because schools are so pervasive and touch the lives of nearly every citizen, they are in a position to reach a wide audience. On the negative side, these lofty expectations can be unobtainable. Our government is tempted to assign responsibilities to schools that are best addressed elsewhere in society.

In recent decades, there has been an erosion of this confidence in education. Currently, many assert that the schools are not meeting these lofty expectations. One of the current debates in society concerns the need to reform education. Maintaining confidence in education is one of the great challenges of educators, who must present convincing evidence to the public regarding their performance.

What Do You Think?

- Do you agree that there has been an erosion of public confidence in the schools?
- What do you think has been the cause of increased criticism of the schools?

Education and Enduring Social Issues

The eminent historian Henry Steel Commager (1976) noted the problem of assigning schools responsibility for enduring social problems. He contends that rather than dealing with these problems, society has been willing to assign responsibility to the schools and then assume that the problem has been addressed. For example, due to increased traffic fatalities following World War II, rather than addressing issues of auto design and highway safety, driver's education was added to the school curriculum. When concern about alcohol and drug abuse became an issue, rather than addressing issues such as advertising and public attitudes, alcohol and drug prevention programs were placed in the schools. When promiscuity and teenage pregnancy grabbed headlines, rather than addressing the media and the prevalence of sexual content, sex education in schools followed. In the 1970s a loss of market share by business and industry to international competitors led to charges that the schools were not adequately preparing students for the world of work so that business could remain competitive. Whenever a problem arises in society, education is often viewed as both a part of the problem and a part of the solution.

The problem with this view is that the schools represent only one influence on the patterns of beliefs and the behaviors of society. Few would deny that education can contribute to the solution of social problems. However, as Altenbaugh (2002) notes, the schools then become the scapegoat if these problems persist.

Schools are limited in what they can do, and giving too many responsibilities to the schools may divert attention from other solutions. For example, if there is a need to improve economic competitiveness, perhaps it would be more effective to question accepted business practices than to place the responsibility on the schools. Schools are likely to have a minor influence on the sexual behavior of individuals if the images portrayed in movies and popular television programs are different from those espoused in the classroom. Billions of dollars are spent advertising "junk" food to children. Asking the school to address healthy eating habits is likely to have limited impact in overcoming these slick and appealing commercials.

Asking the schools to address some of these serious national problems can direct attention away from those central responsibilities. Central questions are what is the role of schools in addressing social issues and can schools have much impact trying to counter popular and pervasive trends?

What Do You Think?

- What do you think the role of the schools should be in addressing important social issues?
- What do you see as some issues that schools are currently being asked to address?

Tensions Between the Primary Institutions in Society

Asking schools to counter popular and pervasive societal trends limits school effectiveness in other areas and creates tensions with other societal institutions. For example, there is a tension between educating individuals with the perspectives of the past and educating individuals for the challenges of the future. Preparing for innovation and change often requires that individuals challenge existing beliefs and assumptions. Addressing areas of injustice inevitably leads to conflict where some of the values and actions of previous generations are called into question.

The result is an intergenerational tension where older generations question the values and actions of younger generations and younger generations challenge the wisdom and beliefs of older generations. One manifestation of this generational tension is the contention of older generations that the schools are not as good as they used to be.

Education and Family Responsibility

An example of how the tensions between social institutions influence education is the debate regarding early childhood education. There is considerable evidence that the early years are extremely important in developing cognitive abilities, self-concept, and social skills of children (Bracey, 2003).

Families have traditionally had primary responsibility for the care and education of children before about age 5. However, there is great variation on the quality of parental care and concern about how well the family is fulfilling its responsibilities. Studies indicate that one in seven Americans claims to have been sexually abused as a child. Ten percent of the newborns are exposed to some kind of illicit drug (Altenbaugh, 2002). The experiences provided by families related to educational readiness tend to vary by social class and family background. One study found that a substantial number of 3-year-olds from poor families were 9 months or more behind in language and intellectual development (Ballantine, 2001).

Several research studies support the value of early childhood education. Among the benefits found for preschool are that those who have preschool experience are less likely to later need special or remedial classes, they have a lower school dropout rate and a lower incident of retention in grade, and they make significant academic gains in such subjects as mathematics and reading. One early childhood education study discovered that the greatest return on investment is providing preschool for 3- and 4-year-old children of low-income families (Ballantine, 2001).

More than half of the nations of the world fund early childhood education for 3- through 5-year-olds. Some nations, such as Israel and China, begin early childhood education earlier and have made it mandatory (Ballantine, 2001). Many attempts have been made to extend mandatory education to the preschool years. For example, the Goals 2000 Project, supported by the Bush and Clinton administrations during the 1990s, emphasized the importance of preschool and contained a "ready to learn" initiative directed at preschoolers.

However, proposals for increased or mandatory preschool in the United States have been met with considerable opposition. Much of the opposition comes from those who see this as an infringement by the schools on the roles and responsibilities of the family (Bracey, 2003).

◆ ◆

Working with Parents
Go to MyEducationLab and select the topic "Family and Community." Read the article "Beyond Instruction." Respond to the questions that are included in the module. Some of the questions are designed to prepare you for your licensure examination.

◆ ◆

Conflict Between Education and Religion

Because both education and religion have a deep interest in the development of youth, conflicts are inevitable. Historically, the conflict between education and religion led to the rise of the private schools, especially Catholic schools. Early on, it was perceived that the public schools were furthering Protestant beliefs so that Catholic leaders felt they had no choice but to create their own school systems.

Over time, legal decisions clarified the separation between church and state. However, this did not eliminate the conflict between church and state. In fact, in some places public schools are viewed as antireligious.

A conflict involving education and religion is the current controversy relating to the science curriculum and the teaching of evolution versus intelligent design. Many religious leaders have long viewed the teaching of evolution as contrary to their religious beliefs. In 1919, the World's Christian Fundamentals Association was formed to oppose the teaching of evolution. Since that time, many efforts have been made to restrict the teaching of evolution; the most famous was the Scopes trial in the 1920s (Altenbaugh, 2002). The basic argument has centered on the idea that "creationism" is a religious theory, not a scientific one. Therefore, teaching creationism amounts to teaching a religious doctrine.

In 1999, the Kansas state school board adopted a science curriculum that essentially replaced evolutionary theory with "intelligent design." Many scientists see intelligent design as just another name for creationism. Proponents claim that intelligent design is not creationism but an alternative theory for explaining the origins of life that should be taught

**Video Viewpoints
9–1**

Science vs. Religion

WATCH: This *Nightline* segment from May 2005 focuses on the debate over the place of evolution in the school science curriculum. This segment deals with the controversy in Kansas about teaching "intelligent design."

THINK: Discuss with your classmates or write in your reflective journal your responses to the following questions:

1. What is your position on "intelligent design"?
2. What should be the relationship between other institutions in society, such as religion, and the role of the school?
3. What are some other cultural issues that are likely to involve conflict between what is taught in the schools and different segments of society?

LINK: What do you think will be the outcome of debates like this on your role as a teacher?

 To view this video, go to the Video Viewpoints DVD and click on this chapter's video: "Science vs. Religion."

in science classrooms. The battle continues to rage in state houses across the nation as proponents of intelligent design, generally religious leaders, lobby to have it included in the science curriculum. Scientists argue that intelligent design is not a "testable" theory and therefore not really science. Learn more about this debate by reading this chapter's *Video Viewpoints* feature.

In summary, as a primary institution in society with a great deal of impact, education is of great concern to many segments of society including parents, politicians, community leaders, business leaders, and religious leaders. For most parents, their children's welfare is their highest priority. They want their children to have the opportunity for a happy and prosperous future. Religious leaders are concerned about the values impressionable young people may learn in school and the relationship of those values to their deeply held convictions. Business and political leaders have a high stake in making sure that the schools are educating individuals who can help keep the nation strong and economically competitive.

As a teacher, you should be aware that it is not likely that all of these constituents will agree on what education should accomplish and how it should be evaluated. You are entering a profession with many "experts" but few clear answers. In fact, some "answers" may be in direct opposition to each other. You will be engaged in a profession that is inherently controversial and evokes strong passions.

SOCIOLOGICAL MODES OF ANALYSIS

Sociologists use three different perspectives to address the functioning and performance of institutions such as education. These three perspectives are

*   the functionalist perspective,
*   the conflict perspective, and
*   the symbolic interactionist perspective.

The Functionalist Perspective

The functionalist perspective analyzes the role of the school system in maintaining an orderly and efficient society. Functionalists contend that if all institutions are funtioning well, then society works well (Curry, Jiobu, & Schwirian, 2005).

Functionalism tends to accept the status quo and assumes that change is relatively slow (Ballantine, 2001). The functional analysis usually focuses on the dominant values in society and emphasizes the benefits of a common language, common values, and the development of useful skills in order to assimilate diverse groups and mold them into a functioning and cohesive society.

Social cohesion is a major concern of interest by those looking at education through the functionalist perspective. **Social cohesion** is a sense of communal belonging and caring that binds together members of a society. This is an especially important topic in the United States because of the diversity of the population. The United States has more than 200 distinct ethnic and racial groups (Curry, Jiobu, & Schwirian, 2005). The functionalist perspective investigates how education is addressing these differences and whether these policies and programs are promoting social cohesion or social disintegration.

Talcott Parsons (1959), a leading American functionalist, saw the school as the social agency that had the basic responsibility for providing society with trained workers. Functionalists assume that all learners have the ability to profit from the school's academic programs. They believe a role of the schools is to serve as a sorting mechanism that eventually leads to the highest ability students getting admitted to the best universities and acquiring the most responsible jobs. This view is based on the assumption that economic rewards are distributed on the basis of individual merit and that schools provide equal opportunities for all (Dougherty & Hammack, 1990).

Functionalism Today

Clearly, functionalism is a dominant perspective for viewing and evaluating education. When there are dysfunctions in society, the schools are quickly viewed as both one of the causes of the problem as well as a part of the solution. For example, as concerns have arisen regarding other institutions in society, such as the social welfare system, the lack of health care for a large number of children, and an overwhelmed juvenile justice system, proposals have called for "full-service schools." **Full-service schools** place numerous functions such as welfare, health care, and juvenile justice at the school site. Once again, the question can be asked, what is the role of the schools in addressing the welfare, health care, and juvenile justice needs of the larger society? Will the addition of these functions to the school site improve the relationships between these societal institutions? Or, will it lead to more responsibility and accountability for the schools, without a commensurate shift in resources?

The functionalist perspective provides some guidance for addressing persistent education problems. For example, when addressing the issue of student failure, the functionalist perspective suggests that the school work in conjunction with other institutions such as the family. Therefore, making parents partners in learning and cultivating school-business partnerships would be recommended. Another recommendation would be to clearly relate education to a practical function such as getting a good job (Lindsey & Beach, 2004).

However, some sociologists question some of the functionalist recommendations. For example, many question the assumption that social stability requires the unquestioned transmission of attitudes and values from one generation to the next (Lindsey & Beach, 2004). Others point out that the functionalist perspective does not adequately address issues such as poverty and ethnicity, two values that have profound impact on school success. In addition, the functionalist perspective may be slow in accounting for societal changes. For example, some critics point out that in an "industrial society," the focus is on the production of goods and the need is for sameness and standardization. However, they now claim that we have changed from an "industrial society" to a "postindustrial society" where the emphasis is on ideas and innovation. Thus, the need is for creativity and individualization rather than sameness and standardization (Curry, Jiobu, & Schwirian, 2005).

Critics of functionalism take issue about the assumption that merit is the primary consideration in the sorting mechanism. They point out that learners do not come to school and compete for jobs on a level playing field. Some students come from affluent families in which they have accumulated a wealth of "cultural capital." **Cultural capital** refers to the attitudes and beliefs, language patterns, amount of material available to the young, and the activities of the family that reinforce the value of education and support learning (Ballantine, 2001). Students from lower socioeconomic classes often lack the cultural capital that allows them to take maximum advantage of opportunities offered by the schools. Therefore, social class may be as important in sorting students into different paths as ability or merit.

Some evidence supports this contention. For example, in one high school study, although the scores on standardized-achievement tests were similar for sophomore students, over 80% of students in the high socioeconomic status group were in the college track as compared to 52% of the students from the low socioeconomic status group (Curry, Jiobu, & Schwirian, 2005).

In summary, the functionalist perspective is an important one. It does influence educational policy and suggestions for reform. On a regular basis business and industry groups issue reports stating that the schools should be doing more to prepare students for the world of work. This is clearly a reflection of the functionalist perspective regarding the primary role of school in society.

What Do You Think?

- What do you see as the benefits and the weaknesses of the functionalist perspective?
- What current school practices can you identify that are consistent with the functionalist perspective?

The Conflict Perspective

The conflict perspective has a very different focus than functionalism. The conflict perspective begins with the contention that power relationships and conflicting interests influence educational policy and practice. Schools are viewed as places where power groups compete for advantage (Pogrow, 2006). It is in the interest of dominant power and status groups to control and shape education in order to maintain their advantages. Therefore, because control of education is basically in the hands of those in power, schools are places that represent the power groups in society and therefore perpetuate social inequality. Factors such as social class, race, gender, and age are viewed as just as important in viewing educational programs and achievements as ability and merit (Macionis, 2005).

The conflict perspective has its roots in the writing of Karl Marx and Max Weber (Ballantine, 2001). Power and dominance are the key concepts of the conflict perspective. Conflict "winners" succeed in having important educational resources dedicated to programs that serve their children.

The analysis of schools from the conflict perspective reveals that schools serving minority groups and the poor tend to be poorly financed and inadequately staffed (Lindsey & Beach,

2004). Their per student budget is often thousands of dollars less than that of more affluent parts of the community and they have a higher percentage of inexperienced or uncredentialed teachers.

People who use the conflict perspective to evaluate education contend that, in general, the schools have been structured to maintain the dominance of the groups who have the most power and who benefit most from the system. There are "insiders" whose status and culture have been reinforced through school experience and there are "outsiders" who face barriers to success (Ballantine, 2001).

For example, most people do not realize that merit in school is usually defined and measured in terms of middle- and upper-class expectations (Curry, Jiobu, & Schwirian, 2005). Therefore, students from minority groups and from lower socioeconomic status groups must adapt to a different set of norms and expectations and that puts them at a disadvantage. Conflict perspective supporters cite the correlation between parents' class standing and educational achievement as evidence of this situation. Upper-class students are more than six times as likely to graduate from college than lower-class students (Curry, Jiobu, & Schwirian, 2005). Because merit and ability are evenly distributed across all social classes, if success was based purely on merit, this disparity would not be statistically predicted.

The Conflict Perspective Today

The conflict perspective provides an important lens through which we can view the educational reform movement and proposals for change. For example, when assessing a proposed change, the main concern would not be social cohesion. Rather, those who look at issues through the conflict perspective would consider who is proposing and supporting the change and which groups are likely to benefit and gain power. They would see educational practices such as standardized testing, English only, and cultural literacy as attempts by the groups in power to sustain and increase their dominance.

It is not that proponents of the conflict perspective are opposed to social cohesion. They would argue that a cohesive and functioning society is one in which all perspectives are heard and in which there is a large measure of social justice.

Proponents of the conflict perspective fear that many school reforms represent self-serving efforts of powerful individuals and groups. Establishing accountability programs that reward schools that perform well on standardized tests is one example. Most schools that receive high scores on standardized tests are located in affluent neighborhoods. Therefore, the schools that are likely to be rewarded with recognition and additional resources are those that serve advantaged young people (Pogrow, 2006). Those likely to be placed on sanctions and have decreased support are schools serving needy learners living in less-affluent neighborhoods.

Gifted and talented programs are frequently the object of criticism by those viewing education through the conflict perspective. Critics claim that the admission to gifted and talented programs is often based on criteria that favor higher social classes. Thus, minority and low socioeconomic status students are often excluded for gifted and talented programs.

Clearly, the conflict perspective has had an increased following in recent decades (Macionis, 2005). Many school programs have been created to respond to concerns of inequality and social injustice. For example, social studies and English classes regularly include multicultural perspectives and multicultural literature. Attempts have been made to include programs such as advanced placement in high schools serving minority students and the poor. In some states, legal decisions have required more equalization of funding based on the needs of the students. Some gains can be noted in decreasing the dropout rate and increasing the aspirations and college attendance rates of nearly all minority groups following the "Great Society" proposals of President Lyndon Johnson.

However, it is equally clear that many of the current proposals to reform education favor the agenda of the established power groups. An increased emphasis on high-stakes testing, on standards applied to all students, and on programs such as vouchers and charter schools generally favors higher socioeconomic status groups.

Those viewing educational issues through the lens of the conflict perspective recommend that more resources should be expended in those schools that serve the neediest in society. These schools need the highest qualified teachers and the lowest student-teacher ratio rather than the least qualified teachers and the largest classes. Efforts should be directed at raising the expectations, the hopes, and the aspirations for low socioeconomic status students (Lindsey & Beach, 2004).

The conflict perspective is not without critics. Although there is abundant evidence that socioeconomic status is a powerful variable in explaining school achievement, there is scant evidence that schools are intentionally serving the power groups of society (Lindsey & Beach, 2004). Some critics accuse the conflict perspective proponents of lacking scientific objectivity in their assertions about the failure of schools to address inequality. Supporters of the conflict perspective tend to ignore the history of education as an institution that has provided upward mobility for individuals from all social classes. Parts of the curriculum do challenge the status quo and address difficult issues such as social inequality (Macionis, 2005).

Others point out that teachers do not view themselves as tools in maintaining class distinctions (Lindsey & Beach, 2004). In fact, many teachers are evidence of the upward social mobility provided by education. Traditionally, teaching has been viewed by women and those in lower socioeconomic status groups as a profession that is open to them, a vehicle to improve their status.

Although it is popular to portray teachers in minority and low socioeconomic status schools as uncaring and "burned out," the fact is that many teachers in these schools are committed to the students they teach and they put forth tremendous effort in trying to raise the aspirations and hopes of their students. These teachers are offended by the assertion that they are merely pawns in a power struggle to maintain class distinctions.

The conflict perspective tends to ignore changes in the role of teachers. In recent decades, teachers have been speaking out on issues of social justice and have been taking political stands (Lunenburg & Irby, 2006). Teachers have become a powerful political

Figure 9–1   Racial/ethnic distribution of public school students enrolling in kindergarten.

There have been significant changes in the composition of students attending public schools. These changes mirror changes in society and have important implications for policies that influence education. Review the chart below and identify the trends and what you see as the implications for schools in the future.

Fall of Year	% White Students	% Black Students	% Hispanic Students	% Asian/Pacific Islander
1974	76.8	15.4	6.3	——
1984	71.7	16.1	8.5	——
1994	65.8	16.7	13.7	2.5
2004	57.4	16.0	19.3	4.1

Source: National Center for Educational Statistics (2006). Participation in Education: Table 5-1.

lobby and the image of the teacher as a timid person who is quietly obedient to the wishes of those in power is no longer accurate.

In summary, those looking at the function of schools through the conflict perspective remind us that we need to view proposals for change from the perspective of *all* members of society, not just from those in power. We need to ask hard questions such as who is proposing this change? why are they making these recommendations? who will benefit? who will be harmed?

What Do You Think?

- As you look at current-reform proposals, who do you see as the potential winners and losers?
- What is your reaction to the conflict perspective as a tool for analyzing and evaluating schools?

The Symbolic Interactionist Perspective

The functionalist and the conflict perspectives look at education at a "macro level." These perspectives view education as an institution and how it relates to other institutions. **Symbolic interactionists** contend that these macro approaches miss the dimensions of everyday school life that shape students' futures (Ballantine, 2001). This perspective changes the focus to the "micro level" or what actually takes place in the classroom. Symbolic interactionists claim that students develop their identities, learn their self-concepts, and develop their hopes and aspirations through interactions with others. This reflects the idea that we learn who we are through the "mirror of others." Therefore, looking at the interactions between students and between teachers and students is critical in understanding the role of school in society (Curry, Jiobu, & Schwirian, 2005).

Symbolic interactionists investigate the formal and informal processes that take place in the classroom. They are interested in the "culture" of the school and the classroom. This involves investigating power relationships between the teacher and the students, the rules that govern classroom interactions, peer relationships and friendship patterns, and how all of these relate to social class and gender (Ballantine, 2001). They are interested in who is rewarded, what is rewarded, and what students are learning through their interactions with others in the school environment. They investigate the relationship of these dimensions to ethnicity, race, gender, and socioeconomic status.

One dimension of interactionism that has received considerable attention is that of teacher expectations and how those influence student achievement. Several researchers have studied how teacher expectations influence the interaction between teacher and student and how that may result in a "self-fulfilling prophesy" so that students behave and achieve in a manner that is consistent with teacher expectations (Good & Brophy, 2003).

Another interesting aspect of the classroom interaction focuses on the cultural background and gender of the teacher and the students. For example, students from cultural backgrounds different than the teacher may exhibit behaviors that are normal for them but are misinterpreted by the teacher so that the teacher concludes that the students are rebellious, disrespectful, or unmotivated.

One example is that in the early elementary grades, most of the teachers are female and the school rules and expectations are often those that are more consistent with the development and socialization of girls. Therefore, boys are disciplined more frequently and may develop more negative self-concepts, negative attitudes toward school subjects such as reading, and less interest in school. Later on, the situation may be reversed (Ballantine, 2001). Females may not be encouraged or rewarded for being engaged in subjects such as mathematics or science. The more active males may be reinforced for their efforts in these subjects and may be more likely to be encouraged to seek a career involving math or science.

Symbolic Interactionism Today

Many current educational practices reflect the symbolic interactionism perspective. It has long been a belief in the United States that students of all races, ethnicities, religious beliefs, social classes, genders, and backgrounds should be educated together in the same classroom. This belief is based on the idea that if diverse individuals interact with each other, they will develop understandings and attitudes that will promote democracy and social cohesion. This perspective has helped to shape many educational policies.

The symbolic interactionism perspective also has an interest in tracking. Symbolic interactionists point out the power of labels in the way individuals identify themselves and in the development of their self-concepts (Lindsey & Beach, 2004). They contend that sorting students into different tracks is often based on criteria other than merit and that tracking can have a profound impact on students.

This focus on the problems associated with tracking has led to a decrease in homogeneous grouping and tracking of students. Consistent with this perspective has been an understanding of the influence of teacher expectations. Over the last decade, numerous teachers across the nation have attended workshops on teacher expectations and student achievement. These workshops have focused on the impact of expectations on teacher-student interactions and student achievement.

Another example of the influence of the symbolic interactionism perspective is the mainstreaming of special education students into the regular classroom. This practice was first required in Public Law 94-142 passed in 1975 and reauthorized as the Individuals with Disabilities Education Act in 1997. Mainstreaming is based on the interactionist notion that placing special education students in the regular classroom would promote interactions between students that would change the expectations and perceptions of everyone. The stigma of placement in special education classes would be reduced and the self-concept and expectations of special-needs students would be enhanced. Regular students would develop respect and positive attitudes toward those with special needs.

Another example of the influence of symbolic interactionist ideas is teacher-preparation programs that include an emphasis on diversity and multicultural education. The intent of this requirement is to increase teacher awareness of cultural and language differences so that they can interact more productively with students and parents from a variety of backgrounds. In addition, the curriculum has been changed to include multicultural and gender-specific content. Once again, the intent is that interacting and discussing the contributions of a variety of groups and genders will result in a more democratic and cohesive society.

The nature of the teaching force is another issue addressed by symbolic interactionism. The concern is that a diverse teaching force is important in improving the interactions between students and teachers and in improving the image and the expectations of culturally diverse students. In recent decades, efforts have been made to attract a variety of racial, ethnic, gender, and social classes to teaching.

Some interactionism ideas have been challenged. For example, there is evidence that students attending same-gender schools achieve at higher levels. Therefore, there has been considerable support for creating same-gender classes and schools. This poses a dilemma. Should the priority be placed on interactions between students from diverse backgrounds and different genders or on higher achievement as measured by standardized tests? It appears that the higher achievement is being given the nod in this debate. On the other hand, research in cooperative learning has indicated that certain types of cooperative learning approaches that include heterogeneously grouped students actually result in higher achievement than homogeneously grouped students.

Other critics contend that interactionists have overlooked data that do not support their contentions. For example, integrating special-needs students in regular classrooms does not necessarily result in positive self-images. For example, if special-needs students are less likely to be chosen by peers for special activities, if there are insufficient additional resources to help them succeed, and if teachers spend less time with them, their self-concepts are likely to be eroded rather than enhanced (Lindsey & Beach, 2004).

SOCIOLOGICAL PERSPECTIVES ON EDUCATIONAL ISSUES

Sociological perspectives are helpful when viewing educational issues and proposals for change. The following two issues illustrate how sociological perspective can help you analyze the issues and gain useful insights.

Web Extension 9–1

Social Perspectives

The following are some Web sites that will allow you to investigate social perspectives on education in more depth.

International Studies in the Sociology of Education

Scholars in many countries focus on social and cultural influences on schools and schooling. The journal *International Studies in the Sociology of Education* is published in the United Kingdom. At this site, you will find articles written by scholars throughout the world that focus on topics related to social influences on education. You can read the articles online.

http://www.triangle.co.uk/iss/

Census Data

Data from the census are very useful in identifying issues and trends in society and education. The Census Bureau published a report on the relationship between schooling and income that is useful in investigating this important link.

http://www.census.gov/population/www/socdemo/fld-of-trn.html

Public Attitudes Toward Education

The Phi Delta Kappa organization publishes an annual poll on education that includes items of interest regarding how the public views the schools. This poll can be found at:

Sociologists are interested in the processes of selecting teachers and the composition of the teaching force.

Laura Bolesta/Merrill

Recruiting and Retaining Teachers

No aspect of education is more important than quality teachers because, of all factors that affect the quality of students and education, teachers have the most impact. This makes the qualities and characteristics of teachers a major concern. For this reason, much attention has been directed toward the issue of teacher qualifications and teacher selection. Sarason (2002) claims that the selection of teachers is the most critical component in improving education.

However, investigating who chooses to become a teacher brings up some interesting issues. The first relates to the way teachers are perceived in society. What is their social standing and their level of respect?

What Do You Think?

- How do you think teachers are viewed by your circle of friends and relatives?
- What might be done to improve the respect and status of teachers?

Although there is widespread verbal support throughout society that teaching is an important profession, teachers are given social status that is inconsistent with this procla-mation. Throughout American history, teachers have been characterized in negative or comical ways. The general image has been that of the spinster schoolmarm or the effemi-nate male (Altenbaugh, 2003).

Teaching has not been viewed as an intellectually challenging profession or one that demands much skill. The image persists that "Those who can do, those who can't teach." Then critics of education and those making decisions about teaching salary often com-plain that teaching does not attract the "best or the brightest." To what extent do these societal images of teachers discourage the best or the brightest to pursue teaching as a ca-reer? For example, one of the authors conducted a research study on individuals entering a teacher credential program. One young woman reported that although she had always had an attraction to teaching, her high school counselor told her, "You're a bright girl, be something. Don't be a teacher." She then chose another career path and only later changed to teaching. Another student who transferred from business to education re-quested that her father not be informed that she had changed because he would be angry.

It has been noted that the values of society can be identified by looking at the alloca-tion of resources. If this is so, the low salaries of teachers would indicate that teaching is not a very highly valued profession. The average salary of teachers is usually far below those of other professions with similar education levels. In some places even the annual income of low educated, nonskill workers exceeds that of teachers. Read this chapter's *A Day in the Life* feature to explore how our focus teacher, Pat, often reflects on teaching as a career.

The status of teachers in society and the low salaries they command are related to one of the persistent problems in American education, a teacher shortage. This shortage has been especially acute in some disciplines such as math, science, and special education. In the case of math and science, individuals who major in these subjects often command much higher beginning salaries in business than teaching.

Changes in society have also impacted the teaching force. At one time education and nursing were the major options for young women who wanted a professional career. Because there were few other options, education could count on a number of bright females entering teaching. However, with a societal emphasis on the elimination of gender dis-crimination, many more options are open to women, and competition for the best and the brightest has increased dramatically.

A DAY IN THE LIFE . . . Are Teachers Paid Enough?

The traffic was heavy as Pat Taylor drove toward home. It had been a rewarding day at school. The students had been very responsive and had been excited about the lessons. Seeing the sparkle in their eyes and hearing the excitement in their voices was really great. As usual, there were the comments and classroom incidents that brought a smile. Kids were great! Although there were problem students from time to time, they actually presented a challenge and one of the most rewarding things in teaching was to see them change and feel like you have made a difference in their lives.

However, Pat's thoughts turned to some other pressing matters. The car needed new tires and that was going to cost a bundle. Increasing gas prices had really put a dent in the monthly budget. It seemed that each month the cost of everything went up while the income stayed the same.

Pat's mind also wandered to the dinner party last Saturday. A couple of Pat's friends from college were there. They were doing well in their jobs and mentioned their promotions and salary increases. One of the guests was a moderately successful businessman. He was driving an expensive car and relished telling everyone about it. During the evening, the subject of education came up and he was quick to condemn educators as unintelligent and lazy. "What can you expect from individuals who choose to be teachers?" he asked. "Individuals with real ambition choose jobs that pay a decent salary. Many of them just choose teaching so they can have the summer off to play around. The problems of education could be simply solved if they had enough knowledge to apply basic business principles."

Reflecting on the dinner party was somewhat depressing. The success of friends was great, but also triggered a bit of envy. The businessman was just an egotistical bag of wind, but his comments were irritating. Putting it all together, the struggle to make ends meet, the success of others in other careers, the lack of respect for teachers in society made Pat wonder about remaining in teaching. Was it worth it?

✓ Disposition Check

In a society where the values of individuals are often measured by the size of their checks, it is only natural to expect teachers will have feelings of inadequacy. This perspective is not just confined to elementary and secondary schools. A few years ago the authors taught at a university where one of the members of the board of regents commented, "If the faculty are so smart, why aren't they rich?"

Few would deny that teachers are underpaid. All teachers get tired of comments about how important teaching is and how noble it is that someone would choose to be a teacher, and then have to stuggle to pay bills. What hurts is that some of the comments of this businessman had an element of truth.

To be sure, there are rewards other than financial ones. Although teachers do have grounds for complaint if they have the disposition to do so, many recognize that teaching can be one of the most rewarding and exciting professions.

As you reflect on this incident,

1. What are your values?
2. What do you find rewarding?
3. Do you have a disposition that will allow you to overcome a societal emphasis on fiscal rewards?

Another societal factor that should be considered is the fact that teaching in the United States continues to be largely a feminine profession. Teaching became a feminized profession in the latter part of the 19th century. It was claimed that females had a natural disposition that made them ideal for teaching. They were defined as more mild and gentle with stronger parental impulses and it was assumed that these qualities made them superior teachers of young children. Teaching was considered as a continuation of the family, and teaching came to be viewed as a vocation belonging to women (Altenbaugh, 2002).

It was also reasoned that women did not have a family to support so they could be hired for less money. In addition, because of their subordinate social position and their perceived submissive nature, it was thought that female teachers would be more compliant in carrying out the directives of the male school administrators (Altenbaugh, 2002).

The proportion of male teachers has been declining in recent years and approximately 85% of the teachers across the nation are female. This continues to support the perception in the United States that teaching is a feminine profession. In addition, the low salaries commanded by teachers can be seen as a continuation of gender discrimination and the notion that they do not need professional-level salaries.

The feminization of education leads to a lack of respect for male teachers. Society does not encourage males to be teachers. When they do enter teaching, it is often expected that they will soon move out of teaching into an administrative role. Therefore, the recruitment of males into teaching is especially difficult.

Another variable related to the teacher shortage is teacher retention. Across the nation, nearly 50% of the teachers leave within the first five years of teaching (Budig, 2006). There are several contributing factors, including low salary, lack of societal respect for teachers, working conditions, the feminine nature of the teaching force, lack of adequate preparation, and changing perceptions about careers in general. For example, one outstanding male teacher, mentored by one of the authors, chose to leave teaching after a few years when his teaching salary did not qualify him for a home loan.

Interestingly, those who apply economic principles to education and claim that competition between schools will improve education do not seem to apply the same logic to the teaching force. It can be argued that making the salary of teachers competitive with other segments of society would have a profound impact on the quality of education and the status of teachers. If teacher salaries were competitive, then more of the best and the brightest would be attracted to teaching. This competition would force out less academically qualified candidates and would improve the talent pool available for hire by the school districts. The increased income would also improve the status of teachers in society.

Many entering teaching do not view it as a long-term career (Budig, 2006). They view teaching as something they will do for a few years before moving on to another line of work. Some suggest that they would consider staying in teaching longer if they felt the conditions of work would improve. Perhaps this is best summarized by the comments of one teacher who stated that if he felt a sense of achievement and if he was paid better, he would probably stay in teaching (Peske, Liu, Johnson, Kauffman, & Kardos, 2001).

If the teacher shortage is to be overcome, attention must be directed to find ways to enhance the status of teaching, to make teaching more attractive to a larger segment of society, and to develop a better balance of intrinsic and extrinsic rewards. This will require serious consideration of those societal perspectives and attitudes that encourage and discourage individuals from becoming teachers.

For several decades, proposals have addressed teacher quality and the teacher shortage. One persistent proposal has been to increase the duration of the teacher-preparation programs. There have been claims that if teacher preparation was extended beyond the undergraduate years and required a graduate education somewhat closer to other professions, such as law and medicine, improved status and prestige would follow. There have been some attempts to implement this perspective. For example, California has required a fifth year for teacher preparation for several decades. However, there is little evidence that this extended preparation has improved teacher status.

One outcome of extended teacher-preparation programs is an increased cost to become a teacher. In addition to another year or so of tuition and costs, those choosing to be teachers are also forgoing a salary for a year. Given low teacher pay, these are costs that will never be returned.

From a sociological perspective, the issue of who would benefit and who would be attracted to teaching should be addressed. It might be predicted that those who would be less likely to be attracted to teaching if program length is increased are those individuals from minority and low-income groups who can least afford the extra cost. This interactionist perspective helps us predict the outcomes of this change. The teaching force is currently predominantly white with a shortage of teachers of color. Would this policy only worsen this situation? What about the interaction between teachers and students when there are few teachers from the students' ethnic group?

This also gives rise to debates about the issue of teacher quality. Advocates of extended teacher-preparation programs point to the complex role of teaching as justification for more depth of preparation and an extended field experience. They believe that the education of our youth is too important to be left to "on-the-job training." However, others see teacher-education programs as a waste of time. They characterize teacher-education programs as "barriers" that perpetuate the teacher shortage. They contend that teacher-education courses discourage individuals with strong academic qualities from pursuing teaching. Individuals voicing this perspective generally contend that subject-matter knowledge is the most important quality for good teaching. As a result, they promote rigorous subject-matter examinations rather than teacher-education coursework as criteria for becoming a teacher. This is the perspective of the "No Child Left Behind" designations of a "qualified teacher."

From a sociological perspective, the debate should be viewed in terms of the impact on the teaching force. What would be the nature of those choosing to be teachers if the major teacher credential requirements were reduced to that of passing a subject-matter examination? What would be the impact on the learning of students if individuals with little or no knowledge of teaching and learning were issued teaching credentials? Will making teaching easier to enter solve the teacher shortage problem or will it only increase the turnover rate? What would be the impact of increasing teacher credential requirements? How would these changes impact the learning of students? Would more rigorous standards improve the status of teachers or would it only lead to an increased employment of substandard or uncredentialed teachers in order to meet the teacher supply problem? Viewing these issues through the lens of the conflict perspective leads to the question, who would be the likely winners and who would be the likely losers to these proposed changes?

School Violence

Another social issue that commands considerable attention is the issue of violence in schools. Incidents such as the shootings at Virginia Tech University, Columbine, and the Amish elementary school in Pennsylvania capture the attention of the nation and shock society. The shooting at Nickel Mines, Pennsylvania, was the third fatal school shooting in the United States in six days ("He Was Angry at Life," October 3, 2006). Public surveys continually indicate that school violence is a major concern that influences public attitudes toward schools. In fact, personal safety is cited as a major concern of those considering teaching as a career.

One of the reasons that violence in school promotes societal shock is that schools are generally viewed as safe havens separate from the problems of society. However, schools are a part of society and if there is violence in society, there will be violence in schools.

The perception of schools as unsafe environments filled with violence does not conform to reality. To be sure, even one incidence of violence is too many. However, compared to other segments of society, schools are relatively safe places. The risk of becoming a victim of violence is about twice as great outside school than it is inside school. School violence is concentrated in about 10% of the schools and only about 9 out of 1,000 students are victims of serious school-related violent crime (Lindsey & Beach, 2004).

Studies that show that about 10% of high school students carry weapons to school and about 20% of middle and high school students report at least one violent crime while

Figure 9–2   **Selecting teaching as a career.**

How do your reasons for choosing teaching as a career compare with the information contained in this section of the chapter? Respond to the following questions.

1. Which of the following were reasons you considered teaching?
   - ____ Working with children and students
   - ____ Love of your subject matter
   - ____ Making a contribution to society
   - ____ Status of teaching in society
   - ____ A convenient work schedule

2. Who had the most influence on your decision?
   - ____ Parents
   - ____ Teachers
   - ____ Counselors
   - ____ Prior experience working with students

3. What is your estimate of males in your teacher preparation cohort?
   - ____ over 50%
   - ____ 25–29%
   - ____ 10–24%
   - ____ Less than 10%

4. What do you see as the status given to teachers in your community, family, and circle of friends?
   - ____ High status, respected
   - ____ Moderate status, "It's okay to be a teacher."
   - ____ Low status, "Why would you want to be a teacher?"

5. How long do you expect you will remain in teaching?
   - ____ 3–5 years
   - ____ 6–10 years
   - ____ Until retirement

6. What is your concern level concerning teacher salaries?
   - ____ Little or no concern
   - ____ Some concern
   - ____ Major concern

---

they were at school help to fuel the view of schools as dangerous places (Lindsey & Beach, 2004).

Fear of violence in schools also impacts the teacher shortage. In addition to discouraging some individuals from entering teaching, the inability to control the classroom and deal with disruptive behavior is a major reason why teachers leave the profession.

Even though there is a general impression that violence in schools is a recent phenomena, student misbehavior and violence have a long history in American education. For example, in 1837 over 300 schools in Massachusetts alone were disrupted by rebellious students. Assaults on teachers and the practice of "putting out the teacher," or locking them out of the classroom, were typical examples of student misbehavior (Altenbaugh, 2002). Consider these perspectives as you complete the Survey in Figure 9–2.

Teachers also contributed to school violence through their responses. Teachers often relied on forms of corporal punishment that today would be considered child abuse. Schoolhouses usually included a whipping post and it was reported that in Boston in 1845, floggings averaged 65 per day in a school with a student population of 400. Moreover, society considered severity as a desirable teacher trait (Altenbaugh, 2002).

What this indicates is that there has been no "golden age" of education when all students came to school with respect for the teacher, had an overwhelming desire to learn, and were well behaved. Violence in schools now, as then, reflects on society as a whole. In earlier days, the physical punishment of children and the cruelty of teachers reflected the culture and societal expectations of the time (Altenbaugh, 2002).

Authoritarian approaches to student misbehavior and violence such as "zero tolerance" can be viewed through the conflict perspective as a power struggle between adults and students in a system where students are powerless. The conflict perspective sees these practices as creating mistrust, student resistance, and an environment that interferes with learning. The contention is that these approaches actually make school less safe because the fear that is generated damages the relationship between teacher and students.

Some sociologists suggest that approaching school violence requires a coordinated effort involving all segments of society. This effort should involve the community and the family. There should be a focus on such dimensions as self-esteem, violence in the media, definitions of masculinity that includes aggression, and the reduction of gang presence in the community (Lindsey & Beach, 2004). You can use Figure 9–2 to reflect on your reasons for choosing a career in teaching.

ARE THE SCHOOLS FAILING?

Because education is such an important part of society, it should not be surprising that there is considerable interest in the performance of schools. Claims that the schools are failing are not new. Many of today's critics would be surprised to learn that the schools they attended were also criticized and labeled as failures. For example, nearly 40 years ago Alvin Toffler, in his book *Future Shock*, noted "The craggy outlines of the new society are emerging from the mists of tomorrow. Yet even as we speed closer, evidence mounts that one of our most crucial subsystems—education—is seriously malfunctioning" (Toffler, 1970, p. 398). Many today would claim that the situation has only grown worse.

Because there are several perspectives through which education can be viewed and there are so many expectations for the schools, there will always be some who view the performance of the schools as inadequate. However, in recent decades the claims of failure have reached unprecedented levels.

Many education critics claim that the nation's public schools are dismal failures. They claim that educational achievement, as measured by the Scholastic Aptitude Test (SAT), has fallen dramatically in the past 30 years, citing international comparisons as evidence of this failure. The media have uncritically echoed these claims so that even many public school supporters assume that the schools are failing.

Much of the current criticism of the schools can be traced to the publication in 1983 of *A Nation at Risk*. This report claimed that the "failures" of the public schools were confirmed by evidence. However, the report did not cite any sources of evidence.

Educational researchers Berliner and Biddle (1995) and Bracey (2003) claim that the so-called failure of the public schools has been manufactured in order to further specific ideological agendas. They present positive data about school performance that have been ignored and indicate how other data have been distorted in order to support the view of the failure of the public schools.

Berliner and Biddle (1995) point out that the SAT is a poor barometer of the success of education and is not intended for this purpose. Bracey (2003) notes that on the SAT, the verbal scores for the 2002 test were precisely what they were in 1981. Furthermore, when the data were disaggregated, the scores for all of the ethnic groups showed increases. The average for white student scores increased by 8 points, for black students by 19 points, for Asian students by 27 points, and for both Mexican and Native American students by 8 points. If the critics looked at the math portion of the test, they would see that the percentage of individuals scoring over 650 has increased by 74% (Bracey, 2003).

How could it be that the overall average remained the same while all subgroups reported an increase? The answer is that a larger percentage of minority students took the test in 2002 than in 1981. For example, in 1981, 85% of the test takers were white. In 2002, 65% of the test takers were white. Because nonwhite students have historically scored lower than white students, increasing the percentage of nonwhite students taking the test decreased the average score even though all subgroups improved. When viewed through this perspective, these data can be interpreted as an indication of the success of schools. More nonwhite students are being encouraged for higher levels of achievement and more have aspirations for higher education prompting them to take the college entrance examinations such as the SAT. In fact, Bracey (2003) concludes that the public schools have educated a more diverse student population while raising achievement levels at the same time. This should be viewed as a major success, not as an indication of failure.

When international comparisons are made, a number of factors must be considered. Those include the sample of the students tested and differences in the curriculum. In some nations, more than 50% of the students enter vocational programs and only selected students are allowed to continue into secondary education. Another example is that in the Third International Math and Science Study (TIMSS), the final year was defined in the United States as the 12th grade. However, other nations included students who would be at levels equivalent to grade 13 or 14, and in one nation, they were as old as college seniors (Bracey, 2003).

Contrary to interpretations of failure, American students are doing quite well. For example, American fourth graders were well above average in the mathematics portion of the TIMSS test and were third in the world on the science portion. In eighth-grade science, 12 nations showed declines from 1995 to 2003, whereas the United States gained 15 points (Bracey, 2006).

An international study of reading skills found that U.S. students were second only to Finnish students at ages 9 and 14. The best readers in the United States outscored the best readers in the 30 other nations tested.

The Organization for Economic Cooperation and Development conducted an international comparison labeled the "Program for International Assessment (PISA)." In this assessment of math, science, and reading literacy, American 15-year-olds scored average with the 28 nations tested. Although critics argue that average is not good enough, it hardly indicates that schools are failing. What the PISA study did reveal were tremendous differences in achievement between rich and poor schools. For example, white students, on the average, ranked 2nd in reading, 7th in math, and 4th in science. However, black and Hispanic students, on the average, ranked 26th in reading, 27th in math, and 27th in science (Bracey, 2003). This seems to indicate that the issue is not a generalized failure of the public schools but a failure to provide a quality education for minority students and schools with large minority populations. This could be used to support the conflict perspective and make the point that it is the powerless groups who are not being served well by the schools.

Evidence of this dual nature of the public school system is reflected in a legal brief filed in California in 2001. The legal action, which was successful in court, cited poor inner-city schools where the following occur:

- Students were forced to sit on windowsills because there were not enough chairs.
- There were chemistry labs with no chemicals, literature classes with no books, and computer classes with no computers.

- There were classes with no teachers. They were taught by a string of substitutes.
- Rats scurried about on bread racks in the school's cafeteria. (Bracey, 2003)

Additional evidence that the public schools are not widespread failures is found in surveys of public attitudes toward schools. Surveys of public attitudes conducted annually by the Gallup organization reveal that over 67% of the parents assign their local school a grade of "A" or "B" (Rose & Gallup, 2007). It is interesting to note that the majority of those surveyed rated their neighborhood schools quite high but the schools in general were rated significantly lower. This could be the result of the overwhelming negative image of the schools reported in the media. The people who have firsthand knowledge of their local schools see them as doing well. However, their images of the schools in general are colored by negative reports, causing them to view other schools as less successful. The issue then appears not to be the failure of the public schools in general.

What Do You Think?

- How do you respond to data reflecting on the success or failure of the schools?
- Why do you think there has been an emphasis on data that are negative about school success?

Why would some individuals and groups deliberately distort and overlook data in order to vilify the public schools? Most citizens like to think that on important matters such as education, politicians and policymakers have the best interest of the people at heart. However, one has only to look at significant events over the past couple of decades to note that individuals are not above giving events a decided "spin" or even stooping to hiding and distorting information in order to further their own political agendas (Pogrow, 2006).

When viewing the claims of educational failure, some individuals are genuinely worried about the status of education. Others have a sincere belief that schools operated by government bodies are just inherently wrong and that privatization of all governmental institutions is the answer. Many well-meaning parents send their children to private religious schools and would like to see these schools receive public funds. Others simply may have misunderstood the data or have been misled.

Berliner and Biddle (1995) identify several other reasons. Some of these reasons reflect sociological perspectives that have been discussed in this chapter. They note that many politicians are private-school graduates with children in private schools. Therefore, they have no loyalty to public schools and, viewed from the conflict perspective, support private education as a means of maintaining their status and power. Another motive consistent with the conflict perspective is the view that many policymakers have led the attack on the public schools in order to divert attention from their failure to address serious social issues. Issues of poverty, racism, and injustice are persistent problems that involve difficult and controversial actions. It is much safer to shift responsibility and blame to the public schools rather than enact controversial and difficult legislation that will address the root of the problem.

From a functionalist perspective, many business leaders would like a trained workforce that would move individuals right into jobs, with little cost or disruption. They would like to have more input and control the goals and the curriculum of the schools. Therefore, being critical of the school establishment and asking for more control to overcome their perceived deficits is a step in furthering their own agendas.

Finally, a tremendous amount of money is spent on education. If the success of schools can be brought into question, a large potential market for other materials and solutions might be created. For example, companies that publish tests have had a great increase in profits as a result of the calls for increased accountability of schools using standardized tests.

Whatever the reasons, suspicions that there are overt efforts to discredit the public schools were fueled when evidence surfaced that a study by the Sandia National Laboratories of the education system commissioned by the first Bush administration was buried when the data indicated that the schools were performing much better than critics claimed. Ignoring positive data and the distortion of data such as those cited above have led many, including Berliner, Biddle, and Bracey, to conclude that there has been a deliberate attempt to mislead the public about the status and success of the schools. Berliner and Biddle (1995) state, "The manufactured crisis" was not an accidental event. Rather, it appeared within a specific historical context and was led by identifiable critics whose political goals could be furthered by "scapegoating education" (p. 4).

In summary, the sociological perspective provides us with some ways of thinking about the role of education in society. These perspectives challenge us to think more deeply about educational issues and the role of school in society. This can be a useful tool in trying to understand the persistent problem of teacher shortage, to place in perspective the issue of school violence, and to understand the possible motives of those who question the success of the schools.

Key Ideas in Summary

- Education is viewed as an important institution in industrialized society linked to the social, economic, and political development of a nation. This creates many tensions between the schools and other institutions and groups in society.
- U.S. citizens have a strong faith in education and view it as important in helping achieve the American dream. This faith has often led to some unrealistic expectations and the assignment of responsibility for social problems and issues whose root causes are outside of education.
- An example of the tensions created between societal institutions is that of early childhood education. Research has indicated that preschool education has important impacts on the education of the children. Some nations have mandated early childhood education at an early age. However, there is much opposition in the United States because some individuals see early childhood education as infringing on the rights of families.
- Sociologists use three modes of analysis to view educational issues. These include the functionalist perspective and the conflict perspective, who view school at a macro level. The interactionist perspective views schools at the micro level by looking at the interactions within schools.
- The funtionalist perspective highlights the major functions of the school in maintaining a functioning society. The perspective looks at socialization, social cohesion, social integration, and the placement of individuals in the social system.
- The conflict perspective views education through the lens of power relationships. The basic premise is that education is a constant struggle between those in power who are trying to keep it and those with little power who are trying to gain it. They investigate class, race, and gender influences on educational policy.
- The interactionist perspective focuses on interactions between teachers and students and how those interactions shape individuals' views of themselves and their role in society. This perspective investigates issues such as rules that govern relationships, teacher expectations, tracking, and gender differences.

- Sociological perspectives are useful in providing insight into educational issues. This insight can be useful when identifying possible solutions. Two issues where sociological research provides insight are the teacher shortage and school violence. A sociological analysis illustrates that solutions to these issues will require collaboration between the institutions of society and even changes in societal values and attitudes.
- Because schools are such important societal institutions, their performance is constantly evaluated. Because schools are expected to achieve a wide variety of goals, some of which are in conflict, it can be expected that some segments of society will find the accomplishments of the schools wanting. In fact, in recent decades there has been a widespread belief that the schools are failing.
- The 1983 publication of *A Nation at Risk* ignited a debate about the failure of public education that continues to influence educational policy. The report and the critics who came later have cited SAT test scores and international comparisons as evidence that the schools are failing. However, other researchers have disputed these claims and have cited data that counter the assertions of failure. They indicate that the "crisis" in education is a manufactured one designed to further the social and political agendas of certain groups.

For Your Initial-Development Portfolio

1. What materials and ideas in this chapter about the role of school in society will you include as "evidence" of your learning in your portfolio? Select up to three separate items of information. Number them 1, 2, and 3.
2. Think about why you selected these materials. As you do so, consider these issues:
   - Specific uses you might make of this information as you consider your role as a teacher.
   - How the various perspectives discussed in this chapter relate to your values and beliefs.
   - Contributions this information can make to your development.
3. Place a check in the chart below to indicate to which INTASC standard(s) each of your items of information relates. (You may wish to refer to Chapter 1 for more detailed information about INTASC.)

INTASC Standard Number										
ITEM OF EVIDENCE NUMBER	**S1**	**S2**	**S3**	**S4**	**S5**	**S6**	**S7**	**S8**	**S9**	**S10**
1										
2										
3										

4. Prepare a written reflection in which you analyze the decision-making process you followed. Mention the INTASC standard(s) to which your selected material relates.

Reflections

1. Which of the three sociological modes of analysis is most consistent with your view of the role of education in society? How does that influence your stance on educational reform proposals?
2. Evaluate your motives for going to college and considering teaching as a career. How were your choices influenced by your social environment?
3. What have been your experiences in labeling, tracking, and teacher expectations? How have these influenced your self-concept and your aspirations?
4. Inequality of schools is a major issue in contemporary education. Various proposals have focused on mandatory busing, vouchers, charter schools, accountability, and high-stakes testing. What are the pros and the cons for each of these proposals in addressing school inequities?
5. What were the influences that led you to consider teaching as a career? What do you think is needed in order to address the teacher shortage?

Field Experiences, Projects, and Enrichment

1. Visit some schools in your area. Do you see any indications of grouping or tracking students based on criteria other than ability?
2. As you observe schools throughout the region, do you see evidence of a difference in facilities and materials according to the socioeconomic status or the ethnicity of the students?
3. Interview some of your classmates. What do they think would be the impact of changing teacher-preparation requirements on those who choose to enter teaching?
4. Discuss with others, both in education and outside of education, the perceived status of teachers. Is the status deserved? What could be done to improve the status of teachers? What impact would that have?

References

Altenbaugh, R. (2002). *The American people and their education: A social history*. Upper Saddle River, NJ: Pearson-Prentice Hall.

Ballantine, J. (2001). *The sociology of education: A systematic analysis* (5th ed.). Upper Saddle River, NJ: Pearson-Prentice Hall.

Berliner, D., & Biddle, B. (1995). *The manufactured crisis: Myths, frauds, and the attack on America's public schools*. Reading, MA: Addison-Wesley.

Bracey, G. (2003). *On the death of childhood and the destruction of public schools: The folly of today's education policies and practices*. Portsmouth, NH: Heinemann.

Bracey, G. W. (2006). The 16th Bracey Report on the Condition of Public Education. *Phi Delta Kappan, 88*(2), 151–165.

Budig, G. A. (2006). A perfect storm. *Phi Delta Kappan, 88*(2), 114–116.

Commager, H. (1976). *The people and their schools*. Bloomington, ID: Phi Delta Kappa Educational Foundation.

Curry, T., Jiobu, R., & Schwirian, K. (2005). *Sociology for the twenty-first century* (4th ed.). Upper Saddle River, NJ: Pearson-Prentice Hall.

Dougherty, K., & Hammack, F. (1990). *Education and society: A reader*. San Diego, CA: Harcourt Brace Jovanovich.

Good, T., & Brophy, J. (2003). *Looking in classrooms* (9th ed.). Boston: Allyn and Bacon.

He was angry at life. *U.S.A. Today*, 2006, (October 3). p. 1 +.

Lindsey, L., & Beach, S. (2004). *Sociology* (3rd ed.). Upper Saddle River, NJ: Pearson-Prentice Hall.

Lunenburg, F. C., & Irby, B. J. (2006). *The principalship*. Belmont, CA.: Thompson/Wadsworth.

Macionis, J. (2005). *Sociology* (10th ed.). Upper Saddle River, NJ: Pearson-Prentice Hall.

National Center for Educational Statistics. (2006). *The condition of education: Participation in education*. Washington DC: http://nces.ed.gov./programs/coe/2006/section1/table.asp?tableID+436 (9-6-2006)

Parsons, T. (1959). School class as a social system: Some of its functions in American society. *Harvard Educational Review, 49*, 297–318.

Peske, H., Liu, E., Johnson, S., Kauffman, D., & Kardos, S. (2001). The next generation of teachers: Changing conceptions of a career of teaching. *Phi Delta Kappan, 83*(4), 304–311.

Pogrow, S. (2006). The Bermuda Triangle of American education: Pure traditionalism, pure progressivism, and good intentions. *Phi Delta Kappan, 88*(2), 142–150.

Rose, L. C., & Gallup, A. M. (2007). "The 39th Annual Phi Delta Kappa/Gallup Poll of the Public's Attitudes toward the public schools." *Phi Delta Kappan, 89*(1), 33–54.

Sarason, S. (2002). *Questions you should ask about charter schools and vouchers*. Portsmouth, NH: Heinemann.

Toffler, A. (1970). *Future shock*. New York: Random House.

CHAPTER 10

How Do Philosophical Perspectives Influence Education?

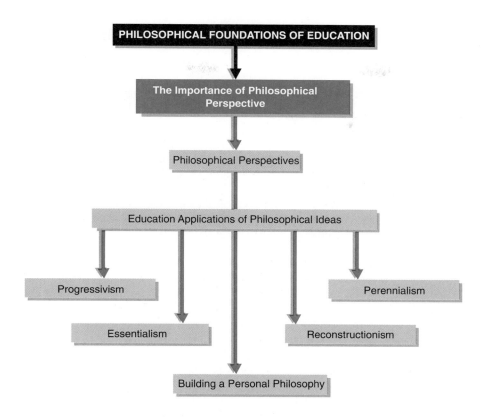

PHILOSOPHICAL FOUNDATIONS OF EDUCATION

The Importance of Philosophical Perspective

Philosophical Perspectives

Education Applications of Philosophical Ideas

Progressivism

Perennialism

Essentialism

Reconstructionism

Building a Personal Philosophy

OBJECTIVES

This chapter will help you to

- state the importance of understanding different philosophical perspectives.

- define basic questions that need to be asked regarding the application of philosophy to the classroom.

- state how different educational philosophies answer basic questions.

- define contemporary applications of different educational philosophies.

- develop a personal statement of philosophy.

The Importance of Philosophical Perspectives

Those entering the world of education soon learn that there is a lack of agreement concerning the purposes of education, what should be taught, who should be taught, and how they should be taught. Beginning teachers are frequently overwhelmed and puzzled by the intensity of the debate. It seems that everyone has an opinion about teaching and learning.

In order to understand the basis for these disagreements, it is important to understand how different philosophical assumptions lead to different conclusions regarding what the practice of education should be. Often, we are unaware of the basis for our beliefs about education and the basis for many of the criticisms (Warner, 2006). As a result, we may find ourselves confused as we address these criticisms and try to articulate our own views. Some individuals are unaware that many of the debates about education are fundamentally differences in philosophical beliefs. Understanding those disagreements enables us to understand criticisms and proposals for change.

To further emphasize the importance of understanding different philosophical perspectives, it is useful to understand how education is changing. For most of the history of education in the United States, teachers had considerable discretion in deciding what and how students would be taught. When the classroom door was closed, the classroom was their domain. Therefore, teacher employers were careful to hire new teachers whose beliefs matched the expectations of the local community. The match was easy because most teachers had a middle-class background that matched the communities where they taught.

For many teachers and administrators, philosophy was a rather abstract and esoteric subject that had little relevance to the daily routines of teaching. This perspective remains popular among many contemporary teachers (Warner, 2006). Those few teachers who held perspectives significantly at odds with those of the local community usually looked for jobs elsewhere. However, the reality today is that both the communities and the teachers' backgrounds are more diverse.

Add to this the fact that in recent decades, education has become a national concern. Politicians have realized that education is a topic that interests a large number of voters. In addition, changes in the way education is funded have shifted power away from local communities. In many places, the influence of teachers over what is taught and how they are to teach has diminished. Individuals outside the classroom, usually at the state and national level, are making more decisions that have a direct impact on teaching and learning. The decisions that these individuals make are often based on philosophical assumptions that may not be understood or challenged. Given the importance of education in society, it has become increasingly critical that educators and the public understand the agenda of policymakers and the implications of their proposals.

Some of the issues that need to be debated include deciding content standards that impact the curriculum for every student in the state, the use of high-stakes testing that can seriously impact the future prospects of all students, tightly prescribed and even scripted curriculums that all teachers are required to follow, and the qualifications of those allowed to be teachers. All of these issues have important implications. Therefore, understanding educational philosophy is no longer merely an academic exercise that entertains university professors. For classroom teachers and the public to evaluate educational proposals they must understand their philosophical roots.

From a personal perspective, understanding the implications of proposed changes can help you decide whether teaching in a particular school and community is going to be personally satisfying. It is far more satisfying in settings where there is basic agreement regarding the purposes and directions of education.

PHILOSOPHICAL PERSPECTIVES

Philosophical perspectives represent clusters of values and attitudes that individuals use to evaluate alternative action options and decide which are preferred. You may rarely have considered your own personal philosophy or how it affects your actions. Conscious thought about your beliefs can help you make more purposeful and consistent decisions about teaching and learning.

What comes to your mind when you hear the term *philosophy*? You may get an image of an arcane subject that deals with issues far removed from the realm of the practical. Some of you may recall unpleasant experiences in undergraduate philosophy courses that required you to confront difficult abstractions. Frustrations in dealing with this kind of content may lurk behind some anxieties you may experience when, during a job interview, the representative of the school district asks, "What is your philosophy of education?"

Philosophy's reputation as a subject that is unconnected to the real world is undeserved. Your philosophical positions help explain your personal reactions to events you confront in your daily life and what you find personally rewarding and satisfying. Philosophy explains your responses to such educational questions as the following:

- What is the purpose of education?
- How should I treat students?
- What knowledge is of most worth?
- Who should decide what is worth knowing?
- What should be included in the curriculum?
- What is the role of a teacher?

Your life experiences have helped you to work out at least informal answers to these questions. In fact, your responses to many of them have become so deeply ingrained that you probably rarely think about them. Your reactions have become part of you because of your interactions with society's customs and traditions. You assume that your patterns of behavior make sense and are natural responses to the world in which you live. However, other people have different life experiences and have developed different views. They also think their perspectives are the natural and logical ones. To help you understand how teachers hold different views, read about our focus teacher Pat, and this teacher's experience working with colleagues in this chapter's *A Day in the Life* feature.

A DAY IN THE LIFE . . . Textbook Selection

It was Pat Taylor's third year of teaching high school American history. Pat had been excited when asked to serve as a representative on the school district textbook selection committee. The texts currently in use were about 10 years old and dated. Pat thought it might be fun to read through some new texts and get some new ideas that could be used in the classroom.

The committee assignment had started off with a meeting of the committee. Attending were teachers from other high schools in the district, the curriculum director for the district, and a couple of school administrators. At the first meeting, the process of the new textbook adoption was explained and a checklist

. . . continued

of criteria for evaluating a text was reviewed. The criteria had been developed by the curriculum director, using checklists that had been previously used. There was some discussion about specific items on the list, and a few changes had been made. The checklist contained a number of items that they had to check as they reviewed each book. It was considerably longer than Pat had anticipated. Pat quickly realized that this assignment was going to involve a lot more than just reading some books and choosing the best. The checklist included items such as the accuracy of the information, making sure the text addressed the state standards, and the readability level of the book. Several items had to be checked to make sure their choice could withstand challenges down the road, including the checking of photographs and illustrations to make sure that a variety of ethnic groups were included. They had to also make sure that the photographs avoided stereotypes. In fact, due to pressure from the nutritional lobby, the state board of education had declared that textbooks could not have pictures that included "junk food." Pat began to understand why so many textbooks appeared bland.

Then a list of the books under consideration was distributed. The first step was for the committee to review the texts and narrow the list to the top three. They each left the meeting with a couple of texts to review.

Using the checklists, Pat spent a considerable amount of time reviewing the texts. Today, the committee was meeting to review the first two books. Pat had especially liked one book and thought the students would find it interesting. When the committee was called to order, the book that Pat liked was the first to be reviewed.

Pat was somewhat taken aback by the comments of the first teacher. "This is a terrible book. It doesn't have enough solid content. We've had enough of 'dumbed down' texts. We need something that is rigorous and demanding." "I disagree," said another teacher. "What we need is a text that is interesting to the students. If they won't read it, the content doesn't matter." Another teacher jumped into the discussion. "I don't like all of the references to the controversial issues in American history. This will only make the students cynical. We need to develop a sense of allegiance and a commitment to our nation. Texts like this will undermine the important citizenship purpose of American history."

Pat was becoming uncomfortable with the adversarial tone that the comments were taking. With such divergent views, how could they ever reach an agreement? Maybe this committee was not going to be as enjoyable as once hoped. As the debate intensified, Pat observed the curriculum director popping a couple of antacids.

✓ Disposition Check

Teaching involves not just working with students in the classroom. Professional responsibilities extend to serving on committees and being involved in making important decisions about the school and the school district. When new teachers find themselves in this role, they are often surprised at the wide variety of perspectives that are brought to the discussion. When this occurs, the excitement that comes from being involved in making an important decision is often replaced with discouragement. One of us was once asked to serve on a very important district-level committee on a topic about which he was quite passionate. He was shocked to discover that no one else on the committee held the same position! Participation with groups like this requires an understanding of why individuals hold different perspectives and a great deal of diplomacy. It is possible to disagree without being disagreeable. Success in education requires that teachers have good interpersonal skills in working not only with students, but with parents and other professionals.

As you review this situation, think about the dispositions and attitudes that would be required in this situation.

1. How do you handle disagreement?
2. Are you able to compromise?
3. What are the things about which you could not compromise?

Individuals have wrestled with these questions and have sought logical answers. This has led to the development of "systematic philosophies." The following section outlines some of these educational philosophies. As you read through them, note those beliefs that are most consistent with your own. Try to remain open to responses that cause you to rethink your assumptions and beliefs.

EDUCATIONAL APPLICATIONS OF PHILOSOPHICAL IDEAS

Education-related systems of philosophy have implications for educational practice. These systems can help you clarify your beliefs about what the goals of education should be, what individuals should be taught, and what methods should be used to teach them. They will help you construct a personal philosophy.

By nature, philosophical systems cannot be scientifically tested. Therefore, none of them has been "proven" to be true. For one person, a given alternative may appear to be based on solid logic and sound arguments, whereas another person may view it as illogical and poorly reasoned. As you read about the systems, consider the assumptions and arguments associated with each one and note those that you consider logical and well reasoned. This exercise will be valuable as you consider educational programs and educational changes.

Progressivism

Progressivism has been an important educational philosophy for a considerable part of the 20th century. One of the main figures identified with progressivism is John Dewey (1902, 1910, 1916, 1938). Note that Dewey lived at a time when education was undergoing profound change. Until the beginning of the 20th century, education was designed primarily for those few who were going on to higher education. It was not assumed that education would be practical. School curricula focused on classical subjects. The general practice of education was that of extensive routine, authoritarian teachers whose word was law, memorization of facts, and no student rights.

Progressivism arose as a reaction to these practices. In addition, the spirit of progress that characterized the close of the 19th century and the early years of the 20th century led to an emphasis on the role of science in improving society.

Dewey was concerned that the schools were out of touch with life and failed to teach individuals how to use knowledge. In his 1916 book, *Democracy and Education*, he claimed that education of that time was not preparing students for their role as citizens. Thus, he proposed an alternative philosophy that would better prepare individuals for the realities of contemporary life. This educational philosophy became known as progressivism.

Progressivism emphasizes change as the essence of reality and the importance of science in dealing with change. Furthermore, in order to prepare students for their role as citizens in a democracy, it emphasizes a strong commitment to the values of democracy.

What Is the Purpose of Education?

Progressivism identifies change as constant in the world. Rather than opposing change, progressive educators believe that individuals need to embrace change and learn how to direct it for the betterment of society. Thus, progressives see a major purpose of education as that of helping individuals learn how to solve problems. In this context, students need to learn the scientific method for defining and solving problems. This means that the active involvement of students is critical.

Progressives also have a high regard for the values and principles of democracy. They consider respect for the individual a basic value of democracy. As a result, progressives define a major purpose of education as that of facilitating the unique development of each individual. This is best done by providing students with the freedom to pursue their questions and interests. It assumes that as individuals develop unique skills and abilities, they will grow to be healthy and intellectually stimulated, with the ability to direct change and become a productive member of society. An important purpose of schools is to teach individuals how to think rather than what to think. In order to develop the values and practices of democracy, schools need to be models that operate according to democratic principles.

How Should Students Be Treated?

Progressives do not view childhood as just a preparation for later life. It is viewed as a unique and important stage in and of itself. All children are viewed as having value and dignity with a right to an education. Therefore, students should be allowed to develop naturally. Their needs and interests must be respected and given priority. Classrooms must allow students the freedom to follow their own interests and find their own answers. The role of the teacher is to help them identify and clarify questions and guide them in their investigations.

◆ ◆

Back to the Whole
Go to MyEducationLab and select the topic "Philosophy of Education." Read the article "Back to Whole" written by Elliot Eisner that makes the case for having a broad-based education focused on the needs of the individuals. Respond to the questions.

◆ ◆

What Knowledge Is of Most Worth?

For progressives, because of the rapid rate of change, knowledge is viewed as temporary, not universal and stable. Rather, knowledge needs to be tested using the scientific method. Thus, the knowledge that is of most worth is knowledge that has been tested by experimentation.

Progressives believe that educated people should know how to adapt to and direct change. Dewey viewed scientific problem solving as the proper way to think and the scientific method as the most effective teaching approach (Gutek, 1997).

Who Should Decide What Is Worth Knowing?

Ultimately, it is the student who decides what is worth knowing. However, this has led to some distortions of the ideas of Dewey and other progressives. Some interpret the answer to this question to mean the only thing that matters is student freedom. They completely eliminate traditional or formal subjects from the curriculum and allow students the freedom to do whatever they desire. Critics of the progressive approach point to these excesses and claim that students do not have the maturity or experience to know what they need to learn. They argue that, left on their own, students will not develop the rigorous knowledge they need in order to prepare themselves to be productive members of society.

However, Dewey indicated that the content of traditional subjects and rigorous knowledge was important. The basic difference is in how this knowledge is to be included in the curriculum. Student interests are used as the beginning point. Building on their interests and questions, the teacher directs students to the content of traditional subjects as they need it to find answers to their questions and concerns. Therefore, rather than introducing a subject, such as history, as a collection of information to be memorized and applied at some later date, it is learned as needed in order to answer student inquiries.

As students grow and encounter more sophisticated issues and problems, they develop a more complete understanding of the subject. The argument is that material learned in relationship to student interests is more likely to be meaningful and therefore learned at a deeper level.

Progressives also favor an interdisciplinary approach to content. Content is not broken into discrete subjects. Therefore, individuals might simultaneously learn history, geography, science, and mathematics as they pursue their interests and quest for answers. The teacher needs to have a breadth of understanding of a variety of subjects in order to guide students to important knowledge.

One example of this approach was observed by one of the authors in a British school. A group of elementary-age students was interested in the Tower of London. The teacher helped them pose a number of questions to guide their search. Then the students decided how to organize the information they found. They researched the history of the tower; drew art sketches of the architecture; developed a scale model map of the area; did some mathematical calculations on topics such as costs, income, and estimated number of visitors; and wrote some essays and poetry. They integrated history, science, mathematics, art, music, and creative writing into an impressive project of which they were very proud.

What Should Be Included in the Curriculum?

Progressives favor a broad curriculum. The curriculum has room for all subjects including the arts and vocational studies. Any subject that is useful to the student in the quest for understanding is a legitimate subject to be included. Because of the extensive use of scientific problem solving, there is a strong emphasis on the natural and social sciences. A part of the role of the teacher is to stimulate student interests by presenting them with realistic questions and problems drawn from the traditional content areas. Students are then taught to generate hypotheses, gather data related to the hypotheses, test the hypotheses, and examine the consequences of each hypothesis. In posing problems and gathering data, the students may be engaged in activities such as field trips, cooperative problem solving, and simulations.

What Is the Role of a Teacher?

Implementing the progressive philosophy requires several abilities. The teacher must find ways to stimulate student interest and move their learning to deeper levels. Some methods for engaging students in learning include exposing them to new scientific and social developments, engaging them in meaningful games or simulations, posing questions that bring to light new or puzzling dimensions of a topic or question, and providing encounters with the world outside the classroom. As one person noted, the purpose of teacher knowledge is not merely to pass information on to the students. The purpose of teacher knowledge is to know the important questions to ask.

Progressives emphasize that schools should teach learners how to solve problems

Progressivism emphasizes student involvement and experimenting in the real world.

and inquire about their natural and social environments. Therefore, laboratory or experimental methods are favored instructional approaches.

What Do You Think?

- What aspects of progressivism are consistent with your views?
- Where do you disagree with progressivism?

Progressivism Today

The 20th century has certainly provided support for many of Dewey's ideas. Change has been a constant and continues to accelerate. This change has been led by advances in science, and the scientific method has been a significant force in the discovery of new knowledge. Research has also supported individual differences. There are significant differences between individuals, and each individual passes through definite stages of development. Children are not simply miniature adults without distinctive learning needs. Children do develop at different rates and they vary in their readiness to learn.

Instructional strategies such as inquiry, project learning, and simulations are consistent with progressive ideas. Classroom management approaches that involve students in the establishment of rules and treating students with respect and dignity also have roots in progressivism.

A recent development related to progressivism ideas is development of constructivism. Constructivism holds that individuals do not passively record and store things in their minds to be recalled at a later date. Rather, individuals continuously reconstruct their concepts and create meaning as a result of the interaction between their prior knowledge and new experience. This is very similar to the progressive emphasis on experience and the importance of allowing students the freedom to search for their own meanings.

However, progressivism has certainly been criticized. The influence of progressivism was seriously weakened in the 1950s by many who complained that the schools had gone "soft" and students were not learning academic content at a level necessary to keep the nation strong (Bestor, 1955). This assertion seemed to be verified when the Soviets launched Sputnik in the fall of 1957. The failure in the space race was blamed on the schools, and a massive educational reform movement was soon launched (Bracey, 2007). Critics claimed that few students were pursuing academic subjects, such as physics, with the rigor necessary to compete with other nations. As a result, education became too important to be entrusted to educators. Curriculum development was turned over to subject-matter experts and there was an increased emphasis on the acquisition of rigorous content in subjects such as science and mathematics.

Some of this criticism was justified because some educators understood or adopted only parts of Dewey's progressive philosophy. Extreme examples of these practices seriously distorted the public's views of Dewey and led to educational practices of dubious significance. Some educators irresponsibly reduced Dewey's thinking to a simplistic "the experience is the thing" slogan, which suggested that involving learners in enjoyable classroom activities was appropriate even in the absence of evidence that serious learning was occurring. Irresponsible classroom practices stemming from an inaccurate understanding of Dewey's work contributed to the development of some suspicions about the entire approach of the progressives.

In addition to a concern about an overemphasis on "experience," some individuals objected to Dewey's work on the grounds that his ideas promoted dangerous "relativism." They believed that enduring bodies of knowledge and truth exist and that Dewey's ideas were contrary to Judeo-Christian beliefs (Gutek, 1997). These critics argued that certain truths and values are universally applicable and valid and that teachers should deliver this fixed body of content to learners.

During the 1970s, there was somewhat of a resurgence of progressive ideas following the publication of a number of books by individuals labeled as "compassionate critics of education." These individuals criticized schools as mindless places that emphasized trivia and the status quo. There was some evidence that students were not making the academic strides that had been predicted. Much of the materials developed by the subject-matter experts simply did not take into account the interests and the motivations of the students. Therefore, students were not motivated and as a result there actually was a decline in students choosing rigorous academic studies.

The publication of *A Nation at Risk* in the early 1980s signaled another change of direction and ushered in a new age of reform based on a "back-to-basics" approach. The intent of the report was to produce a "Sputnik-like event" that would rock the nation. It certainly did this and became a public relations success. The recommendations of *A Nation at Risk* were very much at odds with progressivism and have continued to shape public perceptions of education and educational reform movements.

Today, many educators subscribe to the basic ideas of progressivism. They advocate making learning meaningful by taking into consideration the interests and needs of students. However, many policymakers have a more traditional and conservative view of the purpose of education. The result has been a great deal of tension between large segments of the educational community and the reformers, and the battle between progressive education and traditional education continues (Pogrow, 2006).

Essentialism

Essentialism is the field of philosophy that holds that the primary purpose of schools should be to transmit selected elements of culture to the next generation (Warner, 2006). Essentialism has roots deep in American history. For example, early educational laws in the New England colonies were designed to make sure that students learned those subjects that were essential for reading the Bible and for eluding the snares of Satan. Benjamin Franklin advocated a "practical" education and Thomas Jefferson promoted learning that was considered essential for individuals to be participants in a democratic society.

The term *essentialism* was popularized by William C. Bagley (1941) as a reaction to some of the more extreme variants of the progressive education movement. Essentialism gets its name from a focus on the academic content that is deemed to be "essential" for all students. It is basically a conservative, "back-to-basics" approach that stresses an organized, structured curriculum, and an inculcation of traditional values such as respect for authority.

What Is the Purpose of Education?

Essentialism views the purpose of education as teaching students "essential information and values." The role of school is not to reshape society, but rather to transmit the intellectual knowledge, the cultural heritage, and the moral values defined as necessary to prepare individuals to accept their role as members of society. One of the major purposes of school is to instill the virtues of discipline and hard work.

How Should Students Be Treated?

In the essentialist tradition, the teacher is the authority, not merely a guide. The teacher should establish the rules, maintain strict discipline, and make sure the students are learning

The essentialist philosophy emphasizes teaching students through whole group learning and methods such as lectures.

the specified content of the curriculum. The job of the student is to listen and to learn. All students need to learn the prescribed content, so there should be high academic standards for all students regardless of their prior knowledge or developmental level. Modifying instruction to accommodate individual differences is not a high priority. Thus, there is little support for individualization. Attempts to individualize the curriculum or address student interests are derisively labeled as "dumbing down" the curriculum.

The essentialist teacher should have well-defined lessons focusing on an organized and sequential curriculum. Students should be tested frequently to make sure they are mastering the content. All students should meet high standards and should not be promoted until they have mastered the content. What is usually called "social promotion" is strongly opposed by essentialists.

Essentialists contend that because students are young and immature, they need discipline and pressure to force them to learn. The basic components of the "assertive discipline" approach popular during much of the 1980s and 1990s are consistent with essentialism. In the assertive discipline model, the teacher sets the rules and the consequences and consistently applies them using a "no-nonsense" approach.

What Knowledge Is of Most Worth?

The essentialists hold that there is a core of information and values that all students should learn. The knowledge that is of most use is that which is essential for a person to live well and to contribute to society. This is probably best defined as the "basics." Essentialists claim that their approach is very practical. As society changes, so might what is defined as "essential knowledge." For example, as computer literacy has become important in contemporary society, computer literacy has been defined by essentialists as "essential."

Who Should Decide What Is Worth Knowing?

Who defines what is essential for someone to know in order to be a productive member of society? Should it be university professors or individuals? Should it be CEOs of large corporations? Should it be politicians? Should it be members of the local community? Although there is disagreement about who should define what is essential, essentialists do not give students a voice in the debate.

Who decides what is essential is an important question with serious implications. If essential knowledge is defined by corporate leaders, there is a danger that they will place their narrow concerns for skilled workers and for maintaining the status quo over the broader needs of society.

If politicians are in charge of defining what is essential, they are tempted to define essential knowledge as those areas that support their political values and advance their own political agenda. For example, a few years ago high school students had marched on a state capitol to protest some of the actions of the state legislature. As one of the state senators stood on the steps of the capitol and observed the students, he remarked, "Look at all those students protesting. Let's face it, the social studies has failed." It is quite clear that if he had defined what is essential, questioning the decisions of those in power would not be included.

If university professors define what is essential, as they did during the reform move-ment of the 1960s, their emphasis would most likely center on the narrow content of their disciplines and content required for success in higher education. However important this content might be, it doesn't take into account what is essential for all students, or the broad needs of society.

Throughout the history of American education, local school boards have had signifi-cant input in defining what is considered essential. Local control of education has long been an American tradition. However, this ignores the growing interdependence of the nation and can lead to narrow interests and content that might not be important in the national or international context.

In recent years, many of the high-profile committees established to provide input re-garding education have been composed of corporate leaders. For example, during the 1990s the "Goals 2000 Project" was established at the national level. The purpose of this group was to define what education should be in the year 2000 and to recommend changes. The committee was largely comprised of corporate leaders and politicians.

The emphasis on academic content standards has led to the establishment of com-mittees of scholars in various disciplines that have attempted to define essential content or standards for their respective disciplines. Therefore, content standards have been established for such subjects as science, history, economics, mathematics, and English.

Currently, decisions about what is essential are being made at the state level. Many states have established academic content standards. These standards are usually developed by state boards of education, which are often composed of individuals who are appointed by political leaders. They may include parents, corporate leaders, and educators. Two ques-tions that should be asked are what is the criteria for appointing individuals to these com-mittees and what are their political and philosophical beliefs? The future of education is too important to be left in the hands of unknown individuals who have no accountability.

What Should Be Included in the Curriculum?

As might be imagined, the subjects that are included are those that are often defined as "basics." For example, the basic subjects of reading, writing, and arithmetic should form the main body of content taught at the elementary level. At the secondary level, science, mathematics, English, and history should be the core requirements. Essentialists perceive serious knowledge as residing primarily in the sciences and the technical fields. Unlike the progressives, essentialists place primary emphasis on what is learned rather than on how it is learned. Some contemporary educators attribute the high dropout rate of high school students to their failure to develop such essential skills as writing, spelling, and basic mathematics computation (McCarthy & Kuh, 2006).

Essentialists oppose any subjects they believe move the focus from learning the "ba-sics." Essentialists generally oppose the inclusion of multicultural content because they see it as detracting from essential knowledge of a common cultural heritage. This has led to what some have called the "culture wars." For example, during the late 1980s essentialists supported the development of content standards in American history. However, when the standards were published, essentialists were outspoken in their criticism because they thought the standards included too much emphasis on multicultural content.

Because it is essential that all students reach high levels of English proficiency, essen-tialists usually oppose bilingual programs, claiming that bilingual programs interfere with English proficiency. Once again, this has kicked off a bitter debate between those who contend that teaching in English only is not essential to developing a productive society. In addition, they point to research that indicates that teaching students in their first language and helping them preserve it leads to improved achievement and is essential if the nation is to remain strong in a multilingual world. Essentialists tend to support English immersion and "English only" proposals.

Essentialists believe the arts and humanities are fine for personal pleasure, but they argue that content related to these subjects is not what learners need to prepare them for "useful" adulthood. Many essentialists view these subjects as frills and, when budgets are tight, suggest that they should be the first courses cut. Vocational topics would be supported if they were defined as essential. However, for the most part, they would be opposed because they would "water down" the curriculum.

What Is the Role of a Teacher?

Essentialists contend that the teacher's most important role is to impart information to students and to maintain discipline. Teachers should serve as the intellectual and moral models for the students. The curriculum and lessons should be organized systematically, moving from simple to more complex. All students should be expected to demonstrate mastery. A major responsibility of the teacher is to assess student learning. For their part, students are expected to learn and retain this content. Teacher-centered methods such as the lecture and whole-group instruction are favored, as are any new technologies that are thought to promote quick and efficient transmittal of new information. Authoritarian classroom management and discipline approaches are preferred.

Essentialists contend that students who are left to their own devices will not develop the knowledge and values necessary for them to become productive members of society. Therefore, hard work, discipline, and respecting authority are important values. Because essentialists believe that character development is important and that teachers instruct by example, they are convinced that the character and habits of the teacher must be above reproach.

What Do You Think?

- What aspects of essentialism are close to your views?
- Which perspective, progressivism or essentialism, seems to be closer to your personal philosophy?

Essentialism Today

Given the ascendancy of a conservative political agenda, it should not be surprising that a conservative educational philosophy has also increased in influence. There is no doubt that essentialism is the current dominant philosophical perspective influencing educational practice. A report in the early 1980s that initiated the current reform movement, *A Nation at Risk* was clearly based on essentialist ideas and signaled the dominance of this philosophy in the national debate about education.

This has led to an intense debate between the essentialists and those who have more progressive, student-centered philosophies. Generally, politicians and policymakers tend to favor the essentialist philosophy whereas many educators tend to favor a more student-centered approach. Because the policymakers have the power, the essentialist philosophy is the one driving most of the educational policies and proposals for educational reform.

The essentialist philosophy has led to proposals for change in a wide range of educational issues. These include the current emphasis on academic content standards, accountability, standardized testing, longer school days, the elimination of "social promotion," exit tests for graduation, and a reduction in teacher-education programs. For essentialists, the critical attribute of a quality teacher is depth of content knowledge. Teacher-education programs are therefore seen as a waste of time. Rather than wasting time learning about growth and development, individual differences, and alternative methods of teaching, they believe that teacher preparation should be on academic content.

The "No Child Left Behind" legislation is clearly essentialist. It prescribes a common curriculum, rigorous standards, frequent testing, and high levels of performance for all students regardless of their ability levels. The basic requirement for defining qualified teachers is content knowledge. Knowledge of student development or alternative teaching methods are not viewed as important.

Critics claim that essentialism is a philosophy looking to the past rather than the future. For example, some essentialists have opposed the use of new technologies such as calculators because they fear that such devices detract from students learning basic mathematics operations.

Critics also point out that merely teaching information will not provide students with the problem-solving skills or creativity needed to meet future challenges. When essentialists do change it is often done slowly. For example, a "back-to-basics" charter school near the home of one of the authors resisted the introduction of computers or computer skills until recently because they were viewed as taking time away from learning the essential knowledge of the prescribed curriculum.

Critics further claim that essentialist reform proposals ignore decades of research on topics such as learning theory, individual differences, effective teaching, and the impact of teacher-education programs on teacher quality. They contend that one approach does not fit all situations and essentialists need to recognize the presence of diversity and individual differences. Essentialists counter that the research is incomplete and flawed and is of little use in making policy decisions. Furthermore, they claim that emphasizing diversity leads to divisiveness rather than unity.

It is clear that the essentialists are in charge of the educational agenda at the policy level. Beginning teachers need to understand this. Until there is widespread dissatisfaction by the public and a change in the conservative direction of the nation, it is likely to remain as the dominant philosophical perspective.

Perennialism

The term *perennial* refers to something that is recurring or everlasting. The educational perspective of **perennialism** views truth and human nature as unchanging or constant. So it is that perennialists view education as the discovery and teaching of those underlying and unchanging truths. Perennialists also emphasize cultivating reason and the intellect.

Although perennialists grant that changing times bring surface-level alterations to the problems people face, they believe that human nature and the underlying principles of truth remain unaltered over time. Furthermore, they contend that the experiences of human beings through the centuries have established those truths worth knowing.

Perennialists contend that Western society lost its way several centuries ago. They decry what they see as a trend for society to rely on experimental science and technology—development they fear diverts attention away from enduring truths. Perennialists argue that the growing status of scientific experimentation has led to a denial of the power and importance of human reason.

What Is the Purpose of Education?

The primary goal of education as viewed by the perennialists is that of developing the intellect and the learning of enduring truths or principles that have passed the test of time. They believe that such wisdom is important regardless of the career or vocation a person ultimately chooses to follow. Preparing individuals to be participating members of society who can cope with change is viewed as best accomplished by developing the intellect and learning enduring truths that can be applied to any problem.

Although perennialism shares some common characteristics with essentialism, perennialists condemn essentialists' emphasis on so-called "practical" information. The perennialist points out that what the essentialist considers "essential" is constantly changing. Therefore, a school program focused on the essentials runs the risk of teaching learners information that, in time, will have little relevance for their lives.

How Should Students Be Treated?

A major thrust of perennialism is the discipline of the mind. Therefore, a perennialist teacher should push students to use their minds and develop the powers of reasoning. Emphasis should be placed on helping students think deeply and analytically. The proper way to develop the intellect and the reasoning powers of students is to bring them into contact with great ideas. Merely, presenting them information or providing students with experiences is insufficient. Even though there should be an organized and sequential curriculum and the teacher should be the authority in directing students through the curriculum, students need to be involved, for example, through Socratic dialogue (Copeland, 2005), in order to learn how to think analytically.

All students should encounter the same curriculum with no electives other than possibly a second language. Differentiating the curriculum or tracking students is opposed. Perennialists would support preschool for students who have not developed the prior knowledge to prepare them for encountering rigorous knowledge.

What Knowledge Is of Most Worth?

Because perennialists view knowledge as unchanging, they see the classics of Western civilization as containing those great truths that should be taught. They value knowledge that will challenge the students to develop intellectual skills. The content included in the curriculum should have passed the test of time.

For Internet access to some 18,000 books, see the website http://manybooks.net. For discussion of online books and audio books access see Van Horn (2007).

Who Should Decide What Is of Value?

The issue of deciding what is of value is left to tradition. What scholars have defined as the classics is the knowledge of most value. Perennialists place high value on subjects such as the philosophy, history, literature, the classics, and mathematics. They place the highest value on those subjects that explore the human condition and address enduring questions. In the early years of education, students should be taught the basic skills they will need as they mature and encounter rigorous study. Perennialists do not believe that students are in a position to define what is of value for them to learn.

What Should Be Included in the Curriculum?

A good example of the curriculum favored by perennialists is the Great Books program. They believe that as students read through the works of the great thinkers of history, they will encounter enduring truths and will develop a discipline of the mind that will stand them in good stead for whatever they may encounter in life. Perennialism is often the philosophy of parochial and church-related schools. They believe that the Holy Scripture is the source of enduring truth.

Perennialists oppose diluting the school curriculum in an attempt to make the schools a multipurpose agency. For example, they oppose vocational education programs. They believe this represents a sellout of the purposes of education to the narrow interests of government and business. This concern is directed not only at the public schools but also to colleges and universities. They think vocational training should be attended to by agencies other than the schools.

Perennialists believe that higher education has entirely inappropriate emphases on developing learners' research skills and on preparing them for future careers. In their view, such courses interfere with a more proper focus on a "genuine education" that emphasizes mastery of lasting truths. Many perennialists would like to ban research and practical training from colleges and universities and turn these responsibilities over to technical institutes.

Critics of perennialism criticize the reliance on the classics of Western civilization. They see this as a narrow and constricting education that ignores the contributions of other great civilizations of the world and those of women and minorities. Some perennialists would favor adding some multicultural dimensions to the curriculum, but only after students have learned about Western civilization.

What Is the Role of a Teacher?

Teachers in the perennialist perspective are individuals with a good liberal education. As a teacher, it is important that you be a role model that demonstrates the importance of the intellect and of reason. However, your role is not just one of dispensing information. You need to know how to relate the enduring truths to the lives of students. You also need to know how to get students to delve beyond memorization to that of identifying enduring principles. You need to understand approaches such as Socratic questioning in order to push the students to learn how to analyze and evaluate ideas.

Perennialism Today

There are certainly a number of examples of perennialism. *The Paideia Proposal* by Adler (1982) gave a boost to perennialist ideas. A number of schools have adopted Adler's ideas.

Because there are similarities between essentialism and perrenialism, some of the reform proposals are supported by perennialists. For example, perennialists would support testing and accountability because there is a common body of knowledge to be tested. However, perennialists would emphasize tests that assess thinking and deeper levels of learning, dimensions that are not easily measured using standardized multiple subject test items.

Critics level some of the same criticism at perennialism as they would essentialism. They view perennialism as a backward looking approach that ignores the realities of the contemporary world. In addition, they see perennialism as an elitist and ethnocentric philosophy favoring Western civilization and the students of privilege while ignoring the contributions of other great civilizations.

Is a study of the classics and the Great Books sufficient preparation for students in emerging areas of knowledge? Does one curriculum fit the needs of all students? Is a perennialist curriculum fair to all students regardless of their backgrounds? Will students educated using this approach be prepared to remain competitive with students from other parts of the world? Those questions dominate the concerns of critics. There are no easy answers.

What Do You Think?

- Does perennialism meet the needs of all students?
- Does perennialism meet the needs of society?

Reconstructionism

Reconstructionists, similar to perennialists, believe that society has lost its way. A classic work laying out this basic position is George Counts's 1932 book, *Dare the Schools Build a New Social Order?* However, there is an important difference. Whereas perennialists seek answers from the past, reconstructionists propose to build a new kind of society. They believe that schools should serve as an important catalyst in the effort to improve the human condition through reform. This reform should be based on addressing injustices in society and provide an education that is supportive of all groups.

Reconstructionists are opposed to the ideas of the essentialists. They believe that the "essential" content is composed of obsolete concepts and ideas that are based on the values of existing power groups and maintaining the status quo. They see this as focusing on what is rather than what should be.

Note that much of the **reconstructionism** perspective was developed during the Depression. This was a time when many members of society thought the social institutions had failed them. They believed that all institutions in society needed to be reformed. Like essentialists and perennialists, social reconstructionists believe that the schools need to be changed. However, their objectives and recommendations for change are very different.

What Is the Purpose of Education?

Social reconstructionists see the purpose of education as that of building a just society. They believe that students should critically examine society, especially those controversial topics or "closed areas" of study that are often ignored in the curriculum. Students also need to learn how to make decisions and take action that will produce a better world. Because of the commitment to building a just society, values and moral development are very important.

How Should Students Be Treated?

Social reconstructionists are more student-centered than essentialism or perennialism. They have more confidence in the abilities of students. They believe that students are capable of identifying injustice and searching for solutions. They contend that even though the issues young children may identify are more concrete and related to their lives, as they mature they will develop sensitivity to larger, more abstract concerns. Students need to learn how to identify issues and work for improvement through active involvement. Schools should not be remote institutions dealing with issues in the abstract. Therefore, students need to be involved in identifying issues and problems. They should be given freedom to pursue the information they need to explore and make decisions about the issues they define.

Cleo Photography/PhotoEdit Inc.

Building a better world and being involved in social justice activities are part of the social reconstructionism philosophy.

Reconstructionists are strongly opposed to censorship or limiting the materials that are available for their study. To illustrate the freedom that reconstructionists believe should be given to students, some have suggested that even children in the elementary grades should be given the right to vote in national elections.

To return to the response of a state senator to student protests cited earlier, social reconstructionists would see the protests as an indication that school programs were succeeding.

What Knowledge Is of Most Worth?

The knowledge that has most worth is whatever is information needed to address issues and questions. Some critics contend that students lack the maturity to do this. However, reconstructionists point out that even young children can and do develop considerable depth of knowledge when they are doing something they consider to be important. For example, students who get committed to a topic such as environmental education often develop a depth of knowledge that is astounding even to parents.

Who Should Decide What Is Worth Knowing?

Ultimately, the students make the decision regarding what they need to learn. However, the teacher may use content and information to help identify critical issues that need to be investigated. Teachers should insist that students thoroughly investigate the topic and gather all the relevant information and viewpoints. Reconstructionists contend that such an education is a very rigorous one that pushes students to go beyond simplistic understanding.

What Should Be Included in the Curriculum?

Reconstructionists favor curricula that emphasize creating a world of economic abundance, equality, fairness, and democratic decision making. They see this social reconstruction as necessary for the survival of humankind. The school program should teach learners to analyze all aspects of life and to question rather than accept the pronouncements of those who hold political power. The reconstructionist curriculum draws heavily on insights from the behavioral sciences, which reconstructionists believe can be used as the basis for creating a society in which individuals can attain their fullest potentials.

However, topics such as science and mathematics also have a role in helping students identify issues. For example, a student committed to improving the environment would need to know a considerable amount of science, economics, and political science in order to clearly understand and define the issues.

In one middle school mathematics class, students used mathematics to concretely identify issues of justice. For example, they used mathematics to compare the size of their classrooms, the number of books in the library, and the amount of money spent per pupil with schools in more affluent neighborhoods. In summary, the classroom should be like a "think tank" where many perspectives are focused on current issues and problems.

What Is the Role of a Teacher?

The role of the reconstructionist teacher is much like that of the progressive teacher. However, the focus is not as much on student interests as it is on social issues. Teachers need to have a broad range of knowledge and be up to date on issues. They need to understand the interrelatedness of information. Teachers, like students, need to be inquirers and be engaged in investigating social problems and injustices.

Reconstructionists see the role of teachers as that of raising of the consciousness of students about issues and problems that are important to society. They pose questions to students and provide guidance as they seek data about issues. Young people should be actively engaged in the learning process. Ideally, the classroom should reflect the values of equality and social justice.

One approach that is consistent with social reconstructionism is service learning. In many service-learning activities, students are actively applying knowledge to solve real problems. This active involvement helps students learn that they have a responsibility to be involved and that they can make a difference.

Reconstructionism Today

Elements of reconstructionism can be found throughout contemporary education. Programs that focus on topics such as environmental education, peace education, racism and prejudice, moral dilemmas, and globalism are related to social reconstructionism.

One popular approach that is closely related to social reconstructionism is "critical theory." Critical theory advocates using school to bring about social change. An individual who has helped define and popularize critical theory is a Brazilian educator, Paulo Freire (1921–1997). His most influential work is *Pedagogy of the Oppressed* (1972). In this highly quoted work, educational systems are defined as tools of the dominant class of society for keeping down the masses and for institutionalizing dominant values at the expense of the oppressed. He defined this as the "banking" approach to education where the group in power knows truth and attempts to deposit it in the minds of oppressed.

Freire promoted several educational practices. He strongly emphasized informal educational approaches such as the use of dialogue, making education conversational. Dialogue emphasizes that education should involve people working together rather than one person acting on another. Because it involves respect, dialogue enhances community and the development of social capital.

One of the important outcomes of education for Freire was what was termed "conscientization" or the development of a consciousness of values and issues. Through this, he wanted to give a voice to the oppressed so that a pedagogy of hope would result.

Another contemporary philosophy perspective that is closely related to critical theory and reconstructionism is that of **postmodernism**. Postmodernists claim that there is no one scholarly tradition that is "right" or "true." They believe that some of the traditional philosophical questions and theories are obsolete and meaningless. They contend that how people make sense out of the world depends on the contexts within which they live their lives, including gender and their social setting.

Postmodernists contend that what students learn in schools should vary according to the concerns and priorities of the individual. Topics such as gender studies and ethnic studies are strongly supported because they disclose different views of reality and alternative values perspectives. They also emphasize that students should learn how to question the motives and the political agendas of those pushing reform under the name of "truth."

Social reconstructionists also believe in the importance of dialogue and shared experience. As a result, they emphasize the importance of stories, narratives, myths, and legends as important components of the curriculum. They also support less reliance on science and more on topics such as literature, music, art, and the humanities as ways of finding meaning and purpose.

Social reconstructionism, critical theory, and postmodernism have many critics. Who see these as intellectually "soft" approaches that justify just about anything that one might want to teach. They claim that these approaches give too much authority to the teacher in deciding what should be taught. They contend that the political and social agendas of teachers influence what they teach and that this is little more than "brainwashing." For example, they cite that, in prac-

---

Web Extension 10–1

Philosophy of Education

Following are a few Web sites that can help you gather more information.

http://www.en.wikipedia.org/wiki/Philosophy_of_education

At this site, you will find a general discussion of the historical roots of present-day education-related philosophies. You will find more details about information introduced in this chapter, as well as links to other philosophical orientations, including romanticism and humanism.

http://www.dewey@siu.edu

This is the Center for Dewey Studies. Here you can find more detailed information about the ideas of John Dewy and his continuing impact on education.

http://www.paulofreireinstitute.org

This is the site of the Paulo Freire Institute at UCLA. It contains an abundance of information about the application of the ideas of Paulo Freire.

http://www.c-b-e.org

This is the Web site for the Council on Basic Education. It provides a philosophical perspective related to proposals for reform that are based more on the essentialism and perennialism perspectives.

http://www.oxy.edu/apa/apa/html

This is the site for the American Philosophical Association. Here you can find references to various branches of educational philosophy.

---

tice, these approaches have little difference from the "banking" approach criticized by Freire. The difference, they claim, is that what are banked are teacher biases and values rather than the accumulated wisdom of society. Further, they claim that focusing on the problems of society as advocated by social reconstructionists teaches cynicism and is divisive to society.

What Do You Think?

- Which of the philosophical perspectives discussed in the chapter are closest to your personal philosophy?
- Which elements of each of these philosophical perspectives would you include in your personal philosophy?

In summary, even though essentialism seems to be the philosophical perspective that is driving the current educational reform movement, elements of other philosophical perspectives also have a strong tradition in education. Many of these ideas influence educational practice. The result is that critics of education, regardless of their philosophical orientation, can find something that they can criticize. Therefore, educators can be assured that there will always be editorials, letters to the editor, and speeches critical of education.

♦ ♦

The Case for Diversified Schooling
Go to MyEducationLab and select the topic "Philosophy of Education." Read the article "The Case for Diversified Schooling," that discusses disagreements that arise from different philosophical perspectives. Respond to the questions. Some of the questions are designed to prepare you for your licensure examination.

♦ ♦

The future direction of education will depend on which philosophical perspectives are accepted by the public and are institutionalized into public policy. The debate is an important one that will continue to be heated because it touches strongly held beliefs. An understanding of these perspectives will help you understand and analyze these criticisms and calls for change.

BUILDING A PERSONAL PHILOSOPHY OF EDUCATION

When you are interviewed for a teaching position, you may be asked "What is your educational philosophy?" Why do you think interviewers so often ask this question, and why is it important? Your personal philosophy is not just a written statement. It is a perspective that involves your beliefs and values and becomes the basis from which you make decisions about what is important and about your role as an educator.

As you move toward articulating your personal philosophy, consider what influences your actions. One such influence is what could be called your **personal filter**. An individual's personal filter screens and influences information in ways that are consistent with prior learning, attitudes, and values. These prior experiences affect how you react to, interpret, and assimilate new information.

Your personal filter is an expression of your philosophy of education. It exercises a profound influence on your judgments and attitudes. It is for this reason that many employers ask, "What is your philosophy of education?" They want to know how your beliefs correspond with the goals and purposes of the school district and the community. Read this chapters *Critical Incident* to read about one teacher's educational philosophy.

Your culture, your socioeconomic background, your religious beliefs, and your experiences in school are factors that influence your personal philosophy. You might not have reflected consciously on many of your fundamental convictions. Take time to do so. This philosophic self-understanding will contribute to your development as a teacher.

As you think about your own philosophy, review the questions raised in this chapter. What do you see as the purpose of education? How should you treat those you teach? What knowledge is of most worth? Who should decide what is worth knowing? What should be included in the curriculum? What do you see as the role of the teacher? Compare your answers to those coming from different philosophical perspectives. Which of these positions and ideas do you think are strong or reasonable and which positions do you think are weak and not so reasonable? How sound are your arguments for the positions with which you agree? What merit can you find in those positions with which you disagree? What points do they make that you consider valid?

Critical Incident

What's the Problem?

Roberto Lopez teaches sixth grade in an inner-city school. He believes that young people need to be actively involved in their own education and that they are most interested in learning when they have a voice in deciding what to study. Roberto's instructional program is built around his students' questions and interests. He helps members of his class identify important problems that people face in the real world. Then he helps them learn what they need to know to understand the problems and to think about possible solutions. Often his lessons integrate content from many subject areas.

This afternoon, the school principal, Ms. Fifer, observed Roberto's teaching. After the observation, she and Roberto had a conference that left him upset and confused.

Ms. Fifer told Roberto that although she is impressed with the rapport he has with the students and the ease with which he relates to them, she is concerned about what he is teaching. She believes Roberto is straying too far from the prescribed curriculum. Ms. Fifer pointed out that the adopted curriculum includes key knowledge that the students need to master. She explained that if students fail to learn this information, they will not do well on the state tests. Low student scores will lead to serious problems. Some parents will be angry, the school board will be upset, and the published ratings of the school will suffer.

Ms. Fifer also said Roberto's sixth graders are too uninformed to deal meaningfully with the problems he is asking them to consider. She suggested that the student discussions she heard largely represented a sharing of ignorance and opinions with too few facts to support their ideas. To be able to handle this sort of activity, the students must first acquire a firm understanding of basic information. She added that lessons based on the adopted textbook will give learners information they can use to discuss issues in a more responsible way. At the end of the conference, the principal summarized her feelings by telling Roberto that his actions are denying students access to the textbook-based knowledge they need to discuss issues based on fact and to score well on mandated standardized tests.

Roberto left the meeting very confused. He had believed that he was doing an excellent job. Now, he has been told that he is being irresponsible and is on the verge of harming his students. Roberto finds this hard to accept. He has seen the enthusiasm of the students, and he believes that one of the most important goals of education is to help individuals learn how to make our society better. He is not sure what he should do next.

1. *What do you see as the source of the problem between Roberto and Ms. Fifer?*

2. *What philosophical orientation does Roberto appear to have?*

3. *What philosophical orientation does Ms. Fifer have?*

4. *What do you see as the strong points in both of their arguments?*

5. *What are their basic differences in fundamental values?*

6. *What do you think should be done now?*

7. *What does this situation suggest to you as you begin to think about seeking a teaching position?*

What Do You Think?

- What elements of your personal philosophy are clearly in place?
- How would you respond to a question such as "Tell me about your philosophy of education"?

You may find that there is no one system that you agree with totally and that each system has elements that make sense to you. If so, you have what is termed an eclectic philosophy, one that includes elements of different philosophical systems. However, you should not take this as an opportunity to avoid facing difficult questions and issues. You need to know what you believe and you need to be able to defend your positions. This will provide you with a framework for deciding where you want to teach, how you want to teach, and where you stand on proposals for change.

Key Ideas in Summary

- External pressures of various kinds influence decisions that affect our educational system. Differing philosophical perspectives account for some variance in views regarding the nature of the kind of schools we need.
- Many of the debates and disagreements about schools and the direction they should take are disagreements in philosophy. *Philosophical perspectives* represent clusters of values and attitudes that individuals use to assess varying action options and decide which ones to adopt. As a teacher, conscious thought about your own philosophical perspectives can help you make more focused and consistent decisions regarding what and how to teach.
- *Education-related systems of philosophy* address basic questions and their applications to education. Those basic questions relate to the purposes of education, the nature of knowledge, who should have the authority to decide what is important, what should be taught, and what the role of the teacher should be. Because philosophical perspectives bring together sets of beliefs and values, they are not subject to research and verification. Therefore, as you decide on a philosophy, it is important that you reflect on your values and priorities.
- *Progressivism* is a student-centered philosophy that views change as a constant. The progressives have a great respect for the values of democracy and believe that classrooms should mirror democracy and the respect for all individuals. In order to prepare for their roles in society, students should be actively involved in posing and solving real problems. The scientific method is viewed as important in helping students understand and direct change for the improvement of society.
- Supporters of *essentialism* want schools to provide sound practical and intellectual training that is not diluted by courses that will not prepare young people for citizenship responsibilities and the world of work. They focus on what they consider to be essential knowledge for all students to know. The role of the student is to learn, and the teacher is to be the authority. Essentialism is the philosophical perspective that is currently driving educational reform.
- Advocates of *perennialism* believe there are certain unchanging truths and these truths should be the focus of the school program. They believe these truths are found in the classics of Western civilization. Even though they agree that circumstances change, perennialists contend that this is only superficial and that time-honored principles are still the most important in preparing individuals for their future roles.

- *Reconstructionism* takes the position that society needs to be reformed. Reconstructionists believe that schools should address issues of social justice such as discrimination, poverty, and the unequal allocation of resources. Critical theory is a contemporary perspective that is related to reconstructionism. Critical theory holds that educational systems are often used as a tool to keep down the masses and to institutionalize the values of those in power. Postmodernism is another current approach that rejects the notion that truth is defined by any one class of society. It seeks to include the perspectives of all individuals and the context of their lives, accepting multiple sources of information as sources that help individuals seek for truth and find meaning.

- When you interview for a teaching position, you may be asked to describe your personal philosophy of education. Interviewers know that teachers' philosophies vary and that different philosophical perspectives lead them to make different decisions. Taking time to identify elements of your own philosophy will help you to better articulate your educational priorities and understand your rationale for making decisions.

◆───────────────────────────────────────

For Your Initial-Development Portfolio

1. This chapter discusses content that can be very important for your portfolio. You might want to consider placing a statement relating to your portfolio at the beginning of your portfolio. This does not need to be a complex statement that gets into the intricacies of a particular philosophy. For example, one student had a section titled "This I believe. . . ." In this section the student included a number of quotes about the purposes of education, the nature of students, and the role of the teacher that were consistent with the student's philosophy.

2. What other pieces of evidence of your philosophy might you include in your portfolio? Why did you select them?

3. Place a check in the chart below to indicate to which INTASC standard(s) each of your items of information relates. (You may wish to refer to Chapter 1 for more detailed information about INTASC.)

INTASC Standard Number										
ITEM OF EVIDENCE NUMBER	S1	S2	S3	S4	S5	S6	S7	S8	S9	S10
1										
2										
3										

4. Prepare a written reflection in which you analyze the decision-making process you followed. Mention the INTASC standard(s) to which your selected material relates.

Reflections

1. In this chapter, you learned about several education-related systems of philosophy, including progressivism, essentialism, perennialism, and reconstructionism. When reviewing many of the debates about improving education, you can find elements of these several philosophies in conflict. Think about your personal philosophy and think through your position on these issues. Where do you stand on standardized testing? Do you think the curriculum should include multicultural content? What should be the characteristics of a qualified teacher?

2. Reflect on your background and how it has influenced your philosophical stance. How does your previous experience in school influence what you think is appropriate? What is the influence of your socioeconomic status, your gender, and your ethnicity? How can an understanding on these influences help as you move into teaching?

3. As you begin thinking about your own educational philosophy, how will this information help you? When seeking employment, how might your philosophy influence your choice of school? What kinds of questions might you pose as you view schools where you might be hired as a teacher? What type of school and program do you think would be compatible and personally satisfying?

Field Experiences, Projects, and Enrichment

1. Choose and research a school-improvement idea, for example, standardized testing for all students. What are the philosophical assumptions behind the proposal? What do you see as the logic and the inconsistencies in the arguments for and against the proposal? What kind of language do proponents and opponents use to characterize the proposal? What do you predict will be the consequences if this proposal becomes universal across all schools in the nation?

2. Interview some teachers and administrators regarding their positions on some of the reform proposals. What do you see as the philosophical assumptions they are using to support or oppose a given proposal? How do their philosophical perspectives compare to those in power?

3. Review the Interstate New Teacher Assessment and Support Consortium (INTASC) standards for Beginning Teacher Licensing and Development. Do these standards reflect a particular philosophy of education? How do particular standards relate to a particular philosophical orientation? How do you think proponents of other orientations would define the standards differently?

4. Review state and local school policies and curriculum. You may find it useful to look at your state's curriculum standards. Most state departments of education make this material available on their Web sites. Your instructor may direct you toward other sources. Examine the guidelines to identify elements of philosophical positions in each. Do not be surprised if you find that multiple positions are represented in various places throughout these materials. Which ones seem to predominate? Why do you think this pattern has emerged?

References

Adler, M. (1982). *The Paideia proposal*. New York: Macmillan.

Bagley, W. (1941). The case for essentialism in education. *National Education Association Journal, 30*(7), 202–220.

Bestor, A. (1955). *The restoration of learning*. New York: Knopf.

Bracey, G. W. (2007). "The first time everything changed." *Phi Delta Kappan, 89*(2), 119–136.

Copeland, M. (2005). *Socratic circles: Fostering critical and creative thought in middle and high schools*. Portland, ME: Stenhouse.

Counts, G. (1932). *Dare the schools build a new social order?* New York: John Day.

Dewey, J. (1902). *The child and the curriculum*. Chicago: University of Chicago Press.

Dewey, J. (1910). *How we think*. Boston: D. C. Heath.

Dewey, J. (1916). *Democracy and education*. New York: Macmillan.

Dewey, J. (1938). *Experience and education*. New York: Macmillan.

Freire, P. (1972). *Pedagogy of the oppressed*. Harmondsworth, Penguin.

Gutek, G. L. (1997). *Historical and philosophical foundations of education: A biographical introduction* (2nd ed.). Upper Saddle River, NJ: Merrill/Prentice Hall.

McCarthy, M., & Kuh, G. D. (2006). Are students ready for college: What student engagement data say. *Phi Delta Kappan, 87*(9), 664–669.

Pogrow, S. (2006). The Bermuda Triangle of American education: Pure traditionalism, pure progressivism, and good intentions. *Phi Delta Kappan, 88*(2), 142–150.

Van Horn, R. (2007). "Online books and audiobooks." *Phi Delta Kappan, 89*(2), 154–155.

Warner, A. R. (2006). Philosophies in conflict. A case study in K. T. Henson, *Curriculum planning: Integrating multiculturalism, constructivism, and education reform* (3rd ed.). Long Grove, Il: Waveland Press.

CHAPTER 11

HOW IS TECHNOLOGY
CHANGING EDUCATION?

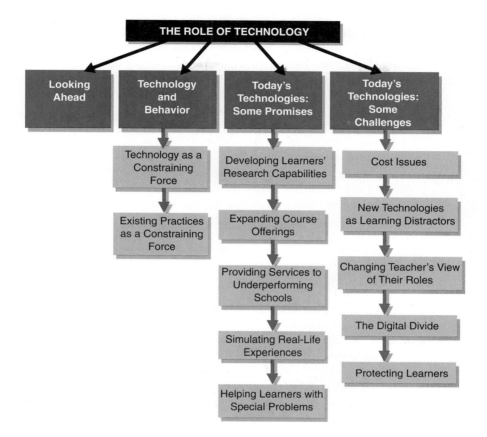

THE ROLE OF TECHNOLOGY

- Looking Ahead
- Technology and Behavior
  - Technology as a Constraining Force
  - Existing Practices as a Constraining Force
- Today's Technologies: Some Promises
  - Developing Learners' Research Capabilities
  - Expanding Course Offerings
  - Providing Services to Underperforming Schools
  - Simulating Real-Life Experiences
  - Helping Learners with Special Problems
- Today's Technologies: Some Challenges
  - Cost Issues
  - New Technologies as Learning Distractors
  - Changing Teacher's View of Their Roles
  - The Digital Divide
  - Protecting Learners

OBJECTIVES

This chapter will help you to

- recognize that effective use of technology requires (1) an understanding of the basic characteristics of available alternatives and (2) a willingness to fit and adapt them to meet the special needs of your own learners and circumstances.
- describe competencies included in technology standards that have been recommended for learners and teachers.
- point out how changes associated with modifications in technologies depend both on the nature of the new technologies and the force of tradition.
- cite examples of ways that today's digital-communication technologies are being used to help learners.
- point out examples of challenges that have accompanied the introduction of new technologies into schools.
- explain provisions of important federal laws that seek to shield learners from dangers that might result from introductions of new technologies into the schools.

LOOKING AHEAD

Project ahead a few years. As you look out over your classroom, you see that most members of your class have chosen to come to school today. Others are working at home. Some of your at-home learners may contact you during the day via e-mail, videophone, or other electronic means if they have questions.

Your classroom has a very different configuration from those in the past. Movable partitions can create different sizes of space. In each section of the classroom you are able to control the lighting and the climate control system. Within each space, sufficient electronic equipment is in place to serve learners' needs. Students can easily access video clips on a wide variety of topics. If they desire, they can make their own videos in place of written reports. All students are supplied with their own computer that allows them wireless access to the vast array of material in the instructional materials center of the school district.

A few individuals are working alone and others are clustered in small groups in areas created by arranging movable visual and sound barriers. As part of your social studies program, individuals and groups in your class are involved in the following activities:

- Using computers linked to the World Wide Web to participate in a virtual archaeological dig in cooperation with learners from other schools
- Engaging in a videoconference with learners in schools in other parts of the country focusing on similarities and differences of their home communities
- Organizing a multimedia presentation using video clips, music, and audio clips to contrast some differences in the lives of young people growing up in an urban part of the United Kingdom, such as London, and a rural section such as the Shetland Islands
- Preparing a recordable CD focusing on important issues facing the state that will feature (1) selected digital-camera pictures taken during a field trip to the state capitol to meet with legislative leaders, (2) information gathered by using personal digital assistants to connect to Internet Web sites featuring state news, and (3) learners' own verbal comments
- Using a computer to write an article titled "Life in the World War I Trenches" based on information accessed from libraries and other Internet sites and from e-mail and, perhaps, videophone exchanges with directors of museums around the world with collections focusing on World War I

How realistic is this picture? This question is difficult to answer. There are places where learners are engaging in these kinds of experiences today. School planners are designing new schools and classrooms that are very different from the static four walls of the typical classroom. Changes in technology have led to dramatic changes in instructional resources and in building materials that allow individuals to rethink the entire educational experience.

However, in other locations, classroom organizational patterns and teaching practices look about the same as they did 50 or more years ago. Some educators are reluctant to embrace new technological changes because they believe it is important for students to learn basic skills so they understand the processes rather than letting technology do it.

In addition, change produces tensions between opportunities to do things differently and the abiding appeal of familiar practices. As an educator, you will be challenged throughout your career to think about issues of change brought about by advancements in technology. Although new advancements bring about new opportunities, they usually create new challenges. History is filled with examples of new technologies that promised to revolutionize education (Baines, 2007). Fifty years ago, a popular view was that television was going to totally change education and that instruction could be delivered inexpensively to wide audiences scattered across the nation. Similarly, in the early 1970s some individuals predicted that early applications of "teaching machines" would allow for complete individualization of teaching and change the role of teacher to that of "instructional manager." Some programs, such as Westinghouse's "Project Plan," attempted to do just that and were tried in a number of schools across the nation. The reason these advancements did not change education in the ways predicted is that they did not consider important learning variables. As you view the claims and the applications of new technology, you will need to consider how well they address important dimensions of learning.

Technology is the application of scientific processes to resources for the purpose of extending our capabilities to meet our needs and wants. What can technology do, and what are its limits? Thomas Glennan and Arthur Melmed (1996), in a report prepared for the Rand Corporation, point out that technology is a means to an end, not a replacement for instruction.

This distinction is not always understood, and sometimes you may even hear a question such as "Are computers in school good or bad for learners?" The question makes no more sense than one focused on an earlier technology such as textbooks. Nobody would think of asking "Are textbooks good or bad for learners?" The only answer you logically can give is "It depends on the quality of the texts and how they are used." Making appropriate use of technologies requires you to go beyond a basic understanding of how they work. You need to think about how their capabilities can be exploited to help a particular group of learners accomplish particular instructional ends. Even when learners have access to excellent technological aids, they still need your guidance to maximize benefits associated with their use.

During your years as a classroom teacher, you will be involved in making numerous decisions related to technology and its relationship to instruction and learning. As background for making responsible decisions, you may find it useful to think about these questions:

- What technological knowledge and skills do you expect your students to acquire as a result of your instruction?
- What happens when there is technological change?
- What are some promises of today's new technologies?
- What challenges do new technologies pose for teachers?
- What possible dangers do new technologies pose for learners?

Web Extension 11–1

International Society for Technology in Education (ISTE)

ISTE is the leading professional organization for educators interested in promoting the use of technology in school programs. At this site, you will find excellent links to information related to topics such as integrating technology in school curriculums, technology standards, promoting technological equity, policies related to technology and schools, and conferences and meetings focusing on technology and education.

http://www.iste.org/

TECHNOLOGY AND BEHAVIOR

When you look at today's classrooms and see that some teachers use many new technologies to support their instruction while others continue to operate much as teachers did decades ago, this point becomes abundantly clear: *Technology alters the limits of what can be done, but it does not ensure progress.* In other words, even though a new technology affords you the opportunity to do something, it by no means guarantees that you will decide to do it. Your decision to change requires understanding that the advantages of the change are significant enough for you to abandon the comfort of the familiar. Supporters of wider use of new technologies in school programs battle constantly to convince reluctant adopters of new technologies that the benefits of proposed changes are worth the psychological adjustments that accompany a break with traditional ways of doing things.

Technology as a Constraining Force

Let's return a moment to the idea that existing technology establishes the limits of what is possible. How has this principle affected what teachers and schools do? Consider pencils. Large-scale manufacture of these tools began only in the late 1860s. Initially pencils were expensive, and schools could not afford to buy them. If you had been teaching in the 1880s, you would have had your learners write on slates. Slates are difficult to write on, do not have much capacity, and are unsuited for lengthy responses. How would you have tested members of your class? Because of the limitations of slates, you probably would most often have used oral exams. The existing technology would have encouraged you to place great emphasis on helping learners develop well-organized oral-presentation skills.

Occasionally, you may have wanted members of your class to write essays. In the 1880s, straight steel pens were available in schools, and you could have assigned learners to write their essays in ink. Paper was expensive, and ink does not allow for easy correction. These limitations would have encouraged you to help learners carefully organize their ideas in their heads before beginning to write.

When inexpensive pencils featuring built-in erasers made their appearance after 1900, some teachers were concerned. Existing technologies had conditioned them to expect learners to do their revisions mentally before committing thoughts to paper. Pencils with erasers allowed young people to make on-the-fly corrections, something that many teachers initially felt resulted in sloppy preparatory thinking. In time, teachers came to appreciate that the multiple revisions made possible by erasers gave learners more opportunities to think about what they wrote than the old revising-in-the-head strategy that was necessary when ink was the only medium available for essay writing.

Over time, many technological changes have raised the limits of what is possible in the classroom. For example, equipment to score tests electronically provided teachers with the possibility of a time-saving correction process. This feature encouraged time-stressed educators to use test types that could be scored using this equipment (multiple-choice, true–false, and other so-called objective tests) rather than essays. Development of technologies such as films, television, personal computers, and the Internet gave learners opportunities to gather information from sources much wider and more diverse than traditional books and teacher presentations.

Existing Practices as a Constraining Force

Though new technologies present opportunities for the education profession to change many traditional organizational and instructional practices, you cannot be sure that education will experience the kinds of radical transformation sometimes envisioned by strong supporters of new technologies. Existing practices are preserved not only by technologies that allow no alternatives but also by tradition. For example, consider the traditional school year.

It has been decades since large numbers of children were needed for summer farm work; yet, with some exceptions, the long summer break remains a fixture of school calendars. Why is this so? The answer lies in the large number of developments and customs that have evolved over the years under the assumption that schools will not be in session during a good portion of the summer months. Among these are the following:

- Development of a large and sophisticated textbook-and-educational-materials industry that has huge inventories of products designed for use over a 9- to 10-month school year
- Assumptions by parents and guardians that children will be free to go on family vacations during the summer months
- School-district schedules presuming that painting, repair work, and other activities associated with building maintenance will occur during the summer months when buildings are vacant
- College and university budgets that assume that large numbers of teachers will pay tuition and attend classes during the summer months
- Summer programs offered by school districts to assist learners who need to retake courses or receive other kinds of help if they are to "keep up" with others in their group when regular school classes begin in the fall

What Do You Think?

- What are some current "traditions" or practices in education that interfere with the application of technology?
- What are some examples of ways that new technologies served as a distractor of educational progress?

You may be interested in other examples of new or better technologies that, for various reasons, failed to win broad-based support. Everett M. Rogers (1995), who has studied innovations for years, points out that the common QWERTY layout of typewriter and computer keyboards is an arrangement that was designed to force people to type slowly. Early typewriters jammed when typists struck keys too rapidly. The QWERTY keyboard positioned letters so that frequently used letters such as *e*, *i*, and *o* required moving fingers off the "home keys"—an action that slowed the typing process.

In the 1930s when improved typewriters did not require typists to type slowly, August Dvorak developed a keyboard featuring an arrangement whereby frequently used letters were all "home keys." Typists who mastered Dvorak's arrangement were able to type faster and experience less fatigue than users of the QWERTY keyboard. Despite these advantages, the older, less-efficient placement of keys on the QWERTY keyboard continues to dominate, even in the first years of the 21st century.

What explains the persistence of this older technology? For one thing, when the Dvorak keyboard was introduced, manufacturers of typewriters had large numbers of models available with QWERTY keyboards. They were reluctant to take on the expense of producing machines with Dvorak layouts, given uncertainties regarding the numbers of users who would buy the machines. Also, by the time Dvorak's keyboard became available, huge numbers of people had mastered the QWERTY keyboard. They felt high levels of comfort with the QWERTY arrangement and, as touch typists, did not feel it worth their time to learn the new Dvorak key arrangement.

To summarize, new technologies provide opportunities, but not mandates, for change. The "build it and they will come" perspective from the Kevin Costner film *Field of Dreams*

Laura Bolesta/Merrill

Technology has opened up a large variety of new approaches to teaching.

might more properly be stated: "Build it and they *may* come." As you think about possibly adopting practices associated with a new technology, you need to weigh potential benefits against such "costs" as (1) time needed to master the new technologies, (2) impact on resources you have available to support other aspects of your instructional program, and (3) the effects on other practices that existing technologies have sustained.

TODAY'S TECHNOLOGIES: SOME PROMISES

Today's communication technologies make it possible for you to arrange for individuals or small groups of learners to work on assignments that vary according to their particular needs. In the past, this kind of individualized teaching was hard to implement. Hence, the practice was to organize learners into groups of 20 to 35 (sometimes more) and house them in a single large space called a classroom. Information basically came from two sources: the teacher and the textbook. Content presented was cut into manageable chunks, and to accommodate this pattern of division, the school day was divided into periods. These learning divisions were gathered together into large entities called units, and textbook authors and teachers developed schemes to cover certain numbers of them during major divisions of the school year.

Newer technologies have overcome some of the constraints that supported these traditional arrangements. In addition to traditional interactions with classroom teachers, learners now have the possibility of gaining information from many other sources. For example, they may receive Web-based instruction from a teacher located hundreds of miles away from the learner. Although learners can continue to receive this instruction in a traditional classroom setting, it is no longer necessary. The technological capability is available for the information to be delivered to learners at home or in numerous other settings (Chou, McClintock, Moretti, & Nix, 1993).

Textbooks increasingly represent just one content source. Further, large numbers of texts, in addition to serving as self-contained knowledge sources, now also function as guides to wider information sources such as the World Wide Web of the Internet. Possibilities are increasing for learners in the years ahead to spend more time in front of computer screens than reading texts.

As a teacher, technology now gives you the ability to function more as an instructional guide than as a primary source of information. You may spend much of your time diagnosing individual learners' needs and helping them develop programs of study that use technologies appropriate for their own learning styles and interests. Ideally, members of your class will engage in considerable self-guided learning. To explore this topic further, read this chapter's *A Day in the Life* feature.

◆ ◆

The Networked Classroom
Go to MyEducationLab and select the topic "Technology in the Schools." Read the article "The
Networked Classroom" to learn how teachers can use handheld devises linked to the teacher's laptop.
Read the article and respond to the accompanying questions. Some of the questions have been
designed to prepare you for your licensure examination.

◆ ◆

New technologies also relieve the need for school days and time to be organized so
rigidly. In the future, you may find your students spending more time at home. When students
are electronically linked to information sources that are located in various world time zones,
they may need to access this information at various times during the school day. Increasingly,
members of your class may spend part of their days at home or, perhaps, in neighborhood
centers where computers are available that will allow them to connect to locations that
have information they need (Rector, 2002).

A DAY IN THE LIFE . . . The Technology Enthusiast

Lorene Boileau, a sixth-grade language arts teacher, has a reputation as an enthusiastic user of instructional
technology. Though Ms. Boileau is known to be a savvy user of computers, the Internet, and other electronic wonders, she recognizes that her increased use of technology presents her with challenges as well as
opportunities.

Ms. Boileau realizes that she now spends much more time planning lessons than she did in her pretech-
nology days. Among other things, she must carefully review Web sites she wishes students to use for her lessons. This must be done every time she wants to use a given site because site addresses often change. Also,
computers and other equipment students will use must be tested. She also must preview software she wants
learners to use to ensure an appropriate fit with her lesson objectives.

Ms. Boileau reports that she must carefully monitor learners when they use computers, particularly
when the computers are connected to the Internet. If even a single learner, either accidentally or purpose-
fully, contacts a pornographic site during a class period and a parent or guardian hears of it, complaints to
school administrators are almost certain. Such parental and guardian concerns can prompt school leaders
to impose restrictive conditions on student use of the World Wide Web—a circumstance that Ms. Boileau
believes has the potential to deny students instructional benefits that can accrue when the Web is appropriately used to support instruction.

Despite these challenges, Ms. Boileau remains convinced that today's technologies allow students to
get experiences they simply cannot get from traditional modes of instruction. She also points out that young
people come to school accustomed to music, animation, and other sensory backups from years of watching
electronically enhanced films, MTV, and other sophisticated audio/visual productions. They take naturally
to learning that engages multiple senses.

For Ms. Boileau, the major attraction of technology-enhanced teaching is that it has the potential to
place responsibility for learning in students' own hands. In technology-rich classrooms, learners are taught
under conditions that engage them actively and promote development of the adult thinking skills of
(1) accessing information, (2) processing information, and (3) applying information. Activities that help
them develop these proficiencies also prepare them for the demands of a technologically oriented workplace that expects employees to know how to locate information, communicate, and work productively
with others.

However, it may be that many students do not want to learn at home. They may want the human contact and the ability to discuss ideas with others. Although students may voice displeasure about going to school, many of them prefer the social atmosphere of school over that of the home. Just because individuals could learn independently does not mean they will choose to do so.

Today, teachers are using digital-communication technologies for many purposes, including (1) reteaching and reinforcing content, (2) providing enrichment experiences for talented learners, (3) individualizing assignments, (4) promoting global perspectives (using World Wide Web sites, encouraging international e-mail pen pals, etc.), (5) and desktop publishing. Let's briefly turn our attention to several more-complete descriptions of other present-day applications of newer communication technologies. These examples relate to

- developing learners' research capabilities,
- expanding course offerings,
- providing services to underperforming schools,
- simulating real-life experiences, and
- helping learners with special problems.

What Do You Think?

- What applications of technology do you see as having the most promise for changing education?
- What applications of technology do you think will face the most resistance?

Developing Learners' Research Capabilities

Helping learners to become more sophisticated thinkers has long been an aim of educators. As early as 1910, John Dewey, a famous educational philosopher, in his influential book, *How We Think*, suggested that learners' thinking skills should be developed by requiring them to follow a series of steps leading from consideration of specific information to formulation of conclusions supported by evidence.

An orientation to teaching that requires learners to engage content personally, think about it carefully, and draw conclusions is constructivism. Constructivism, derived from the work of learning theorists Jean Piaget (Piaget & Inhelder, 1958) and Lev Vygotsky (1962), holds that learners are not passive responders to the environment. Rather, they actively engage the environment and seek to derive personal meaning from this involvement. If you operate in a manner consistent with the constructivist perspective, you will favor lessons that involve your learners in constructing and understanding their own knowledge. New technologies can help you accomplish this.

Inquiry teaching, sometimes called **inductive teaching,** is one approach teachers use to actively engage learners with content they can use as they strive for meaningful and supportable conclusions. Many inquiry or inductive techniques require learners to follow these steps:

1. Describe the essential features of a problem or situation.
2. Suggest possible solutions or explanations.
3. Gather evidence to test the accuracy of these solutions or explanations.
4. Evaluate the solutions or explanations in light of this evidence.
5. Develop a conclusion that is supported by the best evidence.

Though inquiry and inductive techniques have been promoted for many years, new technologies give you options in implementing these approaches that were unavailable to teachers as recently as a decade ago. These techniques require learners to have access to large quantities of specific information. In years gone by, you would have had to assemble this information yourself and make it available to your learners in your own classroom or at some other location within your school building.

Today, the World Wide Web provides opportunities for your learners to access information available at locations throughout the globe. With proper training, they can engage in incredibly diverse activities. For example, you can involve learners in reading diaries of Civil War veterans, looking at paintings housed in the world's finest museums, downloading photographic and other images from famous repositories of these materials, noting how newspapers around the world are covering a common event, and downloading voice and music files. When you engage learners in inquiry activities in this new environment, you do not act as an assembler and presenter of information. Rather, your roles are (1) to guide learners to places they might productively search for information, using tools such as computers connected to the Internet and (2) to monitor their progress, keeping them on task and providing assistance, as needed.

When you use new technologies to develop learners' capacities as researchers, you have opportunities to accommodate their individual learning styles and preferences. For example, you can provide alternative suggestions to individuals in your class who, respectively, prefer to learn (1) by reading prose materials, (2) by looking at photographs and other visuals, or (3) by hearing the spoken word. By teaming learners, you can encourage their use of individual strengths in final projects and reports that require them to develop technology-based multimedia presentations. Using new technologies to investigate problems, identify and weigh evidence, and draw conclusions involves members of your class in the generation of knowledge. Educational specialists who advocate using new technology for this purpose point out that learners find this kind of intellectual engagement motivating (Merrow, 2001).

Expanding Course Offerings

Schools in many parts of the country today use modern communication technologies to bring instruction to learners that, in prior years, could not be delivered. For example, electronic video and audio connections make it possible for courses in such specialized subjects as advanced calculus to be delivered to learners attending small schools where such subjects are not available. Individual small schools often cannot provide classes in specialty areas that would draw only small numbers of enrollees. Today, an instructor from a single location can serve many learners in isolated locations by electronically linking them together using modern video and audio technologies.

One variant of electronically based distance learning features complete courses that are offered over the World Wide Web. In many designs of this type, learners may "log on" to the courses they are taking whenever they are free to do so. In addition to promoting wide geographic dispersion of instruction, Web-based courses allow learners to do assignments at times that are convenient for them. In some places, learners take Web-based courses after normal school hours.

Individuals who have worked with Web-based courses caution that such courses function well when the purpose is to transmit basic information but that they function less effectively when objectives call for individuals to work with others in group activities that require them to engage in higher-level thinking and decision making (Vallecorsa, 2001). Design of Web-based instruction is still in its formative years, and these difficulties eventually may be resolved.

• •

The Virtual School
Go to MyEducationLab and select the topic "Technology in the Schools," then watch the video "Virtual School Advantages." Complete the questions accompanying the video. Some of the questions have been designed to prepare you for your licensure examination.
• •

Providing Services to Underperforming Schools

Over the past 10 years, many states have used test scores and other means to identify schools whose learners have not been performing at acceptable levels. In some places, legislators have adopted policies requiring states to provide young people in these schools with exemplary instruction as a means of improving learner performance. Although legislative mandates of this kind have been well intentioned, state education leaders have found it difficult to comply. Schools in need of assistance often are dispersed in multiple locations throughout the state, and the numbers of expert teachers available to help are limited. With passage of the No Child Left Behind Act of 2001 (2002) this problem has broadened from one affecting some of the states to a difficulty facing educational leaders throughout the entire country.

The No Child Left Behind Act of 2001 requires schools that have failed to produce acceptable learner-achievement scores for three consecutive years to provide additional instructional services such as after-school tutoring if parents request them. Federal funds are available to help schools pay for communication technologies to provide these services.

With the encouragement of the Secretary of the U.S. Department of Education, schools are making plans to deliver these services to learners using the Web and other electronic means (Murray, 2002). John Bailey, director of education technology for the U.S. Department of Education, comments that "the Internet offers . . . the ability to tap into literally the best instructors and the best tutors from all around the country and all around the world" (quoted in Murray, 2002).

Simulating Real-Life Experiences

Simulations have been used in school classrooms for many years. You have participated in examples during your own years as a public-school learner. Simulations give young people opportunities for learning experiences that allow them to experience reality in ways that provide quite a credible illusion of a real-life experience. Learners make decisions that have consequences, but the simulated environment always acts to preserve their personal safety. Simulations also provide opportunities for teachers to allow learners to vicariously experience conditions experienced by people in past times.

New digital technologies have greatly expanded the range of simulations available for use by public-school learners. This range in complexity from relatively simple game-like experiences that are presented to learners on computer disks to hugely ambitious, multiple-day experiences that may require use of Web sites, CD-ROMs, DVDs, televisions, e-mail, and other technologies. Simulations supported by digital technology are now available for virtually all subject areas.

Some technology-based simulations are extraordinarily sophisticated. For example, the Quest Channel, a subscription service, makes available to subscribing school districts and teachers complex "explorations" that link multiple schools and learners with a team of individuals who go to interesting world places in search of answers to intriguing questions. Participating learners use the Web and e-mail to perform background work, to exchange information with "experts" and with other young people (in their own school and in other participating schools), and to see video images provided by the field team. These simulations also provide ways for involved teachers to communicate electronically and share information about learner progress on other issues. During the fall of 2002, the focus was on Christopher Columbus, and learners were involved in such activities as comparing historical accounts of Columbus's voyages with observations of the field team, studying the history of exploration and navigation, learning about cultural groups of the Caribbean, and reading reports in both Spanish and English.

Complex simulations, such as those provided by the Quest Channel, highlight another advantage of technology-supported simulations. They provide a cost-effective way for learners to engage interesting and motivating content. Few, if any, public schools could afford to send an entire class on a trip replicating Columbus's route to the New World. Many can find the money to support a Quest Channel subscription that will allow young people to participate on a highly engaging simulated version of the journey.

Applying Technology in the Classroom

Go to MyEducationLab and select the topic "Technology in the Schools," then watch the following two videos: "Model Inquiry Unit–Part 2" and "Presentation Software in Literature." The first video shows an elementary school classroom that is using the computer to conduct an inquiry into the earthworm. The second video shows a secondary English classroom using presentation software to apply gaming to learning about *Hamlet*.

Respond to the questions that accompany the videos. Some of the questions have been designed to prepare you for your licensure examination.

Helping Learners with Special Problems

Various technologies have long been used to provide assistance to learners who have characteristics that can interfere with their ability to learn. For example, for many years devices called **braillers** or braille-writers that allow users to take notes and produce other prose materials in Braille have been available to learners with severe visual limitations. Learners who are not proficient readers sometimes have had access to audio recordings of important sections of course texts. In some places, enrichment experiences have been provided to bright young people through videocassettes and special computer software available for checking out and working with at home.

Until recently, educators have followed this general sequence in identifying support technologies to use: (1) the general demands of the existing curriculum were examined to identify potential problems that certain categories of learners might face, and (2) technologies were identified that might allow those learners to interact with program materials and profit from them. In other words, the existing curriculum was considered as a "given," and technology was used to accommodate specific learner characteristics to it.

This approach places heavy demands on teachers. For example, in your class you might have learners with conditions requiring you to use a variety of technologies in your efforts to help them learn. One learner might have a physical condition that prevents any movement of arms or legs. Computer-based reading material would help this person, but you would need to develop a system that would allow screen changes to be made by striking a bar with the chin. Another person with very limited vision may require a computer with hugely oversized keys that will "speak" when they are pressed. Other learners may have additional needs to which you must respond. Although technologies are available to assist these learners, the process of accessing needed equipment, making certain that it is being used in ways that relate to the adopted curriculum, and familiarizing learners with use of new equipment can be frustrating and time-consuming.

Web Extension 11–2

Center for Applied Special Technology (CAST)

• •

The Center for Applied Special Technology (CAST) is a not-for-profit organization dedicated to widening opportunities for people with disabilities through innovative uses of technology. You will find much useful information at this site, particularly topics related to using technologies to assist learners in your class who may have disabilities of various kinds. You may find the CAST Newsletter, which is electronically accessible, to be particularly helpful. This newsletter discusses innovative uses of technology in the classroom.

http://www.cast.org/

Today, educational leaders are beginning to challenge this approach of using technologies to help learners cope with a preestablished curriculum. In part, suggestions for a better way have been prompted by revolutionary developments in digital technology over the past decade. Bart Pasha, the research director of the Center for Applied Special Technology (CAST), declares that these changes may affect learning and dissemination of information as much as the invention of the printing press (McHenry, 2002). These technologies make it possible for the initial design of school programs to build in features that will allow learners to access content in ways consistent with their own needs. In working with programs designed in this way, you will no longer need to think about technologies you might need to enable learners with special needs (motor impairments, deafness, profound reading difficulties, visual impairments, etc.) to succeed. The original design of the program will have access channels built in that learners with various needs can use as they seek to master program content.

The term applied to efforts to develop curricula that include built-in access channels for different learners is universal design for learning (UDL). School programs that follow UDL principles seek to do the following (Rose & Meyer, 2002):

- Represent information in multiple formats and media
- Provide multiple pathways for learners' actions and expressions
- Provide multiple ways to engage learners' interest and motivation

School programs that are based on UDL principles try to eliminate barriers embedded within curricula that present problems for learners with certain characteristics. Ways to assist these young people will be incorporated as part of the basic design, and you will receive the information you need as part of your initial orientation to the program.

TODAY'S TECHNOLOGIES: SOME CHALLENGES

According to Tyack and Cuban (1995), most Americans embrace technology because of the potential it offers for solving learning problems. Given this reality, you should not be surprised if you hear or read that today's digital innovations have the power to "transform the school." In part, this hope is based on tangible evidence that teachers, in the past, have incorporated new technologies into their daily instructional routines. Such commonplaces as whiteboards, textbooks for every learner, overhead projectors, and ballpoint pens are examples. It is interesting to note that many of these innovations failed to completely displace earlier technologies. For example, if you visit a school, you may well find both whiteboards and chalkboards. Older video playback units continue to coexist with DVD players.

When teachers have seen legitimate benefits of innovations, they have gradually accepted them as legitimate aids to instruction. On the other hand, sometimes, without input from educators, outsiders have zealously promoted "sure-fire cures" for educational problems (Cuban, 2001; Tyack & Cuban, 1995). These efforts have not always produced the results that promoters of these innovations promised.

Educational policy specialist Larry Cuban (2001) has studied the history of educational innovations. He notes that attempts to install innovations in the school often have featured a cycle including these phases:

1. *Overblown-description-of-potential-benefits phase.* During this phase, supporters of the innovation go public with claims about how the innovative technology will transform education.
2. *Disappointing-research-results phase.* During this phase, reports emerge showing that the innovation has produced fewer beneficial results than its promoters had promised.
3. *Investigate-causes-for-failure phase.* During this phase, further investigation reveals that relatively few teachers have implemented the innovation or that they have implemented it in ways that deviated from its basic design.
4. *Place-the-blame phase.* This phase often features criticism of teachers who sometimes are described as human barriers to the installation of a new technology that, absent their resistance, would do wonderful things for young people.

Cuban (2001) notes that there is little evidence that teachers resist new technological innovations because they fear or dislike technology. Their decisions to use or not use a novel technology are grounded on their perceptions of its utility in helping them discharge their responsibilities. Before embracing a new technology, they want to know how much time they must commit to learn about it. They want assurances that the technology will be applicable to a variety of situations. They need information about how the technology will help them teach content for which they will be held accountable. They want assurances that the needed equipment will work as designed and that immediate help will be available to deal with breakdowns. They want to know whether use of the innovation will undermine their ability to maintain good order in the classroom. Cuban argues that concerns about these issues have often contributed to teachers' disinclination to embrace new technologies enthusiastically.

Web Extension 11–3

FNO—*From Now On:* The Educational Technology Journal

FNO is a monthly electronic journal that publishes articles related to school and teacher uses of technology. You may sign up for a free subscription. Individual issues include descriptions of classroom applications of technology, reviews of books related to technology and education, and other information you may find helpful as you think about integrating technology into your own instructional program.

http://www.fno.org

What Do You Think?

- How comfortable are you with using technology in the classroom?
- What are your personal concerns about using technology as a teaching tool?

Given these concerns, in the long run will teachers embrace computer-based instruction? It is too early to give a definitive answer to this question. However, school leaders are working hard to encourage teachers to embrace computer technology. For example, there is increasing evidence that even less-affluent schools are investing substantial sums of money in high-tech hardware and software. Interests of governmental and business leaders at all levels have acted as an important influence on state legislatures to allocate funds for these kinds of purchases. These funds also increasingly are used to employ technicians to service equipment and to respond to problems teachers have when using it. Although few schools have all the technicians they need, clearly much more help of this kind is available than when technologies associated with films, radio, and television were being actively promoted as agents to improve the schools. Increasingly, too, school leaders are recognizing the need to provide funds to familiarize teachers with new hardware and software and to respond to general concerns related to issues such as classroom management, content accountability, and flexibility of use.

Removable storage media and ever-increasing numbers of schools with connections to the Internet make it possible for you and your learners to access digital information when you need it. The time-flexibility feature of today's new technology stands in marked contrast to characteristics of certain earlier innovations. Finally, if your teacher-preparation program is typical, you will receive instruction regarding how new technologies can be used to support your teaching activities. Ever-growing numbers of teachers have received formal training focused on making good use of new technologies. This situation is in marked contrast to the lack of attention that was given to preparing teachers to work effectively with certain earlier technological innovations.

Cost Issues

Costs associated with embedding new technologies, particularly computers, into school programs strain school budgets. Today, funds to support educational technology in the nation's schools total multiple billions of dollars annually. In seeking these funds, school leaders have struggled to maintain existing operations, while also responding to demands for computer purchases, equipment replacement, new software purchases and upgrades, Internet connections, teacher training, and maintenance services for computer equipment and networks.

If you discuss this situation with central office administrators, you are likely to learn that, because of voter resistance to increased taxes to support school operations, new funds from state legislatures and local taxing authorities have been scarce. In many school districts, financial support for technology comes from multiple sources, including donations from parent–teacher organizations and other school-based groups, private foundations, federal agencies, and grant competitions that award technology-dollars to successful applicants.

In recent years, the role of the federal government has increased support for school technology programs. Though the amount of federal money used to support educational technology varies from state to state, on average federal funds now account for about 25% of the total dollars spent each year for this purpose (*T.H.E. Journal*, 2001). This figure represents a much higher level of federal support for school technology than for other expenses associated with maintaining public education. On average, federal expenditures account for only around 7% of the total annual costs of running our public schools. States and local governments pay virtually all of the remaining expenses.

One particularly important piece of legislation, the **Telecommunications Act of 1996** has been especially helpful to school leaders seeking to expand the numbers of Internet-connected computers in their districts. This law enables individual school districts to apply for funds to support a special e-rate that makes them eligible for discounts that can run as high as 90% on telecommunications and Internet services (Wired News, 2000). This program has made it possible for at least some computers to be tied to the Internet in even our least-affluent schools and school districts.

In general, school districts have found ways to purchase large numbers of computers and to connect them to the Internet. Today, 99% of schools have computers. A national survey completed in 2000 revealed that 84% of teachers had at least one computer in their own classroom. Thirty-eight percent of teachers had two to five computers in their classroom, and 10% of respondents had five or more (National Center for Education Statistics, 2000).

Caution is needed when interpreting the impact of the increase of computers in schools. Simply because computers have become almost-universal features of the school environment does not suggest that everybody has equal access to up-to-date computer technology. Some school computers are too old to accommodate the demands of the latest software. Individual classrooms vary greatly in the numbers of computers available for learners to use. Some learners have access to computers only at school; others, typically from more-affluent families, also have computers to use at home. (You will learn more about differences in access to computer technology in the discussion of the digital divide that appears later in the chapter.) Some schools have found sufficient funds to purchase computers but not to train teachers and learners to use them.

The money issue is important virtually everywhere. School leaders are challenged to find funds for technology-related expenditures in areas not associated with initial hardware and software purchases and connections to networks. In particular, they must work hard to find money to

- replace outdated hardware and software at regular intervals,
- train teachers to make effective use of new technologies,
- provide hardware and software to teachers experiencing difficulty, and
- support technicians to make needed repairs quickly.

One way school systems have responded to the high cost of replacing hardware and software is to lengthen the expected use cycle. In the private sector, computers are replaced, on average, once every three years. Schools have stretched this average to once every five years (Fitzgerald, 1999). This can mean that, toward the end of the replacement cycle, you may be using equipment that limits what you and your learners can do.

If you are expected to use unfamiliar equipment and software, the time required for you to become an effective user will increase. Using computer-based technology to involve learners in sophisticated lessons requires you to have high levels of comfort with both hardware and software. Funding problems that fail to pay for adequate training can undermine the potential effectiveness of even the best-designed instructional-support technologies. In some districts where funds have been insufficient to train all teachers, money has been used to prepare a few teacher experts to help others who have difficulties (Fitzgerald, 1999). In the long run, this is not a good option. Trained teachers who come to the assistance of others divert their time to working with teachers, rather than learners.

When you work with a book or other traditional print material, you can be reasonably confident that nothing will happen to make the information unusable. Computers and programs do not provide this assurance. Occasionally things go wrong. When difficulties arise, immediate help is needed to remedy the situation to minimize interference with your instructional program. Ideally, technicians should be available to provide this kind of help.

Technicians are expensive and scarce. Their turnover rates are high because usually they can command higher salaries from private-sector employers. In response to these circumstances, learners—often individuals who are self-taught "techies"—handle chores associated with troubleshooting computers, networks, and software. A report provided to teachers attending the National Education Computing Conference revealed that today learners, themselves, provide technical support in over half of the nation's school districts (Dean, 2002). Although many young people are quite capable, their tenure within individual schools is limited. Hence, this arrangement provides no year-to-year continuity. In addition, critics wonder whether learners who engage in this kind of technological assistance are doing so at the expense of time they otherwise might be spending in activities more clearly tied to their educational needs.

New Technologies as Learning Distractors

Should young people be permitted to bring electronic pagers, cell phones, portable CD players, MP3 players, personal digital assistants (PDAs), and laptop computers to school? In some places, school districts have adopted policies requiring learners to leave these devices at home. Other school districts are discussing this issue.

Supporters of bans tend to be most concerned about electronic devices that have little potential to be used as an integral part of instructional programs. If you have ever heard a group of teachers discussing pagers and cell phones, you know that some of them are adamantly opposed to learners bringing these devices to class. Among other things, they argue that teachers have worked for years to prevent unnecessary interruptions from school public-address systems. Pagers and cell phones divert learners' attention from their work much the same as voices blaring from public-address-system speakers. Even when buzzers and ringers are turned off and the devices are switched to vibrate mode, learners are distracted when a vibration signals an incoming call. Such interruptions break their concentration and interfere with the learning process ("Should Cell Phones and Pagers Be Allowed in School?," 2001).

Views of teachers who want to keep pagers and cell phones out of their classrooms frequently are at odds with some parents and guardians who argue strongly that their children should be permitted to take these devices with them to school. Among other things, parents and guardians contend that their sons and daughters should have a means of contacting people outside the school when emergencies arise. Sometimes parents and guardians have had difficulty in getting messages passed to their children when they have called the central school office. This situation can be avoided when learners have cell phones or, at least,

David Young-Wolff / Photo Edit Inc.

Rapid adoption of new technologies, such as cell phones, provides both potential advantages and potential problems for teachers.

pagers. Increasing numbers of schoolchildren are raised in homes with a single parent or guardian. Communicating frequently with sons and daughters via cell phones provides these adults with assurances that their children are safe and secure ("Should Cell Phones and Pagers Be Allowed in School?," 2001). Read about how some students use cell phones to cheat in this chapter's *Video Viewpoints* feature.

Although electronic pagers and cell phones have been the most frequent targets of school attempts to keep learners from bringing digital-communication devices to school, some teachers believe that the bans should extend to personal digital assistants and laptop computers ("School Board Weighs Ban on Student Laptops, PDAs," 2002). Many modern PDAs allow two or more users to engage in electronic conversations. Laptops can be used to exchange e-mail messages. Though these uses do pose the possibility that learners' attention will be diverted from assigned school tasks, both PDAs and laptops can be used for legitimate academic purposes. For example, students can use these devices to take notes, gather data from Web sites, and organize information for presentations. Newer PDAs and laptops incorporate features that, collectively, are expanding their potential for integration into the instructional program. For this reason, opposition to learners' use of these devices in school may be diminishing.

Video Viewpoints 11–1

Caught Cheating Using Cell Phones

WATCH: This *Primetime Thursday* segment on student cheating shows students using technology to cheat on examinations. Students claim that the brutal pressure to pass tests and get good grades has led to an increase in cheating.

THINK: Discuss with your classmates or write in your reflective journal your responses to the following questions:

1. What do you see as the causes of cheating?
2. Do you agree that the pressure to learn specific facts in order to pass tests and obtain good grades has led to cheating?
3. What is the ethical responsibility of parents, colleges, schools, and students in this issue?

LINK: What will you do as a teacher to confront the issue of cheating in your classroom?

 To view this video, go to the Video Viewpoints DVD and click on this chapter's video: "Caught Cheating Using Cell Phones."

When you begin teaching, you may find issues related to banning specific kinds of digital-communication devices becoming more complex. Today there are reasonably obvious distinctions among devices such as digital telephones and personal digital assistants, but these differences may be less clear in the future. Functions of numerous one-purpose devices are being blended into single multiple-function devices. For example, some cell phones now function as personal digital assistants and are capable of establishing wireless connections with the Internet. As these devices become common, you and your colleagues will need to weigh their potential educational benefits against their capacity for disrupting the educational process.

Changing Teachers' Views of Their Roles

How are teachers using technologies today? The picture is mixed. Many educational leaders who promote these technologies as levers that can transform schools and engage learners in sophisticated thinking processes despair that many teachers are using computers as little more than electronic replacements for traditional worksheets and drill-and-practice exercises (Foa, Schwab, & Johnson, 1998; Merrow, 2001). On the other hand, in some places these technologies are leading teachers to individualize instruction, tailor programs to particular learner aptitudes and interests, and engage learners in doing highly motivating and important work (Rector, 2002; Roblyer, 2003). Figure 11–1 is a form that you might find useful as you search for material that you can use to enhance your teaching. This form can be duplicated and filed away. (We have used it on a 4×8 file card that can then be filed by topic in a file box.) As you are browsing through the Internet, you can then quickly jot down URLs that are of interest. Then, when you start planning lessons, you can review the file and identify useable resources.

Preparing learners to take advantage of multiple information sources places huge new demands on teachers. For example, if you wish to develop technology-intensive learning, you must commit considerable time to becoming informed about available options and going about the business of organizing learning programs that differ based on individual characteristics of your students. The work required to prepare for and deliver this kind of instruction can be daunting. In response to this situation, many school districts provide in-service training to help teachers become more comfortable as they think about and prepare for increasingly technologically based instructional roles.

Figure 11-1   **Building instructional resources.**

One skill that teachers find useful is that of identifying resources that can be used in the classroom. These resources can include pictures, charts, resource books, Web sites, and lesson ideas. It is a good idea to begin building your instructional resource file so that you will have resources when you begin teaching. Below is a useful tool in keeping track of websites that you might find useful as you prepare for teaching.

1. Subject _____

2. Description of the resource _____

3. Possible uses of the resource _____

4. Appropriate for grade levels _____

5. Cautions related to use in classroom _____

6. URL _____

7. Date last checked _____

Researchers have identified some measures school districts can take to help teachers adapt to and make effective use of newer communication technologies (Foa, Schwab, & Johnson, 1998):

- Providing support for teachers who are early adopters of innovations
- Providing training in how to use new technologies (which is as important as purchasing hardware and software)
- Training and building enthusiasm for technological change among administrators (which is critical if teachers are to receive needed administrative support when they begin using new technologies)
- Providing specific teacher training in the project-based, problem-solving, and constructivist approaches to teaching and schemes for managing classrooms so that individual learners may pursue different instructional ends

The Digital Divide

To have any impact at all, new technologies, must be accessible. Though the past two decades have witnessed dramatic advances in digital communication, different groups of people have responded differently to these developments. Experts who have studied new technologies have discovered enormous differences in the extent to which different categories of people use them. High percentages of people within some groups now actively work with these technologies, and high percentages of other groups scarcely use them at all. The term **digital divide** has been coined to describe this disparity.

The digital divide operates internationally as well as within the United States. For example, one recent study reported that 41% of all Internet users in the world live in Canada and the United States. Though Asia has a much larger total population than the combined total of Canada and the United States, people living on this continent account for only 20% of Internet users. South American Internet users comprise only 4% of the world's total (Digital Divide Network, 2002).

The United Nations, the World Bank, and other organizations interested in promoting more use of technology worldwide are taking steps to make these technologies more accessible to countries with limited numbers of digital technology users. These efforts are taken out of a conviction that countries need technologically literate populations to compete effectively in today's competitive economies. Similarly, the new communication technologies are thought to promote democracies. Because of the capacity it offers to link people, ideas, and government leaders, "the Internet has become both the fuel and the vehicle for a dramatic spread in democracy . . ." (Brown, 2001).

In the United States, a digital divide has been found between people who, collectively, tend to be (1) frequent and extensive users and those who are (2) less frequent and more limited users of newer digital technologies.

For educators, these trends present both positive news and continuing challenges. On the positive side, the growing presence of technologies in school is reflected in data that indicate that young people ages 10 to 25 use computers and access the Internet more frequently than do any other age group (National Telecommunications and Information Administration, 2002). This finding attests to the impact on learners of school systems' efforts to place more and more computers in schools, link them to the Internet, and encourage teachers to integrate their use into the regular instructional program. There is evidence, too,

---

Web Extension 11–4

Digital Divide Network
• •
The Digital Divide Network brings together an electronically linked community of people interested in ensuring access to new technologies to groups that include Native Americans, females, economically impoverished Americans, the homeless, and many others. In addition to feature articles, the Digital Divide Network sponsors an electronic discussion group you can join if you would like to discuss equity and technology issues with others.

http://www.digitaldividenetwork.org

---

that some groups who, a decade ago, were infrequent users of advanced communication technologies now use them routinely. For example, until the late 1990s, fewer females than males used computers and the Internet. Today, these sex-based differences have disappeared (National Telecommunications and Information Administration, 2002).

Some interesting and positive developments indicate that the technology-usage gap is closing between (1) whites and Asian Americans/Pacific Islanders and (2) African Americans and Latinos. In one recent three-year period, Internet use by African Americans grew at the annual rate of 31%, and Internet use by Latinos grew at an annual rate of 26% (National Telecommunications and Information Administration, 2002). Use among whites and Asian Americans/Pacific Islanders has continued to grow, but at a slower rate. Educators and others interested in promoting more use of digital technology hope this trend will continue. If it does, differences in computer use among racial and ethnic groups will greatly narrow in the years ahead.

One aspect of the digital divide that greatly concerns educational leaders is the disparity between the availability of technological equipment in high-poverty schools and affluent schools. One recent study reported that, on average, 16 learners shared a single computer in high-poverty schools. The comparable figure for affluent schools was seven learners (National PTA, 2001–2002). Large numbers of learners per computer in high-poverty schools may limit the types of computer-based learning teachers assign. There also is evidence that computers are used more often in high-poverty than in affluent schools to engage learners in unchallenging drill-and-practice activities (Merrow, 2001).

In thinking about how computer technology relates to families' economic conditions, consider the consequences of some learners having opportunities to use computers at home and others being limited to using them at school. Learners whose parents or guardians have limited incomes have few opportunities to take advantage of digital technologies once they leave the school building. To address this problem, some school districts are keeping school computer labs open during the evening so learners can use them. Many public libraries now make Internet-connected computers available for use by patrons, including students. The private sector also has established some programs to address this issue. For example, Intel's Computer Clubhouse program, which is now in place in 50 locations throughout the country, establishes centers in underprivileged neighborhoods. These centers are designed to help learners from impoverished families develop their computer skills (Goot, 2002).

What Do You Think?

- How serious is the problem of the digital divide?
- What are some specific actions that could reduce the impact of technology on different groups?

In times past, educators worked hard to provide textbooks for every learner. The idea was to provide every child with the basic tools needed to achieve academic success. If new technologies require learners to have access to specialized technological equipment, then the same equity principle that drove the effort to provide all learners with texts will support efforts to ensure that learners, regardless of family income or personal background, have access to these necessary learning tools. Developing ways to diminish and, it is hoped, to eliminate the digital divide may be among the most important tasks you and your colleagues confront in the decades ahead.

Protecting Learners

Digital-communication technologies such as those supporting e-mail and the World Wide Web make it possible for information from almost limitless numbers of sources to be directed to computers that are linked to the Internet. If you use e-mail, you probably are familiar with the problem of dealing with large numbers of unsolicited messages, many of them coming from individuals and firms pushing dubious financial schemes, encouraging you to participate in online gambling, or soliciting your interest in sites that feature pornographic material. When you use the Web pages, you view may feature pop-up ads directing your attention to sites that, in some cases, may not be suitable for learners. Certainly, any search engine can quickly identify dozens of sites with content that many parents and guardians consider unsuitable for young people. In addition, many online chat rooms feature exchanges of obscenities and discussions of topics that responsible adults consider inappropriate for school-age learners.

In addition to concerns about learners' access to inappropriate material, school leaders also fear that some learners may use Internet-linked computers illegally or unethically (Baines, 2007). As a teacher, for example, you do not want members of your class to violate copyright laws nor to find completed term papers that they can copy and submit as their own work. Professional educators also sometimes worry that older learners will use taxpayer-supported electronic equipment and networks to engage in business transactions, for example, through the use of Web-based auction sites.

In response to concerns about possible misuse of digital-communication technology, schools around the country have worked hard in recent years to develop **acceptable-use policies (AUPs)**. Such policies typically make clear distinctions between acceptable and unacceptable learner uses of technology. Often, too, they contain information about sanctions that will be applied to learners who fail to follow established acceptable-use guidelines. These guidelines often differ according to variables including (1) whether learners have completed a class in computer responsibility, (2) learners' grade levels, and (3) whether online work is being done as part of a class assignment. Many lists of unacceptable uses include (1) participation in chat rooms, (2) sending and receiving personal e-mail (unless this is part of an assigned class activity), and (3) posting personal Web pages (unless this is part of an assigned class activity).

AUPs often include lists of the kinds of Web sites learners are forbidden to visit using school computers with Internet connections. Typical examples include Web sites that

- promote violence or illegal behavior,
- feature sexually explicit information,
- provide entry to chat rooms,
- sell term papers,
- allow for copyright infringement or plagiarism, and
- permit users to engage in commercial transactions (National Education Association, 1998)

In a report titled *The Digital Disconnect: The Widening Gap Between Internet-Savvy Students and Their Schools*, investigators Douglas Levin and Sousan Arafeh (2002) report that over three-quarters of young people between the ages of 12 and 17 go online. Thirty percent to forty percent of teenagers fall into a technologically savvy category of elite Internet users. The numbers of young people in this group are growing. These sophisticated users regularly go to the Internet to do school-related work, including locating resources, downloading source materials, collaborating with other class members, and storing papers and notes. Many students in this group express frustration with school policies that are designed to do the following:

- Limit their access to the Internet to specific time periods during the school day.
- Limit their access to the Internet to only a few school computers located in particular rooms (often a computer laboratory).
- Impose content filters that are so restrictive that many legitimate information sources cannot be accessed from school-based computers.

What Do You Think?

- Many school policies regarding limitation of learner access to the Internet are driven by state and federal legislation. Should such legislation exist at all? If so, what kinds of limitations should schools be required to impose on learner Internet access?
- Complaints of learners who were surveyed to gather information for *The Digital Disconnect* report centered on the idea that school policies were preventing them from accessing important Internet content. Are these concerns justified? Why or why not?
- Suppose there were no federal or state regulations requiring schools to limit learner access to the Internet. If you were charged with writing an Internet use policy for learners in your school, what might its provisions be? How would you reconcile (1) the need to maximize the potential for young people to learn from the Internet and (2) the need to prevent harm from coming to learners from Internet content?

Interest in protecting young people from certain kinds of Internet content helped win support for two important pieces of federal legislation you should know. These are the **Children's Internet Protection Act (CIPA)** and the **Neighborhood Children's Internet Protection Act (N-CIPA)**. Both laws are part of Public Law 105-554, a large federal appropriations measure passed in December 2000. Provisions of these acts have important implications for schools.

The CIPA requires schools and school libraries to install filters on all computers accessing the Internet to block materials that (1) are obscene, (2) feature child pornography, or (3) are harmful to minors. School districts must have mechanisms in place to ensure that these provisions are enforced. The law also requires each school to have an adopted **Internet safety policy**. In addition, public meetings must be held to discuss the contents of this policy.

CIPA's companion law, the N-CIPA, focuses on the kinds of information that must be included in the Internet safety policy. The policy must include details regarding:

- access by minors to inappropriate matter on the Internet and Web;
- the safety and security of minors when using e-mail, chat rooms, and other forms of direct electronic communications;
- unauthorized access, including so-called "hacking," and other unlawful activities by minors online;
- unauthorized disclosure, use, and dissemination of minors' personal-identification information; and
- measures designed to restrict minors' access to harmful materials.

Failure to comply with CIPA and N-CIPA can produce negative financial consequences for school districts. Among other things, they may lose their access to the e-rate.

Because you may wish to make considerable use of Web-based technologies in your own classes, you need to learn about specific provisions of your district's acceptable-use policy. You may also have opportunities to participate in periodic revisions of the Internet safety policy. Concerns about protecting learners from potentially harmful Internet content and ensuring that they use the capabilities of the technology responsibly show little signs of abating. It is likely that you, other professionals, parents, guardians, community representatives, and political leaders will devote great attention to these concerns in the years ahead.

Web Extension 11–5

Electronic Portfolios

• •

At this site, Dr. Helen Barrett provides numerous links that feature content about maintaining electronic portfolios. You may be interested in following links to content about (1) teacher education and professional-development portfolios, (2) high school graduation portfolios, and (3) family involvement in early childhood portfolios.

http://helenbarrett.com/

Key Ideas in Summary

- Technology has become such a pervasive feature of our national life that schools are being pressured by business leaders, political authorities, parents, guardians, and other citizens to incorporate more use of today's digital-communication technologies into school programs.
- The leading professional organization advocating on behalf of technology in the schools, the International Society for Technology in Education (ISTE), has developed technology standards for learners and teachers. Increasing numbers of states and school districts are establishing technology standards, many of which are derived from those ISTE developed.
- Technology is not a single instructional methodology. It is a means to an end. Successful applications of technology require you to have a clear instructional purpose in mind and to select a technological alternative that is well suited to the particular needs of your students and each instructional setting.

- Change does not automatically result when new technologies become available. Existing technologies place some restraints on what educators and learners can do. However, traditional practices also act as restraints. As a result, new technologies, although they offer the potential for change, do not always produce change.
- Today's newer digital-communication technologies are being applied in schools to achieve many purposes. Examples include (1) developing learners' research capabilities, (2) supporting expanded course offerings, (3) providing high-quality instructional services to underperforming schools, (4) allowing learners to simulate real-life experiences, and (5) matching instructional practices to characteristics of learners with special needs.
- Teachers rejected some technological innovations in the past because they failed to respond to teachers' needs or created new problems. Though the jury is still out on the fate of newer digital-communication technologies, there are hopes these innovations may take firm root in our nation's schools. These expectations result from the broad societal support for many of these innovations, the willingness of schools to invest in needed equipment, and in the increasing realization that resources to prepare teachers to take advantage of the capabilities offered by these technologies are needed.
- New technologies present some educators with ongoing challenges. Among them are (1) the high costs associated with technology-related equipment and instructional materials, maintenance and replacement of equipment and support materials, and teacher training; (2) within-the-classroom distractions occasioned by learner use and misuse of cell phones, PDAs, and other high-tech equipment; (3) changing the role conceptions of teachers trained before today's digital-technology revolution; and (4) differences in access to computers, the Internet, and the Web outside of school by learners from impoverished backgrounds.
- Concern about possible dangers that can come to learners who have access to the World Wide Web, the Internet, and other modern communication technologies has resulted in the passage of several important laws. These include the Children's Internet Protection Act and the Neighborhood Children's Internet Protection Act. Concerns about learner safety have prompted school districts to adopt acceptable-use policies that spell out acceptable and unacceptable kinds of learner uses of technology.

For Your Initial-Development Portfolio

1. What materials and ideas that you learned in this chapter about *influences of technology* will you include as "evidence" in your portfolio? Select up to three separate items of information. Number them 1, 2, and 3.
2. Think about why you selected these materials. As you do so, consider these issues:
   - Specific uses you might make of this information as you plan, deliver, and assess the impact of your teaching
   - The compatibility of the information with your own priorities and values
   - Any contributions this information can make to your development as a teacher
   - Factors that led you to include this information, as opposed to some alternatives you considered but rejected
3. Place a check in the chart below to indicate the INTASC standard(s) to which each of your items of information relates. (You may wish to refer to Chapter 1 for more detailed information about INTASC.)

INTASC Standard Number										
ITEM OF EVIDENCE NUMBER	S1	S2	S3	S4	S5	S6	S7	S8	S9	S10
1										
2										
3										

4. Prepare a written reflection in which you analyze the decision-making process you followed. In your comments, mention the INTASC standard(s) to which your selected material relates.

Reflections

1. Today's digital technologies make it possible for students to engage in simulated experiences of complex realities. Critic Bill Rukeyser (Philipkoski, 2000) points out that sometimes schools have taken advantage of these capabilities to substitute computer-based simulations for learning experiences that students could experience directly. For example, instead of having students do hands-on work in chemistry labs, some students simply use software to perform simulated versions of experiments. Rukeyser argues that discouraging students from directly interacting with the real world denies them valuable learning experiences. He claims that overuse of computers in schools substitutes artificial learning experiences for ones that have a stronger reality base. Do you agree? If so, how will you decide whether to use computer technology in your own classroom?

2. How might your own initial assumptions about your role as a teacher be influenced by newer developments in digital-communication technology? How do you feel about changes you may have to make in your approach to working with learners? How will you begin preparing for these changes?

3. Bart Pasha, the Center for Applied Special Technology's director of research, suggests that new technologies may have as profound an influence on teaching and learning as the invention of the printing press. Do you agree or disagree? On what do you base your own views about technology's potential impact on school classrooms?

4. Some teachers are excited about new technologies' abilities to help learners. Others are confounded by classroom disruptions that occur when pagers, cell phones, portable computers, and other technological devices interfere with the learning process. In the main, are benefits of newer technologies worth the problems that sometimes accompany them? Why, or why not?

5. As part of your teacher-preparation program, you probably will receive considerable instruction related to incorporating newer technologies into your routine instructional practices. Based on what you know, what, specifically, do you think you need to learn about making effective uses of these technologies as you implement them with your own students? What other sources might you consult in addition to your professors?

Field Experiences, Projects, and Enrichment

1. Interview someone who teaches a grade level and subject area that interest you. Ask how this teacher incorporates technology into the instructional program. What advantages do uses of this technology provide learners? What difficulties, problems, and challenges has this person encountered when incorporating newer technologies into the instructional program?

2. Invite a school principal or central-office administrator to come to your class to discuss issues associated with incorporating more use of technology into instructional programs. What has been the impact on budgets? What kind of an equipment-replacement cycle has been adopted? What provisions have been made to ensure that help is available to teachers when equipment breaks down or software fails to function as designed? Have special arrangements been made to instruct teachers on appropriate uses of new technologies?

3. Visit a professional who has expertise in the area of special education. What kinds of technological aids are now being used to help learners with disabilities and other unique conditions achieve success? To what extent are these aids being used in regular classrooms to help learners with disabilities? How are regular-classroom teachers being prepared to use and manage this equipment effectively?

4. Look again at the ISTE technology standards for teachers and students. To what extent is your own preparation program preparing you to meet ISTE's teacher standards? Do your state and local school district have technology standards for students? How do they compare with those ISTE developed?

References

Baines, L. (2007). "Learning from the world: Achieving more by doing less." *Phi Delta Kappan*, 89(2), 98–100.

Brown, M. M. (2001, October 9). Democracy and the information revolution. *Digital Divide Network*. http://www.digitaldividenetwork.org/content/stories/index.cfm?key=192

Children's Internet Protection Act. http://www.ifea.net/cipa.html

Chou, L., McClintock, R., Moretti, F., & Nix, D. H. (1993). *Technology and education: New wine in new bottles—Choosing pasts and imagining educational futures*. New York: New Lab for Teaching and Learning.

Cuban, L. (2001). *Oversold & underused: Computers in the classroom.* Cambridge, MA: Harvard University Press.

Dean, K. (2002, June 19). Schools' tech support: Students. *Wired News*. http://www.wired.com/news/school/0,1383,53278,00.html

Dewey, J. (1910). *How we think.* Boston: D. C. Heath.

Digital Divide Network. (2002). Digital divide basics fact sheet. http://www.digitaldividenetwork.org/content/stories/index.cfm?key=168

Fitzgerald, S. (1999). *Technology's real cost.* www.electronic-school.com. http://www.electronic-school.com/199909/0999sbot.html

Foa, L., Schwab, R., & Johnson, M. (1998). Introducing technologies into the schools: Triumph or train wreck? *Technology Briefs*. http://www.nea.org/cet/briefs/13.html

Glennan, T. K., & Melmed, A. (1996). *Fostering the use of educational technology: Elements of a national strategy.* Santa Monica, CA: Rand Corporation.

Goot, D. (2002, July 15). Divide is more than digital. *Wired News.* http://www.wired.com/news/print/0,1294,53849,00.html

International Society for Technology in Education. (2000). *National educational technology standards for students: Connecting curriculum and technology.* Eugene, OR: Author.

International Society for Technology in Education. (2002). *National educational technology standards for teachers: Preparing teachers to use technology.* Eugene, OR: Author.

Levin, D., & Arafeh, S. (2002, August 14). *The digital disconnect: The widening gap between Internet-savvy students and their schools.* Washington, DC: Pew Internet & American Life Project.

McHenry, E. (2002, June 1). The digital revolution's new bounty. *HGSE News.* http://www.gse.harvard.edu/news/features/cast06012002.html

Merrow, J. (2001). *Choosing excellence: 'Good enough' schools are not good enough.* Landham, MD: Scarecrow Press.

Murray, C. (2002, August 1). ED: Online courses key to boosting achievement. *eSCHOOL NEWSonline.* http://www.eschoolnews.com/news/showStory.cfm?ArticleID=3870

National Center for Education Statistics. (2000). *Teachers' tools for the 21st century.* Washington, DC: U.S. Department of Education, Office of Educational Research and Improvement.

National Education Association. (1998). Development of student acceptable use policies. *Technology Briefs.* http://www.nea.org/cet/BRIEFS/brief12.html

National PTA. (2001–2002). *Education technology.* http://www.pta.org/ptawashington/issues/ed_tech.asp

National Telecommunications and Information Administration. (2002). *A nation online: How Americans are expanding their use of the Internet.* Washington, DC: U.S. Department of Commerce, Economics, and Statistics Administration.

Neighborhood Children's Internet Protection Act. Bill S 1545 IS. http://www.ifea.net/cipa.html

No Child Left Behind Act of 2001. Public Law 107-110, 115 Stat. 1425. (2002).

Philipkoski, K. (2000, August 17). Costs do not compute. *Wired News.* http://www.wired.com/news/school/0,1383,38079,00.html

Piaget, J., & Inhelder, B. (1958). *The growth of logical thinking from childhood to adolescence: An essay on the construction of formal operational structures* (A. Parsons & S. Milgram, Trans.). New York: Basic Books.

Rector, L. (2002). *A classroom without walls.* http://www.time.com/time/teach/class.html

Roblyer, M. D. (2003). *Integrating educational technology into teaching* (3rd ed.). Upper Saddle River, NJ: Merrill/Prentice Hall.

Rogers, E. M. (1995). *Diffusion of innovations* (4th ed.). New York: Free Press.

Rose, D. H., & Meyer, A. (2002). *Teaching every student in the digital age: Universal design for learning.* Alexandria, VA: Association for Supervision and Curriculum Development.

School board weighs ban on student laptops, PDAs. (2002, June 30). *eSCHOOL NEWSonline.* http://www.eschoolnews.com/news/showStory.cfm?ArticleID=2943&ref=wo

Should cell phones and pagers be allowed in school? (2001, March). *NEAToday Online.* http://www.nea.org/neatoday/0103/debate.html

Telecommunications Communications Act of 1996. http://www.fcc.gov/telecom.html

T.H.E. Journal. (2001, May). First annual state-of-the-states survey. http://www.thejournal.com/magazine/stateofthestates

Tyack, D., & Cuban, L. (1995). *Tinkering toward utopia: A century of public school reform.* Cambridge, MA: Harvard University Press.

Vallecorsa, A. (2001, March 21). Personal interview. Greensboro, NC: University of North Carolina at Greensboro.

Vygotsky, L. (1962). *Thought and language.* Cambridge, MA: MIT Press.

Wired News. (2000, September 12). Feds elated with e-rate. http://wired.com/news/school/0,1383,38729,00.html

CHAPTER 12

WHAT DO YOU NEED TO KNOW ABOUT THE LAW?

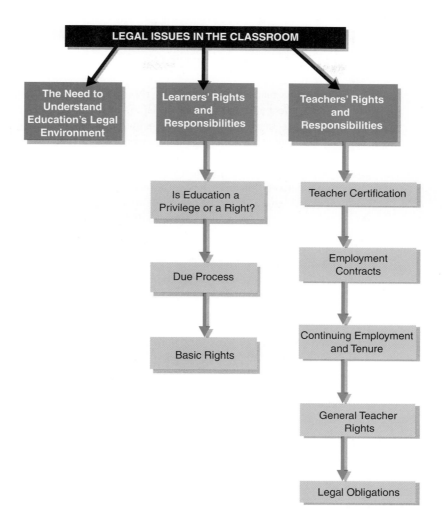

LEGAL ISSUES IN THE CLASSROOM

- The Need to Understand Education's Legal Environment
- Learners' Rights and Responsibilities
  - Is Education a Privilege or a Right?
  - Due Process
  - Basic Rights
- Teachers' Rights and Responsibilities
  - Teacher Certification
  - Employment Contracts
  - Continuing Employment and Tenure
  - General Teacher Rights
  - Legal Obligations

OBJECTIVES

This chapter will help you to

- recognize why today's teachers need to be familiar with the legal context within which they work.
- describe due process protections that students enjoy.
- describe some laws that have extended many constitutional rights of citizens to students.
- recognize the importance of legal issues associated with such issues as teacher certification, continuing employment, and tenure.
- describe some general patterns of court decisions regarding teachers' constitutional rights.
- point out examples of teachers' basic legal obligations.

The Need to Understand Education's Legal Environment

As a prospective teacher, have you ever thought about how laws, regulations, and court decisions will affect your work? Legal decisions and actions have a profound impact on your role as a teacher. Legal considerations begin with your teaching contract; influence your academic freedom as a teacher; determine what you must do when you suspect child abuse; determine what type of material you can use in the classroom without violating copyright law; govern your relationships with students, teachers and others in the school; and even impact your personal life and the decisions you make there. Like any other action involving legal issues, ignorance of the law is not an acceptable defense. In other words, what you don't know about the law could harm you. It could result in loss of a job, loss of a teaching credential, financial loss, and even criminal action.

Legal issues in education are complex and controversial because they involve a conflict between two sets of rights. The courts must balance the rights of individuals, such as parents, students, and teachers with the rights of the school district to establish a productive and safe educational environment. In recent decades there has been much discussion regarding the rights of individuals in the educational environment. For example, in the not too distant past, students have been suspended or expelled from schools because they committed such offenses as wearing makeup to school. A newspaper reporter interviewing a high-ranking official in a state department of education was told that when people choose to become teachers, they must give up certain rights. When asked what rights must be forfeited, the school official replied that any rights demanded by the school board.

More recently, a popular talk show host criticized schools for not automatically expelling any students who caused discipline problems. A newspaper columnist seriously recommended that a local school district simply pass a rule requiring every student to wear a prescribed uniform. All of these examples illustrate the fact that there is widespread ignorance of the legal constraints under which a school district must operate. Although those outside of education might have a limited understanding of legal considerations that govern the action of educators, those who choose teaching as a profession must meet a higher standard of such knowledge.

You have a professional responsibility to know the basics of the law and the implications they hold for your role, your relationship to students, your need to follow an adopted curriculum, and your professional and personal life. Without such information, you might take actions that have serious legal consequences.

As you begin to learn about the general legal environment of education, you need to keep in mind that you are unlikely to find information that tells you exactly how a law will be applied to a particular set of circumstances. Each situation has unique features that may influence how the courts apply laws and previous legal precedents. However, you will find it useful to know and consider some general patterns as you seek to make informed decisions about situations that have possible legal implications.

Learners' Rights and Responsibilities

A few decades ago, there would have been little need to understand legal principles and issues related to your role and the rights of students. Rules and regulations governing teachers and teaching were not complex, and litigation was rare. A legal doctrine known as **in loco parentis** governed relationships between teachers and learners.

According to *in loco parentis*, the school and the teacher acted "in the place of the parent." This meant that school administrators and teachers were assumed to be surrogate parents who would act as if the students were their own children. Essentially, this gave teachers and school authorities wide discretion in how they dealt with students. Their judgment was the final word and few legal actions were brought against educators. In addition, almost no one viewed students as citizens who were protected by the provisions of the U.S. Constitution.

This situation began to erode about four decades ago. A part of this change can be traced to the weakening of neighborhood schools and the distancing of schools and teachers from the local community. Parents who do not know teachers and administrators are less likely to trust them to act as wise parents and accept their judgment as final. As a consequence of pervasive social issues such as the Vietnam conflict and Watergate, where governmental institutions were less than truthful, all governmental institutions, including the schools, became suspect. Some school authorities contributed to the disenchantment when they acted in ways that were clearly not in the best interest of students.

As a result, learners and parents and guardians acting for learners began to bring legal actions that questioned the basic assumptions underlying the *in loco parentis* doctrine. Many of these actions focused on the notion that students did have rights and were protected by the Constitution. Over time, various court decisions increasingly have extended to students the same kinds of legal protections that adult citizens enjoy. As a teacher today, you can arm yourself against potentially unpleasant legal consequences by becoming acquainted with the legal context that currently governs relationships between educators and students.

Is Education a Privilege or a Right?

At the heart of the relationship between legal principles and education is the question of whether education is a right or a privilege. If education is a privilege, then those provisions of the U.S. Constitution protecting the rights of citizens have little application to education. In fact, for most of its history, education has been viewed as a privilege. When legal actions were taken, courts were reluctant to overturn the rules and the actions of school authorities just as they would be reluctant to substitute their judgments for those of parents.

Even if a school policy invaded learners' privacy or deprived them of an opportunity to receive an education, the courts generally were reluctant to substitute their judgments for those of school officials, and school officials had great latitude in making and implementing school policies and rules. If learners were removed from school for violating a school rule or regulation, they had little legal recourse.

The view of schooling as a privilege rather than a right began to unravel in the last half of the 20th century. Several factors led to this fundamental change. For one thing, it became apparent during the latter part of the century that literacy and education had become critical to individuals' economic well-being. Increasingly, denying a person an education was seen as denying that individual the right to economic and social advancement. Thus, it was argued that education should be considered as a "substantial right" to which all citizens were entitled. Add to that the fact that the schools were tax supported. This was used to argue that everyone should have access to public education and that education could not be denied without due process.

Social circumstances also had an impact. During the course of the fighting in Vietnam, many individuals questioned the wisdom of governmental officials, including those charged with managing the schools. One landmark case that brought together the issue of schooling as a right and the wisdom of school officials was *Tinker v. Des Moines Independent School District* (1969).

In this case, a group of learners in the Des Moines, Iowa, public schools wore black armbands to protest the U.S. involvement in Vietnam. When school officials heard of this planned protest, they passed a rule prohibiting the wearing of the armbands. When some students refused to remove them, they were suspended from school.

A couple of the students challenged this action, and the case eventually reached the U.S. Supreme Court. The Supreme Court ruled that once states establish public schools, individuals have a property right to the educational services the schools provide. The Court pointed out that neither students nor teachers leave their constitutional rights at the schoolhouse door. This had enormous implications in that it ruled that students did enjoy the protections of the Constitution and, like other rights, could not be denied unless the specific process of due process was followed. This ruling placed the legal relationship between schools and students in a whole new context and opened to challenge many traditional school policies and actions.

During earlier periods in our history, schooling was legally regarded as a *privilege*. Accordingly, professional educators were free to impose rules and enforce sanctions, including expulsion, without much concern for the legal rights of learners. Over the past few decades, schooling has been redefined as a *right*, and the full protection of the Constitution has been extended to students.

Some people see this extension of rights as reasonable. They point out that, in the past, school officials have acted capriciously to remove young people for arbitrary reasons that had little to do with the safe and orderly operation of the schools. Because education has such a powerful influence on a person's future, they argue that expulsion cannot be left to the whim of an administrator. They contend that this extension of rights has made schools better places.

Recent incidents of violence in schools across America have led others to believe that young people have too many rights and that school officials need more authority to protect the health and safety of students. Some claim that poor discipline in schools is rooted in the loss of authority of school officials. Proposed remedies often include reducing the number of students' legal rights.

What Do You Think?

- Should schooling be defined as a privilege so that professional educators can more aggressively respond to problems without being so concerned about their legal rights?
- How do you respond to the contention that poor discipline is related to the erosion of the authority of teachers and administrators?

Due Process

The Fourteenth Amendment to the U.S. Constitution outlines the principles of **due process.** Due process requires that certain procedures be followed in any action that might put a citizen's rights in jeopardy.

To be entitled to due process individuals must show that they have been deprived of either a **liberty right** or a **property right.** A liberty right refers to the right of people to be free from all restraints except those imposed by law. As applied to schools, liberty rights mean that decisions affecting learners cannot be arbitrary. They must be supported by relevant rules and regulations.

A property right is the right to specific tangible or intangible property. The issue of property rights needs more clarification. Most importantly, you should know that these rights do not always refer to tangible assets. There also can be property rights to names, likenesses, and other kinds of intangibles. People interested in expanding the application of property rights to education have argued that a good education represents a kind of personal property and, hence, it should be regarded as a property right. The basic point is that denying an education to individuals severely restricts their possibilities of economic success and the ability to obtain property. In recent years, various court decisions have supported the idea that education is a property right.

Due process procedures that embed a respect for both property rights and liberty rights seek to ensure that people receive fair treatment in an adversarial situation. Due process imposes requirements such as the following:

- Individuals are not to be disciplined on the basis of unwritten rules or laws.
- Rules and laws are not to be vague.
- Individuals are entitled to a hearing before an impartial body.
- The identity of witnesses must be revealed.
- Decisions must be supported by substantial evidence.
- What this means for teachers and schools is that rules governing learner behavior must be distributed in writing to learners and their parents.
- Whenever a learner is accused of a rules infraction that might result in the loss of a right, the charges must be provided in writing.
- Notice must be given in sufficient time for the learner and his or her representative to prepare a defense.
- A hearing must be held in a timely manner, usually within two weeks.
- Individuals have a right to present a defense and to introduce evidence. An individual may have a right to legal counsel and to confront witnesses. These provisions have been applied differently according to the circumstances and the seriousness of situations (Fischer, Schimmel, & Steelman, 2007).
- Decisions must be based on the evidence presented and must be given within a reasonable period of time.
- Individuals have a right to appeal.

These due process provisions have resulted in significant changes in school practice. Rules must be written and they must be clear. Evidence needs to be gathered, and a formal hearing must be held before an individual can be removed from school. All school districts now have specific procedures in place, based on due process. Simply suspending or expelling students based on the judgment of a school administrator or teacher is no longer permissible.

In a few circumstances rigorous due process is not required. If a discipline situation does not involve a basic right, then due process is not required. For example, expulsion is a serious matter because it denies a learner a right to access educational services. Hence, rigorous due process procedures must be followed in cases that can lead to expulsion. On the other hand, if suspension of a student is for less than 10 days, a less-complex version of due process is required. This involves providing an oral or written notice of the offense and an explanation of the evidence and giving the accused an opportunity to present their views (Zirkel & Richardson, 1988).

WHAT ARE THE BASIC RIGHTS OF STUDENTS?

Examples of rights that now generally are extended to students are:

- the freedom of expression,
- the freedom of conscience,
- the freedom from unreasonable search,
- the right to privacy, and
- special rights for learners with disabilities.

Bob Daemmrich/The Image Works

The constitution guarantees students the same rights as others in society including the freedom of speech.

Freedom of Expression

The First Amendment to the U.S. Constitution provides citizens with a guarantee of **freedom of expression.** This right guarantees that citizens, except in a small number of highly specialized situations, face no governmental restrictions on what they can say. It is one of the most fundamental rights of citizens.

Numerous court cases have focused on the freedom of expression in an educational environment. Freedom of expression cases in education usually focus on student speech, publications, dress, and grooming.

The *Tinker* case, cited earlier, focused on the issue of wearing of black armbands as symbolic freedom of expression. Some critics of the *Tinker* decision predicted chaos in the schools because it gave considerable freedom of expression to students. However, the ruling does not extend unrestricted freedom-of-expression rights to students. In many subsequent court cases, judges have wrestled with the question of when limitations might legally be placed on learners' freedom of expression. The courts have attempted to balance the rights of students for freedom of expression and the rights of the authorities to establish a safe and orderly learning environment.

In general, the courts have ruled that student expression cannot be prohibited simply to avoid discomfort or unpopular viewpoints that might be contrary to those of school officials. However, expression can be limited if it results in material or substantial interference with the operation of the school or the rights of others.

For example, limits on freedom of expression have been upheld when articles of clothing or symbols have led to fights or when the exercise of free speech has acted to disrupt classes. In addition, school officials have the right to punish learners who use lewd and offensive speech or who incite others to fight.

One case that came before the Supreme Court involved a student who, in a nominating speech for a friend running for a student body position, used language filled with sexual innuendo even after being warned by two teachers not to do so. The Court upheld the school district and stated that the public school, as an instrument of the state, may establish standards of civil and mature conduct (*Bethel School District No. 403 v. Fraser*, 1986).

In general, the First Amendment does not protect behaviors of learners who engage in threats of violence (*Deskbook Encyclopedia of American School Law*, 2002). Learners who face legal action after making threats involving shooting, bombing, or otherwise rendering serious harm to others are likely to find little sympathy in the courts.

Hostile Hallways

To gain some more insight into issues of freedom of speech and threats of violence, go to MyEducationLab and select the topic "Ethical and Legal Issues." Read the article "Hostile Hallways" that deals with sexual harassment and the role of the school in dealing with this issue. Respond to the questions accompanying the article. Some of the questions are designed to prepare you for your licensure examination.

Other limits on student freedom of speech involve issues such as "hate speech" and the use of "fighting words." Numerous school districts have established prohibition to speech that threatens, harasses, insults, or offends individuals on the basis of race, religion, gender, or national origin. Proponents of these prohibitions claim that they are necessary to prevent intimidation, violence, and a hostile learning environnment. However, districts must be careful that these prohibitions are not too subjective and go overboard on their prohibitions so that protected speech is prohibited (Fischer, Schimmel, & Steelman, 2007).

In addition, court decisions have ruled that "fighting words," those that by their very nature inflict injury or that incite students to fight are not protected. A similar, and somewhat difficult, area of speech involves threats. Incidents of violence in schools have caused school officials to take threats seriously. However, there have been instances of pranks or other idle comments that have been perceived as threats. The courts have used the standard that a statement is a true threat if a reasonable person would interpret it as a serious expression of an intent to cause harm (Fischer, Schimmel, & Steelman, 2007). Learn more about student threats and schools' zero tolerance policy in this chapter's *Video Viewpoints* feature.

Censorship of student publications provides another interesting freedom-of-expression issue. One case was that of *Hazelwood School District v. Kuhlmeier* (1988). This case centered on the actions of a school principal who censored a school paper article that dealt with teenage pregnancy. The students involved with writing and publishing the article claimed that the principal's action illegally limited their freedom of expression. The Supreme Court ruled that such activities as theatrical presentations and student publications are a part of the curriculum and carry the implicit endorsement of the school. Therefore, administrative leaders responsible for the operation of the school and its programs can legally control expression occurring in this situation. The principal's actions were upheld. However, limitations of expression must be related to legitimate pedagogical concerns.

The content of underground student populations that are published without school sponsorship are not subject to control by school officials. However, the schools can control the time, place, and manner in which such publications are distributed.

Another area relating to freedom of expression involves actions schools have taken to regulate clothing that learners can wear to school. Sometimes dress codes specify the kinds of clothing that are acceptable. In other instances, school districts have decided to deal with the problem by prescribing a school uniform for students. There have been legal challenges both to dress codes and to school-uniform policies.

Video Viewpoints 12–1

Action, Reaction, and Zero Tolerance

WATCH: This *Nightline* video segment focuses on the "zero tolerance" policy of school districts in dealing with perceived threats.

THINK: Discuss with your classmates or write in your reflective journal your responses to the following questions:

1. Do you perceive this action to involve an actual threat?
2. Do rules like this contribute to making schools safe?
3. How would you define a zero tolerance policy that would contribute to school safety but prevent situations such as this?

LINK: How might a teacher prevent situations like this?

 To view this video, go to the Video Viewpoints DVD and click on this chapter's video: "Action, Reaction, and Zero Tolerance."

First, let's consider why school districts have adopted dress codes and uniform policies. Sometimes, school leaders have argued that certain kinds of clothing compromise student safety or threaten the health of others. On other occasions, they have contended that certain kinds of student dress have the potential to disrupt the learning process. These disruptions may relate to clothing being too revealing or displaying gang-related symbols that have the potential for generating conflicts between students.

In considering student dress codes, the courts have wrestled with the question of whether the choice of dress involves a constitutionally protected liberty right. Decisions generally have supported school dress codes when representatives of the districts have successfully demonstrated that their codes contained guidelines that preserved learners' health and safety and prevented discipline problems and school disruptions.

In addition to school regulations related to learners' clothing, some schools and school districts have attempted to impose regulations related to various aspects of personal appearance, particularly hairstyles. Critics have attacked these rules as invasions of liberty rights. Generally, the courts have viewed restrictions on hairstyles as more of an invasion of privacy than regulations related to clothing. Typically, judges in these cases have held that hairstyle is fundamental to personal appearance and restrictions on hairstyle can have important impacts on individuals. In addition, school authorities have found it difficult to prove that hairstyle relates to issues of morality or that particular hairstyles substantially disturb the educational environment (Fischer, Schimmel, & Steelman, 2007).

What Do You Think?

- What is your reaction to dress codes?
- What do you think should be the major consideration in deciding if dress codes are acceptable?

Freedom of Conscience

Controversies related to **freedom of conscience** have centered on several key issues. Among them are concerns related to the teaching of certain content, participation in ceremonies involving saluting the flag, and the free exercise of religion.

In recent years critics of reading materials have contended that certain books advance secular humanism and promote Satanism and witchcraft. The courts have generally upheld the rights of schools to use books that have a legitimate educational purpose. Decisions have reflected the ideas that required books are not advancing some poorly defined religion and that works of fantasy and fiction by well-known authors promote legitimate educational objectives (Fischer, Schimmel, & Steelman, 2007).

Another area relating to freedom of conscience that generates controversy involves saluting the U.S. flag. Supporters of the practice see saluting as a loyalty issue and believe that because the government supports the school, learners should give their allegiance willingly. Some religious groups object to the flag salute, along with others who object on other reasons of conscience. In general, the courts have ruled that learners can refuse to salute the flag on the basis of legal or moral convictions. Taken together, these decisions suggest that a learner's failure to salute the flag does not constitute a serious threat to the welfare of the state. In the absence of a compelling state interest, the courts give precedence to citizens' religious and moral convictions. They have also ruled that learners cannot be required to stand or leave a room while others participate in the flag-salute ceremony (*Lipp v. Morris*, 1978).

The courts have determined that learners can be excused from certain segments of curriculum based on religious or moral grounds. Two principles guide these decisions. The first relates to whether the subject being objected to is essential to some compelling state interest. The second refers to the degree to which school districts have the right to enforce regulations to ensure the efficient and effective operation of the schools. To understand how the first of these principles works, let's look at several issues that have come before the courts.

Although sex education courses are voluntary in many schools, in some schools they are not. Often, these required sex education courses have drawn criticism. In adjudicating complaints about such policies, the courts have had to weigh arguments about how important the state's interest is in having citizens who have adequate knowledge of matters related to sexual relationships. Proponents of required sex education courses often point to the threat of AIDS and the social costs of teenage pregnancy as evidence of compelling state interests in this issue. Opponents contend that issues related to sexual understanding are personal and, sometimes, religious matters, not issues that should concern the state. Court decisions have varied somewhat. The courts have generally supported required sex education programs if there is a provision that allows individual families to remove their children from these classes if they wish to do so.

The courts have found it difficult to accept arguments that the state has a compelling interest in dancing in physical education classes or in ensuring that learners watch particular films. As a result, judicial decisions generally have gone in favor of critics of these practices who have objected to them on religious grounds. It is possible, though, that in a future case school authorities might argue that a particular film presents curriculum content in a way that cannot be easily duplicated. In such a hypothetical case, the court might decide in favor of the film on the grounds that the state has a compelling interest in exposing learners to the content.

As noted earlier, in addition to the issue of whether the state has a compelling interest in some required school experience, courts also consider whether excusing some individuals from required program components of the school program might disrupt the educational process. School leaders often argue that accommodations that must be made for individuals who object to certain requirements create a disruption, require special accommodations for the involved learners, and place a hardship on the schools to find alternative materials and methods. For example, learners who are excused from reading a particular book or passage in an English class must be taken out of the classroom, taught individually, and provided with suitable alternative reading material.

Freedom From Unreasonable Search and Seizure

The Fourth Amendment to the U.S. Constitution protects individuals against **unreasonable search and seizure.** This means that citizens can only be subjected to a search when there is probable cause. **Probable cause** is a legal standard that requires that search actions, including issuing of warrants, must be justified by extraordinarily strong evidence supporting the view that someone is guilty of illegal behavior. Recent concerns about drug abuse and violence in schools have generated new interest in what kinds of searches school authorities legally can conduct.

School officials have a responsibility to maintain a safe educational environment. What is the balance between individual rights and the rights of school officials? Should school officials be required to meet the stringent test of probable cause? Probable cause requires a high standard of evidence to be met before certain actions can be taken. Could the less-stringent test of reasonable suspicion be used instead? Reasonable suspicion requires only evidence that is sufficiently compelling to convince a prudent and cautious individual that some criminal or illegal activity has occurred.

Typically, reasonable suspicion is the standard that has been applied to school searches. Two additional guidelines are applied. These relate to (1) the expectation of privacy and

(2) the intrusiveness of the search. When a search will invade places where an individual has an expectation of privacy, or when it is potentially intrusive, then school officials need to have strong justification that approaches the probable cause test. For example, searching a student's desk is searching an area where there is little expectation of privacy. However, searching a personal possession such as a purse, in which there is a higher expectation of privacy, requires more evidence and justification. Intrusiveness concerns the degree to which a search might come into close contact with the individual's body. The most intrusive of all is a strip search of learners, an action that some states prohibit.

When considering the appropriateness of a search, four tests need to be applied. These relate to

- the target of the search,
- the quality of information that has led to the search,
- the nature of the place to be searched, and
- the nature of the search itself.

More justification for a search can be made when the targeted person or object poses significant potential danger to the learner population. Using this guideline, school authorities have more justification to initiate a search for a gun, bomb, or a controlled substance than for a missing CD player.

Before beginning a search, school authorities must assess the quality of the information they have that leads them to consider initiating this activity. They must weigh the reliability of the information using such criteria as the credibility of the person or persons who gave it to them. For example, if several identified individuals give school authorities similar information, officials have more defensible grounds for launching a search than if information comes from a telephone message from an anonymous caller.

The third test concerns the nature of the place to be searched. If this is an area where there is a high expectation of privacy or where a search is potentially intrusive, then exceptionally solid information is required to justify a search. On the other hand, a proposed search of an area such as a school locker, where there is a low expectation of privacy, can be justified by less rigorous evidence.

The fourth test focuses on the nature of the search itself. If searches of individuals are to be conducted, substantial evidence must be available to justify these actions. In making search decisions, school authorities also have to consider the ages and genders of individuals who may be searched.

The landmark case of *New Jersey v. T.L.O.* (1985) focused on several issues relating to school searches. In this case a female teacher entered a girl's restroom and found T.L.O. (the initials of the student) and another girl holding lighted cigarettes. Because smoking was against the school rules, she took both girls to the school office. When T.L.O. was asked to open her purse, she did so. Her open purse revealed additional cigarettes, drug paraphernalia, and other evidence suggesting she was engaged in selling drugs. T.L.O. claimed that the evidence could not be used against her because her purse was searched illegally. The Supreme Court ruled in favor of the school, rejecting the argument that probable cause was required to initiate this kind of a search. In their decision, the justices argued that school officials met the standard of reasonable suspicion and that this legal standard was sufficient if the case at issue involved a potential violation of either a school rule or a statute law. Because T.L.O. was observed smoking, a clear violation of a school rule, school officials were deemed to have sufficient legal grounds for their search. The fact that cigarettes were easily observable in her purse provided additional justification for the search.

Other questions have arisen when searches involved metal detectors, school lockers, school desks, and student cars. Although there have been no Supreme Court rulings, lower courts have generally applied the principle of reasonable suspicion established in *T.L.O.* The only exception seems to be if a search invades areas where learners have a high expectation of privacy. As a general rule, the courts have upheld searches of school lockers on the grounds that they are loaned to the students and young people have no expectation of privacy in these assigned spaces. In fact, school officials may have a duty to search lockers if they have a suspicion that something illegal or dangerous is being stored in them.

Case law in the area of search and seizure provides school officials with the right to search if there is a reasonable suspicion of wrongful activity. However, given the uncertainty in the applications of these standards, if you find yourself confronted with a situation that might lead you or others to conduct a search, you need to present the situation to a school administrator before acting. This person typically will check with the school district's legal counsel to get some assurance that there is a strong legal basis for the proposed search.

Right to Privacy

In recent years concerns about potential misuses of many kinds of records, including school records, have prompted much interest in a learner's **right to privacy.** For example, some people have worried that a learner who has difficulty with a teacher in the early elementary grades might be stigmatized throughout his or her entire career by records suggesting that he or she is a troublemaker. Worries about possible misuses of records helped win passage of the **Family Educational Rights and Privacy Act** in 1974.

This act requires schools to provide parents and guardians free access to their children's school records. Furthermore, individuals over the age of 18 and those in postsecondary schools have a right to view their records. The law also restricts how schools can distribute those records. Before passage of this law, schools customarily released records to government agencies, law enforcement agencies, and others. Since the adoption of the Family Educational Rights and Privacy Act, school records can be released only after strict guidelines have been followed. Access to records is restricted to personnel within the school and to those who have a "legitimate educational interest."

An implication for you as a teacher is that you need to choose your words carefully when writing comments about learners. Written notes or written comments might become a part of a learner's records that can be viewed by parents and by students who are 18 years of age or older. Parents and adult students can challenge material included in records if they believe it is inaccurate or unfair. Unsubstantiated or derogatory comments that label a student unfairly can lead to legal action. Negative comments about learners must be educationally relevant and have factual support.

You should also be sensitive to other, more subtle ways that learners' privacy might be compromised. Such things as plotting learners' progress on charts that can be viewed by others can be a violation of privacy. You need to handle learner papers carefully and discreetly so that others do not have access to them. Faculty lounges are notorious as places where teachers complain about learners and even parents. You need to guard against this practice. You may find yourself involved in a legal action if parents or guardians suspect you have knowingly spread false gossip that harms a child's reputation.

The Family Educational Rights and Privacy Act also has implications for you when you seek a teaching position. Usually when you prepare your teacher-placement papers with your campus career center, you will be asked whether you prefer an **open file** or a **closed file.** If you choose an open file, the Family Educational Rights and Privacy Act allows you to retain the right to read everything that goes into it. If you choose a closed file, you waive that right. There are arguments for both open and closed files. Some people claim that school district personnel view open files negatively, believing that recommendations will be couched only in highly favorable terms to avoid any possible reaction from the person the file concerns. Others argue that you should not give up the right to an open file because, at some point, you may find it necessary to remove an unfairly negative recommendation that might hinder your employment opportunities. You will need to carefully weigh these issues and make your own decision about whether an open file or a closed file is best for you.

Special Rights for Learners With Disabilities

Before the middle 1970s, many learners with disabilities were excluded from school or were placed in special classrooms. As a result of challenges from parents and guardians of children with disabilities, a series of state and federal laws addressed the needs of learners with disabilities. This legislation brought thousands of learners with disabilities into regular school classrooms for all or part of the school day. (For more information about learners with disabilities and specific legislation related to school services for these young people, see Chapter 6, "What Is Taught and How Is It Taught?")

Provisions of this legislation require school districts to bear the cost of providing educational services to young people with disabilities. To establish compliance, school districts must do more than simply enroll these learners as members of regular school classrooms. They also must provide special equipment and services that will enable learners to derive educational benefits from their school experiences. If the school districts are unable to provide the services needed, they must pay for private facilities. In addition, attorney fees and costs must be paid by a school district if parents have to go to court to remedy an inappropriate placement.

A controversial part of legislation related to learners with disabilities concerns a legal requirement that school districts pay for related services that help support the education of these young people. Related services include developmental, corrective, and other support services and transportation required to help each learner to derive maximum benefits from an education.

The meaning of the term *related service* has been interpreted in different ways. For example, the actual dividing line between a related service and an unrelated *medical service* is unclear. Litigation sometimes has resulted from varying opinions about services that,

These school professionals are meeting with a parent to discuss preparation of an Individualized Educational Program for a learner with disabilities.

legitimately, fall within the related-service category. In one case, the Supreme Court declared that providing a full-time nurse for a student paralyzed from the neck down was a related service that must be paid by a district (*Cedar Rapids Community School District v. Garret F.*, 1999).

In another case, parents of a hearing-impaired learner argued that their child was entitled to the services of a sign language interpreter in order to gain the maximum from her education. Because there was evidence that this learner was receiving some personalized instruction and that her achievement was above average, the Supreme Court ruled that her education was adequate and this related service was not required (*Board of Education v. Rowley*, 1982).

Considerable legal ambiguity continues to surround the related-services issue. It is probable that future court cases will surface as interested parties continue to seek legal clarification.

Compulsory Community Service

An emerging issue related to student rights involves compulsory community service. Many school districts across the country have implemented programs that require a certain number of hours of community service without pay as requirements of graduation. Schools justify these requirements as important components in applying school learning and developing an understanding of the responsibilities of citizenship.

However, some students and parents have protested these requirements claiming that they violate the "involuntary servitude" prohibitions of the Thirteenth Amendment. Some have claimed the right of parents to exempt their children from educational requirements to which they object as a basis for protesting community service activities (Fischer, Schimmel, & Steelman, 2007).

To date, these protests have not been successful. The courts have ruled that as long as these service requirements meet the tests of having an educational purpose and addressing legitimate state interests, such as the development of citizenship responsibilities, they are permissible.

What Do You Think?

- Compulsory community service has been on the rise in many schools. Do you think it should be permissible?

TEACHERS' RIGHTS AND RESPONSIBILITIES

Some legal rights and responsibilities impact the teaching role. Professionals must understand the legal conditions under which they work. Ignoring the legal rights and responsibilities of teachers can result in the loss of a teaching job or even legal actions and penalties. This is one area where what you do not know can hurt you.

What Are the Legal Rights and Responsibilities of Teachers?

Legal rights and responsibilites cover a wide range of issues beginning with the legal provisions of a contract, the impact of personal behavior on continued employment, academic freedom issues, and the reporting of suspected instances of child abuse.

Some areas for which teachers need to understand their rights and responsibilities include:

- teacher certification,
- employment contracts,
- continuing employment and tenure,
- general teacher rights, and
- teacher obligations.

Teacher Certification

The first set of legal requirements you need to know about relates to teacher certificates, licenses, and credentials. Without a proper teaching certificate or credential you will be unable to sign a contract. A teaching certificate, teaching license, or teaching credential confers on the holder the legal right to be hired as a teacher in the state that issues it.

Each state has the right to establish regulations concerning the qualifications of those who will be allowed to teach in its schools. As a result, each state has its own set of requirements. If you are enrolled in a teacher-preparation program in a state other than the one where you wish to teach, you will need to meet the requirements of the state where you wish to be employed. You should contact the department of education in the state that interests you and get information regarding requirements for teachers in that state. By obtaining this information now, you will find the process of getting the necessary credential easier when the time comes for you to file the required paperwork. Today, some states have agreements with others that allow a person with a certificate, license, or credential in one state to easily obtain them in the other states that participate in these reciprocity arrangements.

Holding or obtaining a certificate is not a basic right. The regulations and the requirements of the state must be met and once such a document is issued, the state still retains the right to change requirements. Although many states do exempt teachers who already have certificates from any new requirements, there is no legal obligation for them to do so.

Some individuals have a misunderstanding about credentials. The state authorities, not your college or university, are responsible for establishing the requirements and issuing teaching credentials. Although your college or university will hold you responsible for meeting certain requirements, your institution of higher learning acts only to "recommend" you for credentialing. State authorities make the final decision and issue the documents.

Employment Contracts

Teaching credentials grant specific benefits to those who hold them. For example, holders of valid documents have the right to apply for teaching jobs in their areas of specialization and to be issued a teaching contract. A teaching contract is an official employment agreement between a teacher and a school district that includes information related to issues such as conditions of employment, salary, sick-leave policies, insurance provisions, and complaint procedures. A credential is a "presumption of competence" that indicates to the school district that the individual is eligibile to enter into a contract. This presumption also protects the holder from charges of incompetence that are not supported by evidence.

The requirement to hold a credential as a condition of employment has some important consequences. For example, one individual who had not completed all the requirements for a credential misrepresented this to an employing school district that was trying to fill some teaching positions at the last minute before school started. As a result, the district offered her a contract based on the presumption that she had completed the requirements for a credential. As a general rule, school districts usually require that the credential be presented before finalizing a contract. Usually, a check cannot be issued until the credential is supplied. In this case, because the need for a teacher was great, they issued a contract to the individual before being presented with a valid credential. When they conferred with the state office issuing credentials, they discovered that the individual had not completed the requirements for a credential.

What are the consequences of this situation? The courts have ruled that people who contract to teach with a school district without having a valid teaching credential are "volunteers" who have no right to compensation or other employment privileges. So, the contract was invalid because this individual was not qualified to enter into a contract and she had "volunteered" three weeks of teaching. In addition, she now had established a record of misrepresentation and dishonesty that could provide the state with reasons to deny a teaching credential once she completed the requirements.

When you have been issued an initial teaching credential, you need to check to make sure you know what is required to renew the credential. Usually, additonal requirements must be met in order to keep the credential in force. For example, many states require additional professional development within a prescribed period of time to qualify for a renewal of the credential. If your credential expires and you have not qualified for renewal, you lose your legal right to sign a teaching contract. Every summer some of us have anxious individuals in our office who have failed to meet the renewal requirements and are looking for a solution. In many cases, there is little that can be done.

Continuing Employment and Tenure

Once you have signed a contract, your next concern is continuing employment. You may have been partly attracted to a career in teaching because teaching offers a high degree of job security. This view of security is tied to a feature of educational employment called **tenure.** The tenure principle ensures that an employed teacher has a right to reemployment each year if certain stipulated conditions are met. Not all states and not all districts require or allow the issuance of tenure contracts. There is considerable misunderstanding of tenure and how it functions.

Typically, beginning teachers are issued a **yearly contract.** This contract guarantees the holder employment for a single academic year. The contract is not automatically renewable. Either party can terminate it at the end of the academic year. Typically, school districts inform holders of yearly contracts about mid-April about their employment for the next academic year. Generally, a school district has no obligation to explain its reasons for terminating yearly contract employees. The major exception to this pattern can occur when a holder of a yearly contract has reason to believe a refusal to rehire was based on a school-district objection to a constitutionally protected teacher right. For example, teachers who hold yearly contracts might have a legal case if they can demonstrate that the district's refusal to rehire was based on something such as their religious affiliation or their activity as a member of a teachers' association.

Usually new teachers are hired for a probationary period during which they are issued a series of yearly contracts. When this probationary period is completed and a contract is given for the coming year, a person then has tenure. The intent is that the probationary period will give the school district a period of time to determine if the person is someone they want to employ for an extended time period.

If you are in a district that awards tenure, have completed your probationary period, and have been given a tenure contract, then you have a right to expect employment for an indefinite period of time. You can be dismissed only for reasons specified by law and only after a specified process has been followed.

Tenure was created because of a belief that an open exchange of information and free discussion of ideas are at the heart of our free society. Teachers are in a unique position relative to these values. More than any other professionals, they are in a position to facilitate the exchange and discussion of ideas. The free disussion is important in maintaining a free society. However, teachers' roles in helping learners develop critical thinking skills can be compromised if they hesitate to discuss politically unpopular views because they fear losing their jobs. Tenure was intended to protect teachers from this possibility. For example, teachers have been dismissed because of their involvement in political campaigns, active participation in union activities, using teaching approaches not popular with the school administration, and membership in particular religious bodies.

Another argument has also been advanced for tenure. Teachers' salaries generally are low relative to other professionals with equivalent levels of education. As a trade-off for modest pay levels, tenure laws promise teachers continued employment, even when economic times are not good and states and local communities face severe financial challenges. Supporters of tenure argue that the promise of employment security helps attract people to the teaching profession who, without this feature, might be reluctant to enter a field in which salaries tend to be lower than those in many competing occupations. For example, an acquaintance of one of the authors had been teased by her husband because of her desire to continue teaching rather than taking a higher paying job in the technology sector. She had the last laugh when he lost his job during the downturn of the technology sector shortly after 2000. In fact, a fair number of individuals who lost their jobs actually returned to college to get teaching credentials.

In recent years, some state legislatures have discussed eliminating or modifying tenure laws. Some opponents of tenure argue that the system guarantees lifetime employment and, therefore, protects incompetent teachers. Although school officials in districts with tenure policies must follow challenging procedures to remove a tenured teacher, the claim that tenure guarantees lifetime employment is not true. Tenure laws spell out circumstances in which a tenured teacher can be terminated. These conditions usually include incompetence, immorality, insubordination, conduct unbecoming of a teacher, and physical or mental incapacity. A school district must prove at least one of these allegations in order to remove a tenured teacher. Making a convincing case can be a time-consuming and costly process that requires the systematic collection of data to support the action. For example, one California school district claims that it took eight years and over $300,000 in legal fees to remove a tenured teacher. Critics of tenure point out that some school districts lack the will and the resources to engage the processes needed to remove a tenured teacher.

What Do You Think?

- Should tenure laws be abolished?
- What do you think should be done to make sure incompetent teachers are removed from the classroom?

It is likely that some proponents of educational reform will continue to call for the removal of tenure. Although there are some changes that can be made, care needs to be taken to make sure that changes in the tenure process do not result in the intimidation of teachers and the loss of academic freedoms necessary for the preservation of an open society.

General Teacher Rights

In the *Tinker* case cited earlier, the Supreme Court stated that neither teachers nor students leave their rights at the classroom door. However, as is true in the case of learners, rights of teachers must be balanced with the rights and the responsibilities of the school system (Valente, 1994). Because of the important role that teachers play in the education of impressionable youths, some people believe that teachers should be held to higher standards of behavior and conduct than the typical citizen. In one case that supported this view, a court declared that certain professions, such as teaching, impose limitations on personal actions that are not imposed on people engaged in other occupations (*Board of Trustees of Compton Junior College District v. Stubblefield*, 1971).

As you prepare for a career in teaching, you need to know something about the nature of teachers' rights as they pertain to

- academic freedom,
- freedom of religion, and
- teachers' freedom and lifestyles outside of school.

Academic Freedom

One of the most important and controversial aspects of teacher freedom relates to the concept of **academic freedom.** This refers to your right as a teacher to speak freely about the subjects you teach, to experiment with new ideas, to select the material used in the classroom, and to decide on teaching methods. Courts have held that academic freedom is based on First Amendment rights and is fundamental to a democratic society. Academic freedom protects your rights to evaluate and criticize existing practices in order to promote political, social, and scientific progress (Fischer, Schimmel, & Steelman, 2007).

Because a school board has an obligation to make sure that the adopted curriculum is taught, there is great potential for conflicts between teachers' rights and the obligations of the school board. Generally the courts have ruled in favor of teachers when school boards have tried to prescribe teaching methods. Court decisions have also supported giving teachers wide discretion in the selection of instructional materials. Read this chapter's *Critical Incident* feature to learn how one teacher's instruction is questioned.

In one case school administrators asked an 11th-grade English teacher to stop using a literary work they described as "literary garbage." The teacher defended the selection as an example of literature that was important for learners to read. When she refused to stop using the selection, she was dismissed. The teacher challenged the decision in court as a violation of academic freedom, and the court agreed. The judge ruled that the school district had failed to demonstrate that the use of the material would result in "material and substantial disruption of discipline," so it could not be banned. The opinion further pointed out that teachers have an obligation to defend the selection of materials in light of educational objectives and the age and maturity of their students (*Parducci v. Rutland*, 1970).

Cases related to academic freedom have not always been decided in favor of teachers. For example, the courts have also upheld the rights of a school district to select and eliminate textbooks. In one case, books were removed from a high school reading list because of sexual content and vulgar language. When this action was challenged, the court upheld the right of school district leaders to delete titles from a reading list if their action was based on a legitimate educational concern (*Virgil v. School Board of Columbia County, Florida*, 1989).

The *Virgil* case and others generally have laid down guidelines that require school districts to follow certain processes before rejecting or removing books. Removal decisions must be reached in a constitutional manner, and books cannot be removed simply because school authorities disagree with the ideas they present. In addition, books cannot be taken off the shelves because they are inconsistent with a particular political or religious view, because authorities wish to prevent certain ideas from being discussed, or because they contain content that fails to adopt a particular position on an issue such as racial discrimination (Fischer, Schimmel, & Steelman, 2007).

How Free Is a Teacher to Choose a Teaching Method?

Todd Allenby teaches ninth graders. One of his classes is not motivated, and students' written work has been abysmal. Often, all he gets is a page with the student's name and one or two barely coherent sentences. At the end of last week, he discussed this problem with Darcie Schwarts, another English teacher.

Darcie listened carefully and asked, "Are you letting them write what they want? I find most of my students won't give me much unless they have a personal interest in the topic."

Todd thought about this idea over the weekend. On Monday he began the class with some general comments about how people can become frustrated when they have something to say and nobody listens. Then he announced that the next writing assignment was going to give class members an opportunity to write what they wanted about any subject. He promised that these essays would reach an audience because he would see that every one would be distributed to the entire class. After a few questions, most of the students began to write. Todd collected the papers at the end of the class. He was pleased to note that most were longer than those he usually received.

Todd began reading the papers that night at home. About halfway through, his initial pleasure turned to despair. Although several of the papers gave evidence of serious thinking, a number of them included sexually explicit language. As his stomach began to knot, Todd reflected on his promise to share all of the papers with the entire class. Despite his misgivings, Todd decided that he had to do what he had promised or he would lose credibility. He copied all the papers and circulated them to the class. Two days later, he received a call to report to Dwayne Clark, the school principal. When he arrived at the office, he noticed that several of the essays were spread across the top of the principal's desk.

"Todd," began Mr. Clark. "What in the world were you thinking about? It's bad enough that the students use this language, but to make copies and distribute them in class is too much. Can you imagine what some parents are going to say when they see these?"

"Look," replied Todd. "I'm not thrilled about the content of some of these papers. But, these kids did write something for the first time this year. The public is on our case about not teaching students to write, so we need to figure out how to get the students to do it. I made a commitment to distribute the papers and felt I had to follow through to keep my credibility intact and to continue to get them to write."

"That's a commitment you had no right to make," Mr. Clark replied. "It put you in a position of agreeing to distribute anything, even obscene material. That's not professional. In fact, we cannot tolerate this type of behavior in our district. You need to know that it is a serious matter and that I am going to file a formal complaint to the central office. This situation could lead to an official dismissal hearing."

1. *What are the basic issues involved in this situation? Do you think Todd did the right thing?*

2. *Do you think his approach was reasonable given the class and his past experience with them?*

3. *What might he have done differently?*

4. *How much professional freedom should a teacher have?*

5. *What would you do if you were Todd?*

6. *Is Todd is tenured or untenured?*

7. *How might this make a difference in what happens to Todd?*

The academic freedom you enjoy as a teacher does not give you the right to ignore the course of study for the subject you teach. The material included in the classroom must be relevant to the course and appropriate for the age and maturity of your learners. You might be interested in knowing that teachers have lost academic-freedom cases in situations such as the following.

- A teacher continued to teach sex-related content in a health class because he believed it was of high interest to learners.
- A teacher showed an R-rated film to 9th- through 11th-grade students on a nonacademic day.
- A math teacher encouraged learners to protest the presence of military recruiters on campus.

Academic freedom also extends to the instructional methods you choose. In one case, a social studies teacher used a simulation exercise that evoked strong student responses on racial issues. The teacher was told to stop using the exercise. When she continued, the school board chose not to renew her contract. She took the issue to court, and the court ruled that the district had violated her First Amendment rights and ordered her reinstated (*Kingsville Independent School District v. Cooper*, 1980).

In another case, a high school psychology teacher was fired for using a survey from the periodical, *Psychology Today*. The court upheld the teacher's contention that her firing violated her constitutional right to "engage in a teaching method of her choosing even though the subject matter might be controversial." The school district failed to show that the use of this method caused substantial disruption or that there was a clear regulation prohibiting it (*Dean v. Timpson Independent School District*, 1979).

In summary, though decisions related to academic freedom tend to be situation specific, there are some general patterns. These decisions suggest that as a teacher you have a right to address controversial issues that are relevant to the topic you are teaching. You are also free to choose methods and materials that are appropriate to the age and maturity of your students. However, the materials or methods you select must not be banned by clear school-district regulations, and their use must not result in substantial disruption of the learning process or contribute to a breakdown of discipline.

What Do You Think?

- Why is protecting academic freedom important?
- What needs to be done to protect academic freedom while making sure that the required curriculum is taught?

Grading

Awarding of grades is an issue related to academic freedom. In a litigious society such as ours, students or their parents or guardians occasionally threaten legal action when they are dissatisfied with the grade a teacher has awarded. The courts have usually considered school officials to be uniquely qualified to judge the academic achievement of learners. As a result, they have been reluctant to overturn grading decisions unless there is overwhelming evidence that the grades were given for arbitrary, capricious, or bad-faith reasons. This means you need to have clear grading standards, keep accurate records, and make sure grades are awarded for academic reasons and not as punishment for inappropriate behavior.

School officials may prescribe guidelines for the administration of a grading system. However, the courts have ruled that guidelines may violate teacher rights if they are too prescriptive. In a Minnesota case, the courts ruled as inappropriate a policy stating that an individual teacher could not give grades that deviated more than 2% from the grade distribution of similar classes (*In re Termination of James Johnson*, 1990).

Freedom of Religion

Teachers sometimes face important freedom-of-religion issues. Here are some questions for you to think about that relate to freedom of religion:

- What rights do you have in refusing to teach content that might conflict with your religious beliefs?
- Do you have to lead the Pledge of Allegiance to the flag if doing so is contrary to your religious beliefs?
- Do you have the right to wear distinctive religious clothing when you teach?
- Can you be absent from school in order to observe religious holidays?
- What restrictions can be imposed on you that limit what you can say to learners about your religious convictions?

Several court cases have dealt with these questions. In one case a teacher belonged to a religious group that opposed all references to patriotism and national symbols. She informed her principal that she would not teach any curriculum content related to these topics, nor would she acknowledge national holidays such as Washington's birthday. The school district challenged her right to take this position. Ultimately a federal court ruled that the First Amendment does not provide license for a teacher to teach a curriculum that deviates from the one prescribed by the state. The court went on to point out that although the teacher had a right to her own beliefs, she had no right to require others to submit to her views. To do so would be to deprive students of an expected part of their educational experience (*Palmer v. Board of Education of the City of Chicago*, 1980).

In many places, teachers are required to start the school day with a ceremony that involves the pledge of allegiance. Some teachers have objected to participating in these ceremonies because of religious convictions. In one case, the court upheld the right of the teacher not to participate in the pledge of allegiance (*Russo v. Central School District No. 1*, 1972).

Other freedom-of-conscience cases have focused on the wearing of religious dress by teachers. The courts have usually supported the right of a school district to establish a dress code for teachers that may prohibit the wearing of distinctive religious clothing. Courts have reasoned that such clothing may give students the impression that the school supports a particular religion.

Courts have generally upheld a teacher's rights to take leave for religious holidays as long as two important conditions are met. First, the teacher's absence cannot create an undue hardship on the school district. Second, the amount of time taken off cannot be excessive.

In summary, your religious beliefs enjoy some legal protection, and you cannot be terminated because of your religious convictions or be required to sign an oath or take a pledge that violates your religious beliefs. However, the actions you can take in a school setting that relate to your religious beliefs can be limited if those actions interfere in important ways with the state's interest in educating children.

Lifestyle and Conduct Outside School

When you are employed as a teacher, can your employing school district place restrictions on your out-of-school behavior? Many court cases have focused on issues such as teachers' sexual orientation, live-in arrangements with unmarried partners, and criminal conduct. As stated earlier, the courts have noted that people in certain professions, including teaching, can have limitations placed on them that are not imposed on those of other callings (*Board of Trustees of Compton Junior College District v. Stubblefield*, 1971). This case established the point that certain kinds of out-of-class conduct by teachers can be used as grounds for dismissal.

Criminal conduct is usually recognized as a legal basis for revoking a teaching credential. In most states, those applying for a teaching credential must reveal if they have been convicted of a felony. Even conviction of a misdemeanor may be grounds for dismissal. Most states now conduct a background check on those applying for a credential. Criminal activity of any sort is likely to lead to serious difficulties for any teacher.

As noted earlier, many tenure laws include immorality as a legal ground for dismissing a teacher. In recent years, the courts have developed more careful definitions of the kinds of immoral conduct that are serious enough to warrant dismissal. Recent decisions have required evidence of a tight connection between the private behavior of teachers and their work as professionals.

The courts have generally upheld that out-of-school behavior of teachers may be used for dismissal if their conduct poses a danger to learners or in some way interferes with their effectiveness in the classroom. Situations that result in widespread negative publicity throughout the community are more likely to be seen as interfering with the effectiveness of a teacher than those that receive little or no publicity. Charges of immorality that involve a minor are highly likely to result in dismissal decisions.

Anne Vega/Merrill

Teachers have a responsibility to work cooperatively with other professionals.

> ## What Do You Think?
>
> • Many individuals argue that the behavior of teachers away from school should not have any relationship to their employment status. What is your position?
> • How would you draw the limits on using teacher behavior away from the classroom for employment decisions?

Legal Obligations

Teachers not only have rights, they have legal obligations that accompany their roles. Those legal obligations include reporting cases of suspected child abuse and acting in a professional manner.

Reporting Child Abuse

In recent years, there has been much public concern regarding child abuse. As a result, all 50 states and the District of Columbia have laws requiring mandatory reporting of suspected child abuse by certain professionals. Because teachers are in prolonged contact with young people, they are considered to be in a particularly good position to spot child abuse and are therefore required to report suspected instances of child abuse.

Failure to report can lead to both criminal and civil penalties. A high level of suspicion is not a requirement for mandatory reporting. Legal terms often used to describe the grounds for suspected child abuse include "reasonable grounds," "cause to believe," or "reasonable cause to believe."

Accompanying mandatory reporting is a protection from lawsuits that might arise as a form of retribution for reporting. All states provide some form of protection from lawsuits for mandatory reporters who report their observations in good faith. In most instances, the identity of the person reporting the suspected abuse is not revealed.

Negligence

Acting in a professional manner includes teacher negligence. Failure to act in a professional manner may lead to charges of negligence. **Negligence** is defined as a failure to use reasonable care and/or to take prudent actions to prevent harm from coming to someone. Three types of negligence are:

- misfeasance,
- nonfeasance, and
- malfeasance.

Misfeasance occurs when a teacher acts unwisely or without taking proper safeguards. In these situations, the motives of the teacher might be good but the teacher's actions are unwise or below a professional standard of care. For example, if you ask a very young child to carry a glass container, the child might fall and be cut by broken glass. Although you did not intend harm, a court might decide that you were guilty of misfeasance because you unwisely asked an immature learner to perform this type of a task. As a professional knowledgeable about child growth and development, you are expected to know that there is a high probability that a young child will drop a container.

As stated earlier, a credential carries with it a presumption of competence. This presumption of competence carries with it not only rights but also responsibilities. Those responsibilities include acting in a professional manner.

Nonfeasance occurs when a teacher fails to act when there is a duty to do so. For example, if two members of your class begin to fight, you have a duty to protect these learners from injury. If you make no attempt to stop the fight, you could be found guilty of nonfeasance. A common reason for charges of nonfeasance is when injury occurs when teachers are away from their areas of responsibility. For example, if you are out of the classroom unnecessarily when learners are present and an injury occurs, you could be charged with nonfeasance.

Malfeasance involves actions that are taken to deliberately and knowingly harm someone. In this case the motives of the teacher are called into question. Malfeasance may be charged in a discipline instance when the teacher responds to the misbehavior out of anger or revenge and deliberately harms the student.

To avoid problems associated with negligence you must act as a professional. In deciding cases in this area, courts often test your behavior against what a person with similar professional preparation might do. The fact that you have completed a professional-preparation program and have a teaching credential means that you should have the knowledge you need to make professional decisions. Relying on your own intuition is simply not enough.

In summary, becoming a professional educator requires that you have specialized knowledge. This specialized knowledge includes an understanding of your legal rights and responsibilities and those of students. This is a complex area and new court decisions are constantly changing rights and responsibilities. This is one area where your professional growth is critical. To not keep up with the changing legal environment could result in the loss of your career.

* *

Copyright 101
One of the areas in which teachers regularly violate the law relates to the use of copyrighted material. To obtain information about the impact of copyright law on teachers, go to MyEducationLab and select the topic "Ethical and Legal Issues." Read the article "Copyright 101" that discusses issues and guidelines for deciding what can be legally used in the classroom. Respond to the acompanying questions. Some of the questions are designed to prepare you for your licensure examination.

* *

Key Ideas in Summary

- When you begin your teaching career, you will be entering a profession in which your behavior will be greatly influenced by the legal environment within which today's schools operate. As a professional, you have a need and a responsibility to be familiar with rules, regulations, and laws that govern your actions in the classroom.

- In the past, relationships between teachers and learners were governed by the *in loco parentis* doctrine, which held that school authorities, including teachers, acted "in place of the parent." Under this doctrine, school authorities had few limitations on their authority to make decisions about individual learners. Over time, the *in loco parentis* doctrine has been successfully challenged in the courts. The result is that, today, learners generally enjoy the same constitutional protections that adult citizens possess.

- An important right today's learners have is the right to *due process*. For example, learners cannot be denied access to education unless strict due process guidelines are followed. Due process guidelines also apply, in a slightly altered form, to special education students and parents. Among other things, due process protections ensure that (1) learners cannot be disciplined on the basis of unwritten rules, (2) adopted school rules and regulations cannot be vaguely worded, (3) learners subjected to a disciplinary action are entitled to request a hearing before an impartial body, (4) the identity of witnesses must be revealed, and (5) decisions must be supported by substantial evidence.

- Contemporary students' rights include (1) freedom of expression, (2) freedom of conscience, (3) freedom from unreasonable search, (4) freedom from harassment, and (5) the right to privacy.
- Teachers and school administrators must be aware of the rights of learners with disabilities. Laws require that learners with disabilities have an appropriate placement, that a plan is established that is carefully assessed, and that the schools supply needed related services to help these learners benefit from their educational experiences.
- *Teaching certificates, licenses,* and *credentials* are documents that allow an individual to contract for services as a teacher with a school district. State governments issue these documents. States can change the requirements for obtaining and renewing certificates, licenses, and credentials whenever they wish to do so.
- *Teaching contracts* are binding documents that spell out employment conditions for teachers and that give holders of teaching certificates, licenses, and credentials a "presumption of competence." Typically, teaching contracts clarify responsibilities both of the teacher and of the hiring school district.
- *Tenure* laws have been established to protect teachers from arbitrary dismissal because they have promoted discussions of controversial and debatable ideas. Tenure does not provide a lifetime guarantee of employment. Rather, it specifies the grounds that can be used to dismiss a teacher and places the burden of proof on the school district.
- Teachers enjoy substantial *academic freedom.* Among other things, they have the right to include course materials and teaching methods relevant to the content of the course of study. However, academic freedom is also balanced with the state's right to deliver the prescribed curriculum to learners in the schools. Thus, school districts retain a legal power to place limits on material that is used in class.
- In *freedom of religion* cases, the courts generally have upheld the rights of teachers to refrain from participating in the pledge of allegiance, to take religious holidays, to be free from punishment for their religious convictions, and to be under no obligation to sign an oath that violates their religious beliefs.
- Because of their special relationship with impressionable young people, teachers' rights as individuals are weighed against the right of the state to provide a proper education. Therefore, teachers can be held to a higher level of personal conduct than that expected of the general population.
- Teachers and school officials have a responsibility to report suspected incidents of child abuse, and teachers who fail to do so may face both civil and criminal penalties.
- Teachers sometimes face charges of *negligence,* a failure to act in a professional manner. The three major categories of negligence are (1) *misfeasance,* (2) *nonfeasance,* and (3) *malfeasance.* Misfeasance occurs when a teacher acts unwisely or fails to implement proper safeguards. Nonfeasance occurs when a teacher fails to act when having a duty to do so. Malfeasance occurs when a teacher acts deliberately and knowingly to harm someone.

For Your Initial-Development Portfolio

1. What materials and ideas that you learned in this chapter might you include as "evidence" in your portfolio? Select up to three separate items of information. Number them 1, 2, and 3.
2. Think about why you selected these materials. As you do so, consider these issues:
   - Specific uses you might make of this information as you plan, deliver, and assess the impact of your teaching
   - The compatibility of the information with your own priorities and values

- Any contributions this information can make to your development as a teacher
- Factors that led you to include this information, as opposed to some alternatives you considered, but rejected

3. Place a check in the chart below to indicate the INTASC standard(s) to which each of your items of information relates. (You may wish to refer to Chapter 1 for more detailed information about INTASC.)

ITEM OF EVIDENCE NUMBER	INTASC Standard Number									
	S1	S2	S3	S4	S5	S6	S7	S8	S9	S10
1										
2										
3										

4. Prepare a written reflection in which you analyze the decision-making process you followed. In your comments, mention the INTASC standard(s) to which your selected material relates.

Reflections

1. Review material in the chapter related to *in loco parentis* and the erosion of this doctrine over the years in favor of viewing learners as individuals enjoying the legal protections adult citizens enjoy. Has this change had a positive or negative impact on American education? What evidence and values support your position?

2. Due process requirements place limits on the nature of the rules you will develop for learners in your classroom. Develop a set of classroom rules that references explicit behaviors (a) that you wish to encourage in your classroom and (b) behavior's that you will not allow in your classroom. Think about what you would say to others who might ask about particular difficulties you encountered in attempting to meet the due process requirement that rules be written, clear, and specific.

3. The issue of tenure continues to be hotly debated. Opponents argue that tenure regulations make it extremely difficult for school districts to remove tenured teachers who are not performing up to expected standards. Proponents contend that tenure laws make it possible for teachers to act in a unprofessional way in the classroom without fear that they will lose their jobs if they teach information that may not be popular with administrators, certain groups of parents, or school policymakers. How do you assess the merits of arguments for and against tenure? What is your personal position on the issue, and what led you to this view?

4. Is your own private life your personal business? Do you believe school authorities have a right to hold you professionally accountable (e.g., to threaten you with job loss) if you behave in certain ways outside of normal school hours? How do you react to some court decisions that have supported actions of school districts that dismissed teachers for certain things they did on their own time? Have these decisions been justified? If not, are there *any* circumstances that you might imagine that would justify a school district's decision to fire a teacher for behavior outside of normal school hours?

5. Some people believe (and some courts have supported the idea) that teachers should be held to higher personal and moral standards than other adult citizens. Is this position justified? What arguments can you think of that support this view, and what arguments might you marshal against it?

Field Experiences, Projects, and Enrichment

1. Review copies of professional education journals such as *Phi Delta Kappan* or *Educational Leadership*. Look for articles and features dealing with legal issues in education. Take notes on several articles you read. Summarize this information, and share it with others in your class. Be sure to mention court decisions that may have implications for teachers as they work with learners in school classrooms.

2. Obtain a copy or a summary of the education code for your state. Your professor may be able to help you locate this information. Codes of many states are now available on the Internet. Many state departments of education maintain Web sites. When you locate your state's code, you may be surprised to find that it is quite a lengthy document. Look through the material until you find any existing rules related to such areas as corporal punishment, expulsion, mandatory attendance, teacher tenure, state curriculum, and selection of classroom material. Summarize your findings in a short paper or present your information in another manner as your professor directs.

3. Use a good search engine such as Google (http://www.google.com). Enter the phrase "teaching and the law." You will find many links to books that feature information on this topic. Prepare a list of at least seven titles (author, title, publisher, place of publication, and date of publication). Make copies of your list to share with others in your class. You may find information in these books to be of interest as you seek to learn more about schools' legal environment.

4. Investigate the requirements for a teaching credential in your state. State departments of education often provide this information online at their Web sites. Seek answers to these questions: What are the basic requirements? How long is a credential valid? What needs to be done to keep it in process? What is the process for getting a credential?

5. Invite a school administrator or local teacher-association representative to your class to answer these questions:
   • What provisions are included in the school district's teaching contracts?
   • Specifically, what do contracts say about teachers' rights and responsibilities?
   • Does the school district operate under a tenure policy? If so, what does a teacher have to do to qualify for tenure?
   • If there is a tenure policy in place, what procedures must school district officials follow to seek removal of a tenured teacher?

References

Bethel School Dist. No. 403 v. Fraser, 478 U.S. 675, 106 S. Ct. 3159, 92 L. Ed. 2d 549 (1986).

Board of Education v. Rowley, 458 U.S. 176 (1982).

Board of Trustees of Compton Junior College District v. Stubblefield, 94 Cal. Rptr. 318, 321 (Cal. Ct. App. 1971).

Cedar Rapids Community School District v. Garret F., 526 U.S. 66 (1999).

Dean v. Timpson Independent School District, 486 F. Supp. 302 (E.D. Tex. 1979).

Deskbook encyclopedia of American school law. (2002). Birmingham, AL: Oakstone Legal and Business Publishing.

Family Educational Rights and Privacy Act (FERPA). http//www.ed. gov/policy/gen/guid/fpco/ferpa/index.html 3/20/2003

Fischer, L., Schimmel, D., & Steelman, L. (2007). *Teachers and the law* (7th ed.) Boston, MA: Allyn & Bacon.

Hazelwood School District v. Kuhlmeier, 484 U.S. 260 (1988).

In re Termination of James Johnson, 451 N.W. 2d 343 (Minn. Ct. App. 1990).

Kingsville Independent School District v. Cooper, 611 F. 2d 1109 (5th Cir. 1980).

Lipp v. Morris, 579 F. 2nd 834 (3rd Cir. 1978).

New Jersey v. T.L.O., 105 S. Ct. 733 (1985).

Palmer v. Board of Education of the City of Chicago, 603 F. 2d 1271 (7th Cir. 1979), cert. denied, 444 U.S. 1026 (1980).

Parducci v. Rutland, 316 F. Supp. 352 (m.d. Ala. 1970).

Russo v. Central School District No. 1, 469 F. 2d 623 (2nd Cir. 1972) cert. denied, 411 U.S. 932 (1973).

Tinker v. Des Moines Independent Community School District, 393 U.S. 503 (1969).

Valente, W. (1994). *Law and the schools (3rd ed.)*. New York: Macmillan.

Virgil v. School Board of Columbia County, Florida, 862 F. 2d 1517 (11th Cir. 1989).

Zirkel, P., & Richardson, S. (1988). *A digest of Supreme Court decisions affecting education.* Bloomington, IN: Phi Delta Kappa Educational Foundation.

CHAPTER 13

WHO CONTROLS AND FINANCES EDUCATION?

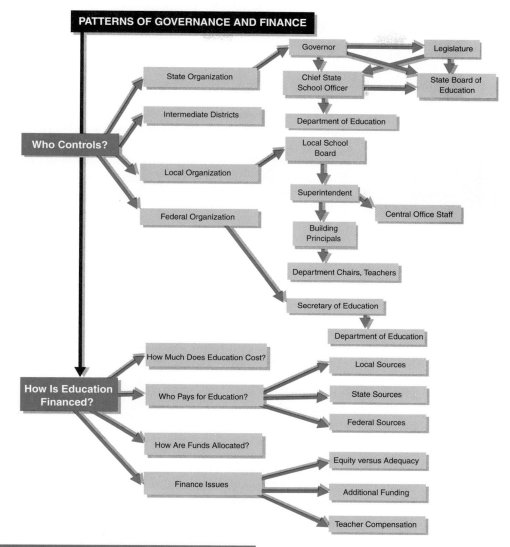

PATTERNS OF GOVERNANCE AND FINANCE

Who Controls?

- State Organization → Governor → Legislature
- Governor → Chief State School Officer → State Board of Education
- Chief State School Officer → Department of Education
- Intermediate Districts
- Local Organization → Local School Board → Superintendent → Building Principals → Department Chairs, Teachers; Superintendent → Central Office Staff
- Federal Organization → Secretary of Education → Department of Education

How Is Education Financed?

- How Much Does Education Cost?
- Who Pays for Education? → Local Sources, State Sources, Federal Sources
- How Are Funds Allocated?
- Finance Issues → Equity versus Adequacy, Additional Funding, Teacher Compensation

OBJECTIVES

This chapter will help you to

- identify the relationship between and define the responsibilities of the local school district, the state, and the federal government.
- state the political implications of different state models of education.
- outline the organization of a typical school district.
- define changes in the federal influence in education.
- state how professional educational associations influence educational policy.

- identify the positive and negative consequences of increased centralization of control over education.
- define the sources of revenue and explain how these impact educational policy.
- explain how shifts from local sources of revenue to state sources have impacted educational policy.
- compare equity and adequacy models for funding education.
- define current teacher compensation plans and proposed with pay for performance plans.

INTRODUCTION

Individuals just beginning to think about education are most interested in how to teach. For them, information related to the governance and finance of education is not on the top of their "need-to-know" list. However, questions concerning who controls education and who finances it are vital issues that influence the future of education and the role of teachers. Governance of education has captured the attention of governors, mayors, state legislators, Congress, and even presidents. Their interest is fueled by the knowledge that education, as one of the primary institutions of society, has an important impact on the political, social, and economic development of a nation. Education has long been used as an instrument of social control and those in power seek control of this important institution. Most recent examples are attempts to control education by different factions in Afghanistan and other Middle Eastern nations.

Although the efforts to control education may be less visible and dramatic in the United States, changes in the control of education are occurring that will have a profound impact on the future direction of education and society. This transformation is taking place quietly with few people challenging it or considering long-term consequences.

In recent decades, business leaders and politicians have begun to realize the importance of education for the economic well-being of the nation, the state, and the local community. Good schools prepare individuals who fuel innovations and help keep business and industry competitive with other parts of the world. Students are the future leaders; there is no doubt that quality of the schools is important for the future of the nation.

States within the nation are also in competition with other states in expanding their economic base. They seek to get business and industry to locate in their state. The quality of the schools is one of the most powerful draws for new investment. As a result, most states have devoted considerable attention to the quality of their schools. Even though this attention has been important in keeping attention focused on educational issues, there is also a downside to all of this attention. Educational issues have become increasingly politicized and decisions tend to be based more on political values than on sound data. One of the outcomes of this has been changes in the governance structure. More politicians and business leaders have tried to find ways to exert more direct control over education.

For example, at the local level, mayors of large cities have been frustrated in their attempts to improve the quality of life in their city because they have limited power over the educational system. They believe they are in a better position to coordinate cross-agency support in order to build an infrastructure that will attract new businesses and residents to their community (Epstein, 2004). Therefore, mayors of many of the large cities have sought to place the school system under their control.

On a more personal level, those who control education define the criteria required to obtain a teaching credential, the general working conditions in the school where you teach, the salary you receive, the curriculum you teach, the materials available for your use, how you are to be evaluated, whether or not you acquire tenure, and how money is to be allocated. Therefore, understanding how schools are governed and who has the power has important social, economic, and political consequences for the nation and its teachers.

The financing of education is also critically important. Education costs comprise a large share of the budget in any state. Therefore, there is intensive debate about the allocation of funds to education. Defining a fair formula for funding education and developing a consistent revenue base are major problems faced by many states. Basic questions concerning funding focus on the following:

- How much money is needed for a quality educational system?
- Who should pay?
- How should the money be allocated?
- Who should be held accountable for the results?

In this chapter the different patterns of governance found across the United States will be discussed and issues related to the financing of education will be considered.

THE STRUCTURE OF EDUCATIONAL CONTROL

The Tenth Amendment to the Constitution of the United States reserves those powers not specifically delegated to the federal government for the states. Because education is not specifically mentioned in the Constitution, governance of education has been delegated to the states. All educational activities within the state are subject to the control of the state. The state enacts legislation binding on all schools, determines financing formulas for the schools, defines criteria for granting and revoking teacher and administrator credentials, establishes curriculum frameworks and content standards, accredits schools, and may determine the textbooks to be used in the schools.

Most states have an **education code,** which is a collection of all of the regulations that govern the operation of the schools in the state. The education code is usually a very large document that covers everything from construction codes for school buildings to standards for credentialing teachers.

The governance of education has evolved into what has been described as a unique form of government that is separate from the traditional political structure (Kirst, 2004). The original rationale for this separate governance structure was to shield the schools from undue political interference (Epstein, 2004).

A key principle has been that of keeping educational decisions free from partisan politics and as close as possible to local community and the parents. Therefore, even though states have the legal responsibility for education, much of the responsibility for the schools has been delegated to local districts under the supervision of a locally elected school board. The usual procedure has been for the state to establish overall policies and directions through legislative action and the state school board. The actual implementation of the policies and the day-to-day operation are delegated to the local level. The assumption behind this local control is that parents and guardians best know the needs of their children and what should be given priority in the local schools.

However, this separate governance structure is not without drawbacks. Few people in a given state understand or participate in the structure of educational governance. For example, the majority of people in a local community cannot identify local school board members and very few participate in school board elections. Usually, only about 10% to 15% of the eligible voters turn out for school board elections (Kirst, 2004). Therefore, the principle of local control and the confusing governance structure that has evolved is being challenged.

Three levels of governance need to be understood when determining who controls education. Those are the local, the state, and the federal levels. In addition, there are other influences that cannot be overlooked. Those include teacher organizations and the business community.

This chapter will start with a discussion of the level with the primary legal authority for education, the state. Then we will discuss the level with the most impact on individual teachers, the local level. The growing impact of the federal government will also be considered, as will influences of other groups such as professional organizations.

State Organization and Influence

Remember that the state has the legal responsibility for education. A number of bodies within the state influence educational policy. These include the governor, the legislature, the state board of education, the chief state school officer, and the state department of education. The amount of influence of each of these bodies varies from state to state according to the state constitution.

State Legislature and Governor

The state legislature is the most influential body in controlling education in a state because this body establishes educational policy and passes the laws that govern education. In every state, numerous bills are introduced in any given year relating to education. In recent years, as interest in education has increased, so has the action in state legislatures regarding education. Most states have had a dramatic increase in the number of bills introduced pertaining to some dimension of education. In some instances court decisions have forced state legislatures to take action. For example, courts' decisions regarding the legality of school financing have prompted legislation in many states.

State governors have the potential for exerting considerable influence on education because they have the power to veto bills that are passed by the legislature. In addition, they can use the power of their office to lobby and influence public opinion and legislative action. For example, Governor Schwarzenegger in California exerted considerable political pressure on voters to pass state bond issues for adding and replacing school facilities.

Together, state legislatures and the governor act on state budgets that contain funding for the local school districts. Many state governors have emphasized education in their elections. For example, their stands on education played a significant role in the elections of Bill Clinton as governor of Arkansas and George W. Bush as governor of Texas. In the 2006 campaigns, education platforms were key issues in the several gubernatorial elections.

Chief State School Officer

Another key education figure within a state is the chief state school officer. This position has different titles in different states. Most common are **state superintendent of education** or "state commissioner of education." This individual is often viewed as the "voice" for education within a state. The actual power of this person varies according to the governance structure of the state. In some states they may have considerable power to influence educational policy and in others they have very limited input. The person in this role is often the executive

Because education is a state responsibility, state legislatures have considerable power in deciding school policies.

Stan Wakefield/PH College

officer for the state board of education and the chief administrator for the state department of education.

State Board of Education

The actual implementation of laws and policies requires a bureaucracy to interpret the laws and implement policies. This is the responsibility of **state board of education**, the state department of education, and the chief state school officer. The state board of education is the body that sets the goals and priorities for education in the state, establishes curricular offerings and state standards, enforces regulations on the local school districts, establishes the education code, and makes recommendations to the governor and the state legislature on educational issues. For example, if members of the state board believe that the standards for obtaining a teaching credential need to be revised, they will work with members of the state legislature to draft a bill addressing this need. In addition, if a bill relating to education is passed in the legislature, the state school board will oversee the implementation.

State Department of Education

The **state department of education** is the body that carries out the work of the state board of education. Because education in a given state is complex, the state department often has a significant number of departments and employees. The state department of education performs tasks such as compiling statistical reports, administering the budget, establishing curriculum frameworks and content standards, establishing standards for teaching credentials, and evaluating existing education programs.

Those entering the education profession will have their most direct contact with the state department of education through the credentialing process. The state department establishes the standards for the teacher-preparation programs, administers any tests required for admission to or completion of teacher-education programs, and teacher candidates usually apply to the credentialing division of the state board for their teaching credential. Because education is primarily a state responsibility, each state has its own requirements for a teaching credential. For example, if you decide to move from the state where you complete your teacher preparation, you will need to meet the requirements of the state you move to in order to obtain a teaching credential. This may mean taking a licensing examination required by that state. Several states have reciprocal agreements that allow an individual with a credential from another state to begin teaching. However, the state may have additional requirements that must be met before the credential can be renewed.

State Governance Models

Understanding how the state board and the chief state school officer are selected in your state can help you understand who has the power to influence educational policy in your state. In reviewing the governance structure of a state, consider who has the most power to control education in the state and how easy or difficult it is to change educational policy. Note if there are checks and balances on the power of the governor and the state legislature. For example, new teachers and the general public are often astounded to learn that some educational policies and practices in the state are not consistent with the findings of research. This is because those making the policies are not selected on the basis of their knowledge about education. Generally, policies are the result of political compromise and influence rather than the findings of solid research.

Several governance models are used by states across the nation. In some states the governor appoints the state board, in others they are elected. In some states the chief state school officer is appointed by the state school board or the governor; in others, they are elected. In total, the state board appoints the chief state school officer in 24 states, the governor appoints them in 12 states, and they are elected in 14 states. The governor appoints all school board members in 25 states and some members in 14 others (Kirst, 2004). The implications are that governors have considerable power to influence education in a large number of states. Look at Figure 13–1 to identify the governance pattern for your state.

What Do You Think?

- What is the governance model in your state?
- Is it an effective model? What are the advantages and the disadvantages?

Figure 13–1   State governance of education.

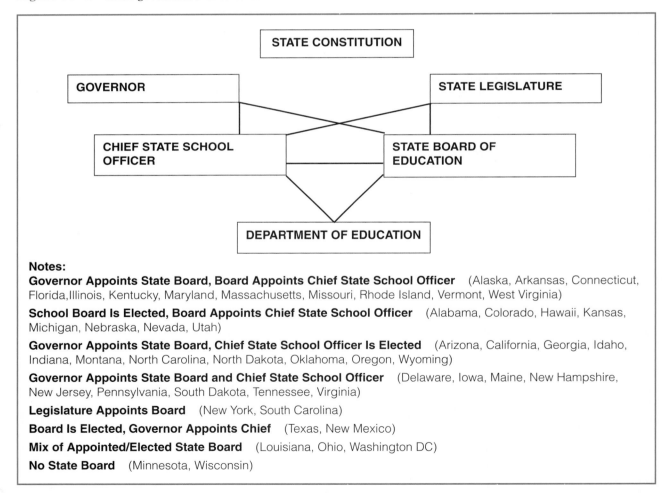

Notes:
Governor Appoints State Board, Board Appoints Chief State School Officer (Alaska, Arkansas, Connecticut, Florida,Illinois, Kentucky, Maryland, Massachusetts, Missouri, Rhode Island, Vermont, West Virginia)

School Board Is Elected, Board Appoints Chief State School Officer (Alabama, Colorado, Hawaii, Kansas, Michigan, Nebraska, Nevada, Utah)

Governor Appoints State Board, Chief State School Officer Is Elected (Arizona, California, Georgia, Idaho, Indiana, Montana, North Carolina, North Dakota, Oklahoma, Oregon, Wyoming)

Governor Appoints State Board and Chief State School Officer (Delaware, Iowa, Maine, New Hampshire, New Jersey, Pennsylvania, South Dakota, Tennessee, Virginia)

Legislature Appoints Board (New York, South Carolina)

Board Is Elected, Governor Appoints Chief (Texas, New Mexico)

Mix of Appointed/Elected State Board (Louisiana, Ohio, Washington DC)

No State Board (Minnesota, Wisconsin)

Source: National Association of State Boards of Education www.nasbe.org.

Local Organization and Power

The daily operation of the schools is the responsibility of the local school districts. They operate the schools, hire the teachers, purchase the supplies, run the buses, build and maintain buildings, and perform all of those tasks related to keeping the schools running.

Local districts are established by the state and are subject to the regulations of the state. The state can change the boundaries, modify the powers of local school board, or even eliminate school districts. In recent years, some states have assumed control of local school districts because of poor performance or financial difficulties.

◆ ◆

The Trouble with Takeovers
Go to MyEducationLab and select the topic "Governance and School Administration." Read the article, "Trouble with Takeovers" that discusses schools that have been taken over by the state as a result of poor performance. Respond to the questions that accompany the article. Some of the questions are designed to prepare you for your licensure examination.

◆ ◆

Currently in the United States there are about 14,000 local school districts governing almost 96,000 schools teaching nearly 50 million students. This represents a dramatic decline in the number of school districts and schools over the past 50 years. In 1940 there were over 117,000 public school districts governing over 226,000 schools. This reduction is the result of school and school district consolidations. For example, in 1940 there were over 113,000 one-teacher schools. In 2003–2004 there were only about 376 (National Center for Education Statistics, 2005, Table 84).

The Structure of Local School Districts

Most school districts share common administrative features. The structure of a local district usually includes a school board, a superintendent, central office staff, school principals, assistant principals, teachers, and school staff.

School Boards.   The legal authority for operating local school districts rests in the hands of the school board. Local school board members are official agents of the state. The local school board is the only body that can legally bind the school district. This means that for any action to be legal, such as contracting with the district for services, it must be approved by the school board. This is important for new teachers to understand because actions such as the employment of a new teacher is not official until the school board has acted and entered the action into the school board minutes. Even though a principal or personnel director may indicate to prospective teachers that the district is going to employ them, the legal decision is made when the school board acts.

The local school board usually consists of elected individuals who reside in the school district. A few school boards are appointed by the mayor. Normally, school board members cannot be employees of the local school district. However, teachers who reside in the district but teach in another district may serve as school board members in the district where they reside. However, the vast majority of school board members are usually laypeople who are residents that live within the boundaries of the school district.

Because education is big business and school districts have large budgets to administer, a fair number of local school board members tend to have business and management backgrounds. Usually, the terms of school board members are staggered so that there are always some continuing members of the board. In spite of the power and the responsibilities of local school boards, members usually serve with little or no compensation.

The local school board has the authority and responsibility for the operation of the local schools.

Local school boards have responsibilities for staffing schools including the selection of the district superintendent, establishing policies and procedures for the daily operation of the schools, developing a budget and keeping the school district solvent, dealing with employee relations such as collective bargaining, developing the curriculum, maintaining community relations, and making decisions regarding such matters as extracurricular activities, requirements for promotion and graduation, grading and reporting procedures, and program evaluation and assessment. Go to this chapter's *Video Viewpoints* feature to read about a school that failed and questions who is accountable for the failure.

The Superintendent.   One of the most important functions of the school board is the selection of the school superintendent. In a few places the superintendent is elected, but that is the exception. Because the board consists of members who have limited expertise in education, the school superintendent is the educational leader of the school district.

Superintendents can have an enormous impact on the local district. Their most important role is that of providing leadership for the local district. The superintendent must advise the school board about educational issues, establishing priorities for the

Video Viewpoints 13–1

Failing Grade

WATCH: This *Nightline* video segment focuses on the failure of a local school high school. The segment discusses the mismanagement of a school district and the difficulty of trying to turn around school failure. In this instance the state took over the school district. They then contracted with a private company to run the schools. They tried opening a charter school and it collapsed. This segment raises the question, Who should be accountable for school failure?

THINK: Discuss with your classmates or write in your reflective journal your responses to the following questions:

1. In what ways does the principle of local control account for the failure of this school district?
2. There are some who believe that the application of market principles by turning schools over to private companies such as the Edison Schools is a solution to school improvement. Why did it not work in this situation? What do you think would required to make it work?
3. If the state has the legal authority for the schools, should the state be held accountable for the failure of this school district? Why or why not?
4. What do you see as steps that should be taken to turn around this district?

LINK: What do you think should be done when a local school board acts irresponsibly?

To view this video, go to the Video Viewpoints DVD and click on this chapter's video: "Failing Grade."

district, supervising school principals and the administrative team, overseeing the development of the budget, maintaining a positive relationship with the local community, and building support for the schools and for district programs. This chapter's *A Day in the Life* feature highlights our focus teacher, Pat, and the election of two new board members.

A DAY IN THE LIFE . . . Trouble on the Horizon

It was another beautiful day as Pat Taylor wheeled into the school parking lot. All materials were ready and the lessons for today were Pat's favorites. It promised to be another good day in the classroom.

Pat really enjoyed teaching here. There was a good faculty and the rapport between the teachers and the administrators was positive. They generally shared the same philosophy and goals.

On the way to the classroom, Pat dropped into the faculty lounge to get a cup of coffee. Pat was surprised at the number of teachers still in the lounge and at the level of anxiety that seemed to permeate the room.

"What's happening?" inquired Pat. Alan Smith, the teacher association representative for the school, spoke up. "You know that yesterday was the school board elections?" "Sure," replied Pat. "I'm sorry that I had an in-service last night and didn't get by to vote." Alan continued, "Well, there was such a light turnout of voters that one of the groups critical of the district was able to elect two of their members to the board." Betty Jones chimed in, "Big deal. That's just school board politics and it doesn't affect me." "Don't be so sure," Alan responded. "They already had one person who supports their agenda on the board and this election gives them a majority. They've already announced that one of their first actions will be to replace the superintendent. They don't like the positive relationship that the superintendent has had with the teacher association. They want someone who will take a hard line in negotiations. In addition, they think we are too liberal and want to move us toward a 'back to basics' approach." "So what?" replied Betty, "I've got tenure. They can't tell me what to teach." "While that is true," Alan responded, "they can make your life much more unpleasant by replacing the principal with someone who shares their perspectives. They can also stop purchasing those supplies and materials that you need to implement your creative ideas."

All of a sudden, a shadow had crossed what had promised to be a good day. Pat wondered if Alan was being overly pessimistic? Could one election really change the tone and direction of the school? Pat had a sinking feeling that things were not going to be the same.

✓ Disposition Check

As a general rule, teachers tend to be individuals with dispositions that make politics unattractive. For example, one of the authors once worked in a urban school. One time on election day, one of the other teachers advised him, "In this election, you'd better not let one hand know what the other is doing." This was offensive because he was a member of an honorable profession and was interested in quality schools. Why should he keep his political opinions a secret?

The fact is that the political climate in a community or school district can have an impact on the satisfactions one gains from teaching. The political climate can change and, if you are in a district long enough, it probably will.

As you reflect on this incident ask yourself,

1. Do my dispositions lead me to be involved or uninvolved in the politics of education?
2. Under what conditions would you become involved?
3. How would an incident like this influence the satisfactions you get from teaching?

As can be seen, the superintendent has a wide range of responsibilities. In some large urban districts with extensive budgets where superintendents must deal with organized special-interest groups and political pressure from mayors and manage a complex organization, school boards have selected superintendents because of criteria other than their educational expertise. For example, the school board for the huge Los Angeles school district has selected a former governor of Colorado and an admiral as superintendents. The school board in Seattle selected a former general. This means that these superintendents do not have the expertise to be the instructional leaders of the school district. They are more like the CEO of a large corporation providing the organizational and management expertise but not the knowledge of the day-to-day activities in the classrooms. In some large complex school districts, the superintendent is not expected to be the instructional leader.

The wide range of superintendent responsibilities also brings a high degree of risk. They must maintain positive support from a wide range of constituents and it is almost inevitable that there will be? some who will disagree with them. The superintendent must maintain a positive working relationship with the school board because the school board can remove the superintendent at any time.

Maintaining strong support on the school board can be difficult in communities where there is conflict and where the composition of the school board frequently changes. Because of the low turnout of citizens for school board elections, special-interest groups can easily influence the composition of the school board by turning out voters who share their views. The election of even one new school board member can change the balance of power on the school board from supportive to nonsupportive. For this reason, the turnover rate of superintendents is quite high. One study found that the average tenure for school superintendents was 6 years (Borja, 2002). If you teach in a school district for any length of time, it is likely that you will work under several school superintendents.

Central Office Staff.   Even though the superintendent is responsible for the daily operations of the school district, the central office staff is a network of individuals with expertise in different areas that advise the superintendent. It usually consists of individuals who have responsibility for business and finance, human resources, curriculum and instruction, facilities, and special services such as federal programs and special education. The size of the central office staff is related to the size of the school district. Small districts may have a small central office staff with individuals having multiple responsibilities. Large districts may have several levels of central office staff including associate superintendents, assistant superintendents, and directors or coordinators.

One issue that often arises in the operation of a school district is that the central office staff tends to be more permanent than the superintendent. Members of the central office staff are usually local individuals who have been in the district for a number of years. Many of them are former teachers and principals who have moved through the ranks to the central office. The result is that most have developed local networks. So, in theory, even though the central office staff is supposed to be supportive of the superintendent, in reality this may not be the case. Some of the central office staff will have more loyalty to local constituents than to the superintendent. Therefore, they may be difficult to work with and may resist the leadership and authority of the superintendent (Hill, 2004). One of the important, and sometimes frustrating, tasks of the superintendent is to win over the central staff members and obtain their support.

School Principal.   Normally, the school principal is in charge of the operation of a local school. Principals are a part of the administrative team and serve under the superintendent and the school board. Although most school principals are experienced teachers who have acquired tenure as a teacher, they do not acquire tenure as a school principal. They can be removed as the principal and returned to other responsibilities, such as teaching, by the superintendent.

Principals usually interview prospective teachers, manage the school budget, supervise and evaluate faculty and staff, take care of necessary paperwork, respond to serious problems, and exert leadership in curriculum and instruction. The responsibilities of the school principal vary somewhat between elementary and secondary schools. Secondary principals typically view themselves more as managers and elementary principals typically view themselves as more responsible for teaching and learning.

Regardless of the level, the role of building principal is demanding. School principals normally must have advanced educational preparation and must possess an administrative credential in order to serve as principal. Because of the complexities of the role of principal, it is a time-consuming job with a high stress level. For this reason, fewer individuals are interested in the job and there are predictions of a shortage of school principals. This definitely opens the door of opportunity for those who have leadership skills and are willing to accept demanding responsibilities.

Effective principals are the instructional leaders for their schools and are of critical importance in establishing a positive teaching and learning climate. The contact of secondary school teachers with the school principal is usually considerably less than that of an elementary teacher. However, at both levels, individuals seeking teaching positions are well advised to consider the leadership abilities of the principal and their priorities before accepting a teaching position.

Assistant Principals.   Depending on its size, a school may have one or more assistant principals. These are members of the administrative team and are accountable to the principal. Large secondary schools may have assistant principals in charge of areas such as instruction and discipline. Because assistant principals in large high schools tend to be more "hands on" than the school principal, it is likely that new teachers in these schools will have more contact with the assistant principal than with the principal.

Normally, the principal is the person who has the authority to recommend the hiring and the retention of teachers to the central office and the school board. Therefore, the school principal is the person who evaluates the new teachers. They may do this in consultation with assistant principals but they certainly have the power to override their recommendations. In other words, they have the power over your employment. It is imperative that you know them and their expectations. You need to know what they expect of you and whether or not you are meeting those expectations.

Department Heads and Team Leaders.   Secondary schools normally have department heads and elementary schools may have grade-level or team leaders. These are teachers who take on additional responsibility for helping address the specific needs of their department or team. At the secondary level there is usually a department head for each of the content areas such as math, English, science, social studies, art, and so forth. At the elementary level there may be first-grade team leaders, second-grade team leaders, and so on. These individuals usually communicate the needs of their area to the administrative staff and communicate wishes of the administration to the teachers in their department or team. Because these individuals are teachers, they normally do not have evaluative responsibilities over other teachers. However, they may serve to mentor new teachers and may advise the school administrators regarding the needs of the new teachers in their area. In large secondary schools, department chairs may be released from some teaching responsibilities, giving them time to perform the duties of the department chair.

● ●

Teaching Teams
Go to MyEducationLab and select the topic "Governance and School Administration," then watch the video "Grade Level Meeting."

● What do the items discussed in the meeting say about the responsibilities of teachers?
● What do you see as the advantages and disadvantages of meetings like this?

● ●

Teachers.   The largest number of professionals in the school will be the teachers. Smaller elementary schools may have only one or two teachers at each grade level. In large high schools the number of teachers may be as many as 100 or more. In an elementary school, it is typical that all teachers know each other and may converse on a regular basis. At a secondary school, teachers may only have a nodding acquaintance with teachers in other departments. Figure 13–2 displays the organization of a typical school district.

Teachers form the informal power structure of the school. Although they do not have formal evaluative functions, the social power structure of teachers in a school can certainly make the life of a new teacher either easier or more difficult. You need to understand that each school develops a particular "culture" that is a combination of the formal and informal power structures. This culture usually includes the written and unwritten rules and

Figure 13–2   Organization of a local school district.

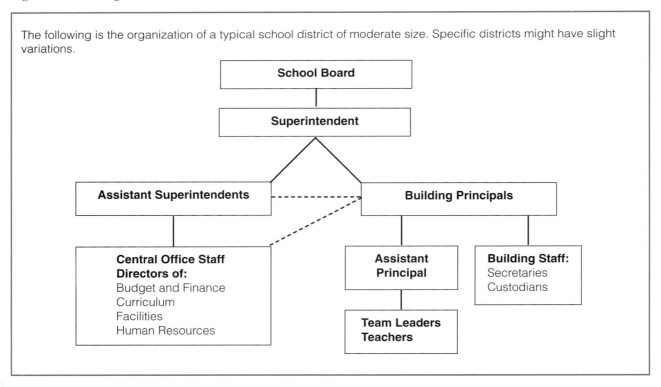

expectations for those working in the school. For example, some schools have a culture that values cooperation and sharing but others do not. In some schools the teachers may have a great deal of trust and confidence in the school administration. In other schools, the administrators, including the principal and the superintendent, are viewed more as adversaries than professional colleagues. These elements of culture can have a tremendous impact on the satisfactions you get from teaching.

What Do You Think?

- Who seems to have the most power in schools where you have been involved?
- What are some examples you have seen of how the school "culture" impacts teachers in the school?

When seeking a teaching position, it is important for you to try to identify the culture and the informal power structure of the school. Is there a sense of trust and cooperation? Are teachers willing to help each other? Do the administrators and the teachers seem to be working toward common goals?

School Support Staff.   An important additional component of any school is the support staff. This usually consists of the staff in the front office and the custodial staff. These are important individuals who keep the school functioning smoothly. The school secretary and the front office staff usually handle all of the records and files, order materials, and take care of supplies. They are the first point of contact when someone enters the school and they can answer most of the questions you might have. The custodial staff keeps the school clean and can help locate needed furniture such as desks, chairs, and filing cabinets. Custodians are often in charge of watching for things such as violations of safety and fire regulations. Needless to say, the support staff is critical in helping you to develop a satisfying working environment. When one of the authors was an administrative intern, one of the first pieces of advice given was to maintain a good relationship with the support staff. You should cultivate a good working relationship with them by treating them with respect.

In summary, not every school and not every school district is alike. Some school districts have dedicated and supportive school boards that work to create a positive teaching and learning climate. They have strong central office staffs that listen to teachers and support them in their efforts. The school administrators are professional and knowledgeable and a there is a positive school culture. On the other hand, there are districts where school board members are often at odds with one another. There is a high turnover of superintendents, central office staffs seem far removed from the realities of the classroom, school principals do not have respect as instructional leaders, and an adversarial relationship permeates the school and the district.

Intermediate School Districts

Another type of school district is considerably less visible than the local school district. This is the intermediate school district. Thirty-three states have intermediate school districts. Across the nation there are a little over 1,400 intermediate units (National Center for Educational Statistics, 2005, Table 86).

In some states, these districts are organized around county lines and in others they are organized by region. The usual role for the intermediate district is to provide services that are difficult for local school districts to provide. For example, intermediate school districts often provide expensive special education and vocational education programs. They maintain resources such as audiovisual libraries and provide in-service training for teachers and administrators. Many intermediate districts have content-area specialists who can assist local school districts in tasks such as curriculum development. Some intermediate districts also provide services such as organizing job fairs to provide an opportunity for local school districts to interact with individuals seeking teaching positions.

In many places the intermediate districts also have responsibility for oversight to make sure local districts comply with state regulations. They track legislation that is passed and help inform local school districts of the rules and procedures that must be followed. They may have the responsibility to monitor the finances of local school districts and have the power to take action if local school districts are fiscally irresponsible.

Intermediate districts do not have responsibilities for hiring or evaluating teachers other than those they might employ for special programs. Although you may not have extensive contact with intermediate school districts, you should check on their activities. They may be posting teaching vacancies for school districts across the region and may have job fairs where you can make initial contact with a number of local school districts. After employment, you might discover that they sponsor workshops that can assist you in your professional growth. When you begin teaching, you should check to see what types of teaching resources the intermediate district provides for teachers in the region.

Federal Organization and Influence

As stated earlier, because the Tenth Amendment to the Constitution assigns authority for education to the states, the federal government has played a relatively limited role in education. Over the years, the most important role of the federal government has been through the federal courts. The federal courts have impacted education by making sure that the rights of citizens guaranteed by the Constitution are not violated. This has led to important legal decisions, such as school desegregation, due process rights of students, family privacy rights, and rights to a fair and appropriate education for all students with disabilities. These were discussed in more detail in Chapter 12. Those legal decisions issued by the Supreme Court apply to all states and school districts. For example, when the Supreme Court ruled that the "separate but equal" doctrine of maintaining separate schools for white and black students violated the rights of citizens, all school districts had to integrate their schools.

In addition to the role of the courts, the federal government has sought to have more direct influence on educational policy at the state and local levels through the issuance of federal reports such as A Nation at Risk. These reports have been used as a forum to focus public attention on educational reform issues. These reports are intended to place pressure on states and local school districts to reform educational practice. In addition, they influence federal priorities and legislation.

In recent years, the federal government has exerted much more influence over education. Increased federal influence has been accomplished through what is called the Constitution's "Spending Clause" (U.S. Constitution, Article I, Section 8, Clause 1). This clause gives Congress the power to tax and spend in order to provide for the general welfare of the people. What this means is that the federal government can influence state policy by attaching conditions to the funds they supply to the states under the claim that it is for the "general welfare of the people." Using this general welfare clause has enabled the federal government to accomplish indirectly what it is prohibited from accomplishing directly (Ryan, 2004).

To illustrate the significance of this spending clause on education and educational policy, the federal government funds more than 60 educational programs (Ryan, 2004). This means there is federal involvement in a wide variety of educational activities. States have the choice of either accepting the funds for these programs and the strings that are attached to each of them, or refusing funding for all of them. Although federal money makes up a small proportion of the total funding in most states (around 7% to 8% of all dollars), the amount is significant enough so that most states comply. For example, "No Child Left Behind" is a federal government initiative that mandates all sorts of requirements, from the qualifications of teachers to the creation of charter schools. Technically, states are not required to follow these provisions. However, if they do not do so, they face the loss of federal funds for all programs. Some state governments that have viewed the requirements of NCLB as overly intrusive and costly have proposed turning down federal funds (Ryan, 2004).

The United States Department of Education

The federal agency with most influence on educational policy is the Department of Education. The role of the Department of Education is to manage educational policy, provide federal leadership on educational issues, administer federal grants and programs, gather and disseminate statistics about education, and support and engage in research.

The growth of the United States Department of Education mirrors the growing influence of the federal government on educational issues. Originally established as an Office of Education shortly after the Civil War, it achieved status as a cabinet-level department in 1979 when President Carter signed legislation creating the department. Previously, the U.S. Office of Education had been a part of the Department of Health, Education and Welfare. However, several other departments had education-related programs. This brought together education-related activities and grants and raised the status of education by making the Secretary of Education a part of the president's cabinet.

The Secretary of Education, as a cabinet-level appointee, plays a major role in advising the president and Congress on educational issues. The secretary is also the person in charge at the Department of Education and establishes priorities for such items as federal grants and research.

Many conservatives opposed the formation of the new department as a growth of federal bureaucracy. For example, one of the campaign issues in Ronald Reagan's presidential campaign was the abolition of the department.

However, as educational issues have become hot political issues, political candidates have increased their attention on education and the political profile of the Secretary of Education has been elevated. Secretaries of Education such as William Bennett, Lamar Alexander, and Roderick Paige have been highly visible in lobbying for educational reform. For example, education was a central feature of the campaign of George W. Bush for president and Secretary Paige was a strong advocate for the "No Child Left Behind" act. A department that once was the focus of criticism by Republicans and conservatives has now become a major player in the implementation of their political agenda.

Other Influences on Educational Policy

Professional Education Associations

Two large professional associations, the National Education Association (NEA) and the American Federation of Teachers (AFT) exert powerful influence on educational policy. Over 80% of all public school teachers across the nation belong to one of the two organizations. The NEA has approximately 2.7 million members and the AFT has about 1.3 million members (Fischer, Schimmel, & Steelman, 2007).

Politicians at the national and state levels have recognized that teacher associations are powerful lobbies with a significant funding base that can turn out large numbers of volunteers and voters. This has given the professional associations considerable political power. At the national level these groups exert influence on the federal government and lobby for educational issues, while state affiliates monitor legislation and lobby at the state level, and local affiliates represent teachers to local school boards.

New teachers will have the most direct contact with the local affiliates of the teacher associations and may be asked to join one of them. This is especially the case in states where professional associations have been given the right to be collective bargaining agents for local teachers. Currently, 35 states have policies that allow for collective bargaining for teachers. Figure 13–3 indicates those states that allow collective bargaining.

This means that a professional association has the right to represent the teachers in a school district and negotiate with the school board for wages and other conditions of employment. The specific responsibilities vary according to state regulations. In some

Figure 13–3   **Status of collective bargaining.**

States That Allow Collective Bargaining		States Without Collective Bargaining
Alaska	Nevada	Alabama
California	New Hampshire	Arizona
Connecticut	New Jersey	Arkansas
Delaware	New Mexico	Colorado
Florida	New York	Georgia
Hawaii	North Dakota	Kentucky
Idaho	Ohio	Louisiana
Illinois	Oklahoma	Mississippi
Indiana	Oregon	Missouri
Iowa	Pennsylvania	North Carolina
Kansas	Rhode Island	South Carolina
Maine	South Dakota	Texas
Maryland	Tennessee	Virginia
Massachusetts	Utah	West Virginia
Michigan	Vermont	Wyoming
Minnesota	Washington	
Montana	Wisconsin	
Nebraska		

Source: Education Commission of the States.

states the regulations governing collective bargaining are relatively general and in other states they specifically identify items that can be negotiated such as evaluation practices, transfer policies, grievance procedures, leave policies, and class size.

When new teachers sign contracts with school districts that have collective bargaining, they will be asked to join the local teacher organization that is the collective bargaining agent for the teachers in that district. The collective bargaining agent is usually the organization that has the largest membership of local teachers. Teachers cannot be required to join and there are some who choose not to do so because of religious or other beliefs. However, if an individual objects to joining the association with the authority to bargain with the school board, that person can still be required to pay a **fair share fee** as a condition of employment. The rationale for this fee is that all teachers in the district benefit from the results of collective bargaining and therefore should help pay for the costs. The fair share fee is viewed as the fee teachers owe the association for the cost of representing them.

What Do You Think?

- What is your view of being involved in a professional teacher organization?
- Do you think it is fair to have to pay a fee to an organization that might take positions other than those you hold?

In summary, although professional teacher associations have no designated governance authority for educational policy, they do have considerable influence and power. Understanding educational issues and change requires that you have a clear understanding of the role of professional teacher associations.

Business Leaders

Business and industry leaders also have a vital interest in the quality of education. A well-educated workforce is vital for their survival. As a result, business and corporate leaders have held prominent positions on national panels calling for educational reform. In fact, business and corporate leaders frequently outnumber educators on these panels. Many state and local communities also have coalitions of business leaders interested in education. Through these coalitions they attempt to influence educational policy. They often lobby state and local politicians and support particular pieces of legislation that they consider desirable.

Many educational reform proposals have originated with business leaders. Often, these proposals are based on business models and apply the economic principles of the market system to educational issues. For example, there has been much support from the business community for voucher plans because they see this as a way of applying competition to educational problems. One of the basic principles of the market system is that competition stimulates innovation and improvement. Thus, they believe that introducing competition in education will improve all schools.

An additional interest on the part of some businesses is the market potential of education. For example, requiring standardized tests as a important element of accountability provides a large market for those firms that develop tests. Similarly, voucher plans open the door for private business to get involved in education and to get a percentage of the funds allocated to education.

There is no doubt that businesses have considerable power and political influence. Their positions will be made known to all policymakers and, for better or for worse, they will be involved in shaping the direction of education.

The Governance Issue: Who Will Control Education?

Local control of education has long been a staple of educational governance across the nation. However, the recent trend has been to centralize the control of education in the hands of the state and federal governments.

Some people think this is a useful trend. They point out that education is a national priority and the quality of education in a given state has national implications. They contend that changes in the control of education are necessary in order to make the nation more productive and competitive, to improve the quality of life in urban areas, to reduce poverty, and to address other social ills (Cuban, 2004).

In some states, efforts have been made to shift some of the power away from state school boards and place education directly under the influence of the governor. At the local level, mayors of several large cities have sought more control over education (Chicago; Washington, D.C.; New York; Los Angeles). They believe that their ability to address urban problems and to make the city attractive to renewal and economic investment is limited because of their lack of power over the school district.

What does this mean for the future control of education? Will these changes in control result in an improvement in educational quality and an improvement in status of education? Will these changes in governance structure eliminate the last vestiges of an attempt to shield education from the partisan politics? These are key questions that need to be thoughtfully considered when changes are proposed.

What Do You Think?

- What do you think these trends toward more centralized control will mean to education?
- What do you see as the benefits and the problems with more centralized control?
- What is the relevance of these trends for choosing a career in education?

Cuban (2004), an educational leader and researcher, opposes the trend to more centralized control. He contends that the typical argument that centralized control is necessary in order to keep the nation competitive with other nations of the world is invalid. He cites data indicating that productivity rates of U.S. workers have increased, not decreased, in the past couple of decades. Therefore, assertions that the schools placing the nation at risk of losing a competitive edge are unfounded. In addition, he cites a study by the World Economic Forum indicating that the United States had the world's second most competitive economy trailing only Finland (p. 108). Finally, Cuban points out that the reforms undertaken at the state and federal levels have generally been unsuccessful.

Cuban further points out that the people who must be involved in the improvement of education are not governors and business executives but the people who do the everyday work at the local level (p. 121). If improvement is to happen, it must take place classroom by classroom and must be supported by teachers and the local community. Regardless of what is done at the state or national level, if it is not supported at the local level, it will fail.

As a part of the argument over more centralized control, it is useful to note that public opinion surveys consistently find that most communities have more trust in their local school board and educators to make sound decisions than they do in state and national political leaders.

In summary, great changes are occurring in the governance of education. There is the potential to reshape who controls education. This issue requires intensive debate in order to protect the interests of all citizens.

FINANCING EDUCATION

An important dimension in understanding education and change, one closely linked to governance, is that of school finance. Control of the finances generally leads to the control of the policies. The costs of education and how money should be allocated are topics of much intense debate. Basically, conservatives have argued that schools do not need more money saying that the solution is more efficient use of money allocated to education.

On the other hand, liberals have argued that money is a major problem. They point out that the per capita funding of education in the United States is considerably lower than that of most of the other highly industrialized nations. They argue that even though additional funding by itself will not result in improvement, substantive change without sufficient funds cannot occur. They further contend that it is money well spent. They state that the money spent on a quality education will reduce the amount needed in other areas such as welfare and law enforcement. In order to understand the debate and to seek solutions, several questions need to be addressed:

- How much does education cost?
- Who pays for education?
- How are funds allocated?

How Much Does Education Cost?

Education is big business. Current expenditures for education across the nation are in excess of $400 billion (National Center for Educational Statistics, 2006). These expenditures cover the daily operation of the schools but do not include capital outlays or the repayment of debt.

Because teachers are the central core of education, it is a labor-intensive activity. The largest cost in education budgets is for instruction and instruction-related purposes. About 60% to 65% of the cost of education is for instruction and instruction-related purposes, about 11% is for administration, about 18% for operations, and about 5% for student services (National Center for Educational Statistics, 2006).

Instruction and instruction-related expenditures are for those activities that assist with classroom instruction and include teacher salaries, librarian salaries, textbooks, supplies purchased for instructional purposes, curriculum development, and assessment. Administrative expenditures are those expenditures for the school district administration including the salaries and costs for the superintendent, school principals, and their offices. Student support expenditures include salaries for nurses, guidance counselors, speech pathologists, and attendance officers. Operation expenditures are those related to the operation and maintenance of the facilities, student transportation, and food services.

When broken out on a per student basis, the average total expenditures per student are about $8,310 per academic year. Instruction-related costs average about $5,492 per student per academic year. Viewed in another way, if the figure of $8,310 is used and a school year of 180 days is assumed, the cost per student per day of education is about $46.00.

One issue related to the cost of education that often escapes the attention of the public is that of **unfunded mandates.** When changes and programs are mandated by either the state or the federal government, they cost money. However, these mandates may not be accompanied by an allocation of funds. For example, one required program that has influenced the cost of education is the delivery of services to special populations. In 1975, the Individuals with Disabilities Act declared that school districts had to provide a "free public education" to students with disabilities. This brought over one million children previously kept at home or elsewhere into the school district. In 2000, it was estimated that the cost for educating these students was about twice the cost for a regular education student (National Association of State Boards of Education, 2006).

Overall, the program has grown from serving 3.7 million children in 1977 to 6.5 million in 1999 or a growth to about 11% of the school population (National Association of State Boards of Education, 2006). At the time of passage, the federal government recognized that this act would result in substantial additional costs to the public schools. The legislation included the intention of the federal government to provide 40% of the costs for education of this special population. However, as of 2002, the federal budget has provided only 18% of the cost. Therefore, over the past 30 years school districts have been required to assume the major share of these additional costs. A significant percentage of local school district budget increases over the past 30 years has gone toward providing an education for students with disabilities.

Across the nation other mandates have been passed either by the federal government or the state that have taken the form of an unfunded mandate. When analyzing the increased costs of education to local citizens, these mandates need to be taken into account.

Who Pays for Education?

There are three main sources of revenue for the public schools. Those involve local sources, the state government, and the federal government. Traditionally, local sources have made the largest contribution, followed by state sources with federal sources providing a relatively small share. However, in recent years, the states have taken on an increased responsibility. This mirrors the shift in control from local to state government. Currently, state governments contribute about 50% and local governments contribute about 43% of the total funding for education (Hoff, 2005).

Some of the changes in increased state responsibility for funding reflect court decisions made over the past two decades regarding how education is financed. For most of the 20th century, the major source of funding for school was the local property tax. Property tax is based on the assessed value of all property found within the boundaries of a local school district. Therefore, the amount of money available for the schools is linked to the property values of the school district. This means that school districts with high-value property such as large businesses, shopping centers, and expensive homes can generate more money than school districts with low-assessed property values. For example, if the property within a school district consists of relatively inexpensive homes and few high-value businesses or industries, a district would struggle to raise sufficient funds for schools. An implication of this model is that those districts serving poorer and needier students, those who generally need more services and better teachers, often have lower-assessed property values and therefore less money to provide services.

This finance model also results in significant variations in per pupil spending from one district to another. In some regions, districts with high-assessed property values spent almost twice the amount of money per student than their low-assessed property value neighbors. For example, in the suburbs surrounding Chicago, the Rondout School District spent $22,508 per student in a recent year where as the Zion Elementary School District spent $8,675 per student (Rado, 2007).

Another issue that has resulted in school funding changes is what has been called the **taxpayer revolt.** This movement started in the 1970s over the concern that as assessed property value increased, so did the tax bill. Therefore, individuals living on fixed incomes, such as senior citizens, were faced with dramatic increases in their tax bills. Because of their inability to pay their property tax, some claimed they would be forced to sell their homes.

In 1978, the California taxpayer revolt led to the passage of an initiative called "Proposition 13," which limited increases in assessed evaluations of property. Several other

A source of additional funding for schools has been to sell advertising space to businesses.

states soon followed this pattern and imposed limitations on property tax increases. In 1989 the highest court in Kentucky ruled that the entire K–12 finance and governance system in Kentucky was unconstitutional. In 1993 the Michigan legislature voted to eliminate local property tax as a source of revenue for the public schools. Across the nation, lawsuits were brought to force more equitable school financing. With the combination of tax resistance and court decisions, financing education began to shift from local property tax to other state revenue sources.

State legislators have usually looked for ways to reduce the percentage of the state budget going to education, so the shift in funding sources has led to a loss of available funds. Therefore, school districts have attempted to cover this loss by instituting a number of fees. For example, they have charged art fees for those in art classes or lab fees for those students taking laboratory classes. One source that has been somewhat controversial is the use of corporate funds for exclusive product rights or advertising. This means that a corporation is given the exclusive right to sell its product or advertise in the school or school district. For example, it might mean that only one brand of soft drinks is available in vending machines on school district property or only one brand of athletic shoes can be worn by athletic teams.

● ●

Commercialized Schools
Go to MyEducationLab and select the topic "Financing Schools." Read the article "The Battle over Commercialized Schools" to obtain more information on how schools have attempted to raise funds through marketing products. Respond to the questions accompanying the article. Some of the questions are designed to prepare you for your licensure examination.

● ●

Another local source has been the implementation of user fees. Students who use buses or participate in certain activities pay fees to help fund the activity. Although it would seem only fair that the users of a service pay for it, it also means that students from low socioeconomic status homes may not be able to participate in some activities because they lack the money to do so.

The loss of funds has also led parent groups to become active in fund-raising in order to provide activities such as field trips, music classes, or supplemental materials. In some cases, the requests of these parent groups in a school district run into the hundreds of dollars! The problem with this arrangement is that less-affluent communities simply do not have the fund-raising capabilities of more affluent communities so their children do not have the opportunity to participate in these activities.

What Do You Think?

- Do you think user fees are an appropriate approach to the need for additional funds?
- What do you think could be done to get more funds?

At the state level funding comes from two primary sources of revenue, income taxes and sales taxes. Forty-one states and the District of Columbia currently collect income taxes. Other sources of revenue for the schools are corporate income taxes, gaming, and a variety of other fees and taxes.

In order to supplement the loss of local revenue, a number of states looked to gaming and state lotteries as a revenue source. However, the amount of money supplied by that source makes a minor contribution to the revenue stream. Except for Nevada, where the revenue from gaming supplies a significant portion of the school budget, only Connecticut, Louisiana, and Rhode Island generate more than 5% of their education revenue from gaming (EdWeek, 2005).

In addition to state and local revenue sources, some additional funding comes from federal sources. Federal revenue to support education usually comes in the form of grants. There are generally two types of grants. One type is a **categorical grant.** These grants are funds that are designated for specific purposes such as technology or vocational education. The categorical grant is the type of grant that has been preferred by the federal government in the past.

The other type of grant is the block grant. A **block grant** provides money and does not specify how the funds are to be spent, leaving the allocation of the funds to the state or the local district. In recent years, the federal government has moved away from categorical grants and has favored block grants.

How Are Funds Allocated?

Different states have different models for determining how to allocate money for education. Most of the funding models are based on the number of students served by the school district. The usual way of determining this is **average daily attendance (ADA).** This requires that school districts keep accurate records on the daily attendance of students and they then submit to the state their ADA in order to receive state funds. Most states specify the number of minutes a student must be in school in order for it to count as attendance.

This funding model explains some school district practices and policies. Because funding is based on ADA, it is in the best interest of the school district to maximize the number of students in school. One technique is to hire school attendance officers who seek to get truant students back in school. Some districts have even instituted "child neglect" charges against parents who have not accepted responsibility for their child's attendance.

Many school boards and central office administrators monitor the housing market in the school district. If people are moving out of the district, it will probably mean fewer students, a lower ADA, and less money. They need to know this as they build a budget. On the other hand, new homes and businesses usually increase the number of students and the ADA.

Understanding that available funds are based on ADA may impact your job search. School districts with tight budgets are often reluctant to hire teachers until they have a firm basis for determining their ADA. Therefore, they may hold off filling some vacant teaching positions until after the new school year has begun and the students have arrived. Then, if necessary, they will hire new teachers and shift the students. Even though this doesn't make for good education, it does help to balance the budget.

ISSUES IN SCHOOL FINANCE

Recent trends in education have generated some finance concerns. One of those is related to the implementation of high-stakes graduation examinations. In the past, a primary consideration of the courts in evaluating school finance plans focused on the issue of equitable distribution of school funds to all school districts across the state. The ADA model met this requirement. The amount of dollars the state allocated per ADA was the same for all students. However, high-stakes graduation tests have changed the focus from what is equitable to what is needed to ensure a quality education for all students.

Equity Versus Adequacy

As states have changed requirements that all students must pass an examination as a condition for graduation, students who have failed this examination have filed legal challenges. They base these legal challenges on the grounds that they were not provided with an education that enables them to pass the test.

The argument advanced in court is that, if states require passage of a competency examination, they have a constitutional obligation to provide an education that prepares the students to achieve the level of competency required for passage. Because students have a variety of educational needs, merely providing the same amount for all students does not meet this standard. The argument is for "adequate" funding rather than "equitable" funding.

Adequacy models begin with the question "What is required to make sure all students are provided with an education sufficient for them to reach the required level of achievement?" This means that the formula for funding the schools needs to take into account factors such as the nature of the student population, the number of at-risk students, the needs of English language learners, and the need for special services and paraprofessionals.

A couple of approaches have been used to define what is adequate. One of those is the "evidence-based model." This approach uses research to identify practices that are successful in promoting student achievement. Estimates are then made regarding how much it costs to implement these procedures. This forms the basis for allocating funds.

Another approach is the "successful schools model." This approach uses the expenditures and practices of the most successful schools in the state and then uses that funding formula to determine what should be allocated to other schools.

A third approach is the "professional judgment model." This model uses groups of educators as focus groups. Programs, practices, and interventions that have support from the research are presented to these groups and they design model schools incorporating the features they believe are essential. An estimate is then made on how much it costs to operate these schools.

To date, adequacy models have led to estimates of expenditures for the schools that exceed current funding levels. For example, in New York the estimated costs for the implementation of an adequacy formula would be an additional $8.4 billion a year. In Maryland, two studies were conducted using different models. One estimated that the state needed to increase spending by 34% and the other by 44% (Hoff, 2005). This has led to opposition from some fiscal conservatives who claim that there is little evidence of a relationship between money and achievement (Baker, 2007).

Is Money Available to Provide Additional Funds?

Regardless of the finance model used to fund the schools, the question remains, "Where can states get additional money in order to address the increased costs required under adequacy models?" Unpredictable funding and a lack of resources have been identified as the most pressing school finance issues.

Some political leaders claim that there simply is not enough money to adequately fund education. In evaluating this claim it might be informative to look at the issue in a broader context. For example, recent estimates are that the war in Iraq is costing about $6 billion a month. This adds up to $72 billion a year or about 18% of the total education costs for the nation for a year.

A recent announcement by the oil companies indicated that they had profits of over $30 billion in just one quarter. This would mean that the yearly profits of just this one sector of the economy would exceed $120 billion a year or about 25% of the total costs of education for a year. The media estimates that the nation spends about $4 billion just to celebrate Halloween.

Our intent is not to claim that oil companies should not make a profit or that the nation should stop celebrating holidays such as Halloween. Rather, the purpose is to point out that money is available for other activities in society. The question then is not whether there is enough money in the society, but, rather, "What are the priorities in spending that money?"

What Do You Think?

- What is your reaction to the assertion that there is insufficient money available to support changes in education?
- Why do you think society has placed education as a low priority for funding?

Teacher Compensation

As previously noted, education is labor intensive and the largest portion of a school district budget is devoted to teacher salaries. Therefore, changing financial models for funding education must address teacher compensation. It is widely accepted that teacher compensation is inadequate and that improving teacher compensation could help solve teacher recruitment and retention problems. Because there also appears to be a research-supported link between teacher quality and student learning (Odden, 2004), revising teacher compensation with a focus on teacher quality has potential for improving education by attracting and keeping quality teachers. This has led to proposals to link teacher compensation with performance.

Traditionally, teacher salaries have been based on what is called a **single salary schedule.** Currently, 20 states mandate a single salary schedule (Olson, 2005). This type of a salary schedule defines the salary of each teacher based on years of experience. There is a base schedule for all teachers who have a valid teaching credential. The salary of a teacher increases a specific amount with each year of teaching experience up to some limit in the number of years of experience.

Most salary schedules include additional steps based on additional education. In this type of a salary schedule, for every additional block of college units completed (usually around 12–15 units) beyond the teaching credential, there is an increase in salary. Sometimes an additional bonus is given for those who obtain a master's or a doctorate.

There are several problems with the single salary schedule. Critics claim that this type of schedule compensates effective and ineffective teachers equally. The contention is that this type of a compensation plan reinforces individuals for putting forth only minimal effort and there is little incentive for improvement. Furthermore, they claim that compensation should not be based on just surviving another year.

Applying some business principles to education, some have suggested changing teacher compensation to a merit pay system where teachers are paid for results. They contend that it is only logical that people should be paid for performing, not just surviving.

However, the claim that merit pay by itself will improve education is based on some questionable assumptions. **Merit pay** is based on the assumption that an individual only puts forth the minimum effort unless an incentive is provided to improve. This may well be the case in businesses where the goals of the employer and the employee are at odds. The goal of a business owner is to maximize production and profit while investing the least amount of resources. The goal of the employee is to maximize income with the least amount of effort. However, in teaching, the goals of the teacher and the organization are more closely aligned. For example, teachers learn that good teaching actually makes their job easier. If students are motivated and challenged, there is increased motivation and fewer discipline problems. Thus, good teaching has the reward of reducing teaching stress and effort. This is consistent with the district goal of providing a quality education. Therefore, increased incentives are not likely to significantly change teaching behavior.

In addition, for merit pay to work, merit must be clearly defined and those in the merit pay system must accept that what is being rewarded is truly meritorious. There must be a clear answer to the question, "Why did X get merit pay?" If meritorious performance is not clearly defined, then the risk is that other variables such as personality and personal attractiveness become the basis for merit.

Clearly defining meritorious performance in education is difficult. What is merit? Is it achieving high student test scores? Should teaching at-risk students be considered? How are counseling and mentoring evaluated? How is problem solving assessed? How are the many roles of teachers weighted in the decision to define merit? Education has multiple purposes and some of the most important purposes are not easily measured on standardized tests.

Merit pay could have a negative impact on the quality of education. If merit is defined solely on test scores, it would be expected that teachers would focus their energies on those things that are likely to impact test scores. Taking time to counsel students or help them with their problems would not be in the best interest of the teachers. Probably the curriculum would be narrowed to focus on those things that are likely to be tested.

What Do You Think?

- Would you favor a merit pay system?
- Would you be in favor of being paid according to how well the students in your class score on a test? Why or why not?
- How do you think merit could be defined in teaching?

The issue of competition between teachers for merit is another issue that complicates the application of merit to education. Unlike the business model where improved performance results in higher production and higher profits, in education there is not a link between improved performance and the additional funds. Thus, there is a fixed amount of money available for teacher salaries and a merit pay plan, so teachers will be in competition with each other for the available funds. Applying this model means that it to your advantage for others to do poorly.

Would this lead to a reluctance of teachers to share their ideas or work with other teachers? Would this be productive in improving education? This leads to an ethical concern. Should a teacher who develops an effective approach or an effective set of materials withhold that from other teachers and thereby limit the learning of students not in their class?

In places where merit pay has been introduced, some schools and teachers have chosen not to participate simply because of this factor. Texas introduced a state grant program to set up merit pay systems for teachers. However, some schools rejected the money because they feared that the money would pit teacher against teacher and that it would have a negative impact on the school. Some stated that they felt the merit pay proposal placed a value on personal gain over the success of the school (Stutz, 2006).

Because of the problems in applying merit pay to education, some variations have been proposed. One proposal has been to change the reward structure from that of the individual teacher to that of the school. In this plan, merit pay would be given to schools that achieve high standards and then passed on to the teachers.

Others have proposed changing merit from just an improvement based on standardized-test scores to include incentives for teachers who increase their knowledge and skill through participation in professional-development activities. Other proposals include incentives for teaching in high need areas.

As you enter the teaching profession, you can expect that considerable attention will be given to teacher compensation plans. Many single salary schedules probably will be replaced. You need to give serious thought to the implications of proposed changes to teacher compensation. The potential exists for some significant changes that can have either a positive or a negative impact on teacher salaries and the quality of education.

Key Ideas in Summary

- The control of education has important consequences. Those who control education can control the political, social, and economic course of society.
- Because of the Tenth Amendment of the Constitution, primary responsibility for education rests with the state. However, using the Spending Clause has enabled the federal government to increased influence on educational policy.
- Local school districts usually have responsibility for the daily operation of the schools. Local school districts exist at the pleasure of the state and can be reorganized or disbanded by the state.
- In the past, a large part of federal influence in education has been through the courts as they enforced the rights of citizens as defined by the Constitution. However, in recent years the federal role has expanded through federal legislation such as the "Individuals with Disabilities Education Act" and "No Child Left Behind."
- Professional teacher associations influence educational policy through their lobbying activities at the federal and state levels. They can deliver funds and volunteers for political campaigns. At the local level, professional associations may exert power through collective bargaining with the local school district.
- Because of the importance of education in the development of a skilled and educated workforce, business and industry have taken a prominent role in calling for educational reform. Business leaders often outnumber educators on important panels.
- There has been a recent trend away from local control of education toward more centralized control. Some support this trend because education is of such national importance. Others worry that this trend will lead to increased political interference in education and increased control over the curriculum and what students learn.
- The cost of education and the methods of financing education have been topics of intense debate. In some states the practice of funding education through property tax has been challenged and funding sources changed. This has led to more dependence on state sources of revenue and increased state control.

- Education is big business and consumes a large part of the state budget. The biggest percentage of educational costs is for instruction and instruction-related programs.
- Different states have different methods for allocating funds. Most of these methods are based on *average daily attendance*. This results in school districts attempting to maximize attendance.
- Traditional funding models in education have focused on equity issues. However, recent court decisions have focused on the issue of adequacy. Adequacy models address the question of how much it will cost to achieve the levels of achievement defined by the state.
- The question of where money will come from to adequately fund education is a perplexing one. This is cited as a major problem by many states. What is needed is a rethinking of national priorities and an identification of ways society is allocating scarce resources.
- Teacher compensation plans are normally based on a single salary schedule where all teachers receive the same amount of compensation. Recent calls have been for merit or performance pay systems. However, there are several issues that must be addressed if merit pay is to be adapted to education.

For Your Initial-Development Portfolio

1. Extend the content covered in this chapter by developing portfolio entries specific to your area or region. Chart the divisions of the department of education in your state and identify the chief state school official.
2. Develop a schema of the local school district where you might be interested in teaching. Identify the school superintendent, key central office personnel, the schools in the district, and the names of the school principals. When you interview for a teaching job, interviewers will be impressed if you have good knowledge of the school district.
3. Research how education is funded in your state. What are the finance issues the state is confronting? What are the primary sources of revenue for education in your state? Place this information in your portfolio. This information can indicate to others that you have a depth of understanding about educational issues.
4. Obtain information about salary schedules from several school districts in your region. This information is useful in helping you understand the salary range that a new teacher might expect.
5. Place a check in the chart below to indicate to which INTASC standard(s) each of your items of information relates. (You may wish to refer to Chapter 1 for more detailed information about INTASC.)

INTASC Standard Number										
ITEM OF EVIDENCE NUMBER	S1	S2	S3	S4	S5	S6	S7	S8	S9	S10
1										
2										
3										

6. Prepare a written reflection in which you analyze the decision-making process you followed. In your comments, mention the INTASC standard(s) to which your selected material relates.

Reflections

1. What is your position on the governance of education? Do you agree or disagree with the trend to more centralized control?
2. How is education governed in your state? What are the pros and cons of this model?
3. What is your reaction to the trend toward having individuals from business, government, and the military serve as school superintendents?
4. How might you go about assessing the "culture" of a school where you are seeking employment?
5. What are the advantages and disadvantages of funding formulas based on equity or adequacy?
6. What is your position of pay-for-performance salary proposals for teachers? Do you think they will lead to improved education?

Field Experiences, Projects, and Enrichment

1. Attend a local school board meeting. Identify the items on the agenda and note the interactions between the board and the superintendent.
2. Go to a local school and identify how that school operates. Are there assistant principals? What do they do? Are there team leaders or department chairs? What do they do? Do teachers believe they have a voice in issues relating to the operation of the school?
3. Investigate the educational issues that are currently under consideration at the state level. What are the bills that are being introduced in the state legislature? Is the governor supporting some educational issues? What are they?
4. Talk with some teachers and get their ideas on teacher compensation plans. Would they favor merit pay? Why or why not? How do they think merit could be defined?

References

Baker, K. (2007) "Are international tests worth anything?" *Phi Delta Kappan*, 89(2), 101–104.

Borja, R. (2002). Study: Urban school chief's tenure is 4.6 years. *Education Week*. February 6, p. 5.

Cuban, L. (2004). A solution that lost its problem: Centralized policymaking and classroom gains. In N. Epstein, (Ed.), *Who's in charge here? The tangled web or school governance and policy*. Washington, DC: Brookings Institution.

Education Commission of the States. (2006). State Notes. http://mb2.ecs.org/reports/Reports.aspx?id=163

EdWeek. (2005). *Sources of state revenue*. http://www.edweek.org/we/qc/2005/tables/17revenue-tl.html 9-06-2006

Epstein, N. (2004). Introduction: Who should be in charge of our schools. In N. Epstein, (Ed.), *Who's in charge here? The tangled web or school governance and policy*. Washington, DC: Brookings Institution.

Fischer, L., Schimmel, D., & Steelman, L. (2007). *Teachers and the law* (7th ed.). Boston: Allyn & Bacon.

Hill, P. (2004). Recovering from an Accident: Repairing governance with comparative advantage. In N. Epstein, (Ed.), *Who's in charge here? The tangled web or school governance and policy.* Washington, DC: Brookings Institution.

Hoff, D. (2005). Elusive answers. *EdWeek*, January 6. http://www. edweek.org/ea/articles/2005/01/06/17revenue.h24.html 10-9-2006

Kirst, M. (2004). Turning points: A history of American School governance. In N. Epstein, (Ed.), *Who's in charge here? The tangled web or school governance and policy.* Washington, DC: Brookings Institution.

National Association of State Boards of Education. (2006). State education governance models. www.nasbe.org 9-07-2006

National Center for Educational Statistics. (2005). Digest of educational statistic tables and figures, Table 84. http://nces.ed. gov/programs/digest/d05/tables/dt05_084.asp 9-06-2006

National Center for Educational Statistics. (2005). Digest of educational statistics tables and figures, Table 86. http://nces.ed. gov/programs/digest/d05/tables/dt05_086.asp 9-06-2006

Odden, A. (2004). *Summary and reflections on 14 years of CPRE school finance redesign research.* Madison, WI: Wisconsin Center for Educational Research, University of Wisconsin–Madison.

Olson, L. (2005). Financial evolution. *EdWeek*, January 6. http://www. edweek.org/ea/articles/2005/01/06/17overview.h24.html 10-09-2006

Rado, D. (2007). Rich school, poor school. *Chicago Tribune*, February 4. http://www.chicagotribune.com/business/content/education/ chi-0702040055feb04,0,7745897.story? 3-05-2007

Ryan, J. (2004). The Tenth Amendment and other paper tigers: The legal boundaries of education governance. In N. Epstein, (Ed.), *Who's in charge here? The tangled web or school governance and policy.* Washington, DC: Brookings Institution.

Stutz, T. (2006). Some schools pass up bonuses. *Dallas Morning News*, October 2. http://www.dallasnews.com/sharedcontnet/dws/news/ nation/stories/DN-meritpay_02tex.ARTO.State.Edition2.3e5bf1b. html 10-02-2006

GLOSSARY

A

Academic Freedom   A right of teachers based on First Amendment that refers to the right to include relevant content in the subject that is taught. It also includes the right to select material and use teaching approaches that are appropriate for the subject.

Academic-Subjects Orientation   A perspective on the curriculum that holds that the school curriculum should be organized around the structure of academic subjects.

Academies   Private secondary schools, first established in the 18th century, that were the primary form of secondary education in the years before a legal basis was established for public support of secondary schools.

Acceleration Programs   Programs for gifted students that increase the pace of learning for the gifted students. Thus, a student may complete a course of study in less time than would normally be expected.

Acceptable-Use Policy (AUP)   A term applied to policies school districts adopt that specify acceptable learner uses of technology.

Accommodation   A term introduced by Piaget meaning how the learning schema of an individual is altered to make it consistent with the environment.

Accountability   The idea that teachers should be held directly responsible for student learning of specific content.

Achievement Gap   A term used to describe the achievement discrepancy between different groups of learners such as Hispanic students, black students, Native American students, Asian students, and white students.

Active Teaching   A term referring to a model of teaching in which the teacher takes direct leadership in presenting new information, monitoring student learning, adjusting teaching, and assessing student learning.

Adequate Funding Formula   A formula for funding education that is based on the funds that are needed to provide students with an opportunity to achieve the standards established by the state.

Advance Organizer   A label or term that a teacher supplies to students before a learning sequence to help them organize the information that is to follow.

Affective Domain   A category of learning that includes learning interests, attitudes, and values.

American Federation of Teachers (AFT)   A national organization for teachers that is affiliated with organized labor.

Americans with Disabilities Act   Federal legislation that extends and defines the civil rights of individuals with disabilities.

Appropriate Education   A principle associated with federal legislation that requires schools to devise educational programs that are responsive to the unique learning needs of students with disabilities.

Assistive Technology   Technology that is used to help individuals with disabilities maintain or increase their functional capabilities.

Attendance Zone   A term used to describe the geographic area students must live in to attend a specific school or school district.

Attention Deficit Disorder (ADD)   A disorder characterized by impairments to one or more of the psychological processes associated with understanding and using language.

Authentic Assessment   A category of assessment that makes judgments about student learning based on their performance on tasks that parallel (as closely as possible) "real-world" conditions.

Average Daily Attendance (ADA)   The average number of students attending in a school or school district.

B

Bacon, Francis   A late 16th and early 17th century educational thinker who advocated the idea that truth could be found, challenged, and modified through systematic observation. He is regarded as the father of the scientific method.

Bell-Shaped Curve   A symmetrical distribution with the greatest number in the center and an even decline moving away from the center in each direction.

Block Grant   A government grant that provides a specific amount of money but allows a school district flexibility to spend the money for a variety of purposes.

Bloom's Taxonomy   A popular way of referring to a classification scheme for educational objectives in terms of cognitive complexity. The scheme was introduced in the book *Taxonomy of Educational Objectives: Handbook I, Cognitive Domain*, written by Benjamin Bloom and others.

Boston English Classical School   The first public high school in the United States. It opened in Boston in 1821.

Boston Latin Grammar School   A private secondary school that opened in 1635 for the purpose of preparing boys for Harvard.

Braille   A system of touch reading developed for individuals with a sight impairment.

Brailler   A device used by sight-impaired individuals to take notes or produce other prose material.

C

Cardinal Principles   A set of principles or goals developed by the National Education Association's Committee on the Reorganization of Secondary Education in 1918. These seven principles influenced educational programs for most of the 20th century.

Carl D. Perkins Vocational and Applied Technology Act   1990 federal legislation that supports the establishment of tech-prep programs.

Categorical Grant   A government grant that designates specific purposes and programs for which the funds might be used.

Charter School   A semiautonomous school, freed from the many regulations imposed on other public schools. They can be established groups who develop a plan and receive permission to operate from the appropriate authorizing body in the state.

Checklist   A data gathering tool that provides information about the presence or absence of targeted behaviors.

Child Protective Services (CPS)   An agency affiliated with the government that is charged with protecting the well-being of children.

Children's Internet Protection Act (CIPA)   A part of Public Law 105-554, passed in December 2000, requiring schools to take actions to block content from the Internet that could be harmful to children. It requires that schools develop an Internet safety policy.

Closed File   A designation of placement files that denies the person access to the information contained in the file.

Cognitive Domain   A category of thinking associated with processing information.

Common School   A term given to Horace Mann's concept of a school for the average person.

Communication-Process Position   A generally rejected explanation for the failure of many minority group children to do well in school. The contention was that their poor performance resulted from their parents' failure to provide intellectually stimulating home environments.

Comprehensive High School   Term used to describe high schools that present a wide range of programs to meet diverse needs of students including college prep programs and vocational programs.

Comprehensive School Reform Demonstration Project (CSRD)   A federal program established by 1997 legislation seeking to promote schoolwide educational reform.

Conflict Perspective   A sociological perspective that views educational decision making as a conflict between different groups striving for power.

Connected Discourse   Verbal communication that features a smooth, logical flow of ideas.

Constructivism   A perspective on learning that holds that learners are passive recipients of information but they construct meanings as they relate new information to what they already know.

Controlled-Choice Plan   A type of student enrollment plan that allows a school district some control of the school choices made by parents and guardians in order to maintain appropriate racial balances at individual schools.

Cooperative Learning: Learning experiences where groups of students work together and learn from each other.

Core-Studies Component   A part of the teacher-preparation program that focuses on developing the general education background of future teachers. It is based on the notion that good teachers need a broad base of knowledge across general subject areas.

Criterion-Referenced Evaluation   An approach that judges the performance of an individual against a predetermined standard.

Cultural Capital   The constellation of attitudes, beliefs, language patterns, and activities of a group that reinforces the value of education.

Cultural-Deficit View   A generally rejected explanation that the failure of students from certain minority groups to do well in school is related to their cultural background.

Culturally Appropriate Practice   Classroom practices that take into account the cultural values of students.

Culturally Responsive Environment   A classroom environment or teaching approach that is responsive to individuals from a variety of different cultural groups.

Curriculum   A term used to identify the specific content of what is taught in a given school program.

Curriculum Leader   Individuals in school districts who have responsibility for designing and implementing the curriculum.

Curriculum Standards   The specific content that is required for every student in a school district or a state. They define what schools and teachers will be held accountable for and usually form the basis for what is to be assessed.

D

Department Chair   A teacher in a middle or high school who is responsible for leading other teachers in his/her subject area.

Dewey, John   A leading educational philosopher who worked from the late 19th century to the middle of the 20th century. Dewey promoted learner-centered education designed to respond to individual student needs as they grew toward full participation in society.

Diagnostic Assessment   Assessment procedures that have as their purpose the diagnosis of student learning and skills.

Digital Divide   A term used to indicate the disparity of access the technology by individuals of different groups—for example, members of affluent and impoverished families.

Due Process   A guarantee provided by the U.S. Constitution that requires certain steps and procedures to be followed before a person is denied rights guaranteed by the Constitution.

E

Education Code   The compilation of state laws and regulations related to education within the state.

Education for All Handicapped Children Act   Also known as Public Law 94-142, this 1975 federal legislation required public schools to provide specific services to learners with disabilities.

Enrichment Programs   Programs for gifted students that provide enriched learning opportunities while maintaining them as members of regular school classes.

Essentialism   An educational philosophy that views the purpose of education as that of providing practical and intellectual training essential for preparing them to be functioning members of society.

Event Sampling   A classroom observation approach that is based on the selection of a particular category of classroom events as the basis for the data-gathering process.

Exceptional Learners   Individuals who have characteristics that differentiate them from individuals with characteristics more commonly found among the general population of students.

F

Fair Share Fee   A fee that professional teacher associations are allowed to collect from nonmembers when the association serves as the bargaining agent for all the teachers in the district.

Family Rights and Privacy Act   This 1974 legislation requires schools to provide parents or guardians (and students over 18 years of age) with free access to school records. The legislation restricts access to these records by others.

Formal-Preparation Phase   Term used to describe the academic training program of teacher-preparation programs.

Formative Assessment   Assessment of learning that takes place during an instructional sequence that provides the teacher with information that can be used to modify instruction.

Franklin Academy   A nonsectarian institution established in 1751 by Benjamin Franklin that offered more practical studies than those normally included in the school curriculum.

Freedom of Conscience   A constitutional guarantee that relates to the rights of citizens in the areas of personal beliefs and religion.

Freedom of Expression   A legal guarantee that allows citizens, except for a small number of exceptions, to make statements.

Full Inclusion   The practice of placing individuals with special needs in regular classrooms throughout the school day while providing them with special help.

Full-Service School   A school that provides a variety of services in addition to education. The services might include health care, social welfare, counseling, and legal support.

Functionalist Perspective   A sociological perspective of education that sees schools as institutions designed to prepare individuals to maintain a smooth, functioning society.

G

Goals 2000   Educate America Act   This 1994 legislation calls for massive efforts to reform American Education by the year 2000 and improve the standing of American students on international comparisons.

Gifted Learners   Students who demonstrate exceptional ability in one or more areas.

Grade-Level Chair   A teacher in an elementary school who is responsible for leading the teachers in the school teaching the same grade.

H

High-Stakes Testing   A term used to describe tests with significant consequences. The consequences may be related to students and their graduation or promotion or related to teachers and their evaluation or pay.

Higher-Level Questions   Questions that require students to engage in complex and sophisticated cognitive processes.

I

Individualized Educational Program (IEP)   A requirement of federal legislation that schools develop and implement a program for each learner with a disability.

Individuals with Disabilities Education Act (IDEA)   A modification and update of the Education for All Handicapped Children Act.

Induction-Years Phase   The beginning phase of a new teacher's career.

Inductive Teaching   Teaching that engages students in looking for patterns and explanations of pieces of information that are given to them during instruction.

Initial-Development Portfolio   A portfolio prospective teachers develop that indicates their growth in skill and knowledge toward effective teaching.

In Loco Parentis   A legal doctrine that indicated that educators serve "in the place of parents." Therefore, the standard used to judge the appropriateness of educator actions was if they acted as a wise parent might act. Although still guiding many legal decisions in education, the doctrine has been modified by court decisions.

Inner Curriculum   The nature of learning that occurs within individuals as they process the formal curriculum.

Input Goals   Goals that focus on the resources provided to facilitate teaching and learning.

Inquiry Teaching   An approach based on inductive logic that requires students to formulate hypotheses and gather data to test them.

In-Service Education   A term used to describe staff development opportunities provided after an individual has been employed by the school district.

Intelligence Quotient (IQ) Test   A test designed to yield a score thought to be representative of the intelligence level of the test taker.

Internal Summaries   Points within a lesson where the teacher pauses to summarize what has been presented up to that point.

Internet Safety Policy   A policy mandated by the Children's Internet Protection Act that seeks to protect children from harmful and illegal uses of technology.

Interstate New Teacher Assessment and Support Consortium   A group dedicated to identifying competencies new teachers should be able to demonstrate and to encourage colleges and universities to emphasize the competencies in teacher-education programs.

J

Jacob K. Javits Gifted and Talented Students Act of 1994   Federal legislation that allocated federal funds to school districts to support the development of programs for gifted learners.

K

Kalamazoo Case   An 1874 legal decision that established the principle that a state had the right to pass laws levying taxes to pay for secondary and elementary education.

Knowledge and Skill-Based Pay (KSBP)   An approach to teacher compensation that considers variables associated with teacher knowledge and ability to positively affect learners' achievement levels.

L

Learner-Centered Orientation   A perspective on curriculum that holds that the knowledge students should learn should be based on student needs and interests.

Learner Portfolio   A purposeful collection of products and performances that indicates student effort and achievement.

Learning Intention   A statement that identifies what students should know or be able to do as a result of instruction.

Learning Styles   Preferred modes of learning that individuals have for learning new content.

Least Restrictive Environment   A principle associated with federal legislation for services to learners with special needs requiring schools to educate them in environments that are the least restrictive possible given their special needs.

Liberty Right   A right of people to be free from all restraints except those imposed by law.

Life-Adjustment Education   An outgrowth of the progressive movement that enjoyed popularity among some school leaders in the years following World War II. The goal of school was to prepare students with experiences that would help them accommodate their world.

M

Mainstreaming   A principle associated with federal legislation that requires delivering educational services in regular classrooms.

Malfeasance   A category of teacher negligence indicating that the actions were taken to deliberately and knowingly harm someone.

Massachusetts School Law of 1642   The first law in America that attempted to make school attendance compulsory. It charged local magistrates with the responsibility for ensuring that parents did not neglect their children's education.

Mental Retardation   People whose intellectual development (1) lags significantly behind that of age mates and (2) whose potential for academic achievement has been found to be markedly lower than that of age mates.

Merit Pay   A teacher compensation plan based on the achievement or performance of the students they teach.

Misfeasance   A type of teacher negligence associated with a person's failure to take proper safeguards to prevent harm from coming to someone.

Modification   Altering tasks for children in order to facilitate their probability of success.

Multicultural Education   A perspective on education that holds that school programs should present students with instruction that honors and respects the contributions of many cultures. It promotes equity of educational treatment to all students.

Multidimensionality   A characteristic of teaching that requires teachers to attend to a broad range of responsibilities in the classroom.

Multiple Intelligences   A perspective that holds that intelligence is not a unitary trait but is composed of multiple dimensions. Therefore, different individuals might be gifted in different dimensions.

N

National Assessment of Educational Progress (NAEP) A program that periodically assesses segments of the nation's learners to ascertain their achievement in various school subjects. It is sometimes referred to as the "nation's report card."

National Defense Education Act   This 1958 legislation was passed in response to the launch of the Soviet satellite, Sputnik. It provided federal support for curriculum reform, teacher training, and other initiatives in order to close what was perceived as an education gap between the United States and the Soviet Union.

National Education Association (NEA)   The largest professional organization for teachers.

Needs-of-Society Orientation   A perspective on the curriculum that holds that what students should learn should be organized around recognized needs of society.

Negligence   A legal term indicating the failure to take prudent actions to prevent harm from coming to someone. Negligence includes three types: malfeasance, misfeasance, and nonfeasance.

No Child Left Behind Act of 2001   This 2002 legislation encompasses numerous actions designed to require all states to develop rigorous content standards, hold schools accountable for the learning of students in all subgroups, and guarantee that all students are taught by "qualified" teachers.

Nondiscriminatory Testing   A principle associated with federal regulations for services to learners with disabilities that requires schools to use multiple measures to determine whether a learner has a disability that requires special services.

Nonfeasance   A type of negligence that indicates that a person failed to act in circumstances where he or she had an obligation to act.

Nonverbal Behaviors   Parts of communication that do not involve the use of words. These may include gestures and facial expressions.

Normal School   A higher education institution specifically designed to educate future teachers.

Norming Group   The group used to establish expected scores for individuals who take standardized tests.

Norm-Referenced Evaluation   A type of evaluation scheme by which the performance or the ability of a person is judged against norms or the performance of a reference group.

Null Curriculum   The messages and lessons that students learn as a result of what is ignored or left out of the school curriculum.

O

Office of Special Education Programs (OSEP)   A component of the U.S. Department of Education that oversees programs for learners with special needs.

Open-Enrollment Plan   A plan that allows a parent or guardian to send a student to any existing school within the school district. In some instances, open enrollment may extend across school district boundaries.

Open File   A category of placement files that allows the person who is the subject of the file to view what is contained in the file.

Outcome Goals   A category of goals that emphasizes the result of instruction rather than the inputs that were provided.

P

Pacing   The rate at which a teacher proceeds through a given lesson.

Paraeducator   An individual hired by a school district to assist teachers in the classroom.

Paralanguage   Those parts of language other than the words. It includes pitch, tone, and rate of speech.

Peer-Evaluation System   A practice that uses peers (other teachers) to evaluate teacher performance.

Peer Group   A term used to describe a group that is similar in age and interests.

Perennialism   An educational philosophy that emphasizes the search for and the dissemination of unchanging principles and enduring truths. It views knowledge as consisting of unchanged principles.

Performance Assessment   A type of learning assessment that uses the performance of an individual on a task that is as close as possible to real-world conditions.

Philosophical Perspectives   Clusters of values and attitudes that individuals use to make decisions about actions that should be taken.

Placement Assessment   Assessment used to determine the entry point for instruction.

Portfolio   An organized collection of artifacts to show a person's knowledge and skills.

Postmodernism   A philosophical position that holds that individuals create knowledge in ways that go beyond the boundaries and constraints of traditional philosophy.

Pretest   An assessment given prior to beginning an instructional sequence in order to inform the teacher about what a student may already know.

Pretraining Phase   The processes and experiences of prospective teachers that may influence their attitudes and skills prior to the beginning of a formal preparation program.

Probable Cause   A rigorous legal standard that prescribes the level of evidence that must be present in order for authorities to take actions such as obtaining a search warrant.

Professional-Education Component   A part of the formal teacher-preparation phase that focuses on the content and experiences designed to help individuals plan, deliver, and assess instructional programs.

Progressive Education Movement   An approach to education that was especially popular in the 1920s and 1930s. It drew inspiration from the ideas of John Dewey and emphasized that the schools should respond to the needs of students.

Progressivism   As applied to education, a philosophical perspective that emphasizes change as the essence of reality and that educated persons have the insight and problem-solving skills needed to adapt to change.

Property Right   A right to specific tangible or intangible property.

Proposals Relating to the Youth of Pennsylvania   In this 1749 work, Benjamin Franklin proposed a new kind of school, practical and free of all religious ties.

Psychomotor Domain   A learning category that focuses on muscular coordination, manipulation, and motor skills.

R

Rating Scales   An assessment device that allows observers to judge the quality of observed behaviors using a range of descriptors.

Raw Score   A student's score based on the number of correct answers that has not been statistically adjusted or treated.

Reconstructionism   A philosophical perspective that holds that the role of education should be to build society.

Reliability   A concept that refers to the extent to which individuals performing an assessment arrive at similar conclusions.

Right to Privacy   Learners' legal rights to privacy while in the school setting. It specifically relates to those places where students have a high expectation of privacy and to the records kept by the school.

Rigorous Assessment   Comprehensive assessment procedures that require individuals to use sophisticated thinking processes.

Risk Factors   Those characteristics or conditions that place students at risk of failing.

S

Salary Schedule   A document produced by a school district that describes the criteria used to determine salary levels.

Scholastic Achievement Test   A test used by higher education to make entrance decisions.

School–Business Partnership   The relationship between a school and a business for the purposes of enhancing the quality of educational programs.

School Choice   A policy that allows parents and guardians to choose the school their child will attend regardless of the location of their residence.

School Climate   The general atmosphere within the school. It takes into account interpersonal relationships between individuals in the building and the expectations individuals have for themselves and others.

Scoring Rubric   A set of guidelines that provides clear definitions used to rate performances.

Sense of Efficacy   The feelings of competence or power. People with a high degree of efficacy believe that they can make a difference.

Single Salary Schedule   A uniform salary schedule for all teachers in a school district that bases teacher compensation on such factors as years of experience and education level.

Social Cohesion   A sense of communal belonging in which members of the same group work together with little disagreement and have the same goals and purposes.

Socialization   The process that teaches individuals the values, norms, and their role in society.

Special Education Teachers   Those teachers who have specialized preparation to teach students with special needs.

Spending Clause   A provision of the U.S. Constitution that allows Congress the power to spend funds for the general welfare of the people.

Staff Development   Efforts of organizations to provide additional education and training to employees. Also called "in-service education."

Standardized Test   Tests that have been developed and used on representative populations of individuals in order to establish norms and expectations against which the scores of an individual can be compared.

Standards-Based Education   A movement that bases resource allocation and evaluations of schools and teachers against clear and measurable standards.

State Board of Education   The body that has the authority and responsibility for implementing educational policies within the state.

State Curriculum Standards   State-adopted elements of the curriculum that are required for all students in the state.

State Department of Education   The department of state government that implements the policies and procedures of the state board of education.

State Superintendent of Education   The chief educational official in a state. Sometimes called the state commissioner. This officer might be elected or appointed.

Stem   In assessment this term refers to the first, or cueing portion of a test item that precedes the answer options.

Structure-of-the-Disciplines Approach   A curriculum variant of the subject-matter orientation that places the emphasis in the curriculum on students learning the structure and organization of the academic disciplines they are studying.

Summative Assessment   Assessment procedures that are used at the conclusion of a learning sequence in order to determine the amount of student learning that has taken place.

Symbolic Interactionism   A sociological perspective on education that focuses on the interactions within a school and classroom. Of special interest are the interaction patterns as they relate to gender, ethnicity, and socioeconomic status.

Systemic Reform   The belief that significant improvement requires simultaneous change in all parts of the system.

T

Task Analysis   The systematic breakdown of a task into components and how they need to be sequenced in order to achieve the desired task.

Taxonomy   An classification scheme. Educational objectives can be classified into cognitive, affective, and psychomotor taxonomies.

Taxpayer Revolt   A movement in several states that sought limits on taxes, especially property taxes, which have been the foundation for school funding.

Teacher's Aid   See paraeducator.

Teachers' Dispositions   Perceptions and attitudes of teachers that influence their views of students, their views of education, and their beliefs about the role of a teacher.

Teaching Contract   An official and legal employment agreement between a teacher and a school district that includes information related to the terms of employment, the nature of the assignment, the salary, sick leave, health care plans, and other expectations. It is binding on both parties.

Teaching Credential   A document issued by the state that indicates a person is able to teach in the state. It may be called a certificate or a license.

Teaching Specialization/Academic Major   The part of the teacher-preparation program that focuses on the academic subjects and content a person expects to teach.

Teaching Team   A group of teachers who collaborate, plan, and deliver instruction to a group of students.

Technological Literacy   A capability of a person who has the basic understanding and skill to use technology at an acceptable level of proficiency.

Technology   The scientific application of to resources to meet student needs and wants.

Telecommunications Act of 1996   Federal legislation that provide funds to help schools integrate modern communication technologies into instructional programs.

Tenure   A principle guaranteed by law in some states and as policy in some school districts that ensures that employed teachers who reach certain minimum experience requirements can only be dismissed under certain stipulated situations and provides them with due process in appealing a negative employment decision.

Time Sampling   An observation approach that is based on recording what is happening in a classroom at certain specified time intervals.

Tinker v. Des Moines Independent School District (1969)   This is a landmark legal case that established the point that both students and teachers enjoy constitutional protections in the school environment. This case involved freedom of speech and whether a school district could prohibit students from wearing symbols that signified their opposition to the war in Vietnam.

Total Immersion   A type of program that places individuals with limited English proficiency in an instructional program that is only delivered in English.

U

Unfunded Mandate   A regulation or requirement placed on school districts by governmental agencies that is not accompanied by a funding source to pay the costs associated with the mandate.

Unpredictability   A characteristic of teaching that refers to the fact that teachers work in environments where unexpected occurrences are common. One dimension of unpredictability is that student reactions, behaviors, and comments vary from day-to-day.

Unreasonable Search and Seizure   A constitutional guarantee that protects individuals for searches and seizure of property unless rigorous evidentiary conditions are met. These guarantees extend to the school and classroom.

Use Fees   Fees that school districts charge students for participation in certain services. For example, user fees have been levied for riding the bus or for participation in certain extracurricular activities such as athletics or band.

V

Validity   A measurement concept that focuses on the degree to which an assessment tool measures what it is intended to measure.

Vouchers   An approach to school choice that gives parents tax money that they can cash in at the school of their choice to pay for the education of their child. The school can be either public or private. It is advocated as a means of introducing competition between schools as a means of improving them.

W

Whole Language   An approach to literacy education that contends that reading, writing, listening, and speaking are all important parts of the language process and that they should be taught as a single, integrated process.

Within-Individual-School Segregation   A pattern that can occur within a school in which members of some groups are overrepresented and members of other groups are underrepresented regardless of the diversity of the total school population.

Y

Yearly Contract   A contract type that offers a position to a teacher one year at a time with no guarantees or legal obligations to renew the contract at the end of each year.

Z

Zero Rejects   A principle associated with federal regulations for services to learners with disabilities and requires the schools to enroll all children between certain ages regardless of their disabilities.

NAME INDEX

SUBJECT INDEX

A

Abused students, 94–95
  reporting, 334
Academic freedom, 329–331
Academic-subjects curricula, 145–147
Acceleration programs, 133
Acceptable-use policies, 304–305
Accommodation, 123
Accountability, 21. *See also* Assessment
Achievement gap, 91
Active teaching, 153
ADD, 128, 129
Adolescent behavior, 101–102
Affective domain of learning, 183–184
African Americans, 131
  history of education, 217–218
  special education and, 130–131
  technology-usage gap and, 303
AFT, 32, 38
Alaska Natives, 131
ALL Handicapped Children Act, 120
Allocation of funds, 362–363
Alternative assessment, 190–191
American Federation of Teachers, 32, 38
American Indians, 131
  history of education, 210–211
American Society for Training and
  Development, 49
Americans with Disabilities Act, 120
ASCD tutorials, 157
Asian Americans, 131
  technology-usage gap and, 303
Assessment, 173
  authentic assessment, 190–191
  school reform initiatives, 63
  students. *See* Student assessment
  teachers. *See* New teacher assessment;
    Teaching portfolios
Assessment plans, 173–174
  criteria, development of, 184–185
  educational outcomes. *See* Educational
    outcomes
Assistant principals, 351
Assistive technologies, 130, 295–296
Association for Supervision and
  Curriculum Development, 157
ASTD, 49

At-risk students, 96
Attendance zones, 64
Attention deficit disorder, 128, 129
AUPs, 304–305
Authentic assessment, 63, 190–191
Average daily attendance, 362

B

Bell-shaped curve, 175
Bethel School District No. 403 v. Fraser, 318
Bilingual education, 14
Block grants, 362
Bloom's Taxonomy, 182–183
Board of Education v. Rowley, 325
*Board of Trustees of Compton Junior College
    District v. Stubblefield,* 329, 333
Boards of education
  local school boards, 347–348
  state board, 345
Bodily-kinesthetic intelligence, 17
Boston English Classical School, 215
Boston Latin Grammar School, 212
Braillers, 295
Braille-writers, 295
Brown v. Board of Education, 114
Business leaders, influence of, 357
"Business roundtables," 75

C

Cardinal Principles, 220–222
Carl D. Perkins Vocational and Applied
    Technology Act of 1990, 74, 75
CAST, 296
Categorical grants, 362
*Cedar Rapids Community School District v.
    Garret F.,* 325
Cell phones in school, 13
  cheating with, 300
Census data, 245
Center for Applied Special
    Technology, 296
Central office staff, 350
Certification of teachers, 326
  emergency teaching certificates, 119
Changing society
  chart depicting challenges, 3
  constancy of, 58

  coping with. *See* Coping with changes
  reformation of schools. *See* School reform
Charter schools, 68–70
Cheating using cell phones, 300
Checklist(s) assessment tool, 191
Child abuse, 94–95
  reporting, 334
Child Protective Services, 94–95
Children's Internet Protection Act,
    305–306
Choice of schools. *See* School choice
Church and state, 237–238
CIPA/N-CIPA, 305–306
Civil War to 1900, 216–218
Clarity
  teacher clarity, 157
  teacher questions, 158
Class history, 12
Classroom diversity, 13–14. *See also*
    Multicultural education
  benefits of, 109–111
  case for, 278
Classroom favoritism, 118
Classroom immediacy, 10–11
Classroom observation, 159–160
  coding systems, 162–163
  event sampling, 160
  expertise, development of, 165
  frequency counts, 161–162
  narrative approach, 160–161
  seating-chart systems, 163–164
  time sampling, 160
Classroom questioning, 158–159
Classroom simultaneity, 10
Classroom teachers, 45–46. *See also*
    Teachers
Closed files, 323–324
Coding observation system, 162–163
Cognitive domain of learning, 182–183
Collective bargaining, 356
Colonial America, 210
  Middle Colonies, 212–213
  Native American cultures, 210–211
  New England Colonies, 211–212
  Southern Colonies, 213–214
Commercialized schools, 361
Commissioner of education, 344–345
Common school, 215